SAN DIEGO

SAN DIEGO

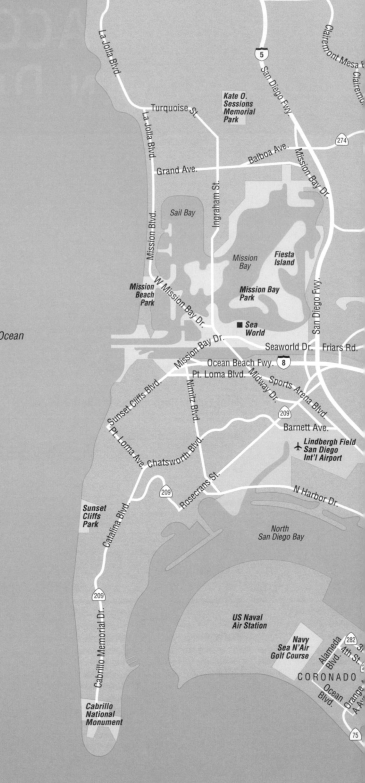

Pacific Ocean

La Jolla Blvd

Turquoise St.

Kate O. Sessions Memorial Park

San Diego Fwy.

Balboa Ave.

Mission Bay Dr.

Grand Ave.

Ingraham St.

Sail Bay

Mission Blvd.

W Mission Bay Dr.

Mission Bay

Fiesta Island

Mission Bay Park

Mission Beach Park

■ Sea World

San Diego Fwy.

Mission Bay Dr.

Seaworld Dr.   Friars Rd.

Ocean Beach Fwy.

Pt. Loma Blvd.

Sports Arena Blvd.

Midway Dr.

Sunset Cliffs Blvd.

Nimitz Blvd.

Barnett Ave.

✈ Lindbergh Field San Diego Int'l Airport

Pt. Loma Ave.   Chatsworth Blvd.

Chatsworth Blvd.

Rosecrans St.

Sunset Cliffs Park

Catalina Blvd.

N Harbor Dr.

North San Diego Bay

Cabrillo Memorial Dr.

US Naval Air Station

Navy Sea N'Air Golf Course

Alameda Blvd.   4th St.

CORONADO

Ocean Blvd.

Orange A Ave.

Cabrillo National Monument

ORIENTATION

Travel to the edge of America and you end up in San Diego, wedged between the **Anza-Borrego Desert**, the **Mexican border**, the **Pacific Ocean**, and the Orange County–Los Angeles sprawl. The nation's seventh-largest city is tucked so far down in the southwest corner of the map it often escapes attention and is rarely mentioned in the national news, almost as if it exists only as a backdrop for major events.

San Diegans hosted the **1998 Super Bowl**, showing off palm trees and tans to football fans on the East Coast huddled between their fireplaces and TV sets. Sailors watched the best boats from all over the world flap their sails in San Diego's winds during the **1992 and 1995 America's Cup** races. The Republican Party chose San Diego for its **1996 Republican National Convention**. Each time the city shows up on TV, the population rises. Visitors love San Diego, and with good reason. The city is so mellow, pretty, and laid-back that stress just melts away. There's never been an earthquake as intense as those in Los Angeles and San Francisco—just a few tremors to remind locals of their faults. And San Diego escapes the flooding, fires, and tension that plague other parts of Southern California. Nothing dramatic happens here, which drives some of San Diego's 1.25 million residents to distraction. But it drives others to create great science, art, theater, and literature. There's a reason Dr. Seuss and Dr. Salk both took up residence here.

San Diego's history is lightly buried under its modern façade. The beach-front lawns, cascades of bougainvillea, and sky-high palms all came from elsewhere. The region's original Kumeyaay residents lived in a brown landscape of rocks, chaparral, and sand. In 1769 Spanish explorers and missionaries chose San Diego's **Presidio Hill** for their first fort and Franciscan mission in what was then known as **Alta California**. The early settlers built their first homes and shops at the base of the hill in what is now called **Old Town**. The developers of the mid-1800s moved their centers of commerce to the shores of San Diego, laying the foundation for today's downtown. By the late 1800s, San Diego's first building boom was on, to be followed every few decades by another.

San Diego's first big national attention-getter was the **1915–1916 Panama-California Exposition**, designed to celebrate the opening of the Panama Canal. The exposition's greatest effect on the city was an architectural one. Several of San Diego's most significant buildings were built during that era, from the Spanish-Moorish palaces in **Balboa Park** to the Spanish-Colonial–style **Santa Fe Depot** downtown. Stroll through the park on a Sunday morning, or better yet on a weekday in late afternoon, and enjoy the sights; it's one of the city's greatest attractions. But ultimately, San Diego's heart is at the beach. Grab a pair of in-line skates and cruise the **Mission Beach Boardwalk**, or sip a cappuccino by **La Jolla Cove**. Build a bonfire on **Coronado's Silver Strand**; ride the waves on a boogie board in **Ocean Beach**. Once the sand gets between your toes, you'll be hooked.

For culture and culinary thrills, visit the village of **La Jolla**'s tony galleries and trendy cafés. Do as the locals do and order a glass of white wine and seared ahi at **George's at the Cove** overlooking the water, or cruise **Prospect Street** in a limo. For more exciting nightlife, head downtown, where the white sails of the **San Diego Convention Center** glow against a neon-laced skyline. Take your chances on getting a table at one of the cafés in the **Gaslamp Quarter**, where shops and cafés stay open past midnight.

Got a few more days? Drive to the **Cleveland National Forest** and ride mountain bikes through **Julian**. Pose beside a blossoming ocotillo cactus in the Anza-Borrego Desert; go sleigh-riding on **Mount Laguna**. And don't forget to cross the border into **Tijuana** for a taste of Mexico.

Area code 619 unless otherwise noted.

Getting to San Diego Airport

Lindbergh Field is on the shores of **San Diego Bay**, 3 miles northwest of downtown. The wisdom of having a major international airport so close to the city has been debated for decades, but it certainly is convenient for visitors, who have a 5-minute cab ride to downtown hotels. Taxis to other destinations are another story—you can easily run up a hefty fare heading north or east (see below). The airport has three terminals, the **East**, **West**, and **Commuter** terminals, with transportation between provided by the Red Bus Shuttle. Be forewarned that you cannot walk to the Commuter Terminal from the main airport. Ask which terminal your flight is leaving from before heading to the airport.

AIRPORT SERVICES (AREA CODE 619)

24-Hour Operations	686.8065
Airport Harbor Police Dispatch	686.8000
Currency Exchange	295.1501
Customs and Immigration	557.6275, 557.5370
Ground Transportation	686.8070
Information Recording	231.2100
Lost and Found	686.8002
Paging	686.8076
Parking	291.1508
Traveler's Aid	231.7361

AIRLINES

Aeroméxico	238.1320, 800/237.6639
Alaska Airlines	800/252.7522
America West	800/235.9292
American Airlines	800/433.7300
British Airways	800/247.9297
Continental Airlines	800/523.3273
Delta Airlines	800/325.1999
Frontier Airlines	800/432.1359
Midwest Express	800/452.2022
Northwest Airlines	800/225.2525
Southwest Airlines	800/435.9792
United Airlines	800/241.6522
US Air	800/428.4322

Getting to and from Lindbergh Field

BY BUS

San Diego Transit's bus 992 "The Flyer" (685.4900, 233.3004, 800/262.7837) runs between all of the airport's terminals and downtown every half hour between around 5:00AM and midnight. There is an excellent web site at www.sdcommute.com that details bus routes and times.

BY SHUTTLE

Shuttles can be found at the transportation plazas across from Terminals 1 and 2. Companies that provide door-to-door shuttle service from the San Diego airport are Xpress Shuttle (222.5800, 800/427.7483), Cloud 9 Shuttle (505.4950, 800/974.8885), All-City Shuttle (800/690.9090), and Supreme Shuttle (295.1863).

BY LIMOUSINE

Limousines are not commonly used for airport transportation in San Diego. A limo from the airport to La Jolla is a very expensive option. Companies providing limousine service are listed below.

Limousines by Linda	234.9145
Olde English Livery Service	232.6533, 800/468.6066
Paul the Greek's Limo	589.2299, 287.6888

BY CAR

From the airport, take **Harbor Drive** to downtown and to **Interstate 5** (**I-5**) north, which goes to Old Town and La Jolla and connects with **Interstate 8** (**I-8**) to the beaches and **Mission Valley**. To get to the airport from downtown, take Harbor Drive; from other areas, take I-5 to the airport exit and follow the signs through a convoluted series of right turns to Harbor Drive and the airport entrance. Ask in advance which terminal your airline is in so you can take the proper entrance to the airport. Entrances are clearly marked.

RENTAL CARS

The following car-rental companies have counters at the airport. They're generally open between 5:30AM and midnight.

Alamo	297.0311, 800/327.9633
Avis	688.5000, 800/230.4898
Budget	498.1144, 800/527.0700
Dollar	234.3388, 800/800.3665
Hertz	220.5222, 800/654.3131
National	497.6777, 800/227.7368

How To Read This Guide

SAN DIEGO ACCESS˙ is arranged by neighborhood so you can see at a glance where you are and what is around you. The numbers next to the entries in the following chapters correspond to the numbers on the maps. The text is color coded according to the kind of place described:

Restaurants/Clubs: Red

Hotels: Purple | **Shops: Orange**

🏛 Parks/Outdoors: Green | **Sights/Culture: Blue**

♿ Wheelchair accessible

Wheelchair Accessibility

An establishment (except a restaurant) is considered wheelchair accessible when a person in a wheelchair can easily enter a building (i.e., no steps, a ramp, a wide-enough door) without assistance. Restaurants are deemed wheelchair accessible *only* if the above applies *and* if the restrooms are on the same floor as the dining area and their entrances and stalls are wide enough to accommodate a wheelchair.

Rating the Restaurants and Hotels

The restaurant star ratings take into account the quality, service, atmosphere, and uniqueness of the restaurant. An expensive restaurant doesn't necessarily ensure an enjoyable evening, whereas a small, relatively unknown spot could have good food, professional service, and a lovely atmosphere. Therefore, on a purely subjective basis, stars are used to judge the overall dining value (see the star ratings at right). Keep in mind that chefs and owners often change, which sometimes drastically affects the quality of a restaurant. The ratings in this guidebook are based on information available at press time.

The price ratings, as categorized at right, apply to restaurants and hotels. These figures describe general price-range relationships among other restaurants and hotels in the area. The restaurant price ratings are based on the average cost of an entrée for one person, excluding tax and tip. Hotel price ratings reflect the base price of a standard room for two people for one night during the peak season.

Restaurants

★	Good
★★	Very Good
★★★	Excellent
★★★★	Extraordinary Experience
$	The Price Is Right (less than $10)
$$	Reasonable ($10–$15)
$$$	Expensive ($16–$20)
$$$$	Big Bucks ($21 and up)

Hotels

$	The Price Is Right (less than $100)
$$	Reasonable ($100–$175)
$$$	Expensive ($175–$250)
$$$$	Big Bucks ($250 and up)

MAP KEY

• City/Town	
95	Interstate Highway
30	US Highway
Entry 1 Number	
73	State Route
10	Mexico Highway
▲ Mountain	Freeway
	Tunnel
Point of Interest ■	Main Road
	Secondary Road
	Unpaved Road/Pedestrian Passage
	Trolley Line

BY TAXI

Taxis line up at the transportation plaza and the fares are the same for all cab companies. The fare to downtown is inexpensive (usually between $10 and $12); to Mission Valley and the beaches, it's still lower than what you might expect in most major cities (about $20 to $25). But if you're headed for La Jolla and other outlying communities, the shuttles are a better deal.

BUS STATION (LONG-DISTANCE)

Buses are not as popular here in autoland as they are on the East Coast, and bus travel seems popular primarily among those who simply can't afford to get around any other way. The **Greyhound Lines** terminal is downtown (120 W Broadway, at First Ave; 239.3266, 800/231.2222; baggage, 239.9231). Taxis are available at the bus station.

TRAIN STATION (LONG-DISTANCE)

The historic **Santa Fe Depot** (1050 Kettner Blvd at Broadway; 239.9021) is one of downtown's loveliest buildings. **Amtrak** (800/872.7245) travels from downtown to Los Angeles, with two San Diego stops in **Solana Beach** and **Oceanside**. The ride from San Diego to Los Angeles, which takes about 3 hours, is a gorgeous one, past crowded and secluded beaches, through small towns, alongside the congested freeway, where drivers eye you with envy. There are nine daily departures, beginning at approximately 6AM. The ticket office is open daily between 5:30AM and 10:30PM.

The **Coaster** commuter train (info 685.4900, 800/262.7837) from downtown to the coastal communities in **North County** departs from the **Santa Fe Depot** and stops in Old Town, **Sorrento Valley**, **Solana Beach**, **Encinitas**, **Carlsbad**, and **Oceanside**. The morning train departs downtown at 6:33 and 7:45AM; afternoon trains depart between 2:15 and 4:20PM.

Getting Around San Diego

BICYCLES

Dedicated bikers have no problem pedaling anywhere in San Diego, though it takes considerable time to get from one community to another. Most cyclists transport their bikes to a particular area. Popular biking spots include downtown's **Embarcadero**, the trails throughout Mission Bay, the Mission Beach Boardwalk, Coronado, and La Jolla. For a free map of bike trails throughout the county call **Bikeways Map** (231.2453).

Bike rentals are available from any of the following companies: **Bikes and Beyond** (1201 First St, at the Ferry Landing, Coronado; 435.7180), **Hamel's** (704 Ventura Pl at Mission Blvd, Mission Beach; 858/488.9168), **Rent-A-Bike** (641 17th St, between Harbor Dr and First Av, downtown; 232.4700).

BUSES

Public buses are not a good mode of transportation if you're in a hurry or traveling farther than 10 miles; they are more popular with commuters than sightseers. Some buses have bike racks, making them a good option for visiting the beaches and bay. For information on routes and fares, call the **San Diego Transit Information Line** (info, 233.3004, 800/266-6883).

There are various passes available for purchase. The Day Tripper Pass is a 1-day pass, good for unlimited trips on buses and trolleys. Passes are sold at the **Transit Store** (102 Broadway, at First Ave; 234.1060). The store is open Monday through Friday, 8:30AM until 5:30PM, and Saturday and Sunday, 10:00AM to 4:00PM; passes also can be ordered ahead by mail.

Regional bus companies that serve areas outside the city include **National City Transit** (474.7505), **Chula Vista Transit** (476.9914), **Coronado Strand Route** (427.6438), and **North County Rural Bus System** (760/966.6500). The **Southeast County Rural Bus System** (478.5875) provides access to rural county towns.

DRIVING

You don't need a car if you're staying within a particular area, such as downtown, Coronado, or La Jolla, but a car is essential if you plan to see more of San Diego's sprawling attractions. Don't go near the freeways until you have studied your maps and memorized your routes: Southern California drivers get a thrill out of speeding up around entrance and exit ramps, scaring the daylights out of timid tourists. If you're determined to drive under 65 mph, stay in the far right lane or you'll be terrorized by natives intent on maintaining a steady 80. Freeway traffic slows to a crawl during morning and evening rush hours. Downtown traffic isn't bad, but the beaches and Mission Bay are a nightmare on summer weekends. Right turns on red lights are allowed except where noted as prohibited.

FERRIES OR BOATS

Ferries travel between downtown and Coronado, and the water taxi is a great way to get from **Harbor Island**,

Shelter Island, Coronado, and downtown hotels to the Convention Center. The **San Diego–Coronado Bay Ferry** (234.4111) runs every hour on the hour between 9:00AM and 9:00PM. **San Diego Water Taxi** offers on-call taxi service daily between 10AM and 10PM (235.8294). **Harbor Hopper Water Taxi** (858/488.2720, 800/300.7447) runs between May and September, 9AM through 7PM.

PARKING

Most major beaches, Mission Bay, and **Balboa Park** have free parking lots, which fill up quickly on sunny weekends. Downtown has several metered lots along the waterfront and inland. You can usually find a space on the street if you look hard enough, but pay attention to the posted signs—many of the best spots permit only 15-minute parking. Meters all over town are closely monitored. Don't bother running back to throw more change in the machine; a 2-hour space is a 2-hour space, period. Downtown meters accept only quarters.

TAXIS

Unless you're traveling solely within downtown, taxis are yet another unsatisfactory means of transportation. Fares are steep and distances great between major attractions. There is no shortage of taxis at the airport, train and bus stations, and hotels and amusements, but don't expect to just flag one down at the beach. To arrange a pickup call: **Coronado Cab Co.** (435.6211), **La Jolla Cab** (858/453.4222), **Orange Cab** (291.3333), **San Diego Cab** (226.8294), or **Yellow Cab** (234.6161).

TOURS

Old Town Trolley Tours (298.8687 or 800/868-7482) offers 2-hour, narrated, eight-stop tours of downtown, Old Town, **Balboa Park**, and Coronado. Passengers can get off the trolley and reboard whenever they wish, which also makes it an efficient way to get around the city. The company also offers specialty tours, such as the Ghost and Gravestone tour, featuring a haunted house and San Diego's oldest graveyard. Tickets are available at the **International Visitor Information Center** (First Ave at F St; 236.1212) and at trolley stops. **Gray Line Tours** (491.0011) offers daily narrated tours of San Diego. The **Gaslamp Quarter Foundation** (233.4692) offers walking tours of downtown's historic district. **San Diego Harbor Excursion** (234.4111) has narrated tours of San Diego Bay. The **Natural History Museum** (232.3821) in **Balboa Park** offers nature walks of the park's canyons and gardens. **Baja California Tours** (454.7166) specializes in tours below the border to **Rosarito** and **Ensenada**, and often has special tours to Tijuana. **San Diego Mini Tours** (477.8687) offers daylong tours of San Diego, including the major attractions; tours combining San Diego and Tijuana; and tours to Tijuana, Rosarito, and Ensenada.

Horse-drawn carriage tours and transportation in downtown are available through **Cinderella Carriages**

THE MAIN EVENTS

January

Martin Luther King Day Parade takes place downtown around the 14th.

February

The annual **Buick Invitational Golf Tournament** at **Torrey Pines** attracts top golfers on the PGA tour.

March

The **Ocean Beach Kite Festival** features kite building, decorating, and flying contests for all ages.

St. Patrick's Day is celebrated in bars and restaurants throughout the city on the 17th. The downtown parade is usually held the weekend before the 17th.

April

The **San Diego Padres** baseball season begins; 881-6500.

The annual **San Diego Crew Classic** brings racing teams to the waters off **Crown Point** at **Mission Bay**.

Art Walk is a 2-day event along 1.5 miles of scenic downtown, showcasing works of visual and performance artists.

The **Borrego Springs Grapefruit Festival** celebrates the desert's leading crop with music, food, arts and crafts displays, and carnival rides.

The **Coronado Flower Show** transforms the entire city into a floral display, with contests for the best front-yard gardens, floral specimens, and displays.

The annual **Earth Day** celebrations are held at **Balboa Park** with booths, displays, and live entertainment.

Day at the Docks features free boat rides, fishing contests, and displays of fishing gear at the **San Diego Sportfishing Landing** in **Point Loma**.

May

Cinco de Mayo is a national Mexican holiday celebrated with fiestas at **Old Town** on the 5th.

The annual **Pacific Beach Block Party** brings the beach boys and girls off the sand and onto **Garnet Avenue** for food, live music, and crafts exhibits.

June

The **Indian Fair** brings Native Americans from throughout the Southwest to **Balboa Park**'s **Museum of Man** for art, culture, and music demonstrations.

The **Del Mar Fair**, held between mid-June and 4 July, transforms the **Del Mar Fairgrounds** into a massive carnival with midway rides, livestock and gardening displays, concerts, food booths, and more.

The annual **Ocean Beach Festival and Chili Cook-Off** closes **Newport Avenue** to traffic for a day of concerts, crafts shows, children's games, and llama rides.

July

Fourth of July celebrations typically last a week or more throughout the city. The **Coronado** parade is one of the biggest events, and fireworks displays are held in

(239.8080). To check out the scenery from above, contact **Corporate Helicopters** (858/505.5650) or **Barnstorming Adventures, Ltd.** (760/438.7680, 800/SKY.LOOP), for aerial tours in vintage planes.

TROLLEY

Public transportation in San Diego is extremely inefficient, time-consuming, and confusing, except for the extremely efficient, inexpensive, worldwide model of excellence: the smashing red **San Diego Trolley**. The **Blue Line** services Mission Valley to Old Town and downtown, then south all the way to the **San Ysidro**–Tijuana border; the **Orange Line** loops around downtown, then heads out to **Santee** in the eastern part of the county. For information, call 231.8549 or 685.4900 or visit the trolley web site at www.sdcommute.com/service/trolleypage.htm.

WALKING

San Diego is a great walking city. In fact, strong legs and sturdy shoes are essential for thoroughly touring some areas, especially **Balboa Park** and the **Zoo**. Distances are too great to walk from one community to another, but there are terrific local walks within downtown, Coronado, La Jolla Cove, Balboa Park, and the neighborhoods of uptown. And, of course, the **Mission Beach Boardwalk**.

FYI

ACCOMMODATIONS

Downtown hotels, best for business travelers or those seeking a central location, are fully booked when large conventions are in town. Mission Valley and Old Town have some of the most reasonably priced hotels, and both have easy freeway access. Hotels at the beach

Ocean Beach, Coronado, Chula Vista, La Jolla, and Rancho Bernardo.

The **Over-the-Line Tournament** is a rowdy, bawdy demonstration of athletic skill and hedonism held at **Fiesta Island** in Mission Bay for 2 weekends in July.

The **San Diego Lesbian and Gay Pride Parade** runs down **University Avenue** through **Hillcrest**.

The **Annual US Open Sandcastle Competition** brings out the best in sand artists as they create castles, dragons, and superstructures along the sand at **Imperial Beach**.

The **Del Mar Race Track**'s opening day is a lavish affair, with San Diego's elite decked out in fashionable summer wear to herald the beginning of racing season, which lasts to mid-September at the **Del Mar Race Track and Fairgrounds**.

August

SummerFest La Jolla presents chamber music concerts and educational programs.

The annual **Body Surfing Contest** brings championship body surfers to **Carlsbad Beach**.

September

San Diego Street Scene is a weekend-long street festival attracting top-name musical groups to downtown's **Gaslamp Quarter**.

The annual **La Jolla Rough Water Swim** is for all ages and takes place at beautiful **La Jolla Cove** in the new **Scripps Park**.

The **Miramar Air Show** fills the skies with screaming jets and aerial acrobatics.

The **Julian Apple Harvest** draws urban folk to the mountains for apple cider and apple pie.

October

The **Columbus Day Parade**, usually held on the weekend closest to the 12th, is downtown.

The **Haunted Museum of Man** brings terror and thrills to **Balboa Park**.

November

The **Mother Goose Parade** is San Diego's largest and most beloved parade, held in **El Cajon**.

December

Christmas parades are held in **Pacific Beach, Coronado, Chula Vista, La Jolla,** and **Ocean Beach**.

Christmas on the Prado transforms **Balboa Park** into a nighttime wonderland with a Swedish St. Lucia candle procession and ethnic food booths scattered around, usually held the first weekend in December.

San Diego Harbor Parade of Lights features yachts, tugboats, military carriers, and sailboats all decked out in lights, floating along the harbor. It's usually held the second and third Sundays of the month.

areas and Mission Bay tend to be busiest during the holidays and summer months. Many vacation-oriented hotels drop their rates between Labor Day and Christmas. **San Diego Hotel Reservations** (858/627.9400, 800/SAVE.CASH, 800/728.3227) offers reservations at hotels throughout the county, often at reduced rates.

The **Bed & Breakfast Guild of San Diego** (523.1300) offers a list of accommodations in the area. The **Beach Connection** (858/456.9411) and **San Diego Vacation Rentals** (296.1000, 800/222.8281) can arrange house and condo reservations.

AREA CODES

As San Diego grows, so does the number of area codes. For the purposes of this guide, unless it is otherwise indicated, assume that the area code is 619. As you venture northward, you will find the area code changes to 858, then eventually to 760. When that's the case, we will add that information.

CLIMATE

San Diego has often been called the only area in the US with perfect weather. The average annual temperature is 70 degrees, and the average day is sunny and mild with low humidity. Seasonal changes are hard to detect unless you've been here a while, and something as dramatic as rain is treated as a major event. Rain showers occur between January and March, and the dreaded June Gloom has the beaches socked in with fog much of the day.

DRINKING

The legal drinking age in San Diego is 21. Bars usually stay open until 2AM. Beer, wine, and liquor are sold in supermarkets.

HOURS

Throughout this guide, opening and closing times for shops, attractions, coffeehouses, and so on are listed by

Phone Book

EMERGENCIES

Ambulance/Fire/Police 911
AAA 800/400.4222
Auto Impound 531.2844
Auto Theft 531.2000
Dental Emergency 800/917.6453
Hospitals
   Children's Hospital 858/576.1700
   Sharp Cabrillo Hospital 221.3400
   Sharp Memorial Hospital....................858/541.3400
Locksmith (AAA 24-hour referral number) ....
....800/400.4222
Pharmacy (24-hour) 800/627.2866
Poison Control 543.6000

VISITORS' INFORMATION

American Youth Hostels (downtown) 525.1531
Amtrak..800/872.7245
Better Business Bureau 858/496.2131
Convention & Visitors' Bureau 232.3101
Disabled Visitor Information 858/279.0704
Greyhound Bus 800/231.2222
Police (nonemergency)....................................531.2000
San Diego Transit 233.3004,
....685.4900, 800/262.7837
Time..853.1212
US Customs 557.5360
US Passport Office....................................310/575.5700
Weather...289.1212

day(s) only if normal hours apply (opening between 8:00 and 11:00AM and closing between 4:00 and 7:00PM). In all other cases, specific hours are given (e.g., 6AM-2PM; daily, 24 hours; noon-5PM).

MONEY

San Diego banks are typically open Monday through Friday between 9AM and 4PM; some large branches are open on Saturday mornings. Banks do not commonly exchange foreign currency, except for the major branches downtown. **Thomas Cook** (Horton Plaza, downtown; 800/287.7362) exchanges most currencies. **American Express** has offices in Mission Valley (297.8101) and La Jolla (858/459.4161). Exchange dollars for pesos at the **Casas de Cambio** (Change Houses) on either side of the border.

MONTH	AVERAGE TEMP (°F)		RAINFALL
	High	Low	Inches
January	65	46	1.88
February	66	48	1.48
March	66	50	1.55
April	68	54	0.81
May	70	57	0.15
June	71	60	0.05
July	75	64	0.01
August	77	66	0.07
September	76	63	0.13
October	74	58	0.47
November	70	52	1.25
December	66	41	1.73

PERSONAL SAFETY

Pedestrians from other cities might be shocked by how San Diegans obey crossing signs. The police actually do cite people for jaywalking and crossing against the light. The most common crimes tourists deal with are car theft and robberies; keep all your belongings stashed out of sight and your doors locked.

PUBLICATIONS

San Diego's one major daily newspaper, the *San Diego Union-Tribune*, covers the arts, entertainment, and restaurants. Its Thursday *Night & Day* section has listings of events in San Diego and Baja. The *Reader* is distributed free on Thursdays at restaurants and shops and contains information on dining and entertainment.

RESTAURANTS

Restaurants in San Diego are generally casual, with few requiring jackets and ties for men. Waits can be long, especially in downtown's **Gaslamp Quarter** and in La Jolla; reservations are strongly advised for weekend dinners. Most establishments accept credit cards.

SHOPPING

Galleries and boutiques abound in the **Gaslamp Quarter**, Old Town, **Hillcrest**, and La Jolla.

SMOKING

Smoking is prohibited in public buildings, stores, restaurants, bars, and even at the stadium. Be aware that in health-conscious California, you're likely to offend someone even when you're lighting up outdoors.

STREET PLAN

The ocean provides a perfect geographical landmark to the west; if it's on your left, you're heading north. Most attractions are located near the coast.

TAXES

San Diego's sales tax is 7.5% on all purchases except groceries. The hotel tax is 10.5%.

TICKETS

Ticketmaster (Charge-By-Phone, 220.8497) is a computerized ticket center for concerts and sports events; there are several outlets around town, or you can charge your tickets by phone.

The **San Diego Performing Arts League's Arts Tix** (28 Horton Plaza, downtown; 497.5000) sells half-price, day-of-performance tickets on a first-come, first-served basis. They are also a Ticketmaster outlet.

TIME ZONES

San Diego is on Pacific Time, 3 hours earlier than New York and 3 hours later than Hawaii.

TIPPING

A 15% tip is standard in restaurants and taxis, and $1 per bag is expected by hotel porters. Concierges antici-pate tips based on the extent and quality of their services. Hotel housekeepers appreciate $1 for each night's stay.

VISITORS' INFORMATION CENTERS

The excellent **International Visitor Information Center** (236.1212), on the **First Avenue** street-level side of **Horton Plaza**, is open Monday through Saturday between 8:30AM and 5PM and on Sundays in June, July, and August between 11AM and 5PM. The **San Diego Convention and Visitors Bureau** will send brochures and a good visitor's guide magazine on request. Write them at 401 B Street, suite 1400, San Diego, CA 92101; call 232.3101; or go to its web site at www.sandiego.org. The **San Diego Visitor Information Center** (2688 E Mission Bay Dr, off I-5, Mission Bay; 276.8200) is open daily between 9AM and dusk and is filled with brochures; clerks can help you make hotel reservations. For travelers with disabilities, **Accessible San Diego** (P.O. Box 124526, San Diego, CA 92112-4526; 858/279.0704; www.accessandiego.com) operates an information hotline with complete info on access to tours, hotels, attractions, and businesses.

BALBOA PARK

In a wise and prescient move, San Diego's early developers reserved 1,200 acres of rugged canyons and hilltops just outside downtown for a community park (and made the smart decision to hire the city's premier horticulturist, Kate Sessions, to design the landscape). Actually, they also had commerce in mind. **Balboa Park**'s first Spanish-Colonial buildings were constructed for the **1915–1916 Panama-California Exposition.** Several of the exhibition's structures are still in use, including the **Cabrillo Bridge,** the **California Building** (topped by the tiled **California Tower**), the **Administration Building,** and the **Chapel of St. Francis,** all part of today's **Museum of Man.** Fairgoers entered the

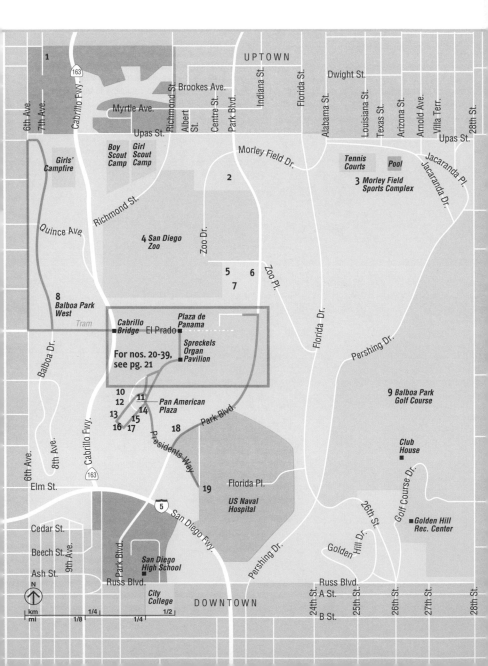

park via the Cabrillo Bridge over the former **Cabrillo Lake** (now the **Cabrillo Freeway**) and walked past the California Building, whose 200-foot-high blue-and-white-tile dome is still a San Diego landmark. The fair was designed to celebrate the opening of the Panama Canal by bringing attention, money, and fame to a struggling port city of some 40,000 residents. The fair was such a success that it was kept open for another year; and in 1935–1936, a second exposition brought further lasting developments to the park.

The leaders of the first exposition had an immense curiosity about the world. Their purpose, as stated in a letter from Colonel D.C. Collier, director of the exposition, to Dr. Edgar L. "Bull" Hewett, architect of the exhibits, was "to illustrate the progress and possibility of the human race . . . for a permanent contribution to the world's progress." The exhibitions included stelae from the Maya ruins of Guatemala (now located in the Museum of Man), a Panama Canal Extravaganza showing ships sailing through a miniature canal, model farms, tea plantations, and a small menagerie that became the impetus for the world-famous **San Diego Zoo**, today the city's most popular attraction.

The **1935–1936 California Exposition** was less erudite than the first, and far more prurient. The post-Depression populace wanted glamour, excitement, amusement, and titillation. So Sally Rand danced with her fans on a platform over the lily pond, 76 of the smallest people in the world lived in Midget Village; and Alpha the Robot frolicked for the cameras with Queen Zorine of the nudist colony. The exposition's midway of rides and exhibitions extended south from the **Spreckels Organ Pavilion** to the **Ford Bowl** (now the **Starlight**), where the best symphonies of the time played under the stars. For added culture, the **Globe Theatre** presented 40-minute adaptations of Shakespeare's greatest plays. The midway's centerpiece was the completely round **Ford Building** (now the **San Diego Aerospace Museum**), where new autos rolled off a modified assembly line.

The military took over the park during World War II, and when they returned it to the city after the war, the place was in a shambles. Plans to destroy many of the original buildings raised such a public outcry that the idea was shelved. Over the next 3 decades, the structures were gradually refurbished to house museums and offices, and the park itself grew under the watchful eye of civic leaders and community groups.

Since the late 1940s Balboa Park has evolved into San Diego's cultural centerpiece, with most of the city's major museums housed in its Spanish-Colonial palaces. The Old Globe Theatre, a theatrical treasure built in 1935, was destroyed by an arson fire in 1972. The current Old Globe Theatre, inaugurated in 1982, is a faithful replica of the 1915 theater, which in turn was a copy of the Elizabethan Globe Theatre on the River Thames in London. The **Globe Theatres** (now comprised of the Old Globe Theatre, Cassius Carter Center Stage, and the Lowell Davies Festival Theatre) have been the launching pad for scores of famed thespians.

The park is also a great place for sports lovers, who flock to **Morley Field** for facilities ranging from archery to disc (aka Frisbee) golf. For serious golfers, there's an 18-hole golf course, and hikers will be thrilled with the many nature trails winding into the canyons.

If coming by car, try to get to the park before 10:00AM—especially on summer and holiday weekends. Free parking is available at the following locations: in front of the **San Diego Zoo**; behind the **Alcazar Garden, Reuben H. Fleet Space Theater, Spreckels**

Restaurants/Clubs: Red | **Hotels: Purple** | Shops: Orange | **Outdoors/Parks: Green** | Sights/Culture: Blue

Organ Pavilion, and Natural History Museum; in the center of Pan-American Plaza; on the west side of Cabrillo Bridge; and at Inspiration Point on the south side of the park across Park Boulevard from the museum area. A free tram stops at these lots, most of the park's attractions, and across Cabrillo Bridge (see "Tired of Tramping Around? Take the Tram" on page 27. The park's museums and other major sights are all within walking distance of each other, but only the hardiest hikers should plan on trekking from the museums to the Morley Field Sports Complex and the Balboa Park Golf Course. There is parking, however, at several lots within the sports complex.

1 MARSTON HOUSE

George Marston, founder of Marston's department store and a civic leader, donated his 15.85 acres to **Balboa Park** in 1925. His daughter, Mary, followed her father's legacy by deeding the 1905 family home and 4.5 acres at the northwest edge of Balboa Park to the city in 1974 but died shy of her 108th birthday in 1988, before the house became a museum. Architects **Irving Gill** and **William Hebbard** had made the house a showplace of the American Arts and Crafts movement, and Marston's downtown department store became the sole agent for the original Craftsman furniture that was displayed so well in his home. Most of the furnishings are gone now, but the San Diego Historical Society has been gradually restoring and refurnishing the 8,500-square-foot house's 16 rooms, creating a house museum devoted to Arts and Crafts furniture and decorative objects. ♦ Admission. F-Su, 10:00AM-4:00PM. 3525 7th Ave (between Upas St and Pennsylvania Ave). 298.3142

2 VETERANS MEMORIAL CENTER AND MUSEUM

Navajo, Hopi, and Zuni Indians lived in a mock village on this site during the 1935 exposition, and rumor has it they nearly starved until fair officials realized someone should provide them with food. Some 12 years later, with funds raised from the sale of lumber from military barracks that were no longer needed, this memorial—designed by **Sam Hamill** and John S. Siebert—was built. Historical objects, artifacts, documents, and memorabilia dating back to the Civil War are on display. Veteran's groups hold meetings here, and the expansive lawns surrounding the memorial are popular for spur-of-the-moment football games. ♦ Free. Daily tours. Park Blvd (between Morley Field Dr and Zoo Pl). 239.2300

3 MORLEY FIELD SPORTS COMPLEX

This complex has evolved over the decades into a one-stop sports fix, with a swimming pool; velodrome for cyclists; shuffleboard, boccie, and *petanque* (a French ball game) courts; an archery range; and 25 public tennis courts. And if you've never played disc golf, this 300-acre canyonland wilderness is the place to try it. A guaranteed workout, the game involves throwing a Frisbee over treetops, across canyons, and down riverbeds into wire baskets hanging from poles. Pros carry two or three flying discs of different weights, but you can get by with one. ♦ Fee for some facilities. Hours vary; pool daily, June-Aug. Parks and recreation office: 2221 Morley Field Dr (at Pershing Dr). 692.4919; tennis information, 291.5248; pool information, 692.4920

4 SAN DIEGO ZOO

San Diegans are rightfully proud of their zoo, an internationally acclaimed 100-acre zoological and botanical center in the heart of the city. The zoo's first animals were left behind after the **1915-1916 Panama-California Exposition**, from whence **Balboa Park**'s ecological and architectural legacy grew. Dr. Harry Wegeforth, who served as a surgeon during the exposition, is said to have commented upon hearing a lion's roar, "Wouldn't it be wonderful to have a zoo in San Diego? I believe I'll build one." Wegeforth's dream came true in 1916 when his newly formed zoological society was given the animals. In 1921 the zoo received a parcel of land on the north side of the park, and these animals (which had been in various locations around the park) were moved to the new zoo in 1922. The exposition's **International Harvester Exhibit Building**

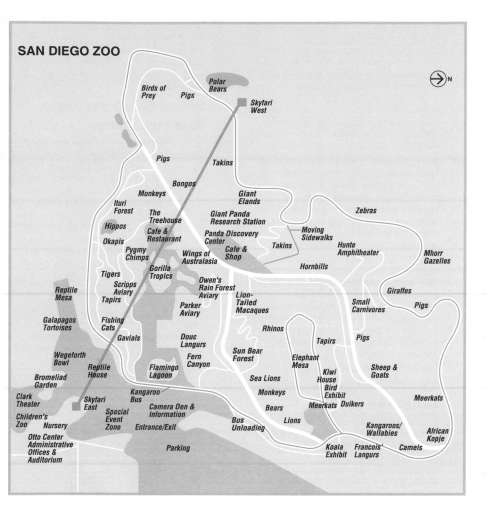

SAN DIEGO ZOO

became a reptile exhibit, and outdoor grottoes for bears, seals, lions, and tigers were built with donated funds. During the 1930s several buildings were constructed through the Works Projects Administration; architect **Louis J. Gill** donated his time to oversee the design. The zoo now has 4,000 animals of 800 species, and an accredited botanical garden filled with an outstanding collection of trees, plants, and flowers. The Zoological Society of San Diego, which also operates the **San Diego Wild Animal Park** near Escondido, has 250,000 member households and 130,000 child memberships—far more than any other zoo in the world—and at least 3 million visitors pass through the zoo's gates each year. The society is dedicated to the conservation of animals, plants, and ecosystems worldwide through its Center for Reproduction of Endangered Species (CRES).

The animals live in ecosystems, or climate zones, that are built to provide conditions as similar as possible to those of their native habitats. With the exception of the snakes, all the animals are outdoors. The plants—over 6,500 species of them—are as colorful and varied as the animals. Wander down the paths signposted **Fern Canyon**, **Orchid Basin**, and the like. Your senses will quickly become immersed in the sights, smells, sounds, and feel of fertile soil, blooming flowers, screeching gibbons, and stray peacock feathers found along the way. It takes quite a bit of energy to explore the entire zoo on foot, as the walkways go up and down steep canyons. Transportation options (all charge a fee in addition to the park entrance admission) include the **Skyfari** aerial tram that travels from near the **Reptile House** on the zoo's east side to the **Horn & Hoof Mesa**

Restaurants/Clubs: Red | Hotels: Purple | Shops: Orange | Outdoors/Parks: Green | Sights/Culture: Blue

on the west side. The tram, 180 feet above ground, gives an illuminating overview of the zoo, Balboa Park, and the downtown skyline. Another alternative is the 40-minute **Guided Bus Tour**—double-decker buses with drivers well versed in the habits of giraffes, elephants, lions, and bears—that passes by many of the exhibits. A third choice is the **Kangaroo Bus Tours**, offering an unlimited number of rides throughout the zoo. It stops at eight locations and runs every half hour.

There are several restaurants and take-out food stands scattered around the grounds, most with outdoor shaded tables and chairs. Indoor dining is available at **Albert's** and **Sydney's Grill** restaurants (see below). Soft drinks, ice cream, and popcorn can be purchased at snack carts throughout the zoo. In addition, coolers and picnics are permitted (just don't bring glass containers or alcohol); the largest picnic area is the **Rainforest Grove** by the **Children's Zoo**. Stroller and wheelchair rentals are available at the zoo entrance. ♦ Admission; deluxe package includes passes for the Guided Bus Tour and the Skyfari aerial tram. Daily, extended hours during the summer. 2920 Zoo Place (at Park Blvd). 234.3153. www.sandiegozoo.com

Within the San Diego Zoo:

CHILDREN'S ZOO

Beware of billy goats nibbling your purse, and allot plenty of time for the kids to go nose to nose with a bunny. The two nurseries, behind glass walls, are a guaranteed pleaser—who can resist a toddling orangutan dragging a stuffed Big Bird at his side? The exhibits are all placed at a child's eye level, and even the restrooms have kid-size toilets and sinks. The **Naked Mole Rat Colony**, showing the tiny pink moles running through Plexiglas tubes and tunnels, is one of the most popular exhibits. Friendly goats and lambs allow children to pet and stroke them unceasingly while tolerating squeals and occasional howls from timid toddlers.

TIGER RIVER

Sprinklers hidden amid jungle vines in this area provide a constant mist that grows

heavier through the day, much like a rain forest. You'll spot kingfishers swooping toward the river to fish, and Indochinese tigers roaming hillsides behind glass. This is a good place to rest in the cool shade and watch the tigers interact.

PACIFIC BELL GIANT PANDA RESEARCH STATION

On a 12-year loan to the United States from China since 1996, male Shi Shi and female Bai Yun delighted the zoological world by producing an offspring, Hua Mei, in 1999. The only giant panda born in the Western Hemisphere in a decade, the baby has thrived under the attentive care of its mother and a devoted cadre of keepers. On busy summer days, a long line of zoo patrons winds around in front of the exhibit, patiently waiting to catch a glimpse of the three pandas eating bamboo and rolling around in the grass. If you just can't get enough of the cuddly-looking creatures, log on to the zoo web site (www.sandiegozoo.com) and check out the Panda Cam. The lines for this exhibit are long on holidays and busy weekends. If you're determined to get a close-up view, head here first.

SUN BEAR FOREST

The antics of the ursine inhabitants of these woods are legendary and are best caught in early morning and evening. Natural actors, the bears have an intense sense of playfulness and wreak constant havoc with the trees and grasses that are meant to make them feel at home. Don't miss the nearby well-established colony of lion-tail macaques who preen and play all day.

ITURI FOREST

Completed in May 1999, this exhibit simulates the vast Ituri Forest of the northeastern Democratic Republic of Congo (DRC). Hippos, okapi (relatives of the giraffe that can clean their ears with their long, blue-black tongues), monkeys, and a host of birds call this steamy place home. Illustrated panels and a recreated Mbuti camp demonstrate how these people of the forest interact with the indigenous animals and plants.

African Rock Kopje Exhibit

A simulation of an outcropping of volcanic rock that juts up from the African plains, this exhibit houses klipspringers (small antelopes), pancake tortoises, and other creatures who seem to blend imperceptibly into the landscape.

Koalas

Among the zoo's most popular residents, these Australian marsupials pose charmingly among the eucalyptus leaves they devour at a rate of a pound per day for each 13- to 15-pound animal. The San Diego Zoo has the largest koala colony outside Australia. The koalas are often asleep, camouflaged in the tree leaves. There's a TV screen at the exhibit that gives you a more close-up view of their antics.

Gorilla Tropics

Environmental sounds taped in the African rain forests soothe these gorillas in their recently remodeled jungle environment filled with African grasses, wildflowers, and fallen trees on the ground begging to be clambered over.

Scripps Aviary

When the aviary was dedicated in 1923, it was advertised as the "world's greatest flying cage." Spanning a hillside some 90 feet high, the aviary is made of blue mesh covering a forest of trees that shelter 200 colorful African birds.

Hummingbird Aviary

Hundreds of jewel-tone hummingbirds whir through this enclosure covered with screens, oblivious to the two-legged creatures who come to see them. It's a nice place to rest and a great challenge for photographers.

Animal Shows

Shows held at the **Wegeforth Bowl** and **Hunte Amphitheater** include performances by California sea lions, leopards, and emus. If you're lucky, you might even be invited down to the stage to be part of the show. You won't find seals balancing beach balls here; the emphasis is much more educational, yet it's still thoroughly entertaining.

Hippo Beach

It's amazing how graceful a 2-ton hippo can seem when it's immersed in 130,000 gallons of water. This habitat allows viewers to watch through a 105-foot-long observation window as hippos swim in the water and walk on the bottom of their pool. Above water, the hippos frolic in an African river valley setting while humans watch from beside a group of 12 giant hippo sand sculptures.

Polar Bear Plunge

A 2.2-acre summer tundra habitat for arctic animals—including Siberian reindeer, arctic birds, and the ever-popular polar bears—was installed in 1996. Kalluk and Tatqiq, brother and sister bears rescued in Alaska in 2001 after their mother was killed, can be observed diving and swimming underwater from a glassed-in viewing area.

Flamingo Café

$ This is the most conveniently located of the zoo's restaurants—near the entrance. It serves decent soups, salads, and sandwiches at reasonable prices. Floor-to-ceiling windows provide a great view of the flamingo lagoon. ♦ American ♦ Daily, lunch

Sydney's Grill

$ Located between the koala and elephant exhibits, this eatery offers burgers, kid's meals, a variety of salads, as well as hot entrées. ♦ American ♦ Daily, lunch

Albert's

★$$ The **Treehouse** in **Gorilla Tropics** is the setting for this gourmet restaurant where diners can feast on Caesar salads and grilled meats and fish. It is also the only place in the zoo with a full bar. ♦ Californian ♦ Daily, lunch

5 Balboa Park Railroad

Though the half-mile ride on this train is not terribly thrilling, the track runs through a pretty eucalyptus grove between the **San Diego Zoo** and **Spanish Village**. ♦ Fee. Daily, 11AM-

5PM, mid-June–Labor Day; Sa-Su, school holidays, 11AM-4:30PM, Labor Day–mid-June. South side of Zoo Pl (west of Park Blvd). 239.4748

6 BALBOA PARK CAROUSEL

There are a few brass rings amid the iron loops, and most everything else—from the hand-carved unicorns to the military band organ—is just as it was when the Herschell-Spillman Company 1910 carousel was brought to the park in 1922. The 13-mile-an-hour ride lasts 5 delightfully old-fashioned minutes. ◆ Fee. Daily, 11AM-6PM, mid-June–Labor Day; Sa-Su, school holidays, 11AM-5:30PM, Labor Day–mid-June. South side of Zoo Pl (west of Park Blvd). 460.9000

7 SPANISH VILLAGE

One of the park's more serene enclaves, this artists' village was designed by **Richard Requa** in 1934 to resemble a typical Spanish Renaissance neighborhood, with 39 cozy cottages housing gift shops. The army used the cottages as offices and medical clinics during World War II, causing over $13,000 in damage. In 1942 a group of artists and artisans took over, creating an art colony by installing studios and shops in 35 cottages. Today painters, potters, and sculptors continue to display their talents and wares throughout the week, although some of the cottages are open only on the weekend. Check out the mineral and gem displays and consider purchasing a painting of the **California Tower** as a souvenir. ◆ Daily, 11AM-4PM. 1770 Village Pl (west of Park Blvd). 233.9050

8 BALBOA PARK WEST

The strip of park along what is now called Sixth Avenue, across the Cabrillo Bridge from

You'll find great mementos at Balboa Park's museum and zoo shops. The Museum of Man has Guatemalan weavings and worry dolls; and the San Diego Museum of Art offers quality classic, modern, and ethnic objets d'art, posters, books, and cards. Kids love the kaleidoscopes, holograms, and science kits at the Reuben H. Fleet Science Center and the dinosaurs at the Natural History Museum. The Aerospace Historical Center's shop sells airplane models and great bomber jackets for babies. The International Gift Shop at the House of Pacific Relations has a good selection of ethnic arts and crafts. For the best overall shopping, the San Diego Zoo comes out on top. You'll find beautiful T-shirts; an eclectic collection of books, toys, and stuffed animals; and an impressive selection of folk art pieces from Africa and Latin America.

El Prado, is used mostly as a community park, with playgrounds, picnic tables, and long stretches of road for roller skating, jogging, and bicycling. Marston Point, at the southwest point of this area, overlooks a downtown skyline and harbor that would overwhelm George Marston, to whom the point was dedicated in 1924. A flagpole and flag were donated by the Free and Accepted Masons on Flag Day in 1927, when only a scattering of buildings blocked the view out to sea and the point was still part of a 17-mile bridle trail running through the park. ◆ Bounded by the Cabrillo Bridge and Sixth Ave and by Elm and Upas Sts

9 BALBOA PARK GOLF COURSE

Golfers had staked their claim in the park in 1915—even before the first exposition—behind what is now the **Natural History Museum**. They used sheep to keep the chaparral from covering their dirt course, until the poundmaster (an early-day animal control officer) raised a fuss. The powers behind the fair convinced the golfers to move southeast, where they doggedly cleared a 9-hole course (and created a duffer's nightmare called the **Rockpile**) in time for the fair. In 1920, the course was upgraded and extended to 18 holes; in 1934 a local work relief project and the Work Projects Administration built a clubhouse and resodded the course, which is still very much in use today. You'll find a fascinating cross-section of San Diegans here, and great views of the park and downtown. ◆ Greens fee. Daily, 6:30AM-5PM. Golf Course Dr (at Pershing Dr). Pro shop: 239.1632; computer reservations, 570.1234

10 BALBOA PARK CLUB

The **Rapp Brothers** designed this building for the State of New Mexico's exhibition at the 1915 fair after the Mission Church of Acoma. The original church had been built by the Franciscans and their newly christened followers in 1529. New Mexico's visitors to the fair were so impressed by the building that they modeled Santa Fe's New Mexico Museum of Fine Arts after it. In 1934, artist **Belle Baranceanu** covered the west wall with a mural depicting the facets of youth and education, and **Richard Requa** supervised remodeling for the building's reincarnation as the **Palace of Education** for the fair the following year. Before the mural stands the Frederick W. Schweigardt fountain—the *Four Corners of American Democracy*—with sculptures personifying the concepts of Church, Community, Home, and School. During World War II, the Admiral Kidd Officer's Club took over, holding dances on a floor big enough to hold 2,250 waltzers. Today dancers once again grace the ballroom as local folkloric and ballroom dance clubs rent the facilities and

FREE TUESDAYS

A thorough tour of **Balboa Park** can be expensive, as most museums charge an entry fee. A good way to save money is by purchasing a Passport to Balboa Park, available at the **Balboa Park Visitors Center** in front of the **Timken Art Gallery**. The $30 passport covers admission to 13 of the museums and is valid for a week. Alternatively, visit the park on a Tuesday—most museums have free admission one Tuesday of each month, as follows:

1st Tuesday

Natural History Museum

San Diego Model Railroad Museum

Reuben H. Fleet Science Center (fee charged for Space Theater)

2nd Tuesday

Museum of Photographic Arts

Museum of San Diego History

3rd Tuesday

San Diego Museum of Art

San Diego Museum of Man

Japanese Friendship Garden

Mingei International Museum

4th Tuesday

San Diego Aerospace Museum

San Diego Automotive Museum

San Diego Hall of Champions

House of Pacific Relations International Cottages

take advantage of the great sound system's 42 speakers. The San Diego Police Department has an **Outreach Station** near the front door. ♦ Free. M-F. Pan-American Rd W (at Pan-American Plaza). 235.1100

11 HOUSE OF PACIFIC RELATIONS INTERNATIONAL COTTAGES

This cluster of cottages was built by **Richard Requa** for the 1935 exposition as an exhibition of common people's homes during Mexico's colonial period. At the following year's exposition, representatives from the various countries exhibiting at the fair used the houses as headquarters. Hosts in costumes representing each nation held open houses, displaying crafts and serving their indigenous foods. When the fair ended, the concept continued. Today, volunteers from Sweden, Scotland, Mexico, and other countries offer exhibits in the cottages about their countries' cultures, histories, and traditions. International travelers are delighted to find a taste of home here, and domestic visitors are equally thrilled with discovering new cultures. Other special events include music and dance festivals, the **Ethnic Food Fair**, and **Christmas on the Prado**, a celebration held in early December that features carol singing, brightly colored lights, and creatively decorated Christmas trees. ♦ Donation. Su, noon-5PM. South of the Organ Pavilion (between Pan-American Rd W and Pan-American Rd E). 234-0739

12 PALISADES BUILDING

Richard Requa first designed this Indian pueblo in 1934 as the **Woman's Palace** and then the **Entertainment Palace** for the 1935-1936 fair. Now, resident puppeteers work their magic with marionettes, hand, rod, and shadow puppets at the **Marie Hitchcock Puppet Theater**, which occupies part of the building. ♦ Admission. Shows: W, Th, and F, 10AM and 11:30AM; Sa, Su, 11AM, 1PM, 2:30PM. Northwest side of Pan-American Plaza. 685.5045

13 SAN DIEGO AUTOMOTIVE MUSEUM

An 1886 Benz and 1981 Delorean, plus assorted Ferraris, Lamborghinis, and Model T's, fill this Maya-New Mexico pueblo. The building was originally designed by **Richard Requa** for the 1935-1936 exposition to house exhibits from various states around the US; during World War II it was the **National Armory**. After the war, the building became San Diego's first convention center. When more modern facilities were constructed downtown in 1964, this place was closed to commercial meetings and was used for dances, floral exhibitions, and the like. In 1988, it once again became a museum. There's a great collection of motorcycles and an engine room exhibiting car engines. A research and resources library contains historical data and periodicals. If you come by on a

---

Restaurants/Clubs: Red | Hotels: Purple | Shops: Orange | Outdoors/Parks: Green | Sights/Culture: Blue

Sunday afternoon, you may catch an additional outdoor display of automobile collectors' treasures. ♦ Admission. Daily. West side of Pan-American Plaza. 231-2886. www.sdautomuseum.org

14 SAN DIEGO HALL OF CHAMPIONS

Architect **Richard Requa** let loose his fascination with the Maya in 1934 when he designed the US government's **Federal Building** for the 1935–1936 fair to resemble the Maya Palace of the Governor in Uxmal, Mexico. The building was renovated in 1999 and is now home to the San Diego Hall of Champions, devoted to the region's many sports heroes. Over 40 sports are represented in the hall, with 70,000 square feet of display area spread over 3 levels. The **Breitbard Hall of Fame** honors athletes from or made famous in San Diego, including baseball's Don Larsen, swimmer Florence Chadwick, basketball's Bill Walton, and America's Cup champion Dennis Conner. The **Time Out Café** serves up deli sandwiches, salads, and soups. There is also a store where you can purchase sports memorabilia, clothing, and coffee-table books. ♦ Admission. Daily. 2131 Pan American Plaza (at Presidents Way). 234.2544. www.sandiegosports.com

15 MUNICIPAL GYMNASIUM

Another **Richard Requa** building from the 1935 exhibition, this gym underwent a $155,000 restoration in 2001 to refinish the basketball court floor and upgrade the rims and backboards. The court is open for basketball lessons and games. ♦ Free. 1–9PM, weekdays; 9AM-4PM, weekends. 2111 Pan American Plaza (southeast side). 525.8262

On seeing the grounds of the 1935 Exposition, retiree Joseph E. Dryer said, "Truly, this is heaven on earth." In 1940 he started the Heaven on Earth Club, an early-day tourism bureau aiming to perpetuate the civic impetus from the fair and promote San Diego.

The Park is nearly square. It is one and 1/2 miles across. The skyline to the north is outlined by chains of mountains 10,000 feet high. To the southwest, the Coronado Islands are weird, fantastic forms in the unlimited space of ocean. To the northwest is Point Loma. Beyond are glimpses of the Pacific, and below the beautiful San Diego Bay covering twenty-two square miles in this wonderful land. —the *New York Evening Post*, 1902

16 SAN DIEGO AEROSPACE MUSEUM

It may be nearly 70 years old, but the circular 1935 **Ford Building** designed by **Walter Teague** is still the most Modernist structure in the park. Blue lights encircling the outer walls give the building the appearance of a spaceship hovering over the park at night. The Ford Motor Company set up an automobile assembly line in the building for the 1935 fair and called the exhibition the Palace of Transportation. Other modes of conveyance were added in 1936. The 251st Coastal Artillery held classes here in 1940, and during World War II the City School and Convair Aircraft Company set up a vocational school for aircraft training. When the building housing the **San Diego Aerospace Museum** burned down in 1978, this seemed like an appropriate new home. The **International Aerospace Hall of Fame** and the San Diego Aerospace Museum share the cavernous curving hall, where everything from human-propelled planes to space capsules dangles from the ceilings and walls. A 1935 Juan Larrinaga mural depicting the stages of transportation, from a sphinx being dragged by slaves to a locomotive powered by steam, encircles the inner walls. Exhibits include biographies and photos of famous aviators and an interesting *Women in Aviation* exhibit. If you need a break from the overwhelming assemblage of aircraft, step into the center open-air courtyard for a few minutes and imagine the fairgoers of the 1930s strolling amid the Art Deco fountains and lamps. ♦ Admission. Daily. 2001 Pan-American Plaza (south end). 234.8291. www.aerospacemuseum.org

17 STARLIGHT BOWL

Even the roar of jets following the flight path right over this outdoor auditorium hasn't halted the popular productions of the **Starlight Musical Theatre**. On summer evenings there's hardly an empty seat in the house during productions of *Music Man*, *Fiddler on the Roof*, and other such fare. The performers simply freeze midstanza when a plane passes by, then carry on. Visiting musicians, from rock and reggae bands to symphonies, are less blasé but usually get turnout crowds when they appear here. The light opera organization began performing at the bowl in 1948 but abandoned it in 1967, when increased jet traffic became unbearable. Other stages just weren't as popular, however, and the group moved back in 1975. Originally designed by **Vern D. Knudson**, the most recent improvement to the bowl was a $1.2 million stage house, completed in 1997. It provides space for moving scenery while protecting the original outdoor theater. ♦

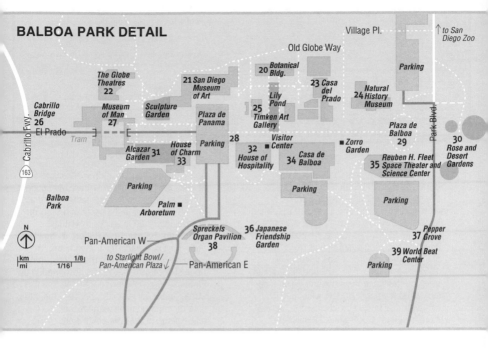

BALBOA PARK DETAIL

Village Pl. • ↑ to San Diego Zoo

Old Globe Way

20 Botanical Bldg.
23 Casa del Prado
Parking
Natural 24 History Museum

The Globe Theatres 22
21 San Diego Museum of Art
Lily Pond
25 Timken Art Gallery

Cabrillo Bridge 26
El Prado Tram
Museum of Man 27
Sculpture Garden
Plaza de Panama
Plaza de Balboa 29
30 Rose and Desert Gardens

Alcazar 31 Garden
House of Charm 33
Parking
28
Visitor 32 Center
House of Hospitality
Casa de 34 Balboa
Zorro Garden
Reuben H. Fleet 35 Space Theater and Science Center

Parking
Palm ■ Arboretum
Parking
Parking

Balboa Park

N ⊕
Pan-American W —
Spreckels Organ Pavilion 38
36 Japanese Friendship Garden
Pepper 37 Grove
39 World Beat Center

km 1/8
mi 1/16
to Starlight Bowl/ Pan-American Plaza ↓ — Pan-American E
Parking

Admission. Shows: Tu-Su, 8PM, mid-June–early Sept. Pan-American Plaza (south end). Box office, 544.7827. www.starlighttheatre.org

18 **CENTRO CULTURAL DE LA RAZA**

Brilliantly colored murals depicting Mexico's history and the current concerns of Mexican-Americans cover the outer walls of a water tank built during World War II. It was here that a group of Hispanic artists found a base after being moved out of the **Ford Building** in 1970 to make way for the **San Diego Aerospace Museum**. Muralists from throughout California joined creative forces in the early 1970s, producing a vivid testimonial to their legacy. The center has studio space for local artists and holds a ballet, folkloric dance classes, and a variety of concerts, plays, and performances by Latino artists. ♦ Free. W-Su, noon-5PM. 2004 Park Blvd (near Presidents Way). 235.6135

19 **INSPIRATION POINT**

The US Navy had control of this hilltop with a good view of the downtown area until 1992, when it closed the original **Naval Hospital** and built a new facility at the foot of the hill on Pershing Drive. The original hospital buildings were remodeled to serve as offices. The major draw here is the large lot with free parking. The park tram stops here frequently. ♦ Park Blvd (at Presidents Way)

At Inspiration Point:

BALBOA PARK MANAGEMENT CENTER

The San Diego Department of Parks and Recreation is responsible for the hands-on supervision, maintenance, and planning that keeps the park a pleasurable public space. The office staff handles questions about the park's facilities and permits. ♦ M-F. 235.1100

BALBOA PARK ACTIVITY CENTER

Opened in 1999, the activity center is the newest building at Balboa Park in over 3 decades. Designed by local architect **Rob Wellington Quigley**, the center is a 38,000-square-foot multipurpose gymnasium built to accommodate table tennis, volleyball, and badminton. Tournaments on the state and national level are held here. The Sports Information Office for the City of San Diego Park and Recreation Department is located at the center. ♦ Daily; call for hours. 2145 Park Blvd. (at Inspiration Point Way). 858/581.7100

20 **BOTANICAL BUILDING AND LILY POND**

Designed by **Carleton Winslow** and **Gerald Wellington**, this structure and pond (originally

---

Restaurants/Clubs: Red | Hotels: Purple | Shops: Orange | Outdoors/Parks: Green | Sights/Culture: Blue

called **La Laguna**) were built as a garden display for the 1915 fair. The building was closed during and after World War I; it reopened for a short time in the 1930s, when hundreds of yellow canaries were caged beside floral displays inside the building. The edifice was closed again during World War II and remained so until it was restored in 1957. At that time, new redwood lathing was used to strengthen the structure, which measures 250 feet long, 60 feet wide, and 75 feet high. The building was closed for several months in early 2002 while 12 miles (or 70,000 lineal feet) of redwood lath was replaced. Inside, sunlight streams over towering tree ferns; waterfalls and fountains are covered with moss and delicate orchids; and in spring, tulips and lilies abound. The plants are clearly labeled, giving local gardeners a chance to explore new treasures for their plots at home.

Pastel yellow, pink, and blue lotuses and lilies bloom in the 257-foot-long pond, also known as the Reflecting Pool, that stretches from El Prado to the **Botanical Building**. During World War II, the pond was a swimming pool for patients of the **Naval Hospital**; during the summer of 1945, over 22,000 San Diego children also made this their swimming hole. Today artists, musicians, magicians, and mimes set up shop on weekends for the crowds beside the pond. A truly beautiful spot, the lawns surrounding the pond are popular with loungers, sunbathers, and locals who come here to relax and read the Sunday newspapers. ◆ Free; closed on Th. Between the Casa del Prado and the Timken Art Gallery. 235.1100

San Diego Museum of Art

21 San Diego Museum of Art

Above this museum's ornate entryway are the coats of arms of San Diego, California, Spain,

and America, statues of Spanish painters Murillo, Zurbarán, and Velázquez, and a giant curved seashell, representing the shell that carried St. James to the coast of Spain. The façade, designed in stages by **William Templeton Johnson** and **Robert W. Snyder** between 1924 and 1926, was meant to resemble the buildings of the 16th-century Spanish Renaissance. It was decorated in the Plateresque style, derived from the Spanish word *platero* (silversmith), because the intricate ornamentation resembles the refinements of the silversmith's art.

The museum was known as the **Fine Arts Gallery of San Diego** until 1978, when curators found that visitors assumed the museum's collection was for sale. The name was then changed, though the membership is still called the Fine Arts Society. Between the 1920s and the 1940s, much of the gallery's internationally acclaimed collection of Italian Renaissance and Spanish Baroque paintings was donated by Anne R. and Amy Putnam, two sisters who devoted their lives and estates to collecting important paintings. During World War II, the paintings were loaned to several other US museums, and the gallery became a 423-bed military hospital. When the patients moved out, William Templeton Johnson was commissioned and paid $5 a day to get the galleries back in shape.

Thanks to the largesse of several San Diegans, the museum's permanent collection has continued to grow. Spanish Baroque paintings, 19th- and 20th-century European paintings, and works by contemporary California artists comprise the bulk of the museum's holdings. Architects **Robert Mosher** and **Roy Drew** designed the **West** and **East Wings**, in 1966 and 1970, respectively, for Asian arts and sculpture. The **May S. Marcy Sculpture Garden** was designed in 1972 by **Marie Wimmer** and **Joseph Yamada** to provide needed space to update the museum's growing sculpture collection, including works by Henry Moore and Louise Nevelson.

The museum presents exciting and unusual traveling exhibits; recent ones have included a

SAN DIEGO MUSEUM OF ART

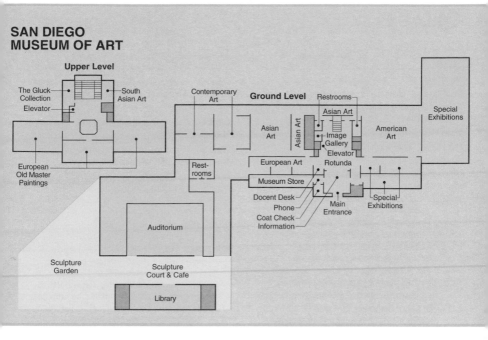

fascinating display of picture frames from 1860 to 1960. One popular exhibit displayed psychedelic rock posters; another covered the works of Grandma Moses. Each spring, the museum presents **Art Alive**, with floral designers, artists, and gardeners creating arrangements of flowers and greenery to express their interpretations of the museum's artworks. The exhibit draws enormous crowds; proceeds benefit the museum's educational programs. Jazz, chamber music, classical guitar, and other concerts are held at the museum frequently, along with various lecture series.

Harking back to its role as a landscaped plaza at the 1915 exposition, the parking lot in front of the museum is called the **Plaza de Panama**. The museum marks the northern side of the plaza; the **Spreckels Organ Pavilion** is at its south end. ♦ Admission. Tu-Su. 232.7931. ⑤ www.sdmart.org

22 THE GLOBE THEATRES

The **Old Globe Theatre**, in its many incarnations, is the heart and soul of this theatrical triplex. Modeled by **Richard Requa** after England's Elizabethan Globe Theatre on the Thames, it was the site, during the 1935-1936 exposition, of what many an Anglophile considered a theatrical abhorrence. Although the building itself was a faithful reproduction, the plays were far less traditional. The **Old Globe Players**, a group of energetic and versatile actors, presented *Streamlined Shakespeare*—40-minute condensations of the bard's top plays, with each actor changing character up to five times a day. After the fair, the troupe took their tremendously popular show on the road and appeared at expositions and theaters around the country.

Built as a temporary structure for the exposition, the theater was sold to wreckers in 1936 for $400. Fans raised $10,000 to buy the building back and reinforce it as a permanent playhouse. In 1949 a farsighted B. Iden Payne, Shakespearean scholar and director, began a summer series of Shakespeare's plays (in their entirety) that became the cornerstone for the theater's enduring success. The **Old Falstaff Tavern**, where fairgoers in the 1930s quaffed their brews by the fireplace, became the **Cassius Carter Centre Stage** in 1968. The theater was named for a local attorney who attended every performance and was said to have memorized every line of Shakespeare.

Restaurants/Clubs: Red | Hotels: Purple | Shops: Orange | Outdoors/Parks: Green | Sights/Culture: Blue

CHILD'S PLAY

In the unlikely event that the beaches, bays, playgrounds, and parks aren't enough fun, here are a few more guaranteed child pleasers:

Feed the baby goats and watch the primate infants in the glass-enclosed nursery at the **Children's Zoo** in the **San Diego Zoo**.

Crawl through the net tubes under showers of water at **Sea World**'s **Shamu's Happy Harbor**.

Splatter paint on a dilapidated pickup truck at the **Children's Museum/Museo de los Niños** in **downtown**.

Snorkel amid golden garibaldi at **La Jolla Cove**.

Search for starfish and anemones at the tide pools under the **Ocean Beach Pier**.

Alter images at the computer-generated mirrors at **Balboa Park**'s **Reuben H. Fleet Space Theatre and Science Center**.

Gape at the mummies in **Balboa Park**'s **Museum of Man**.

Wrangle the controls away from a grownup at the **Model Railroad Museum** in **Balboa Park**.

Screech and **scream** full force on the **Giant Dipper** roller coaster in **Belmont Park**.

In 1978 **Balboa Park** was struck by its second arson fire in just a few months, and the entire Globe complex was destroyed. By December 1979 ground had been broken for a new and better complex that was still modeled after the first. In 1982 the new **Old Globe Theatre** became the centerpiece of three stages, which also included the **Cassius Carter Stage** and the outdoor **Lowell Davies Festival Theatre**, where summer-night performances of plays like *The Night of the Iguana* are enhanced by animal cries from the zoo next door. Over the years, scores of famous actors and actresses have begun or advanced their careers here under the direction of Executive Director Craig Noel and Artistic Director Jack O'Brien. Both Dennis Hopper and Hal Holbrook starred in *Merchant of Venice*; Neil Simon premiered two of his works at the Globe. *Into the Woods*, *Play On!* and *The Full Monty* all went on to Broadway after successful runs here.

In 1950 fences were built on both sides of the Cabrillo Bridge to prevent the despondent from jumping to their deaths; at least 50 people had been successful by that time, causing a local cynic to post a sign on the road below the bridge reading "Beware of falling bodies."
—Florence Christman,
The Romance of Balboa Park

Zoo leaders have always been creative in their quest for new occupants. In 1938, San Diego Zoo director Belle Benchley sent a weekly jar of fleas from the dog pound to a flea circus in New Jersey in exchange for several rare snakes.

The Tony award–winning Globe Theatres produce 14 plays annually. The complex includes an excellent gift shop with puppets, T-shirts, books and videos on theater topics, and even Cliff's Notes for those not quite familiar with Shakespeare. **Lady Carolyn's Pub** serves salads, sandwiches, desserts, and coffee drinks 1 hour before performances. ◆ Theater tours Sa-Su, 10:30AM. Tour fee. El Prado (between the Museum of Man and the San Diego Museum of Art). 239.2255; tour info, 231-1941 ᴄ

THE PRADO
AT BALBOA PARK

23 CASA DEL PRADO

This edifice was the inspiration of Bea Evenson, who founded the Committee of 100 in 1967 to preserve **Balboa Park**'s architecture. Originally erected in 1914 as the fair's **Food and Beverage** building (another **Carleton Winslow** design), it was used by the navy during both world wars and as offices for civic groups in between. The building became temporary headquarters for the **San Diego Public Library** between 1952 and 1954. Like many of the park's structures, it fell into disrepair over the years. The city could barely keep up with maintenance and restoration of the many buildings left from the two expositions, and this was one of those to fall by the wayside. The civic groups using the building's offices gradually found more modern space, and the edifice was virtually abandoned in the 1960s.

The structure was declared unsafe and closed after a moderate earthquake in 1968. Before it was sold to a wrecking company for $25, members of the Committee of 100 carefully removed much of the statuary from the original building and had it recast for what is standing here today. Architect **Richard George Wheeler** was already familiar with the park's buildings from the 1915 exposition—he had sketched them as a child—when he designed the current structure.

Like its forerunner, this edifice combines copies of various Mexican and Spanish buildings, including chapels from the Catedral Metropolitana in Mexico City and a patio in Querétaro, Mexico. The ornaments and embellishments on the façade include the face of Neptune, the figures of St. Jerome and Queen Isabella, and a veritable covey of cherubs.

A 680-seat auditorium houses the **Junior Theatre** and other performing-arts organizations. The San Diego Floral Association sponsors garden shows in the building on most weekends throughout the year, with some impressive displays of orchids, bonsai, and cacti. ◆ Between the Natural History Museum and the Lily Pond. Junior Theatre box office, 239.8355. ఠ www.juniortheatre.com

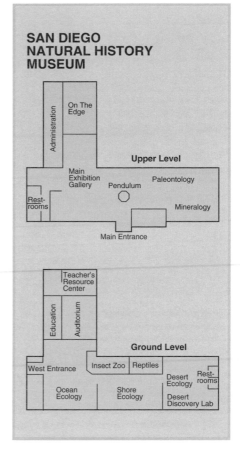

24 NATURAL HISTORY MUSEUM

The San Diego Society of Natural History was founded in 1874 but didn't have a permanent setting for its collection until Ellen Browning Scripps donated $125,000 for a museum in 1931. **William Templeton Johnson** designed the structure, which was completed in 1933. For many decades, the museum housed displays on the region's minerals, endangered and extinct animals, and desert and seashore life. In 1991, the museum's leaders adapted a new approach to their mission, focusing on the binational region of San Diego and Baja California, Mexico. It contributed to the making of the IMAX film *Ocean Oasis* about the Sea of Cortez, and established the Biodiversity Research Center of the Californias.

At the same time, the museum embarked on a building campaign, which resulted in a renovation and addition that more than doubled the size of the building. The new wing, which opened in 2001, was designed by the **Bundy and Thompson** architectural firm of San Diego. Its most striking feature is a soaring glass-fronted entrance and atrium with balconies and vast display areas. Exhibits include a full skeletal cast of a *Tyrannosaurus rex*, a collection of fossils and live snakes and lizards called Natural Treasures Past & Present, and a Kid's Habitat with interactive games.

The museum's society also offers biological expeditions throughout the county, as well as walks through the park's canyons and educational whale-watching boat trips. The new north entrance atrium sits beside a Moreton Bay fig tree that is said to be over 150 years old. A fence surrounds the tree's rambling roots. ◆ Admission. Daily. Between Park Blvd and the Casa del Prado. 232.3821. ఠ www.sdnhm.org

25 TIMKEN ART GALLERY

Mrs. Appleton (Timken) Bridges and her husband were major benefactors of the **Fine Arts Gallery** (now the **San Diego Museum of Art**) from 1925 through the 1940s. When

THE BEST

Hugh M. Davies
David C. Copley Director, Museum of Contemporary Art, San Diego

Fort Rosecrans National Cemetery for the spectacular view and sense of serenity. A great place to watch the whale migration in January.

Centro Cultural Tijuana (CECUT), an impressive cultural center with a marvelous multimedia display of the history of the Californias. Fine café, IMAX theater, state-of-the-art concert and lecture hall. Easy to reach over the border.

Border Field State Park for a true sense of what it feels like to live on the border between the US and Mexico. A simple fence—*la linea*—runs all the way to the ocean, separating the two countries. Also, there is a beautiful bird sanctuary there and a festive, convivial atmosphere.

Top of **Mount Soledad** in **La Jolla** for the 360-degree view of San Diego.

Timken Art Gallery in **Balboa Park**, a jewel box of a museum with a great repository of European old masters, Russian icons, and historical American paintings.

Salk Institute—Louis Kahn's architectural masterpiece—for the magnificent vista of the sea framed by a timeless building.

The truly challenging and visually splendid south course at **Torrey Pines Golf Course**.

First white corn in July from **Chino's** in **Rancho Santa Fe**.

Exploring the **tide pools** in **La Jolla** on a Sunday afternoon with my children.

Guy Fleming Trail at **Torrey Pines State Park**.

Third baseline seat for a night baseball game at **Qualcomm Stadium**, with its old-fashioned grass and newfangled lights.

Strawberry-banana gelati from **Gelato Vero** in **Hillcrest**.

Sautéed English sole and Pinot Grigio at **Sante Restaurant** in **La Jolla**.

Going to see the **Neville Brothers** at **Belly Up Tavern** in **Solana Beach**.

Playing darts and eating Scotch eggs and chips at the **Prince of Wales Pub** on India Street.

Chicano Park murals in **Barrio Logan**.

Banker's Hill, especially the **Spruce Street pedestrian suspension bridge**.

The **Fishery Restaurant**, Cass Street, **Pacific Beach**, finest fresh fish and seafood, five draft beers and strong wine selection, raw oysters followed by mahimahi. Unpretentious and excellent.

Mrs. Bridges died, Anne and Amy Putnam took over the major support of the museum, donating works by old masters from their collection. In the 1950s, the sisters founded the Putnam Foundation under the direction of their attorney Walter Ames (who had been Mrs. Bridges's lawyer in the 1920s). Sometime later, either the sisters or their lawyer had a falling out with the Fine Arts Gallery, and Ames convinced the Timken family to create a foundation, build a museum, and move the remarkable Putnam collection to the new space. The result was this small, unobtrusive building designed by **Frank Hope** in 1965. Be sure to stop in the **American Room** to see *Cho-looke, the Yosemite Fall*, a painting by Albert Bierstadt. The **European Rooms** display priceless paintings from the 14th to 19th centuries, including works by Rembrandt, Rubens, Pisarro, and Cézanne. But the gallery's real treasures are to be found among the *Russian Icons*—elaborate altar screens and small panels used to section off a space for private religious devotions in the home. ♦ Free. Closed Monday and the month of September. 1500 El Prado (between the Lily Pond and Plaza de Panama). 239.5548. www.gort.ucsd.edu/sj/timken/

26 CABRILLO BRIDGE

Designed by **Thomas B. Hunter** as a dramatic entrance to the 1915 fair, this cantilevered bridge is a truly heartwarming sight at Christmastime when it is strung with colored lights. The first passenger to cross the bridge was Franklin D. Roosevelt, then secretary of the navy. At that time, it spanned a barren canyon that was transformed from the city pound into a glassy pond reflecting the **California Tower**. The pond is now a freeway, and the bridge is busy with cars, bicycles, in-line skaters, and pedestrians vying for space. Though the walk across is hardly as serene as it once was, the view—from the shrouded canyon walls to the Coronado Bridge—is still impressive. ♦ From Sixth Ave to the California Quadrangle

27 MUSEUM OF MAN

Located in the original entryway to the park, this gallery—originally called the **San Diego Museum**—was established in 1915 to continue the archaeological and anthropological work that was begun for the fair. The museum's main exhibits are housed in the **California Building**, designed by **Bertram Goodhue** and **Carleton Winslow** for the 1915 exposition. The building, one of the most

TIRED OF TRAMPING AROUND? TAKE THE TRAM

With parking at a premium in **Balboa Park**, and with a large distance to cover to get the most enjoyment out of a visit here, the best way to get around the park is by tram. Not only does it travel across a wide area and run frequently, but it's free! The red tram—with large windows, wooden seats, and brass railings—goes from the parking lot at **Inspiration Point** at the far southeast side of the park to the **San Diego Zoo** at the northeast side and across **Cabrillo Bridge** to **Balboa Park West** (see map on page 21). It operates daily every 8 to 12 minutes between 8:30AM and 6PM (hours are extended during the summer).

architecturally impressive in the park, is topped by the 200-foot-high **California Tower**, where the Westminster Chimes continue to sound the quarter-hour on the carillon. The elaborate façade includes full-size sculpted figures of Father Junípero Serra, Sebastián Vizcaíno, and Father Luis Jaime—California's first Christian martyr. Much of the rest of the park has been built to carry on the ornamental Spanish-Colonial theme that Goodhue created with this building back in 1915.

Bull Hewitt, the museum's first director, had convinced the Smithsonian Institution and the School of American Archaeology to support a $100,000 comprehensive exhibit called *The Story of Man through the Ages* for the 1915–1916 exposition. Archaeologists, physical anthropologists, and ethnologists were dispatched to Peru, Central America, Africa, Central Europe, Siberia, the Philippines, and the Southwest US to collect the 5,000 specimens of ethnological importance that still comprise the core of the museum's permanent collection. Under the museum's sky blue dome is a cast replica of the grand stela (carved pillar) at the Maya ruins in Quirigua, Guatemala. The museum's original stela was remolded in 1999 by local artist Tony Neff. It took him 2 years to replicate the intricate Mayan symbols on the 21-foot-tall monument, which was moved ever so gingerly back to the museum in 2001. Its carvings of Maya gods and legends are more distinct than on the original stela, which suffered from being exposed to the jungle's elements.

Among the permanent collection is an exhibit on the Kumeyaay Indians, San Diego's original residents. *Lifecycles and Ceremonies* includes a hands-on, high-tech lesson in biology and reproduction. There are also exhibits on the costumes and rituals of San Diego's many ethnic communities, and one focusing on the sun gods and mummies of ancient Egypt, complete with a real human mummy. The Children's Discovery Center features *Discover Egypt*, an interactive learning experience for kids. The exhibit highlights the role of archaeologists and anthropologists in interpreting ancient Egyptian culture. Children can listen to a description of mummification as told by the Egyptian god Anubis or decipher a message written in hieroglyphics. ♦ Admission. Daily. 1350 El Prado (between Plaza de Panama and Cabrillo Bridge). 239.2001. ⅗ www.museumofman.org

Within the Museum of Man:

CHAPEL OF ST. FRANCIS

Built in Spanish-Colonial style for the 1915 fair, this chapel was used for weddings and as a military chapel during World War II, but was never consecrated. The frontispiece above the altar echoes the fanciful façade of the museum, with sculptures of *Our Lady and Child* and *St. Francis Xavier.*

ADMINISTRATION BUILDING

Located adjacent to the **California Building**, this was the welcoming point for the 1915 exposition. **Irving Gill**, San Diego's premier architect at the time, began designing the building in 1911. Midway through Gill's work, the park's overseers shifted their focus from a modernistic, minimalist style to the more ornate design of New York architects **Bertram Goodhue** and **Carleton Winslow**, who added Beaux Arts balconies and filled the structure with intricate Baroque ornamentation. The grand lobbies and spacious offices were used for international receptions during the fair and as a military hospital during World War II. In 1978 the city planned to demolish the building, which had been vacant for years. The state intervened, saying it was included with **Balboa Park**'s other architectural treasures in the National Register of Historic Places and could not be destroyed. A mid-1990 restoration opened up more gallery space for displaying the museum's collection.

28 EL CID

Anna Hyatt Huntington's 23-foot-tall sculpture of Rodrigo Díaz de Bivar (known as El Cid)—the chivalrous Castilian who drove the Moors from Spain in the 11th century—was donated to the **Fine Arts Gallery** in 1927. **William Templeton Johnson** designed a limestone pedestal for it, and in 1930, *El Cid* took up residence between the gallery and the **Spreckels Organ Pavilion**. A smaller Huntington sculpture of *Diana* stands by the entrance to the **San Diego Museum of Art**. ♦ El Prado (near the House of Hospitality)

29 PLAZA DE BALBOA

The fountain in this plaza soars 50 to 60 feet in the air, foaming white against the cloudless blue sky. A wind-sensing device cuts the volume of water when the wind blows, protecting all those who pose for a souvenir snapshot from becoming wet. ♦ Between the Space Theater and the Natural History Museum

30 ROSE AND DESERT GARDENS

A footbridge over Park Boulevard leads to these gardens on the edge of Florida Canyon. The rose blossoms are often the backdrop for weddings, and the blooms on the cacti to the north are stunning. Smaller gardens are scattered throughout the park and are well worth exploring. ♦ Park Blvd (at Florida Canyon)

31 ALCAZAR GARDEN

Depending on the season, snapdragons, zinnias, and calendula splash color through the beds of this hidden garden, one of the prettiest resting spots in the park. Designers Requa & Perry patterned the gardens after those surrounding the Alcazar Castle in Seville, Spain. Moorish-style fountains are inlaid with turquoise, yellow, and green tiles, and the cement benches near the flowerbeds are

---

Christmas on the Prado is the most beloved annual event in San Diego. The official celebration usually takes place the first weekend of December, bringing the park alive on winter nights. Colored lights sparkle along Cabrillo Bridge, carolers and the crowds sing, and even *El Cid* looks as if he should be sporting a big red bow. The museums, with free admission, display imaginative Christmas trees; many serve goodies such as popcorn, hot cider, hearty soup, and caramel apples.

Some say Bigfoot visited San Diego in the late 1800s, but proof of his presence has yet to be found.

---

perfect for reading and relaxation. ♦ Behind the House of Charm (south side of El Prado)

32 HOUSE OF HOSPITALITY

The prettiest part of this elaborate complex—said to resemble the Hospital of Santa Cruz in Toledo, Spain—is the courtyard's tiled fountain, wherein sits *La Tehuana de Tehuantepec, Mexico*. This serene señorita, pouring water from her rounded jar, was created from a 1,200-pound block of limestone by sculptor Donal Hord for the 1935 fair. Her visage has been photographed unceasingly ever since. The structure, designed in 1915 by **Bertram Goodhue** and **Carleton Winslow**, was first used as the **Foreign Arts Building**, then as headquarters for the Women's Executive Committee. It was restored and refurbished in 1935 by **Sam Hamill** and used for community organizations, banquets, receptions, and dances, except during World War II, when its cavernous dining rooms and hallways served as dorms for 600 military nurses. In 1995 the building underwent a $15 million, 2-year reconstruction, keeping true to the original design of both the interior and exterior. ♦ 1549 El Prado (between Casade Balboa and Plaza de Panama)

Within the House of Hospitality:

THE PRADO RESTAURANT

★★ $$ Restaurateurs David and Lesley Cohn, who own several popular San Diego restaurants, worked wonders with the park's landmark restaurant. The setting is exquisite, with a warm, wood-beamed dining room and a sunny terrace overlooking the park's gardens. The menu draws upon Balboa Park's heritage with an emphasis on Latin cooking (with Italian touches). It's one of the few places where you can get a good pisco sour—practically the national drink of Peru—and chicken with Oaxacan *mole* sauce. The Cohns also operate the **Balboa Park Food and Wine School** at the House of Hospitality, with classes on sushi making, food as an aphrodisiac, and other enticing topics. ♦ Latin/Italian ♦ Daily, lunch and dinner. Reservations recommended. 557.9441. www.balboawinefood.com

BALBOA PARK VISITORS CENTER

Located in the northeast corner of the House of Hospitality, the 1,200-square-foot visitor center was remodeled in late 2001 to better accommodate the approximate 500,000 people who pass through every year. It is staffed largely by volunteers who field a phenomenal array of questions and answers about the park. Be sure to pick up a copy of the fine map and guide to the park and to browse through the center's collection of books and pamphlets. There's also a retail counter with souvenirs and sundries (including postcards and postage stamps) for sale. ◆ Daily. 239.0512

33 HOUSE OF CHARM

During the first exposition, this Mission-style building—designed by **Carleton Winslow** in 1915—housed displays of American Indian arts; during the second, it held souvenir stands. It fell into disrepair and was saved from the wrecking ball by the Committee of 100. Restoration began in 1994 with workers making meticulous plaster casts of the exterior ornamentation so they could faithfully reproduce Winslow's original design. New tenants set up operation in the building in 1996 and have made it one of the most gorgeous structures in the park. ◆ 1439 El Prado (next to the Alcazar Garden)

MINGEI INTERNATIONAL MUSEUM

33 MINGEI INTERNATIONAL MUSEUM

Once housed in a shopping mall, this museum of world folk art, craft, and design never ceases to enthrall its fans with fascinating exhibits. The permanent collection includes works by many of Mexico's most famous folk artists, along with 12,000 art objects from 100 countries. Exhibit themes range from American Shaker arts to hand-carved and painted carousel horses to Indonesian and Chinese textiles. The museum has produced several books and videos on various subjects, including kites as art and the Japanese arts of daily life. As might be expected, the shop is packed with irresistible finds. Admission; Tu-Su, 10AM–4PM. 239-0003. ◆ 1439 El Prado (next to the Alcazar Garden). www.mingei.org

34 CASA DE BALBOA

This building's many incarnations include stints as the **House of Commerce and Industries** for the 1915 fair; the **Canadian Building**, complete with a colony of beavers building a dam, for the 1916 fair; the **Museum of Natural History**, 1922–1935; the **Palace of Better Housing** (with displays of electric lighting phenomena that gave the building the moniker "the Electric Building") for the 1935–1936 exposition; a military

hospital during World War II; a setting for bake sales, dog shows, and other community endeavors between 1949 and 1965; and home of the **Aerospace Museum** in 1965. A devastating arson fire in 1978 destroyed the original 1914 **Bertram Goodhue** building. In 1978, **Richard George Wheeler** created a faithful reproduction, complete with sculptural details copied from bits and pieces of the original building found in the charred rubble. ◆ El Prado (between Zorro Garden and the House of Hospitality). ♿

Within the Casa de Balboa:

SAN DIEGO HISTORICAL SOCIETY MUSEUM

Founded in 1928, the San Diego Historical Society achieved a decades-long dream in 1989 with the establishment of this museum and permanent home for the society's research archives. Rotating exhibitions on San Diego's history—focusing on the region's American period beginning at the end of the Mexican-American War in 1846—are displayed in the galleries. Those interested in the park's early days should be sure not to miss photographs of the expositions. ◆ Admission. Tu-Su. 232.6203. www.sandiegohistory.org

SAN DIEGO MODEL RAILROAD MUSEUM

Various railroad clubs set up working model train exhibits here, using tracks, trains, and dioramas to replicate the railroad lines that once existed throughout Southern California. Wheels clatter, whistles blow, and the museum's basement quarters reverberate with the sounds of trains in motion. Train buffs have been known to settle in for the day, ignoring the sunshine and fun up above. It's easily one of the park's most popular shows, and the gift shop is sure to lure the kids. ◆ Admission. Tu-Su. 696.0199. www.sdmodelrailroadm.com

MUSEUM OF PHOTOGRAPHIC ARTS

Designed by **David Raphael Singer** in 1983, this museum is one of the world's best for photography, film, and video. It is well known for its permanent collection of 3,000 photographs and daguerreotypes tracing the history of photography, and eclectic selection of visiting shows. Traveling exhibitions in the past have included *Abelardo Morell and the Camera Eye* and *The Model Wife*, presenting photographs of well-known artists featuring their wives as models. The exhibits usually combine images from the museum's collec-

THE BEST

George Varga
Pop Music Critic, *San Diego Union-Tribune*

When asked in previous years how I liked living in San Diego, I invariably responded: "The weather is awful, but the thriving cultural scene makes up for it." In truth, the once-moribund cultural scene here has grown dramatically and could soon rival our usually picture-perfect weather. The following list reflects both perspectives.

The **Coronado Bay Bridge**, the largest freestanding bridge on the West Coast, affords a panoramic view of San Diego to the north, the **South Bay** and **Tijuana** to the south, and **Coronado** itself to the west. Be sure to visit **Hotel del Coronado**, where the classic Billy Wilder film *Some Like It Hot* was shot in 1958. Nondrivers can take the slow but quaint **Coronado Ferry**.

The **Gaslamp Quarter** in downtown San Diego boasts some of the city's best restaurants and nightclubs. For food, check out **Portobello** (one of the finest Italian restaurants in an area overrun with them), **Croce's Restaurant & Jazz Bar** (outstanding orange roughy), and—just beyond the **Gaslamp**—**Pokez**, a down-to-earth eatery specializing in Mexican vegetarian cuisine. For music in the Gaslamp, there's jazz and more at the all-ages **Dizzy's**, the **Juke Joint Cafe**, **Croce's**, **Lilo's**, **Martini Ranch**; techno at **Ole Madrid** and the subterranean **Onyx Room**; blues at **Croce's Top Hat** and **Patrick's II**; and Latin at **Sevilla** and the **Grant Lounge**. The **Casbah**, San Diego's fabled alternative-rock mecca, is a short distance away in Middletown.

Other top nightclubs that boast regional and national talent include the **Belly Up Tavern** in Solana Beach, **Cane's** in Mission Beach, and **Blind Melons** and the **Cannibal Bar** in Pacific Beach. Shelter Island is home to the outdoor **Humphrey's Concerts by the Bay**, which since 1982 has annually hosted some of the biggest names in music. **Chula Vista**'s **Coors Amphitheatre**, with a seating capacity of nearly 20,000, is the area's largest venue. **Java Joe's** in Ocean Beach is one of the most intimate, and it's where such homegrown stars as Jewel, Steve Poltz, and Jason Mraz got their start.

The hoity-toity crowd likes to go to **Bertrand's At Mr. A's** for drinks and a high-rise view of the city. But those in the know favor the **Park Manor Suites' Top of the Park**, a far more earthy setting with a comparable view and much more colorful clientele. A few blocks away is **Fifth & Hawthorn**, a favorite dining spot of actors from the nearby **Old Globe Theatre**, and the upscale **Laurel** (where reservations are essential). The nearby Hillcrest area offers some arresting dining options, most notably **Arrivederci** (for Italian), **Lotus** (for Thai), the **Crest Cafe** (for American favorites), **Ichiban** (for easy-on-the-budget Japanese fare), and **Cafe on Park** (for some of the biggest breakfasts around). Hillcrest is also where you'll find **Off the Record**, one of the county's two best stores for alternative-music fans (the other is **Lou's** in Encinitas), as well as **Spruce Street Forum**, which each year brings the world's leading cutting-edge music artists to town.

Balboa Park and the adjacent **San Diego Zoo** are both worth a visit. But don't overlook the **Botanical Building** (one of several park landmarks featured in Orson Welles's classic film *Citizen Kane*), the **Museum of Photographic Arts**, or the quintessentially California **Frisbee Golf Course** at nearby **Morley Field**.

Rare-book devotees must visit **Wahrenbrock's Book House** downtown, which counts Michael Jackson and Bruce Hornsby among its avid customers. Those seeking difficult-to-find folk, blues, and jazz recordings should head directly to **Folk Arts Rare Records** in Kensington, where proprietor Lou Curtiss boasts a music library so large and varied that the Smithsonian Institution frequently calls on his services.

Finally, no stay in San Diego is complete without a trip to **Tijuana**, where Carlos Santana grew up, which is just 15 miles away by trolley. Avoid the touristy glitz of **Avenida Revolución**, the city's main drag. But do visit the **Centro Cultural**, the jai alai arena, and the **Hipódromo de Agua Caliente** race track. And be sure to check out Tijuana's **Nortec Collective**, whose Mexican music–tinged techno style has drawn international acclaim. Members of the collective regularly perform at various area venues, which also showcase such top local talents as Almafa, Othli, Natural, Nona Delichas, and the memorably named Los Kung Fu Monkeys.

---

tion with those of the show. Various film and lecture series are open to members and the public. ♦ Admission. Daily. 238.7559. www.mopa.org

CAFE IN THE PARK

$ The muffins at this small bakery are so good they typically sell out by noon, but you can get sandwiches, veggie burgers, snacks, and drinks throughout the day. ♦ Café ♦ Daily, breakfast and lunch. No credit cards. 237.0322

35 REUBEN H. FLEET SPACE THEATER AND SCIENCE CENTER

This wonderland of hands-on gadgetry and gimmicks is sure to entrance child and adult alike. **Louis Bodmer** followed Spanish-Colonial design with this 1973 building but added an artistic flourish with a cast parapet that looks like crocheted lace. Inside, the building is devoted to all things scientific and spacey.

The center's benefactor Reuben H. Fleet grew to love San Diego while stationed here as an aviator during World War I. After the war, Fleet started an aircraft company in Rhode Island in 1923 but moved it to San Diego in 1935. Here he became a community activist and benefactor, and after years of talk with other civic leaders about San Diego's need for a hall of science, Fleet donated $400,000 to turn the idea into a reality. This complex—a space theater and science center—is one of the most exciting and popular attractions in the park. The space theater's 75-foot dome was the first Omnimax theater in the world. Multimedia planetarium shows are paired with Omnimax films that make you feel like you're soaring through space or sailing the high seas in a storm. A planetarium show is presented in the theater the first Wednesday of every month.

The science center is filled with interactive exhibits geared toward children and adults. There are computers altering facial images, bolts of electricity zapping between terminals, water splashing from resonance bowls that vibrate with sound, a virtual reality exhibit that puts you in the middle of a meteor shower, and the ever-popular whisper chamber that projects the softest voice across a room. The **Galileo Café** is located off the east rotunda in the Reuben H. Fleet Science Center with tables outside next to the fountain. The menu includes soups, sandwiches, and pastries. The museum store is a gadget lover's nirvana packed with everything from ultra-expensive telescopes to bargain-priced lava lamps. ♦ Admission. M-Tu; W-Th, Su, 9:30AM-8PM; F-Sa, 9:30AM-11:30PM. Between Park Blvd and Casa de Balboa. 238.1233. ♿ www.rhfleet.org

36 JAPANESE FRIENDSHIP GARDEN

The first phase of this garden, which will eventually cover 11 canyon acres east of the **Spreckels Organ Pavilion**, includes a traditional Japanese sand-and-stone garden, with raked gravel walkways and young bamboo and pine groves. Designer Takeshi (Ken) Nagajima started the project in 1990; when completed, it will also feature a formal teahouse, cultural pavilion, and more elaborate gardens. Currently in the garden is an exhibit house built in the Sukiya (tea taste) style used for teahouses. The building has copper shingles and clay tiles on the roof and sliding cedar doors, and inside is a model of how the garden will look when it is finished. ♦ Admission. Tu-Su. Northeast of the Spreckels Organ Pavilion. 232.2780

37 PEPPER GROVE

Originally established in 1910, this stretch of parkland has been used over the years by such groups as the Girl Scouts and the Marines, but its heyday was between 1938 and the outbreak of World War II. At that time, a Works Project Administration project turned the grove into an outdoor dance hall, with a band pavilion, cement dance floor, benches and tables, and live dance music on Saturday nights. The war ended the frivolity, but the sound of laughter returned to the grove with the addition of playground equipment and picnic tables in 1967. This is one of the park's few play areas for children, with plenty of playground equipment and picnic areas. ♦ Park Blvd and Space Theater Way

38 SPRECKELS ORGAN PAVILION

No sound is more characteristic of **Balboa Park** than the music of the world's largest outdoor pipe organ that echoes through the canyons. Sugar magnates John D. and Adolph B. Spreckels donated the $35,000 organ (built by the Austin Organ Company of Hartford) for the 1915 fair. The organ is housed on a raised stage under a carved archway, designed by **Harrison Albright** in 1914, and is protected from the elements by a 12-ton metal curtain. Pillared walkways form Corinthian colonnades in a half-circle around a seating area for 2,400 music lovers. A 20-horsepower electric blower provides the air to operate the organ, which can be heard 2 miles away or more when weather conditions are correct. Balboa Park has had seven official organists since 1915. The current organist, Carol Williams, faced intense competition for the job in 2001. When awarded the position, she said, "I feel as if all my life I've been trained for this job."

Free organ concerts are offered on Sunday afternoons throughout the year and on Monday evenings in the summer. An enormously popular series of weekly summer concerts by military bands, jazz ensembles, and Dixieland quartets is presented weekly during the summer in the pavilion. And if you're lucky, you may just happen to wander through the park when the organist is practicing her repertoire—you'll get a whole new feeling about Balboa Park. ♦ Free. Pavilion: Daily; Su, 2–3PM; Mon concerts: mid-June-Aug, 7:30PM. South of El Prado and the Plaza de Panama. 702.8138. www.serve.com/sosorgan

39 WORLDBEAT CENTER

A multicultural nonprofit organization, the **WorldBeat Center** is dedicated to African music, arts, dance, sculpture, and education. The center offers African dance and drumming classes and sponsors reggae concerts and cultural events. ♦ 2100 Park Blvd at Pepper Grove. 230.1190. www.worldbeatcenter.org

Restaurants/Clubs: Red | Hotels: Purple | Shops: Orange | Outdoors/Parks: Green | Sights/Culture: Blue

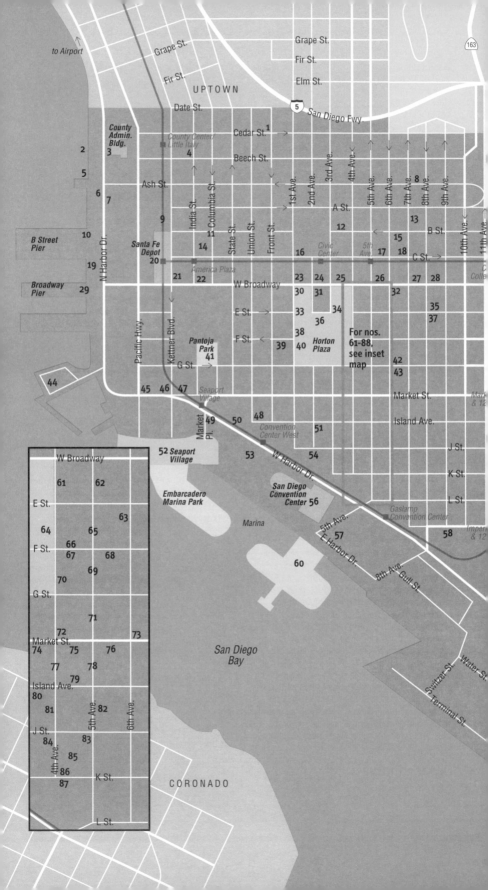

DOWNTOWN

After decades of intense development and restoration, downtown San Diego has emerged as a vibrant neighborhood with attractions that last long after banking hours. The city center is now a magnet for travelers, conventioneers, and locals who once abhorred the thought of leaving their safe, secure neighborhoods and venturing into the evil Big City. Few can resist the magnificent **San Diego Convention Center** on the waterfront, and **Horton Plaza**, the Disneyesque shopping center. Streets are filled with pedestrians long into the night, thanks to the proliferation of trendy cafés and nightclubs in the historic **Gaslamp Quarter**. Cruise ships, sailboats, and US Navy aircraft carriers fill **San Diego Bay**, facing a shimmering skyline of windows dedicated to the view.

The bay has served as San Diego's focal point since the first Spanish conquerors disturbed the peaceful camps of the Kumeyaay Indians along the fertile coastline. Portuguese explorer Juan Rodríguez Cabrillo, sailing under the Spanish flag, discovered San Diego Bay on 28 September 1542 and named it San Miguel. Sebastián Vizcaíno rediscovered the bay on 10 November 1602 and renamed it San Diego in honor of the Spanish saint San Diego de Acalá, whose feast day is celebrated on 12 November. When Spain's first explorers and missionaries settled in San Diego in 1769, they bypassed the harbor and built their mission and fort on a hill overlooking what is now called Old Town. For nearly a century, the bay was a rustic landing station for San Diego's pioneers. But in 1850 an ambitious financier, William Heath Davis, envisioned a great seaport that could someday rival San Francisco as the queen city of the Pacific Coast. He convinced the army to build a supply depot and began raising prefabricated houses along the new dirt streets of downtown. Unfortunately, his fortunes ran out long before his city could become established, and the few wooden structures by the bay became known as **Davis's Folly**.

Davis's dream wouldn't die, however. In 1867 Alonzo Erastus Horton bought 960 acres of mudflats and sagebrush and called the area **New Town**. Within 2 years, the city had an infrastructure of sorts, free lots for churches, free whitewash for homeowners, and **Horton's Wharf**, **Horton's Bank Block**, and the luxurious **Horton House Hotel**. Alonzo E. Horton had built himself a city that belied the naysayers' label of **Horton's Folly**.

Today, as in Horton's day, the bay is what first captivates visitors to downtown. The area that stretches along **Harbor Drive** from the international airport at **Lindbergh Field** to the mock sails atop the San Diego Convention Center has been the focus of considerable development since the early 1980s. Along the waterfront, high-rise hotels and high-price condos pierce the sky between parks. An overhead sign at the foot of **Fifth Avenue** by the San Diego Convention Center marks the entrance to the **Gaslamp Quarter**. Here in downtown's first center is a cluster of renovated historic buildings housing some of the city's best restaurants and clubs. Central downtown is marked by **Horton Plaza**, the fantastical shopping center surrounding the original park and fountain of the plaza of old, dedicated to the city's father in 1909 with a plaque that reads "Fountain for the People of Broadway." Downtown's main boulevard since the late 1800s, **Broadway** is losing its tattoo parlors and dive bars to hotels, modern business centers, and a court-house. North of Broadway, business goes on as usual in established offices and banks as the red **San Diego Trolley** whooshes by.

Development continues in downtown, at an amazing pace. City planners have mapped out seven development districts within an area that only a few decades ago seemed like a ghost town, except during office hours. Each district is undergoing massive change, with everything from public parks to exclusive condos under construction. The East Village, long neglected, will be the site of a new baseball stadium and several large hotel and residential complexes. The **San Diego Convention Center** in what's now called the Marina District was expanded to nearly double its size in a 2.5-year project completed in September 2001. Little Italy, a neighborhood formed by Italian immigrants northwest of downtown, is undergoing a complete face-lift and is becoming an exciting dining and entertainment area. And the Gaslamp Quarter, where Horton first plotted his folly, is now a wildly successful model of urban renewal. It seems there's no shortage of visionaries in downtown, and no end to its possibilities.

1 RADISSON HOTEL HARBOR VIEW

$$ You can't beat the freeway access—at the base of the I-5 ramp into downtown—from this waterside member of the worldwide chain. And if you don't have a car, the hotel's complimentary shuttle will get you to and from the airport, **Horton Plaza**, and **Seaport Village** quickly, saving you from dealing with the waterfront traffic jams. Some rooms in the 22-story tower have views of the harbor, and the heated outdoor pool on the third floor gives an interesting perspective of the county court-house and jail. The 333 rooms and suites are pleasantly subdued in a contemporary pastel and light mahogany theme, and the restaurant serves breakfast, lunch, and dinner daily. ♦ 1646 Front St (between W Cedar and W Date Sts). 239.6800, 800/333.3333; fax 238.9461 &

2 SAN DIEGO BAY AND THE EMBARCADERO

Ⓟ If you drive from the airport into downtown, you'll be riding beside San Diego Bay, where aircraft carriers, cruise ships, sailboats, ferries, and water taxis jockey for space. On clear, sunny Saturdays the horizon is nearly obliterated by billowing sails; at night, the murky dark water reflects the skyscrapers' lights. A pathway popular with joggers and strollers runs beside the bay and its many attractions, winding from the pier where the historic ship *Star of India* is docked, south to **Embarcadero Marina Park**. An ambitious redevelopment project along the waterfront will result in a bayfront esplanade with large park areas and new shops and restaurants. The project is still in the planning stages.

3 SAN DIEGO COUNTY ADMINISTRATION BUILDING

Few downtown towers are as graceful and elegant as this Spanish Colonial-Beaux Arts complex, especially when it's flooded with columns of light at night. At the west entrance, Donal Hord's sculpture, *Guardian of the Water*, portrays a pioneer woman carrying a water jug on her shoulder—perhaps the only public art beloved by all San Diegans. The motto "The Noblest Motive Is the Public Good" is inscribed over the west entrance, with its floor of gold and azure tiles; "Good Government Demands the Intelligent Interest of Every Citizen," reads the mosaic in the foyer floor. Designed by architect **Sam Hamill**, the 10-story administrative center was built on 18 acres of prime waterfront land during the Depression with $1 million from the Works Progress Administration; President Franklin Delano Roosevelt dedicated the building in 1938. If you are in the mood to get married, there is a gazebo on the west side of the building with a lovely view of the water where the county performs civil ceremonies. ♦ 1600 Pacific Hwy (between W Ash and W Grape Sts). County administration offices, 531.5880

4 LITTLE ITALY

India Street, the heart of San Diego's Italian community, is undergoing extensive redevelopment. The revitalized area has become a desirable urban neighborhood within walking distance of downtown. The trolley line runs near here, and parks, pedestrian promenades, and schools have been constructed and/or improved. There are several condo and apartment buildings under construction in the area. Several old pizza parlors, bakeries, and bars have long drawn fans to this area (see the Uptown chapter).

Restaurants/Clubs: Red | Hotels: Purple | Shops: Orange | Outdoors/Parks: Green | Sights/Culture: Blue

THE BEST

Chef Bernard Guillas
Marine Room, La Jolla

Enjoying an early morning espresso in the bar at the **Marine Room**, watching the dolphins in the surf at La Jolla Shores.

Fishing on a local lake and never catching anything.

Walking downtown **Oceanside** because it is still old-fashioned and funky.

Picking your own strawberries in **Carlsbad** and eating them while walking through the **Flower Fields**.

Shopping for fresh fish at **99 Ranch Market**.

Enjoying the change of seasons in **Julian** while eating fresh apple pie.

Playing golf at **Torrey Pines** and looking over the 13th fairway to **Black's Beach**.

Walking through **Balboa Park**, enjoying the museums.

Morning at the zoo, sharing my newspaper with the monkeys.

Dinner and cocktails in the **Gaslamp Quarter**.

Summer jazz concerts at **Thornton Winery** in **Temecula**.

San Diego Bay harbor cruise at sunset.

Jewel Ball at the **La Jolla Beach & Tennis Club** is a blast.

Hot-air balloon ride over the **Del Mar Fairgrounds**.

A day with the ponies, always betting on the donkey.

Visiting local farmers in the morning mist.

Afternoon stroll through the **San Diego Mission**.

Martini at **Four Seasons Aviara**.

Riding the carousel at **Seaport Village** and taking the ferryboat to **Coronado Island**.

Now, antique shops, design stores, and trendy cafés are beginning to turn Little Italy into an extension of downtown. Bordered by Ash and Laurel Sts and by Columbia St and Harbor Dr

5 MARITIME MUSEUM

Volunteers have been staffing this organization since 1958, when a group of enthusiastic volunteers calling themselves the 40 Thieves set to work on the *Star of India*, now the cornerstone of the museum's collection of historic vessels, navigational tools, scale models, and a replica of Cabrillo's vessel. The group is headquartered on the *Berkeley* ferry. Admission. Daily, 9AM-8PM. 1492 N Harbor Dr (at W Ash St). 234.9153

At the Maritime Museum:

STAR OF INDIA

Built in 1863, this is the oldest iron merchant ship afloat in the world. It is the undisputed masterpiece of the bay, and easily the most popular attraction. The main mast soars 139 feet into the blue sky, the 205-foot-long hull is built of more than 1,000 tons of Swedish iron, and 15,000 square yards of white canvas unfurl into her sails. Christened the *Enterpe* at the Isle of Man, the vessel made 21 trips around the world and served as a ferry for immigrants from England to Australia and as a courier on the East Indian trade route. In 1906 the ship was registered in the US as the *Star of India* and used as a cannery tender, shuttling Asian laborers from San Francisco to Alaskan canneries. It made its last journey to Bristol Bay, Alaska, in 1923,

and was retired to float and disintegrate in San Diego Bay in 1926. In 1959, an enthusiastic group of volunteers set to work stripping the deck, polishing the figurehead, and restoring its dignity. The vessel's sails captured the wind on 4 July 1976 for its first journey in 50 years; it sails approximately once a year now with a crew of 60 volunteers on deck and in the rigging.

THE BERKELEY

An 1898 propeller-driven ferry as ornate as any riverboat on the Mississippi, this was the **Southern Pacific Railway**'s only misguided attempt at building a ship of this type. The unwieldy 289-foot-long boat could carry 1,709 passengers but had a difficult time maneuvering between the San Francisco and Oakland piers on its daily route. The ferry's moment of glory arrived when it carried shiploads of refugees from the 1906 earthquake and fire in San Francisco to the relative safety of Oakland. The **Maritime Museum**'s offices are located on the ship's main deck, with carved wood paneling, plate glass mirrors, and stained-glass windows in the clerestory.

THE *MEDEA*

Captain MacAllister Hall of Torrisdale Castle, Scotland, commissioned this iron-hulled, steam-powered yacht in 1904 for his grouse and deer hunting soirées off the Scottish isles. Members of Parliament and other such British gentry have owned it from time to time, and the boat patrolled the English Channel for submarines during World War I. In 1969, Paul and Olive Whittier spotted the ship covered with snow and ice off the coast of Sweden. Enchanted, they bought it, had it restored in Canada, and in 1973 donated the yacht to the **Maritime Museum**.

6 STAR OF THE SEA

★★★★$$$$ Candles glow, crystal glistens, and the chatter seems ever so refined in this elegant dining room suspended over the water. Once a wood-paneled, old-guard establishment, the restaurant was totally remodeled in 1999 and is now one of the most fashionable dining rooms in town. Huge windows provide unobstructed views of the bay, and sleek lighting fixtures resemble sails floating above the tables. Chef Brian Johnson is a master at preparing fresh seafood. Start your meal with ahi tartare, then move on to lobster-tail butter poached with wild mushrooms or sautéed sea scallops with goat cheese and onion tart. Save room for the liquid-center chocolate cake—a divine dessert. ◆ Seafood ◆ Daily, dinner. Reservations strongly advised. 1360 N Harbor Dr (between W Broadway and Ash St). 232.7408

7 RUTH'S CHRIS STEAK HOUSE

★★$$$$ This branch of the famed steakhouse chain was the first downtown restaurant to champion the resurgence of thick, juicy steaks. A dab of butter sizzling atop your rib eye wipes out any pretensions of healthy dining. This is the place to throw caution to the wind and forget dietary and financial concerns. The side dishes are as impressive as the steaks—spinach lovers must try the creamed spinach. The wines by the glass are very pricey. Just order the bottle and take a cab back to your hotel. You'll be too full to walk anyway. ◆ 1355 N. Harbor Dr (between W Broadway and Ash St). 233.1422

8 EL CORTEZ

The dilapidated and abandoned El Cortez Hotel at Seventh and Ash Streets was the epitome of elegance and style when it was built in 1927. In 1956 architect C.J. Paderewski designed the first outside glass hydraulic elevator in the world for the hotel, and over the decades generations of San Diegans have danced under the stars in its Sky Room. The hotel's most colorful owner was evangelist Morris Cerullo, who used it as an international ministry school. The hotel fell into disrepair until the J. Peter Block Companies purchased it and created a tower of classy luxury apartments. The hotel's Don Room is available for events and is the only part of the hotel that is open to the public. ◆ 702 Ash St (at 7th Ave). 338.8338 (building manager). www.elc.cc

9 RAINWATER'S

★★★$$$ A popular spot with the power-lunch crowd for its classic American chop-house fare, this restaurant has spacious private booths and freestanding tables in the middle of it all. This is one of the best places in town for stick-to-your-ribs, soul-satisfying steaks, chops, and fish. A midday repast in the old style might include dry martinis, oysters, and a perfect filet mignon or the lunch special of chicken potpie or meat loaf. Dinner would be steamed mussels, a massive Caesar salad, and Maine lobster. Killer desserts like Southern-style pecan pie should follow all meals for the full (and filling) experience. And best of all, the wait staff greets strangers with the same graciousness given the politicos and business honchos who consider Rainwater's their private club. ◆ American ◆ M-F, lunch and dinner; Sa-Su, dinner. Reservations recommended. 1202 Kettner Blvd (between West B and West A Sts). 233.5757

10 B STREET CRUISE SHIP TERMINAL

Cruise ships bound for the Mexican coast and Panama Canal provide a jarring contrast to the navy carriers home from sea duty docked across the bay. ◆ N Harbor Dr (between W Broadway and W Ash St)

11 W HOTEL

$$$ Any feelings of inferiority San Diegans might have felt about their downtown can be put to rest. The classy W chain wouldn't consider building a hotel in a second-rate city. This 19-story pleasure palace is scheduled to open in 2003 with 261 rooms. ◆ State at B St. 888/625.5144. www.whotels.com

12 4TH & B

Dowtown's best (for now) concert venue attracts top-notch musicians of every breed, from jazz to hip-hop to Latin rock. There are several bars, lounges, and concert halls in the converted bank building. ◆ 345 B St (at Third Ave). 231.4343, 231.2131. www.4thandb.com

13 SYMPHONY TOWERS

Copley Symphony Hall sits at the base of these twin glass and red-granite towers designed by **Skidmore, Owings & Merrill** in 1989. The lobby for the **Marriott Suites** hotel is on the 12th floor; other giants have moved in above; and the **University Club**, one of the oldest private clubs in downtown, is on top. ◆ 750 B St (between Seventh and Eighth Aves). 231.7721

Restaurants/Clubs: Red | Hotels: Purple | Shops: Orange | Outdoors/Parks: Green | Sights/Culture: Blue

Within Symphony Towers:

Copley Symphony Hall

The **San Diego Symphony** has the distinction of owning this performance hall set in a magnificently restored theater. The original Rococo–Spanish Renaissance **Fox Theatre** (designed by **Weeks & Day**) opened in 1929 with the talkie *They Had to See Paris* to a celebrity crowd including Buster Keaton, Jackie Coogan, George Jessel, and the film's star, Will Rogers. Walt Disney loved the theater so much he opened all his movies here. Like most of downtown's old theaters, it steadily disintegrated over the decades and seemed destined for destruction until a developer bought the entire block in 1984 and sold this building to the **San Diego Symphony**. The **Deems/Lewis** architectural firm was hired to handle the renovation. The 12-foot-wide chandelier—which held eight chorus girls and the accordion-playing orchestra conductor on opening night—and the 26,000-pipe organ were also restored, giving longtime San Diegans a jolt of nostalgia for the Fox. The symphony performs from October through May at this 2,225-seat theater. It also hosts a SummerPops series at the Navy Pier. ◆ 1245 Seventh Ave (between B and A Sts). Box office, 235.0804 ♿

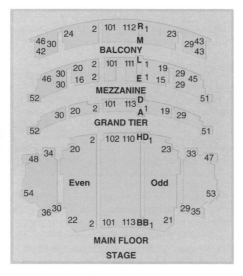

13 Marriott Suites

$$ The hotel's lobby is on the 12th floor, so entering can be a bit disconcerting until a bellhop comes to your rescue and takes you up in the elevator. Classical music befitting **Copley Symphony Hall** plays throughout the pink-and-green marble lobby and atriumlike lounge connecting the office tower with the hotel. The rooms aren't overly lavish, but they're ideal for business travelers who like having a handsome wood desk to work on (with a convenient view of the television, a telephone, and French doors to separate it from the bedroom). All 264 rooms are suites; some have conference tables in the living room area, and all have refrigerators and coffeemakers. The **Renditions** restaurant serves breakfast, lunch, and dinner daily. ◆ 701 A St (between Eighth and Seventh Aves). 696.9800, 800/228.9290; fax 696.1555

14 Karl Strauss' Brewery & Restaurant

★★$ Brewmaster Karl Strauss, who perfected his skills for 44 years at the Pabst brewery, made San Diego's first participant in the microbrewery craze a winner. The stainless-steel tanks are visible from the long bar; the smell of malt and hops fills the air. Homemade brews, ranging from pale ale to amber lager, are available on tap in small sampler glasses, 12-ounce glasses, pints, and 23-ounce schooners. Accompaniments include great Cajun-spiced fries, German sausage with red sauerkraut, and decent burgers. The **Bakery & Cafe** (same phone) next door features the brewery's wood-oven–baked breads, pâtés, cheeses, and salads. ◆ Eclectic ◆ Daily, lunch and dinner. 1157 Columbia St (between West C and West B Sts). 234.2739

15 La Gran Tapa

★★★$$ Elegant brass and wood décor, and a menu featuring classic tapas prepared with only the best ingredients, are featured at this dining spot. You can run up a phenomenal tab as you graze through the menu and wine list, or you can curb your curiosity and stick with the fragrant garlic soup and *empanadillas* (tiny turnovers packed with spicy potato or sausage). Come with a large group for a night-

When the San Diego Trust and Savings' downtown headquarters closed, some longtime clients were allowed to keep the doors to their safe-deposit boxes. The vault holding those boxes is now a meeting room in the Mariott Courtyard hotel.

A linear park called Tweet Street is in the works for the edge of Cortez Hill at the edge of Interstate 5. The city is creating pathways lined with birdhouses to encourage humans and their winged friends to enjoy downtown's natural attributes.

C. Arnholt Smith built the Westgate Hotel in 1970 after prominent Republicans told him San Diego did not have the proper hotels to host the Republican National Convention.

long culinary fiesta. ◆ Spanish ◆ M-F, lunch and dinner; Sa, dinner; closed Sunday. Reservations recommended. 611 B St (between Seventh and Sixth Aves). 234.8272

16 SAN DIEGO CONCOURSE

Downtown San Diego hit the big time in the mid-1960s when office towers began piercing the sky. **Sam W. Hamill** designed this new city center, which opened in 1964. In 1974, the official name became the **Charles C. Dail Concourse**, in honor of the mayor who pushed for the building's construction, though few San Diegans ever refer to it by that name. The **San Diego Convention Center** (see page 49) has drawn away many of the crowds, but the concourse is still in heavy demand for smaller conventions, crafts shows, spiritualist fairs, and the like. Most city offices are located here, and an information center in the main lobby assists residents in getting licenses, permits, and so on. The **Civic Theatre** within the concourse is used for traveling plays and concerts. Its main salon was dedicated in 1980 to Beverly Sills, a strong supporter of the **San Diego Opera**, which performs its spring series here. ◆ Information center, M-F; box office, M-F. 202 C St (between Second and First Aves). Information center, 236.6500, box office, 236.6510

Within the San Diego Concourse:

DOWNTOWN JOHNNY BROWN'S

$ Office workers cram into this casual bar for after-work beers, pool games, and burgers. The walls and ceilings are covered with memorabilia from local sports teams. The best burger, topped with avocado, Ortega chiles, and jack cheese, is named for the San Diego State University's Aztec football team. Stop here for a cheap meal before a concert or play at the **Civic Theatre**. ◆ American ◆ 232.8414

17 COMPUTER MUSEUM OF AMERICA

So you think your Mac is obsolete, right? Be thankful you're not working on a 1920s Burroughs comptometer or even a 1980s Kaypro. Even nontechies are taken by the name of this extensive museum and wander through the door. Science and nature TV shows and publications find it to be a tremendous resource, as do computer groupies. ◆ Donations. 640 C Street (between Sixth and Seventh Aves). Tu-Su. 235.8222. www.computermuseum.org

18 SEVENTH NEAR B

★$ Study your morning news over a latte and bagel or chat with the waitresses from Costa Rica while you wait for your double espresso at this narrow coffeehouse in the business district. Office workers keep a running tab on honor cards when they run in for a fueling. The menu includes good, quick breakfast items (try the fruit, yogurt, and granola parfait) and sandwiches and salad. ◆ Coffeehouse ◆ M-Sa. No credit cards accepted. 1146 Seventh Ave (between C and B Sts). 696.7071

19 SAN DIEGO HARBOR EXCURSION

This company offers 1- and 2-hour harbor cruises throughout the day, as well as dinner cruises on summer weekend nights. Whale-watching excursions are conducted by trained naturalists twice daily during January, February, and March. Call the recorded info line for times. ◆ Fee. 1050 N Harbor Dr

---

Restaurants/Clubs: Red | Hotels: Purple | Shops: Orange | Outdoors/Parks: Green | Sights/Culture: Blue

(between the Broadway and B St Piers). 234.4111

19 HORNBLOWER DINING YACHTS

Come aboard one of the yachts in this fleet for a dinner cruise of the harbor with dance music, or a Sunday brunch cruise with a lavish spread of fruits, salads, meats, and pastries. Call ahead to find out which boat will be sailing; the yachts are available for private parties as well. ♦ Fee. 1066 N Harbor Dr (between the Broadway and B St Piers). 686.8700

19 SAN DIEGO BAY FERRY

When the arching blue Coronado Bridge opened in 1969, the venerable ferry to Coronado stopped running until 1987. Now the *Silvergate* and the *Cabrillo* ferry passengers a mile across the bay from downtown to Coronado's east shore, where restaurants, shops, bike rentals, and trolley tours are available at the **Ferry Landing Marketplace**. ♦ From downtown daily on the hour; 9AM-9PM, Su-Th; 9AM-10PM, F, Sa; from Coronado daily on the half hour. Fee. 1050 N Harbor Dr (at W Broadway). 234.4111

20 SANTA FE DEPOT

The 1915–1916 exposition's most lasting contribution to downtown is **John R. Blakewell**'s Spanish-Colonial–style train station, with its blue, yellow, and white glaze-tile dome echoing the vision of **Balboa Park**'s landmark **California Tower**. There was an earlier train depot at the site, considered to be the best of its kind in the 1880s, but it wasn't up to par with the exposition's grand schemes. Fortunately, this 1915 depot is on the National Register of Historic Places, and plans in the late 1960s to replace it with a high-rise were thwarted. The depot was refurbished in 1983 by **Tucker Sadler**, and is considered so spectacular that celebrity balls and special events are held in the spanking-clean station with its polished wood benches, tiled wainscoting, and polychrome wood beams. The **Coaster** express rail line runs from the depot up the coast eight stops to Oceanside, and **Amtrak** operates trains to Orange County and Los Angeles (with nationwide connections in LA) from the depot. The Museum of Contemporary Art, San Diego, plans to take over the station's baggage building for use as exhibit and workshop space. ♦ 1050 Kettner Blvd (between W Broadway and West C St). Amtrak reservations, 800/872.7245; arrivals and departures recording, 239.9021; Coaster reservations, 800/262.7837; information, 685.4900

21 AMERICA PLAZA

Three architectural firms collaborated on this 500-foot-high office tower spearing the sky with what looks to some like the business end of a Phillips screwdriver. A crescent-shaped glass-and-steel canopy covers the trolley tracks that run along the base of the tower from the **San Diego Convention Center** through downtown. There's plenty of underground parking, and the **Amtrak** depot is right across the street. Two other office towers are under construction at the plaza. ♦ 600 W Broadway (between India St and Kettner Blvd) &

21 MUSEUM OF CONTEMPORARY ART, SAN DIEGO

The main branch of this fine museum is in La Jolla; these smaller downtown halls feature special exhibitions and pieces from the museum's collection. There's a first-rate selection of art books, posters, and cards in the museum shop. The museum's facilities will be expanded over the next few years to include the Baggage building at the **Santa Fe Depot** across the street. ♦ Tu-Th, Sa-Su; F, 11AM-8PM. 1001 Kettner Blvd (between W Broadway and C St). Museum offices, 234.1001; recorded information, 454.3541

22 ARMED SERVICES YMCA

Downtown's original Y is dwarfed by high-rise office towers and construction cranes. It is being redeveloped to hold 260 single-room-occupancy units, including several for low-income tenants. ♦ 500 W Broadway (between Columbia and India Sts). 234.5252 &

Downtown's artists and gallery owners band together each spring to present the annual Artwalk, with special gallery shows, performance art, and a street fair. It usually takes place during a weekend in April.

The carnation is the official flower of San Diego.

San Diego County is the leading avocado producer in the US.

the BRISTOL
San Diego

23 THE BRISTOL

$$ You certainly won't have any trouble waking up in one of these bright, cheery rooms with red walls, yellow and orange

bedspreads, and pop art. Somehow, it all comes together, and the 102 rooms are a pleasant change from standard hotel décor. The rates are great and the location is a bit quieter than at other downtown hotels. Try to sneak a peak at the top-floor Starlight Ballroom with its retractable roof. It's used for private parties. There's live jazz in the lobby on Friday nights, and California cuisine is served in the **Daisies Bistro**. ♦ 1055 First Ave (between Broadway and C St). 232.6141, 800/662.4477; fax 232.6148. www.thebristolsandiego.com

24 WESTGATE

$$$ The lobby of this hotel is a re-creation of the anteroom of Versailles, where French nobility awaited the attention of King Louis XV. Baccarat crystal chandeliers, Kerman Persian carpets, and 18th-century chairs and desks fill the public spaces, whereas the 223 guest rooms are furnished with European antiques from the Louis XV, Louis XVI, Georgian, and English Regency periods. Guests are fittingly treated like royalty, and you almost expect a curtsy or bow whenever you enter a room.

This property was the crowning jewel of financier C. Arnholt Smith's dynasty, though he ended up losing money on it. Smith hired architects **Fujimoto & Fish** in 1970 and spent $14.5 million on the structure while his wife toured Europe collecting $2.4 million in period antiques. Smith sold the complex for $14.7 million in 1974. Today the hotel is popular with European and Latin American travelers accustomed to gracious accommodations and impeccable service; for example, guests receive fruit baskets in their rooms. It's a good location for a special night at the theater or symphony. The main restaurant, **Le Fontainebleau**, is a study in gracious propriety and gourmet cuisine. Make reservations way in advance for the Friday-night seafood soirée or Sunday champagne brunch. The **Plaza Bar** has live entertainment most nights. ♦ 1055 Second Ave (between Broadway and C St). 238.1818, 800/221.3802; fax 557.3737

25 WYNDHAM U.S. GRANT HOTEL

$$ This hotel offers grandiose nostalgia at its best, with crystal chandeliers dripping with sparkling lights, marble gleaming with the luster of age, and a gentrified, refined air. The décor in the 280 rooms and suites could be considered stuffy, with wingback Queen Anne chairs and two-poster beds, and interior rooms can be very dark. The suites, however, have fireplaces and Jacuzzis. If you dine in the venerable **Grant Grill** and entertain acquaintances in the ever-so-elegant lounge, you'll be following the tradition of former guests Charles Lindbergh, Albert Einstein, and Harry S. Truman.

The history of this landmark goes back to Ulysses S. Grant Jr., a young man with a dream of creating a monument to his father's memory that would also glorify the son. To do so, Junior razed the original structure on the site, the massive **Horton House**, and hired **Harrison Albright** to create this masterpiece dedicated on 15 October 1910 to President Ulysses S. Grant. Albright gave full reign to his fantasies of an Italian-Renaissance palace, fashioning it from marble, steel, and cement, with a nine-story tower, two seven-story wings, 400 rooms, 200 baths, a saltwater swimming pool, and a ladies' billiard room.

Over the decades, the hotel has been both a fantastic monument and a financier's nightmare. The structure's quirks and limitations have haunted all of its owners—and there have been quite a few over the years. The hotel has changed frequently during its lifetime, with various remodeling projects that enlarged the rooms and reduced their number from 400 to 280. The swimming pool is gone, but the ambience of Old World gentility remains. ♦ 326 Broadway (between Fourth and Third Aves). 232.3121, 877/999.3223; fax 232.3626. www.wyndham.com/USGrant

Within the U.S. Grant Hotel:

GRANT GRILL

★★★$$$$ Beginning in the 1940s, this posh pub with cushy booths displayed a sign reading "Gentlemen only until 3 o'clock." This tradition held firm until 1969, when seven women insisted on being seated for lunch. They reached their desired goal of integration 3 years later, when a $1 million lawsuit charging violations of the Federal Civil Rights Act was filed. Today the grill honors the seven intrepid interlopers with a plaque.

This staid, conservative dining room relies on traditional fare, expertly prepared. Lobster bisque, mock turtle soup, crab cakes, pan-seared salmon, and the restaurant's legendary steaks and chops are all good choices. The chef prepares lowly fish tacos—covered with a lime sauce, pepper jack cheese, and guacamole—and the ever-popular Grant Grill burger at lunch. The wine list features several Californian, French, and South American red wines to accompany the hearty fare.

The adjacent lounge is an ideal quiet spot for an after-work martini; live jazz groups play on weekend nights. A serene, courtly manner prevails, though the dress code is no longer in effect. ♦ American Continental ♦ M-F, lunch and dinner; Sa-Su, dinner. Reservations recommended. 239.6806

26 COURTYARD BY MARRIOTT

$$ Blessed be the investor group that purchased downtown's grandest historic bank and turned it into a one-of-a-kind hotel. The original San Diego Trust and Savings bank was designed by **William Templeton Johnson** in 1927. Originally there was a shooting gallery on the 14th floor with a steel backstop, soundproof walls, and FBI offices. San Diego's first aviation beacon flashed from the building's cupola.

Many of the bank's Italian Romanesque Revival details have been restored, and the sweeping marble lobby with painted coffer ceilings and bronze teller cages separating customers from clerks is essentially intact. A restaurant occupies much of the lobby, whereas the boardroom and original vault are now meeting rooms. The hotel has 246 rooms that echo the building's design with deep red carpets and heavy drapes while providing up-to-date amenities for business travelers. ♦ 530 Broadway (between Sixth and Fifth Aves). 530.4000, 800/321.2211; fax 446-3010. www.courtyard.com/sancd

27 WAHRENBROCK'S BOOK HOUSE

Books pack shelves on three stories in this shop specializing in rare, used, and

"Information" Anderson, aka Adolph H. Anderson, was hired by the San Diego Electric Railway Company in 1915 as a public relations gesture. From his booth at Horton Plaza, he researched and answered some 22 million questions about San Diego and transportation over a span of 33 years.

The *Spirit of St. Louis,* flown by Charles Lindbergh in his 1927 New York–to–Paris flight, was built by San Diego's Ryan Airlines in 60 days.

The Jessop clock in Horton Plaza was built by clock maker Claude D. Ledger in 1906. When Ledger died in 1935, the clock stopped running. It was restarted, but it stopped again on the day of Ledger's funeral, prompting an entry in *Ripley's Believe It or Not.*

antiquarian books. Owner Chuck Wahrenbrock is a downtown denizen beloved by writers and book collectors. ♦ Tu-Sa, 9:30AM-5:30PM. 726 Broadway (between Eighth and Seventh Aves). 232.0132

28 SUSHI DELI

★★$ The setting of this Japanese eatery is like a no-frills diner where clients belly up to the counter or squeeze into an empty seat and recite their orders with accuracy and speed. The best deals are the platters, which all include rice, salad, and a couple of entrées—like ahi sashimi and teriyaki chicken. The sesame chicken and mixed tempura plate are great, as are the California rolls—if you don't mind artificial crab—and you can always get a good, cheap American breakfast of bacon, eggs, and toast. ♦ Japanese ♦ Lunch and dinner; closed Su. 828 Broadway (between Ninth and Eighth Aves). 231.9597

29 BROADWAY PIER

This World War II pier was renovated as a berthing area for visiting naval vessels. There are controversial plans to create a museum within the retired Midway aircraft carrier and dock it here. Protesters would prefer to keep the water view unobstructed. ♦ W Broadway and N Harbor Dr

30 DOBSON'S

★★$$$$ The official watering hole of downtown's bigwigs, this place even has brass plaques for regulars over the booths. Owner Paul Dobson—who is also a skilled matador—has created an elegant, cozy pub resplendent with beveled glass and lustrous mahogany. The best seats are at the edge of the upstairs balcony overlooking the bar; the best meal is the exceptional grilled salmon. If you're on a budget, sit at the bar and order a California Chardonnay and the mussel bisque *en croûte* (thick mussel soup with a pastry crust on top), a puffy, fragrant bowlful of culinary ecstasy. ♦ French ♦ M-F, lunch and dinner; Sa, dinner. Reservations recommended. 956 Broadway Circle (at Broadway). 231.6771

30 SPRECKELS THEATRE

Harrison Albright was commissioned by John D. Spreckels to design this Chicago School–style neo-Baroque theater to commemorate the opening of the Panama Canal and the **1915–1916 Panama-California Exposition**. The theater originally had 1,915 seats in honor of the exposition; subsequent remodeling reduced the capacity to 980. It still has outstanding acoustics and is one of the best concert venues in town, though not popular with the big names seeking massive crowds. ♦ 121 W Broadway (between Second and First Aves). 235.0494

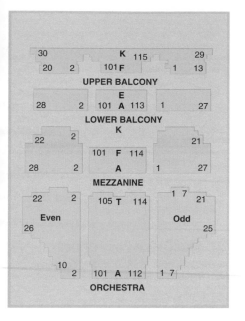

31 NBC

The local NBC affiliate took over the **Home Savings Tower** on Broadway in 2002, creating a center for public excitement with their street-level studio. Locals now gather in front of the building in San Diego's version of the *Today Show* crowd, and crews often tape news segments amid the crowds. 225 Broadway (at Second Ave). 231.3939

Within the NBC Building:

DOWNTOWN INFORMATION CENTER

Information on downtown developments and housing is available at this office in the **NBC Building**. The large model of downtown with labels for current and upcoming development projects is immensely informative and helps newcomers figure out the lay of the land. Visitors and locals can join the tours of the downtown redevelopment district that the center offers on the first and third Saturdays of each month. ◆ M-Sa. Reservations required for tours. 225 Broadway (at Second Ave). 235.2222

32 ON BROADWAY

High rollers hobnob with visiting celebrities at this classy nightclub in one of downtown's oldest high-rise bank buildings. The Renaissance-Revival building from the 1920s seems well suited to its latest incarnation. The gleaming marble floors and gold inlaid ceilings create a mood of opulence enhanced by the well-dressed patrons who must pass inspection by the doorman before forking over the cover charge. The two-story club is separated into eight rooms, from quiet lounges to a billiard hall to a disco dance floor. Expect long lines, unless you're a VIP. ◆ Cover. F-Sa. 615 Broadway (between Seventh and Sixth Aves). 231.0011. www.onbroadwayeventcenter.com

33 WESTIN HORTON PLAZA

$$$ If shopping is a major activity when you travel, then this is the hotel to drop your bags in. Set smack up against **Horton Plaza**, this place is low on frills and high on volume. There are 450 rooms decorated in pastels, a fitness center, small pool, two rooftop tennis courts, and a restaurant. Tour buses and taxis fill the driveway roundabout, which features a weird obelisk sculpture and fountain with water spurting out of plaster pelicans. ◆ 910 Broadway Circle (at First Ave). 239.2200, 888/625.5144; fax 239.0509 &

34 BALBOA THEATER

Plans have been approved to rehabilitate this circa-1923 stage theater and reopen it for performances—but that's hardly news. The building was nearly razed in the flurry of redevelopment when **Horton Plaza** went in but was designated a historical landmark and protected. Various individuals and agencies have tried to restore the theater, but the cost of bringing the building up to current standards is prohibitive. The original theater, designed by **William Wheeler** in 1924, had two 20-foot-high waterfalls inside that flowed freely during intermissions. The tiled dome echoes the form of the domes on the **Santa Fe Depot** and the **California Tower**. A tile mosaic in the sidewalk at the entrance depicts Balboa discovering the Pacific Ocean. The building is closed to the public. ◆ Fourth Ave (between E St and Broadway)

35 SAN DIEGO PUBLIC LIBRARY

This main library is San Diego's greatest civic embarrassment, a pitifully underfunded, outmoded structure that librarians knew would soon become outdated even as it opened in 1954. There was little money in architect **William Templeton Johnson**'s budget for ornamentation on the reinforced concrete façade, except for two cast concrete bas-reliefs picturing the cultural heritage of East and West as sculpted by Donal Hord. The building has only five stories, no parking, and no room to grow. Its warmth and wealth of tables and chairs are attractive to the many homeless living in nearby streets, and library users and

---

Restaurants/Clubs: Red | Hotels: Purple | Shops: Orange | Outdoors/Parks: Green | Sights/Culture: Blue

staff have grown accustomed to having their heartstrings and wallets tugged constantly. Continuous political wrangling has stalled the planned $145 million new library on city-owned land at 12th and J near the ballpark. The city has already paid architect Rob Quigley a sizable amount to begin the design process, and his design has won raves from architects and library users. In July 2001, the city council voted to back the proposed site and allocate another $1 million to Quigley to proceed with the architectural plans. But the future of the library has yet to be firmly established. ♦ M-Th, 10AM-9PM; F-Sa, 9:30AM-5:30PM; Su, 1-5PM. 820 E St (between Ninth and Eighth Aves). 236.5800 &

36 LYCEUM THEATRE

In San Diego's thriving theater scene, the **San Diego Repertory Theatre** company stands out for its innovative, imaginative productions, iconoclastic humor, and cast of longtime supporters and participants. The troupe was founded by artistic director Douglas Jacobs and producing director Sam Woodhouse in 1976 at the **Sixth Avenue Playhouse**, a cold, uncomfortable former church where crowds gathered to witness such delights as *Rap Master Ronnie*, an irreverent look at the Reagan years. In 1986, the **Rep** became the resident managers of this venue, which offers two separate stages—the 545-seat **Lyceum Stage** and the 260-seat **Space**. Eight productions a year are performed at the **Lyceum Theatre**, either by the Rep itself or by visiting companies. Sometimes too experimental for San Diegans' tastes, the Rep has come close to demise a couple of times. But philanthropic forces always manage to rescue this worthy cause. ♦ Admission. 79 Horton Plaza (on Broadway Cir). Administrative office, 231.3586; box office, 544.1000 &

Adjacent to Horton Plaza:

TIMES ART TIX

Purchase same-day half-price tickets for concerts, symphony performances, and plays at this small booth outside **Horton Plaza**.

Discounts are also available on tickets to most major attractions and tours. ♦ Tu-Sa. 28 Horton Plaza (on Broadway Cir, between Fourth and Third Aves). 497.5000

37 SAN DIEGO POST OFFICE

Designed in 1936 by **William Templeton Johnson** as San Diego's postal service headquarters, today this Art Moderne post office is a large branch serving the downtown area. ♦ M-F. 815 E St (between Ninth and Eighth Aves). 232.8612

38 INTERNATIONAL VISITOR INFORMATION CENTER

An excellent resource for travelers and locals, this center is staffed by volunteers who speak several languages (other translators can be contacted by phone). In addition to offering basic tourist information in an extremely helpful manner, the staff provides informative literature from the **San Diego Convention and Visitors Bureau**, including a great selection of brochures from budget hotels. Tickets for the **Old Town Trolley Tours** (see Orientation chapter) and area attractions are available here. ♦ M-Sa, 8:30AM-5PM; June-Aug, 11AM-5PM. Horton Plaza (First Ave and F St). 236.1212

39 ATHENS MARKET TAVERN

★★★$$ Mary Pappas and her Greek kitchen crew were downtown denizens of a small taverna long before the influx of beyond-hip restaurants drove rents sky high. They subsequently moved to this place—filled with sunlight, chatter, and the same captivating smells—that looks onto a small park by the **Federal Building**. A perfect, if somewhat unbalanced, meal for four would include creamy *taramasalata* (a whipped caviar dip), Greek salad heavy on the feta and olives, *loukanikos* (savory sausage from a Pappas family recipe), luscious leg of lamb, and if you still have room, some honey-drenched baklava and thick Greek coffee. ♦ Greek ♦ M-F, lunch and dinner; Sa, dinner. 109 West F St (between First Ave and Front St). 234.1955 &

40 WESTFIELD SHOPPINGTOWN HORTON PLAZA

Dedicated to Alonzo Horton in 1910, the original Horton Plaza was a small park on Broadway across the street from the **U.S. Grant Hotel**. It had a fountain designed by Irving Gill that boasted colored lights, flowing water, and three plaques on its base commemorating Juan Rodríguez Cabrillo, Padre Junípero Serra, and Alonzo Horton. Today, the park and fountain front this complex, which fulfilled shopping mall magnate Ernie Hahn's dream of an urban amusement park for well-heeled adults—filled with shopping, entertainment, and dining thrills. Architect **Jon Jerde** took Hahn's concept and turned it into a multitiered fantasyland of arches, cupolas, and gargoyles. Designer Deborah Sussman, using a palette of dusty rose, sky blue, vivid yellow, and muted rust, created an explosion of color that set tongues wagging. Traditionalists were horrified by this Disneyland plunked into the center of their city.

But shortly after it opened in 1985, suburbanites and travelers started flocking to downtown like never before. The plaza became a six-block-square, five-story-high neighborhood—a self-contained community with shops, restaurants, the **Westin Hotel**, galleries, movie theaters, street vendors, and 2,300 parking spaces. Nearby condominium and apartment complexes echo the colors and forms of the plaza, and other neighborhoods far from the city (and beyond the border) have adopted the plaza's distinctive look. This is not the place for quick one-stop shopping; in fact, you could skip the stores altogether and still while away the better part of a day just finding your way around. At each corner is yet another spectacle.

If you park at the plaza, be sure to memorize the floor you're on (e.g., avocado, pepper, and onion) and take note of the shops closest to your car. The plaza and parking lot have an extremely confusing layout, with the floors staggered in uneven levels; you can see where you want to go, but getting there is a whole different matter. Parking is free for 4 hours with validation from the movie theaters or the **Lyceum Theatre**, and for 3 hours with proof from the shops and dining spots.

Restaurants and a 14-theater complex are on the top floor; the major department stores (**Nordstrom** and **Macy's**) have entrances on the streets bordering the plaza—Broadway, G Street, and Fourth and First Avenues. Apartments, shops, and restaurants line the Fourth Avenue side of the plaza at street level, integrating this massive development with businesses in the **Gaslamp Quarter**.

There are over 100 small shops selling everything from kites to cutlery. Considerable dining options are on the plaza's top floor overlooking the harbor. Take-out stands line the south side, where tables and chairs are clustered along the banisters. **Wonder Sushi** has the healthiest selection of quick snacks among the kiosks serving Japanese, Greek, Italian, and Mexican fare, along with all-American corn dogs and cheese-covered french fries. Be sure to note architect **Tom Grondona**'s whimsical award-winning design for **Claudia's**, which serves sublime cinnamon rolls. ♦ Daily. Bounded by Fourth and First Aves and by G St and Broadway. 238.1596 ⑊

Within Horton Plaza:

PANDA INN

★★$$ Stylish, with an elegant interior and a view of downtown's changing skyline, this dining spot is much more upscale than most Chinese restaurants. Mandarin and Szechuan specialties—chicken in garlic sauce, fish fillets in spicy black bean sauce, and tea-smoked duck—fill the menu. ♦ Chinese ♦ Daily, lunch and dinner. Reservations recommended. Top level. 233.7800 ⑊

LA SALSA

★★$ This authentic restaurant serves terrific Mexican dishes prepared with your health in mind. Tacos are soft—not fried—and made with fresh yellow or blue corn tortillas; the chicken variety is wonderful. The black beans are fresh—not fatty refrieds. There is a salsa bar with several varieties made daily, ranging from mild to red hot. Wash it all down with a cold Mexican beer. ♦ Mexican ♦ Daily, breakfast, lunch, and dinner. Top level. 234.6906

41 PANTOJA PARK

⑪ The oldest park in downtown San Diego, this pretty spot near the bay was originally dedicated in 1850 as the **Plaza de Pantoja y Arriaga**. A central plaza in William Heath Davis's ill-fated plan to turn the settlement of San Diego into a flourishing city, it was named for the pilot of a 1782 expedition that charted San Diego Harbor. The view of the bay is now blocked by buildings, and the park is surrounded on three sides by condos and office towers. There are large trees and perfectly manicured lawns, but no park benches or picnic tables. A statue of Benito Juárez, a gift from Mexico, was erected in 1981. ♦ Bounded by Columbia and India Sts and by West G and West F Sts

42 VILLAGER LODGE GASLAMP

$ A good place to set up housekeeping if you're in town for several days, the **Villager**

Restaurants/Clubs: Red | **Hotels: Purple** | **Shops: Orange** | **Outdoors/Parks: Green** | **Sights/Culture: Blue**

has 104 rooms with microwaves, small refrigerators, and coffeemakers. There's a laundry room on the property, but no restaurant or pool. ◆ 660 G St (between Seventh and Sixth Aves). 238.4100, 800/598.1810; fax 238.5310. & www.villagerlodge.com

43 PANNIKIN

Former owners Bob and Gay Sinclair turned this 1909 redbrick and timber Davidson furniture warehouse (designed by **D.S. Harbison**) into the headquarters for their coffee importing business in 1976. The Pannikin empire grew to several locations, and the Sinclairs eventually parceled off the business to several interested parties. Former employees now own this venerable shop and coffeehouse with its delightful assortment of imported curiosities, many with a coffee theme. Up front is a cluster of comfy couches for coffee sippers and a huge selection of blends from around the world available by the pound for home brewers. ◆ Daily. 675 G St (between Seventh and Sixth Aves). 239.7891

44 TUNA HARBOR

Tuna fishing was a lucrative industry in San Diego between the 1940s and the 1960s, and Portuguese and Italian fisherfolk unloaded their catches here at what was then called the **G Street Mole**. The tuna fleet is now nearly extinct, and today this is home to an enormous two-restaurant complex with one of the biggest parking lots in downtown. Both dining spots offer a smashing view of the bay, and on warm days the bayside patio bar is a great place to soak up the sun. ◆ 750 N Harbor Dr (between W Market St and W Broadway). 232.3474

Within Tuna Harbor:

THE FISH MARKET

★★$$ This downstairs eatery has bustling oyster and sushi bars and several sections of tables and booths, many with a view of the water. You can't go wrong with any of the grilled fresh fish or pasta dishes. ◆ Seafood ◆ Daily, lunch and dinner. 232.3474 &

TOP OF THE MARKET

★★$$$ White linen tablecloths, roses in bud vases, and glistening crystal make this upstairs dining room far more elegant and refined than its downstairs sister. Most tables have at least a glimpse of the waterfront—the best seats are on the deck and worth reserving in advance. Seafood is imported from all over the world, and diners can choose Maine or Australian lobster, New Zealand or Washington oysters, Holland Dover sole, Mississippi catfish, and a variety of caviar. The smoked tuna, ahi, and dorado are moist and flavorful. A few nonseafood choices are

available as well, including a veal chop and rack of lamb. The extensive wine list includes champagnes by the glass and a wide variety of after-dinner drinks. ◆ Seafood ◆ Daily, lunch and dinner. Reservations recommended. 234.4867 &

45 EMBASSY SUITES

$$$ This is one of the best deals near the **San Diego Convention Center** for those who like spacious rooms. All 337 suites have separate living rooms, mini-kitchens, and work areas. The neon bull's-eye atop the 12-story neoclassical Mediterranean tower ensures you won't lose your bearings at night. All rooms open onto an atrium filled with palm trees, koi ponds, and fountains. The best breakfast bargain in town is in the hotel's atrium restaurant, where hotel guests are served a complimentary all-you-can-eat breakfast buffet—eggs, meats, pastries, pancakes, juices, and coffee. ◆ 601 Pacific Hwy (at W Harbor Dr). 239.2400, 800/EMBASSY; fax 239.1520 &

46 CINDERELLA CARRIAGE CO.

Elegant horse-drawn carriages are available here for leisurely tours of downtown. It's the perfect way to get to and from the **Gaslamp Quarter** without hassling with parking or panhandlers. You can also arrange for a special tour, including a pickup at your hotel. ◆ Fee. Daily, 11AM-midnight. 801 W Market St (at W Harbor Dr). 239.8080

47 KANSAS CITY BARBEQUE

$ It doesn't get any funkier than this—a rattletrap shack beside the railroad tracks, made famous as a flyboy hangout in the movie *Top Gun*. Be prepared for a heavy dose of spice and grease in the barbecued ribs, chicken, and hot links served with slices of Wonder bread and onion rings. The food does not inspire rave reviews, but the décor is still popular with Tom Cruise fans. ◆ Barbecue ◆ Daily, lunch and dinner. 610 W Market St (at Kettner Blvd). 231.9680

48 CHILDREN'S MUSEUM SAN DIEGO/MUSEO DE LOS NIÑOS

All the signs and exhibits in this museum are labeled in both English and Spanish in a deliberate attempt to welcome San Diegan children who speak both languages, as well as the younger generation from neighboring Tijuana. A majority of the displays emphasize imaginative, interactive play—kids seem to be particularly entranced by the opportunity to splatter paint all over the 1955 Dodge pickup truck and to play Queen for a Day onstage, sitting on a giant throne. Several construction projects are planned for the museum's lot, and it may close for a while until it is moved into new digs in the same area. ♦ Admission. Tu-Sa, 10AM-4PM. 200 W Island Ave (between Front and Union Sts). 233.5437 &. www.sdchildrensmuseum.org

49 MANCHESTER GRAND HYATT SAN DIEGO

$$$ The slim, cream-colored tower of this hotel rises 40 stories above the waterfront like a sleek obelisk, standing tall against its neighboring mirrored spires. City leaders and the **Skidmore, Owings & Merrill** architectural group planned the space specifically to be pedestrian-friendly—a 2-acre park and 1,200-space parking lot covered with trellises and vines were incorporated into the hotel's design. The 875 rooms and suites are much like those in other members of this worldwide chain, but the third-story pool has a great view of San Diego Bay, and the **Top of the Hyatt** bar also boasts a spectacular vista. There's also a fitness center, several nice shops, and three restaurants. A second 33-story tower is under construction and slated to open in the summer of 2003. ♦ One Market Pl (at Harbor Dr). 232.1234, 888/591.1234; fax 239.5678 &.

Within the Grand Hyatt San Diego:

SALLY'S

★★ $$$ Chef Stephane Voitzwinkler's wonderful French Mediterranean creations are a striking contrast from the unimpressive fare of most hotel dining rooms. Try the meaty crab cakes, seafood paella, any fresh fish, and all the desserts, prepared in an open kitchen in full view of the diners. The din inside the sparsely decorated restaurant can be deafening at night when the live band is playing; the patio tables with a view of the marina are far more peaceful. ♦ Mediterranean ♦ Daily, lunch and dinner. Reservations recommended. 687.6080

50 KING PROMENADE

A long-awaited project to tie the waterfront's various buildings with a linear park was recently realized with the construction of this wide sidewalk lined with trees and flowers and plenty of park benches. It runs along the east side of the **Bayside** trolley line, past the **Children's Museum of San Diego/Museo de los Niños**, and residential condo buildings. Its public art celebrates the accomplishments of Dr. Martin Luther King Jr. The **Children's Park**, across from the Children's Museum, is a restful stop with grass, trees, and a reflecting pool. ♦ W Harbor Dr (from Eighth Ave to Kettner Blvd) &.

51 ISLAND INN

$ Architect **Rob Wellington Quigley** has become one of the nation's leading designers of budget-price hotels for both tourists and urban residents. Featuring 198 studio units, this place has all the amenities of the **J Street Inn** (see below)—kitchenettes, private baths, a gym, laundry, reading room, and low rates. There's no dining room, but the neighborhood's best eatery is next door. ♦ 202 Island Ave (at Second Ave). 232.4138; fax 232.4183 &.

51 CAFE 222

★★ $ Restaurateur Terryl Gavre prepares great veggie burgers, grilled meat loaf, pumpkin waffles, and orange-and-pecan pancakes in the open kitchen of this small, colorful café. Downtown workers mingle with European travelers at sidewalk tables, sharing money-saving tips over fare that would cost twice as much in the **Gaslamp Quarter**. Gavre is the restaurant critic for *San Diego Metropolitan*, a downtown paper, and has loads of ideas on the best places to eat whatever you desire. ♦ American ♦ Daily, breakfast and lunch. 222 Island Ave (at Second Ave). 236.9902 &.

51 SAN DIEGO CHINESE HISTORICAL MUSEUM

The first Chinese mission building in San Diego houses a collection of historical artifacts covering the establishment of the Chinese community in San Diego and Baja California, along with 700 books on Chinese history. Behind the building is a peaceful Asian garden with a stream. ♦ Tu-Su. 404 Third Ave (between J St and Island Ave). 338.9888

52 SEAPORT VILLAGE

A farsighted developer staked out 14 acres of prime waterfront land in 1980 and hired architect **Norbert W. Pieper** to create this theme-park shopping and dining complex with tropical landscaping by Wimmer, Yamada & Associates. A shingled replica of the Mukiltea Lighthouse in Everett, Washington, and the 1890 hand-carved Broadway Flying Horses Carousel give a historic feeling to the village. There's enough variety in the 75 shops and sufficient dining options to occupy most folks' attention; mimes, jugglers, balloon sculptors, magicians, and fire painters offer further entertainment. A long grassy jetty thrusts from the boardwalk shopping zone into the bay, where picnickers, kite flyers, bicyclists, and strollers while away the day here. Others

---

Restaurants/Clubs: Red | **Hotels: Purple** | **Shops: Orange** | **Outdoors/Parks: Green** | **Sights/Culture: Blue**

come here for concerts, fireworks displays, and other scheduled celebrations. In addition to a few restaurants, there are food stands serving Mexican, Chinese, Italian, deli sandwiches, burgers, and hot dogs. Tables are scattered near the carousel and waterfront.

The village will undergo a $40 million expansion in the near future, adding more restaurants and shops. One proposal by the San Diego Unified Port District is renovating the nearby Mission-style **police station**, built in 1939 and abandoned in 1987 for new quarters. Most city tours include a stop at the village, and the Orange Line of the San Diego Trolley connects it with the **San Diego Convention Center** and C Street downtown. ♦ 849 W Harbor Dr (at Pacific Hwy). Offices, 235.4014; recorded events line, 235.4013 &

Within Seaport Village:

EMBARCADERO MARINA PARK

At the beginning of this wide sweep of grass out over the bay is the *Morning Statue*, Donal Hord's sculpture of a fisherman. Magicians and musicians perform nearby, and the lawns here are a good spot to escape the crowds at the village and relax over a peaceful picnic. Concerts and fireworks displays are held here on holidays.

SEAPORT VILLAGE SHELL COMPANY

As the name suggests, this is the place to buy *objets* made from shells: night-lights from cowry shells, nautiluses set in stained glass, and mother-of-pearl earrings. ♦ Daily, 10AM-9PM. 234.1004

UPSTART CROW AND COMPANY

Great books, fragrant espresso, and an upstairs reading room with comfortable chairs are the draws at this wonderful place to escape to when it's not crowded. ♦ Su-Th, 9AM-10PM; F-Sa, 9AM-11PM. 232.4855

CAPTAIN'S COVE

All the accoutrements for a nautical attitude—carved mermaid figureheads, brass ship's lanterns, and so on—are here for the asking. ♦ Daily, 10AM-9PM. 234.5050

SWINGS N' THINGS

Hang out on high-quality hammocks and swinging chairs from the Yucatán and Brazil while the others are shopping. ♦ Daily, 9:30AM-9:30PM. 234.8995

GREEK ISLAND CAFE

★★$ This is the best informal dining spot in the village. Enjoy well-prepared Greek roasted chicken, salads, and gyros while seated at bright blue picnic tables on the boardwalk by the bay. ♦ Greek ♦ Daily, lunch and dinner. 239.5216

53 SAN DIEGO MARRIOTT HOTEL & MARINA

$$$$ The **San Diego Convention Center** was barely a dream when developer Doug Manchester hired architects **C.W. Kim** and **Hope Consulting** to build this mirrored-tower hotel in 1983. It now has two towers and multiple meeting rooms, banquet rooms, and ballrooms. This is the most convenient place to stay if you're holding court at the convention center next door, but be sure to reserve your room way in advance. The views from the expensive upper-level suites are astounding, and all guest rooms feature a vista of either downtown or the bay. The lagoonlike pool area can be remarkably peaceful for a hotel with 1,355 rooms, and the yachts in the marina are a captain's dream. There are several restaurants and bars and a fitness-beauty center. ♦ 333 W Harbor Dr (at Front St). 234.1500, 800/228.9290; fax 234.8678 &

54 J STREET INN

$ Another **Quigley** design, this sleek, modular inn proves that comfort, safety, and economy can be attractive. The 221 studio units have queen-size beds, small kitchenettes with microwaves and refrigerators, bathrooms with tubs and showers, and cable TVs. The complex includes underground parking, an exercise room, laundry facilities, a reading room, and outdoor patios, but no restaurant. Best of all, it is only three blocks from the waterfront. Weekly and monthly rates are available. ♦ 222 J St (at Second Ave). 696.6922; fax 696.6922 &

54 MORTON'S OF CHICAGO

★★★★$$$$ Tucked in the lower level of an ultraexpensive condo tower, this bastion of beef has the ambience of a private club where waiters know their clients' wishes and whims. All diners are treated with subdued courtesy (none of that "Hi. My name's River and I'll be serving you guys" chumminess here). The food is sublimely decadent and the menu, a cause for serious deliberation. Start with the smoked salmon and a Caesar salad, move on to a steak or prime rib with perfect steamed asparagus, then finish with New York cheesecake. If you can still stand, adjourn to the handsome bar for a snifter of brandy. ♦ Steakhouse ♦ 285 J St (at Second Ave). 696.3369. www.mortons.com

55 29 VILLA MONTEZUMA

At the turn of the 19th century, Golden Hill was an elite address for wealthy pioneers and

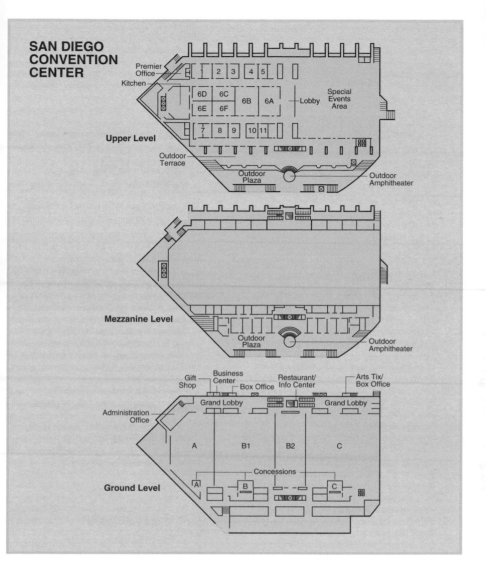

SAN DIEGO CONVENTION CENTER

Premier Office
Kitchen

Upper Level

6D | 6C | 6B | 6A
6E | 6F

Lobby
Special Events Area

Outdoor Terrace

Outdoor Plaza
Outdoor Amphitheater

Mezzanine Level

Outdoor Plaza
Outdoor Amphitheater

Gift Shop
Business Center
Box Office
Restaurant/Info Center
Arts Tix/Box Office

Administration Office

Grand Lobby
Grand Lobby

A | B1 | B2 | C

Concessions

Ground Level

was filled with Victorian houses. Although the neighborhood still boasts such homes, many are run down and others renovated. The most impressive of all is this villa, faithfully restored by the San Diego Historical Society as a museum, showplace, and romantic wedding setting. An elaborate Queen Anne, this mansion was designed by **Comstock & Trotsche** in 1887 for Jesse Shepard, a mystic, spiritualist, poet, author, and pianist. Shepard spared no expense on carved redwood and walnut, brass hardware fireplaces, and stained-glass windows. Easily the most opulent home of its time, the villa is a delight for those who enjoy immersing themselves in the grandeur and spirit of the past. ♦ Admission. Sa-Su, noon-4:30PM; last tour, 3:45PM. 1925 K St (between 20th and 19th Sts). 239.2211

56 SAN DIEGO CONVENTION CENTER

City planners wanted a striking, bold, distinctive convention center, and this winged giant—built in 1989—rising like a futuristic underwater terminus from the bay certainly fits the bill. A partnership of architects from

Restaurants/Clubs: **Red** | Hotels: **Purple** | Shops: **Orange** | Outdoors/Parks: **Green** | Sights/Culture: **Blue**

San Diego, Los Angeles, and Seattle designed the 760,000-square-foot center with a cruise ship theme in mind, incorporating a roofless 100,000-square-foot top deck covered with white Teflon-coated sails. The **1996 Republican National Convention** was held here, bringing international attention to the area. The center underwent a $216 million expansion, doubling its size to 2.6 million square feet. The project took 2.5 years, with the center reopening in September 2001. Auto, home and garden, and travel shows are often held here. The building is also open to nonconventioneers; just check in with guest services at the front door and ask for an informal tour. A steep stairway and an enclosed funicular lead to the top, where you can cross and descend to the waterfront. ♦ 111 W Harbor Dr (between Third Ave and Front St). 525.5000. www.sdccc.org

57 CHART HOUSE

★★$$ The **Chart House** chain is known for restoring cherished historical sites and turning them into successful seafood and beef restaurants. The company outdid itself at this venue—a peaked-roof wooden structure resting on 30 pilings in the bay at the city's original steamship wharf. In the mid-1800s, newcomers to San Diego arrived here at the foot of Fifth Avenue at the entrance to what was known as New Town. The wharf was the area's center of activity, and San Diego's rowing club's headquarters was dedicated here on 1 January 1900. Through the first 4 decades of the 20th century, the club held regattas and tournaments, but at the end of World War II, some question was raised about the practicality of having a social club in the busy San Diego Harbor. For another 20 or so years, the members held on to their wooden clubhouse suspended over the bay, but they finally moved to Mission Bay in 1974. Downtown preservationists fought against the destruction of the building, which eventually was renovated, designated a historic site, and turned into this dining spot. Ship's hulls, crew boats, nautical gear, and a wonderful display of period photographs fill the restaurant, and there is a small dock for diners arriving in their yachts. Their recently revamped menu includes more seafood; the seared peppered ahi tuna is a good bet. The signature chocolate lava cake, served warm at your table, is worth the calories. ♦ Seafood ♦ Daily, dinner. 525 E Harbor Dr (between Sixth and Fifth Aves). 233.7391 &

58 EAST VILLAGE

The focus of downtown's ongoing redevelopment has shifted to this long-neglected area of warehouses, freight yards, and dirt plots now called **East Village**. A 46,000-seat baseball stadium is scheduled to open in time for the 2004 season, although lawsuits and funding problems have halted progress several times. The ballpark is the impetus for several other developments in the area, including large and small hotels and housing structures. The city is also beautifying Twelfth Avenue to make it a Park to Bay Link connecting the waterfront with Balboa Park. Best of all, if everything goes as planned the area will also be home to a new main public library—a project backers have been pushing for over a decade. ♦ Bordered by Harbor Dr and E St and by 17th St and Sixth Ave

59 JAMES R. MILLS BUILDING AND TROLLEY TRANSFER STATION

The Swiss clock atop the spire of this gray-and-red 10-story office building, parking lot, and trolley station has become a commuters' landmark. Passengers using the ever-expanding trolley system make connections here (it's sure to be mobbed when the ballpark opens), where there are newsstands, comfortable benches, and plenty of security guards. The award-winning building, designed by **Delawie, Bretton and Wilkes** in 1989, is named for the city's longtime champion of public transportation. ♦ 1255 Imperial Ave (at 12th Ave). 233.3004

60 EMBARCADERO MARINA PARK SOUTH

This 22-acre waterfront park incorporates a grassy strip at **Seaport Village** and this broad lawn south of the convention center. Fishermen dangle their lines at the park's pier, and downtown workers bring their lunches for a break in the outdoors. ♦ Marina Park Way (at E Harbor Dr)

GASLAMP QUARTER

An overhead sign spanning the foot of Fifth Avenue at Harbor Drive marks the entrance to the **Gaslamp Quarter**, downtown's most popular dining, shopping, and entertainment enclave. The Gaslamp's transformation from a seedy, sleazy near slum to an upscale attraction has gained acclaim from dining critics and urban planners around the country. Its streets are jam-packed on weekend nights—a sight that would have made Alonzo Horton beam with pride. When Horton established his New Town in 1867, its center was along Fifth Avenue, where runaway horses galloped through dirt streets lined by saloons and brothels. As downtown prospered, the center of commerce shifted toward Broadway, and the original buildings of Horton's frontier town fell into disrepair. The area became known as the Stingaree, a red-light district.

When city planners started focusing on downtown redevelopment in the 1970s, the Gaslamp Quarter, as the area south of

Broadway around Fifth Avenue was known, looked like prime turf for rampant destruction. But San Diegans protested and formed the Gaslamp Quarter Foundation, which oversees the area and protects downtown's heritage. The quarter was designated a National Historic District in 1980 and now encompasses a 16-block area with brick sidewalks, wrought-iron benches, gas street-lamps, and street signs with distinctive brown lettering. The beautifully restored historic buildings were built between 1870 and 1930 in a variety of styles—including Frontier, Victorian, Italian Renaissance, Romanesque, Chicago Commercial, Oriental, Modern, International, and Spanish Renaissance—and today house restaurants, offices, and shops.

The Gaslamp has become hip, trendy, and ever so cutting-edge. Its proximity to the **Convention Center** makes it the obvious evening destination for thousands of out-of-towners who can spot the brightly lit Gaslamp Quarter sign at the foot of Fifth Avenue from their convention hotels. Discerning diners have their pick of dozens of restaurants—the dining and nightlife scenes are constantly changing. Club hoppers roam from pubs to martini bars to late-night dance venues. Shops stay open until 10PM or even midnight on weekends, and limos, Beemers, taxis, and pedicabs cruise the streets. Many restaurants offer valet parking, and several parking lots have opened or are under construction. The trolley also stops nearby, which helps ease the congestion.

Roving bands of kids with too much time and too little money are drawn to the neighborhood, as are transients and the homeless. Given the popularity of venues pushing large volumes of alcohol, the ambiance can become rather edgy, especially late on weekend nights. The police presence is significant, with cops patrolling the streets on horseback, bicycles, and foot. Keep your wits about you and carry ID and only as much cash as you're willing to spend (plus a bit of plastic). You'll find an ever more intriguing selection of shops, hotels, and eateries. New businesses are always opening—a two-story Borders Books is in the works at Sixth Avenue and G Street and a Marriott Hotel is planned for J Street between Fifth and Sixth Avenues. Several annual celebrations are held in the neighborhood, including a big Mardi Gras parade and Street Scene, an immensely popular music festival held every September. Call the Gaslamp Quarter Association, 614 Fifth Avenue, for information at 233.5227 or visit www.gaslamp.org. The area is bounded by Sixth and Fourth Avenues and by West Harbor Drive and Broadway.

Traditional Japanese Delicacies

61 SANBAN

★★$ Japanese students and office workers jam the booths in this tiny Japanese restaurant known for its fresh sushi. The caterpillar and rainbow rolls are works of art and so inexpensive you'll be tempted to order everything on the sushi menu. The noodle and curry dishes and rice bowls are filling and excellent. This isn't gourmet fare, but it's fresh, authentic, and served with generous smiles. ♦ Japanese ♦ M-Sa, lunch; Tu-Sa, lunch and dinner. 933 Fourth Ave (between E St and Broadway). 237.0546

IN THE GASLAMP QUARTER

62 DAKOTA GRILL & SPIRITS

★★$$ Noisy and busy with two stories of dining areas and live piano music, this place serves good Southwestern cuisine with sauces and spices that sometimes work and sometimes don't. Try the red-chili calamari rings, wood-fired wild mushroom pizza, baby-back ribs, and the blackened rib eye. ♦ Southwestern ♦ Daily, lunch and dinner. 901 Fifth Ave (at E St). 234.5554. & www.cohnrestaurants.com

62 PRAVA

$$$ This stylish boutique hotel was once a time-share property. Now guests can book 56 rooms with kitchenettes and plenty of space—the suites even have washers and dryers along with Egyptian cotton sheets and Sharper Image radios and CD players. Amenities include a fitness center and spa services. If you're staying a while or prefer to prepare your own meals, this is a good choice. ♦ 911 Fifth Ave (at E St). 233.3300

63 RAMADA INN & SUITES

$$ The *Saint James* name still stands out in bright lights atop this 1913 hotel building. When first designed by the architectural firm of **Henry, Harms, and Preibisuis**, the hotel was elegant and entirely up to standard, according to advertisements of the day.

Restaurants/Clubs: Red | Hotels: Purple | Shops: Orange | Outdoors/Parks: Green | Sights/Culture: Blue

Probably the commerce enacted therein was of a more illicit type during the Stingaree years; later, the hotel became a flophouse. New owners renovated the hotel in the 1980s, investing $2.5 million in the lobby alone, with its crystal chandeliers and old-fashioned elevators. The hotel never quite caught on as a luxurious hostelry but has 99 rooms and suites with character at an affordable price. ♦ 830 Sixth Ave (between F and E Sts). 234.0155, 800/664-4400; fax 235.9410. www.stjameshotel.com

64 BANDAR

★★★$$ Behrooz Farahani moved his family from Iran to San Diego a decade ago and used his skills as an architect to transform one of the **Gaslamp**'s historic structures into a fabulous contemporary restaurant. The aromas of saffron, cilantro, charbroiled onions, and simmering sauces immediately allert the taste buds as you enter the fashionable dining room. The menu offers an irresistible array of homemade yogurt and shallot appetizers, salads with feta cheese, and entrées served with lovely layers of white and gold basamati rice. Choose the **Bandar** special so you can sample both the chicken and lamb skewers, and have someone in your party order one of the veal stews. ♦ Persian ♦ Daily, lunch and dinner. 825 Fourth Ave (between F and E Sts). 238.0101. & www.bandarrestaurant.com

65 FIO'S

★★$$ A hit from day one, this powerful enterprise (more than 30 partners, many active on the local scene) continues to be one of *the* dining spots in which to see and be seen. Perhaps the partners were empowered by the spirit of George Marston, a founding father who hired the **Stewart Brothers** to build this Italianate-Victorian building for his Marston's department store in 1881. Seating is in well-spaced booths or at the pizza and cocktail bars. Best bets are the angel-hair pasta with fresh basil and pine nuts, linguine with smoked scallops, and four-cheese pizza. ♦ Northern Italian ♦ Dinner, daily. Reservations recommended. 801 Fifth Ave (at F St). 234.3467 &

65 CROCE'S RESTAURANT & JAZZ BAR

★★★$$ Ingrid Croce, widow of singer-songwriter Jim Croce, dedicated this restaurant and jazz club to the memory of the man who created "Bad, Bad Leroy Brown." Since she first opened it in 1979, Croce has expanded her business into every corner of the 1890 Romanesque **Keating Building** and on down the block. She's become an industry of her own, with a cookbook aptly titled

Thyme in a Bottle. Son A.J. Croce plays the piano in a bluesy New Orleans style that has made him a recognized musician in his own right. **Croce's** was one of the first successful restaurants and clubs in the **Gaslamp**, and it continues to fill with loyal diners. The contemporary American menu features pasta, fish, seafood, beef, chicken, and lamb dishes, and there is an extensive wine list. Sit in the glassed-in dining room or at the sidewalk tables. Live rhythm-and-blues groups play nightly at the adjacent **Croce's Top Hat Bar & Grill**, with such national acts as Maynard Ferguson, Rita Coolidge, and Arlo Guthrie appearing for special engagements, with or without A.J. Croce, who's on his fourth album and a steady rise to fame. Groups also appear at the **Jazz Bar**. The cover charge for acts is included in entrée dinners at the restaurant. ♦ Contemporary American ♦ Daily, breakfast, lunch, and dinner. 802 Fifth Ave (at F St). 233.4355. & www.croces.com

65 ROGER'S ON FIFTH

★$$ The city's first granite building, designed by **Clements & Stannard** for the Bank of Commerce in 1887, is still one of the **Gaslamp**'s finest. The 1983 renovation (one of the first in the Gaslamp Quarter) of the edifice's ornate façade, with bay windows, terra-cotta bas-relief Second Empire decoration, and twin cupolas, was faithfully overseen by Don Reeves. The building houses a restaurant named and owned by former mayor Roger Hedgecock, now a controversial conservative talk-show host. It's a hangout for his cronies and serves traditional American fare with a bit of flair. ♦ American ♦ Daily, lunch and dinner ♦ 835 Fifth Ave (between F and E Sts). 702.0444. & www.rogersonfifth.com

65 SAN DIEGO HARDWARE

If you can't find that special widget here among the 50,000-piece inventory, you might not find it anywhere. The business has been family-owned since 1892 and moved to this location in 1910. Check out the window display of fascinating doorknobs and handles—it's enough to make you want to remodel your kitchen. ♦ M-Sa. 840 Fifth Ave (between F and E Sts). 232.7123. www.sandiegohardware.com

65 THE ONYX ROOM

Descend the stairway to this underground cocktail lounge reminiscent of the stylish 1950s. Red upholstered barrel chairs are clustered around cocktail tables where hip patrons sip pink squirrels, old-fashioneds, and other classic cocktails. The live music ranges from acid jazz to high-energy dance music. Visiting DJs spin the vinyl most nights; Tuesdays are reserved for jazz jam sessions. The dress code prohibits baseball caps, gym shoes, and other casual attire. ♦ Cover. Closed M. 852 Fifth Ave (between F and E Sts). 235.6699

66 PATRICK'S II

Live jazz and blues are played nightly here in one of downtown's oldest bars, tucked into a small space off F St. ♦ Cover, F-Sa. Daily, 9AM-2AM. 428 F St (between Fifth and Fourth Aves). 233.3077

67 STAR OF INDIA

★★$$ Peaceful and serene, this small restaurant is a pleasant change from the frenetic nighttime activity in the **Gaslamp Quarter**. There's a wide variety of vegetarian dishes, from *palak paneer* (spinach with cheese cubes) to *bengan bhartha* (eggplant baked in a clay oven), and the fiery meat dishes from the tandoori oven go well with a cold Taj Mahal beer. The lunch buffet is inexpensive and quick. Champagne is included in the buffet price on weekends. ♦ Indian ♦ Daily, lunch and dinner. 423 F St (between Fifth and Fourth Aves). 234.8000 ♿

68 KIYO'S

★$$ Inside this unobtrusive little storefront is a Japanese fantasyland with paper lanterns and banners. Kiyo presides over a handsome wooden sushi bar, arranging whatever ingredients you want into sushi that's shaped into rolls, flowers, and leaves. The sashimi, particularly the ahi, is delicious, and the smoked eel is also splendid. ♦ Japanese ♦ M-Sa, dinner. 531 F St (between Sixth and Fifth Aves). 238.1726

69 PACIFIC GASLAMP STADIUM 15

Should the **Gaslamp** action become overwhelming, you can always step into this 15-screen movie house that dominates a corner lot. The building is way too massive for the corner it commands and jars with the surrounding architecture. There is valet parking. ♦ 701 Fifth Ave (at G St). 232.0406 ♿

69 OSTERIA PANEVINO

★★$$ Frequent downtown diners consistently rate this trattoria among the better of the area's Italian eateries. The narrow dining room and sidewalk tables are popular in the evening when diners linger over stuffed foccacia, gnocchi, sublime spinach ravioli, and costini—short ribs braised in a red wine sauce. The menu and décor are meant to transport diners to Tuscany. The tables inside that are near the exposed brick walls are the best if you're seeking the European ambiance. ♦ Italian ♦

Daily, lunch and dinner. Reservations recommended. 722 Fifth Ave (between G and F Sts). 595.7959. ♿ www.osteriapanevino.com

69 OLE MADRID CAFE

★★$$ About as hip as a tapas bar could be, this spot covers two stories and a sidewalk patio. The tapas—especially the mushroom or chicken and garlic—are good, as are the pasta and paella, but the food isn't nearly as important as whom you know and how you're dressed. Stick with black and you'll fit in fine. ♦ Tapas ♦ Tu-Su, dinner. 755 Fifth Ave (between G and F Sts). 557.0146

69 THE BITTER END

Jeans, sandals, hiking boots, and other casual wear are forbidden in the upstairs lounge of this stylish bar. The code relaxes a bit for the main bar and the **Underground** dance club, where the music rocks and the crowd is young and exuberant. ♦ Cover, Th-Sa. 770 Fifth Ave (at F St). 233.4603 ♿ www.thebitterend.com

70 LE TRAVEL STORE

Owners Joan and Bill Keller created what may have been the first shop geared completely to travelers' needs in Pacific Beach in 1976. The business moved from Pacific Beach to Horton Plaza in 1985, then became one of the pioneers on Fifth Avenue in 1994 when they restored a 1907 brick building. Local travel aficionados and tourists from all over the world stop by to peruse the excellent display of books, luggage, and the latest gadgets. The extensive line of Eagle Creek gear is enough to make you donate your old backpacks and roll-aboards. There's a travel agency in the back of the shop, and the Kellers now have a mail-order business at their web site (your purchases can also be shipped from the on-site facility). ♦ Daily. 745 Fourth Ave (between G and F Sts). 544.0005. ♿ www.letravelstore.com, www.luggage.com

71 Z GALLERIE

Hip furnishings and home accessories give you an idea of how downtowners furnish their lofts. This is a good place to pick up a housewarming gift. ♦ Daily. 611 Fifth Ave (at Market St). 696.8137

71 THE YUMA BUILDING

Designer Marsha Sewell and her husband lovingly restored this 1888 brick structure, the only single-family home in the **Gaslamp**. The blue, cream, and dusty rose paint job brings out all the details of the ornate façade, and the building is one of the loveliest restorations in the district. It houses Sewell's design business and a retail shop. 631 Fifth Ave (between Market and G Sts)

The Elephant's Trunk
www.theelephantstrunk.com

Within the Yuma Building:

THE ELEPHANT'S TRUNK

Gorgeous ikat weavings from Indonesia and Thai silk wall hangings are draped on the walls of this shop packed with imported furnishings and accessories. The collection includes Burmese rice baskets, mango wood vases, marble Buddhas, and, of course, elephants in every imaginable design. ◆ Daily. 631 Fifth Ave (between Market and G Sts). 515.1115

71 JIMMY LOVE'S

★★$$ Dining and dancing come with a sense of style at this classy restaurant that caters to a well-dressed, over-30 crowd. There's live jazz, R&B, or disco most nights, and the menu offers a bit of everything, from gourmet pizzas to New York steak Bordelaise. The restaurant takes up two stories of the old city government building, built in 1887. ◆ American ◆ Daily, dinner. 672 Fifth Ave (at G St). 595.0123 ৬

72 CHEESE SHOP

★★★$ Downtowners consistently praise the gargantuan sandwiches made with the freshest meats and cheeses, the lavish fruit and cheese plate, and the ever-satisfying chocolate-chip cookies and brownies. The owners had to move from their long-time digs but remain **Gaslamp** veterans. Locals wouldn't consider buying their sandwiches anywhere else. ◆ Deli ◆ Daily, breakfast and lunch. 627 Fourth Ave (at Market St). 232.2303

73 PARK IT ON MARKET

Gaslamp business owners and visitors were thrilled when this 500-space parking garage opened near the main dining and shopping area. The rates are lower than at many of the lots in the area, and the lot is guarded. ◆ Sixth Ave (at Market St). 232.1271

74 BAYOU BAR & GRILL

★★$$ Owner-chef Bud Deslatte brings his Cajun and creole recipes to San Diego by way of New Orleans. Killer jambalaya, smoked sausage, red beans and rice, and Mardi Gras pasta with shrimp and crawfish over linguine all go well with a Blackened Voodoo beer. The peanut-butter pie is a must for dessert. The tables are a bit too close for private chats, but the dining room is bright and comfortable, with green wainscoting against white walls and a long bar at one end of the room. There are also sidewalk tables on Market Street and live entertainment Friday and Saturday nights. ◆ Cajun ◆ Daily, dinner. Reservations recommended. 329 Market St (between Fourth and Third Aves). 696.8747 ৬

75 GASLAMP BOOKS AND MUSEUM

Wyatt Earp was the **Gaslamp**'s most famous resident. Ken Cilch has compiled a museum of Earp's life in this used-book store and has authored a book on Earp's years in San Diego. Step inside for a whole different view of the **Gaslamp**. ◆ 413 Market St (between Fifth and Fourth Aves). 237.1492

76 HOSTELLING INTERNATIONAL DOWNTOWN HOSTEL

$ The location and price are ideal, and this hostel has private rooms as well as dorm spaces. There are kitchen facilities, a dining area, and a main lounge where you can trade info and tips. ◆ 521 Market St (between Sixth and Fifth Aves). 525.1531; fax 338.0129. www.hostelweb.com

77 ROBSON GALLERY

One of the most established galleries in the **Gaslamp**, the Robson showcases oils, watercolors, and drawings by emerging and established artists. ◆ Tu-Sa. 535 Fourth Ave (between Island Ave and Market St). 234.7356

77 CAFÉ SEVILLA

★★★$ This small tapas bar is usually packed by 10PM, so it's a good idea to arrive early. Some of the tapas are displayed along the bar, but don't overlook the menu for such savory delights as garlic-and-oil-drenched olives stuffed with anchovies, decent fried paella, and spicy hot potatoes with tomatoes and peppers. Enjoy it all with a pitcher of fruity sangria. The adjacent restaurant is quieter, though still filled with diners feasting on *conejo a la catalana* (baked rabbit) and *cordera a al cordobesa* (roasted lamb). **Club Sevilla** in the basement hosts live music nightly ranging from Spanish rock to salsa and merengue bands. The club holds a tango dinner show on Friday nights and a flamenco dinner show on Saturday nights. ◆ Spanish ◆ Club Sevilla: cover for live music. Daily, dinner and late-night meals. Reservations recommended for flamenco shows. 555

Fourth Ave (between Island Ave and Market St). 233.5979. www.cafesevilla.com

paintings, and applied arts. ♦ Tu-Su. 520 Fifth Ave (between Island Ave and Market St). 235.0700

CH1VE
cuisine moderne

77 CHIVE

★★★★$$$$ Local critics have used every imaginable adjective to describe this totally chic eatery. *Daring, bold, brazen, innovative,* and *sophisticated* are all appropriate descriptions for the dining room, cuisine, and clientele. Owner Tracy Borkum took one of the **Gaslamp**'s most treasured old buildings—the Royal Pie Company—and hired architect Graham Downes to transform the brick warehouse into a room that is both minimalist and inviting. The menu features "Cuisine Moderne," which translates into innovative twists on familiar themes. Salmon, for example, is slowly baked with five spices. Crab is shaped into fritters served with pistachio-vanilla dipping sauce. Lasagna is a free-form affair made with ahi and chanterelle mushrooms. The surf and turf combo comes with ruby beet salad, and oysters on the half shell are topped with a pearl of caviar. It's all quite edgy and interesting enough to keep adventuresome diners captivated. ♦ Cuisine Moderne ♦ Daily, dinner. 558 Fourth Ave (between Island Ave and Market St). 232.4482. ♿ www.chiverestaurant.com

78 BLARNEY STONE PUB & RESTAURANT

★$ This place is a touch of Old Ireland in the New West, with Guinness on tap and live music Thursday through Sunday nights. The food is unexceptional—soups, sandwiches, steaks, and a traditional corned beef and cabbage dinner—but it's worth a visit for the ambiance. ♦ Irish ♦ Daily, lunch and dinner. 502 Fifth Ave (between Island Ave and Market St). 233.8519

78 GOLDEN PACIFIC ARTS

Looking for the perfect bauble to please your mate? Go no farther than the jewelry cases at this tasteful gallery. Tourmaline, topaz, lapis lazuli—you name it. You'll find your favorite stone in a unique setting, many appropriate for men as well as women. The artists on site can design whatever you wish as well. The gallery also features handblown glassware,

THE ♥ PAPERIE

78 THE PAPERIE

Need a thank-you card, wrapping paper, or diary for your notes? You'll be tempted to invest in paper products—so temporary and yet so essential—including classy business cards and printed invitations, origami supplies, lampshade kits, even supplies to design your own paper. ♦ M-Sa. 534 Fifth Ave (between Island Ave and Market St). 234.5457. www.thepaperie.com

78 THE FIELD

★★★$ Pubs have popped up all over the **Gaslamp**; this one truly feels like a bit of the old country. The brogues are heavy, the beers are dark, and the music is both lively and sentimental. Were it not for the lack of smoke layering the air, you'd think you were in Galway. The owners shipped the farming tools and other implements decorating the interior from Ireland and designed a menu that lauds the lowly potato. Boxty dishes featuring grilled potato pancakes wrapped around chicken or imported bacon with melted cheddar cheese, deserve acclaim, as do the full Irish breakfasts with black pudding. The bartenders make the heart flutter. ♦ Irish ♦ Daily, lunch and dinner. 544 Fifth Ave (between Island Ave and Market St). 232.9840. www.thefield.com

78 THE CUBAN CIGAR FACTORY

There are several cigar and smoke shops in the neighborhood. This was the original, where master cigar makers from Cuba roll aged Cuban seed tobaccos from the Dominican Republic and Honduras. Check out the humidor. ♦ Daily. 551 Fifth Ave (between Island Ave and Market St). 238.2429

78 BLUE POINT COASTAL CUISINE

★★$$$ Firmly established on a prime corner, this seafood house was the first in the neighborhood to offer an oyster bar—the seafood tower of saltwater delicacies satisfies those who've come to San Diego expecting to eat piles of fresh fish. The tempura shrimp and asparagus is a pleasant change from grilled catch of the day, as is the Thai calamari. Rack of lamb, steaks, and duck keep carni-

---

vores happy. Call ahead and reserve a comfy booth for your group. ◆ American ◆ Daily, dinner. 565 Fifth Ave (between Island Ave and Market St). 233.6623. ᚖ www.cohnrestaurants.com

79 WILLIAM HEATH DAVIS HOUSE

The Gaslamp Quarter Historic Foundation is headquartered here in the former home of William Heath Davis, the chief backer of the failed 1850 attempt to develop San Diego. Alonzo Horton, who was more successful with New Town in the 1870s, also lived in this two-story Cape Cod saltbox house, which was moved to its current location in 1984 and restored as a museum of late-18th-century life. The foundation is planning a $500,000 enhancement to improve the rooms and research facilities, create a visitor center and gift shop, and improve disabled access. Information, brochures, and tours of the **Gaslamp Quarter** are available from the volunteers staffing the place. Guided tours are offered on Saturday mornings at 11 AM. ◆ Donation. Tu-Su, 11AM-3PM. 410 Island Ave (between Fifth and Fourth Aves). 233.4692

80 HORTON GRAND HOTEL

$$ Half Victorian, half Baroque, this hostelry is an odd apparition. The hotel is made up of two historic buildings connected by a porchlike atrium furnished with wicker and ferns: the original **Horton Grand**, designed in 1888 by **Comstock & Trotsche**, and the **Brooklyn Hotel**, also known as the **Kahle's Saddlery Hotel** and once the home of Wyatt Earp. **Gaslamp** savior Dan Pearson and **Wayne Donaldson**, architect for many of the area's renovations, decided to save both buildings from destruction by dismantling them and relocating them to the heart of the **Gaslamp Quarter** in 1970. The resulting 108-room hotel (with an additional 24 suites with kitchenettes added on later) is a smashing success. The rooms and suites all have queen-size beds, gas fireplaces, and lace curtains. Weddings are common in the central courtyard. High tea is served Thursday through Saturday in the **Palace Bar**, which is also a jazz venue on weekend nights. The restaurant, **Ida Bailey's**, is named for the infamous madam whose fashionable bordello once stood here. Roger the ghost is said to hang out in room 309. ◆ 311 Island Ave (between Fourth and Third Aves). 544.1886, 800/542.1886; fax 239.3823. ᚖ www.hortongrand.com

81 HORTON GRAND THEATRE

The Gaslamp Theatre Company set up residence in this former paper-box factory, presenting an impressive roster of new playwrights' works. Today, the theater is home to an open-ended run of *Triple Espresso*, a comedy that's become an institution in several cities. ◆

Admission. 444 Fourth Ave (between J St and Island Ave). 234.9583

82 ROYAL THAI CUISINE

★$ History buffs can't resist a close look at this odd three-story brick building constructed over three periods in history and architecture starting in 1874. Iron columns support the walls—five bricks thick in some places. As the **Nanking Cafe**, the restaurant was a favorite of sailors and their dates, who dined and smooched in booths behind beaded curtains. Today you can enjoy good Thai fare while lazing amid floral upholstered booths and tall palm and bamboo trees. ◆ Thai ◆ Daily, lunch and dinner. 467 Fifth Ave (between J St and Island Ave). 230.8424

83 SPLASH

East Coast fashionistas might find the clothing here to be a bit too ethnic and hippielike for their tastes. But the beaded vests, flowing Indonesian skirts, velvet scarves, and skimpy cocktail dresses suit the **Gaslamp**'s anything-goes attitude. ◆ Daily. 376 Fifth Ave (at J St). 233.5251

84 COST PLUS

If all the costly wares in the **Gaslamp** boutiques have you down, stop into this warehouse filled with moderately priced furnishings, glassware, imported gifts, wines, and just about any other special treat you might crave (including wine and chocolates). The store validates parking. ◆ Daily. 372 Fourth Ave (between K and J Sts). 236.1737

85 DICK'S LAST RESORT

★$ A restaurant-bar of many moods, this place is very popular with office workers, families, and youthful partyers. The ambiance is at its calmest during lunch, when sunlight streams onto the peaceful patio and lawyers, bankers, and secretaries relax over huge salads and sandwiches. In the early evening, families take advantage of the inexpensive children's menu (which comes with balloons and instructions for folding the paper into an airplane to shoot through the dining room) featuring bountiful portions of messy barbecued ribs, chicken, and crab legs. The party mood grows more frenetic as night falls; on weekends, college students and convention-eers wait in long lines to join the fun, fueled by tequila shooters and pitchers of beer. There are entrances on both Fourth and Fifth Avenues. ◆ American ◆ Daily, lunch and dinner. 345 Fourth Ave (between K and J Sts). 231.9100

86 HIGHLIGHTS

Longing for a perfectly engineered Tizio desk lamp or a glowing gold sconce? The display at this minimalist gallery will fill you with desire. All the finest lighting designers are represented. ◆ M-F. 301 Fourth Ave (at K St). 232.6064

BRIDGEWORKS

87 BRIDGEWORKS

Long before the **Convention Center** consumed the waterfront, the Pacific Coast Steamship Company operated a depot and wharf at the foot of Fifth Avenue. The dilapidated warehouses and industrial buildings that took over the site were replaced in 2001 by the **Bridgeworks** complex, which has won several awards for its striking brick, glass, and steel architecture. 401 K Street (at Fourth Ave)

Within Bridgeworks:

HILTON SAN DIEGO GASLAMP QUARTER

$$ You don't have to buy a downtown loft to feel like a sophisticated urbanite. The **Hilton's Enclave** has 30 suites and lofts with soaring ceilings, high windows that let in plenty of natural light, brick and burnished-steel accents, and original paintings by local artists. These creative spaces have a few more creature comforts than most lofts, however, including plush beds with Frette linens, whirlpool tubs, velvety couches, and chocolates on the down pillows at night. The hotel's 245 regular rooms also have a modern, artsy décor and all the right touches, including windows that open to views of the city. The **New Leaf** restaurant is an ideal place for conventioneers and **Gaslamp** workers to gather at the breakfast bar and buffet or on the terrace by the King Promenade. Drinks by the two-sided fireplace in the lounge are the perfect beginning for your evening's Gaslamp crawl. The hotel's rooms and public space offer a pleasant respite from the nearby convention hotel giants. ◆ 401 K Street (at 4th Ave). 231.4040, 800/774.1500; fax 231.6439. ь www.hilton.com

ROYALE

BRASSERIE · BAR

88 ROYALE BRASSERIE

★★$$$ The spread of oysters, mussels, and crab on ice at the entrance to this California-style French brasserie are a sign of great things to come. The burnished wood, brass, and glass room bustles with a sophisticated buzz as well-dressed diners share appetizers of Pernod-cured salmon or steak tartare followed by veal and frog's legs and mussel entrées. Solo diners and large groups of diners may feel more comfortable in the clubby bar or on the terrace, sampling the plate of four imported cheeses or a bowl of spicy seafood soup. Local foodies are thrilled by the menu—an exciting departure from more trendy fare. ◆ French ◆ Daily, dinner. 224 Fifth Ave (at the King Promenade). 237.4900 ь

88 ARTESIA DAY SPA AND SALON

Are your feet and eyes tired from touring or working? Book a pedicure (with exfoliation and massage), a facial designed to diminish those bags and circles under your eyes, or a hot stone massage that will melt your tense muscles. The spa is light and airy yet soothing with its subdued music and lighting. A visit here may be the best lunch break you could take. ◆ Daily. 240 Fifth Ave (between Harbor Drive and K St). 338.8111

Restaurants/Clubs: Red | Hotels: Purple | Shops: Orange | Outdoors/Parks: Green | Sights/Culture: Blue

CORONADO

Though Coronado is often referred to as an island, it is really a peninsula connected to the mainland by the narrow isthmus of highway and sand called the **Silver Strand**. The Coronado Islands are actually offshore and to the south, in Mexican waters; this bit of land was named after that island chain. Coronadans don't refer to their hometown as an island but rather as "The Village," despite its 34,000 residents.

Coronado does seems like a village, a self-contained island community where multiple generations of old-line families live next door to each other on quiet, tree-lined streets. Within its 5.3-square-mile radius, the city has at least 18 public parks—some no larger than a good-size living room in one of the area's stately old mansions—and 28 miles of sandy beach line its shores on the **Pacific Ocean** and **San Diego** and **Glorietta Bays**. The US Navy frames Coronado to the north with the **North Island Naval Air Station** and to the south with the **Naval Amphibious Base** on the Silver Strand. Downtown San Diego is just a 5-minute ferry ride across the San Diego Bay to the east; **Point Loma** is visible to the west.

Residents speak of San Diego as a foreign entity; their city was incorporated in 1890 and has withstood outside intervention ever since. As a rule, Coronadans are faithful to tradition, respectful of local lore, and resistant to change. It's a remarkably safe and thoughtful community, steeped in a colorful and stimulating history that never ceases to fascinate newcomers and old-timers alike.

The history of Coronado begins with Elisha S. Babcock Jr. and Hampton L. Story, two hunting buddies who (as the story goes) became enamored in the 1880s of their hunting grounds on what appeared to be an island in San Diego Bay. On boat trips across the bay, they gradually began to envision a full-scale, spectacular resort where quail and jackrabbits roamed free on scruffy, barren land. Babcock and Story (with additional investors) purchased the peninsula for $110,000 in 1885; by 1887 they had sold $1 million in property, laid out streets and a pipeline to carry fresh water under the bay to the settlement, named it Coronado, and begun construction on the **Hotel Del** (as residents familiarly call the **Hotel del Coronado**). Despite booming land sales, Babcock and Story were broke by 1900, and John Diedrich Spreckels took control of the hotel. Spreckels was the son of Claus Spreckels, called the "Sugar King" for the fortunes he amassed selling Hawaiian sugar in San Francisco. J.D. Spreckels commenced to reign over Coronado's most prosperous and glamorous era, when millionaires built mansions along the waterfront and travelers from all over the world visited the hotel and the adjacent glorified summer camp called **Camp Coronado** (later **Tent City**).

Spreckels combined his many investments to create an irresistible vacation destination conveniently accessible to his railroad lines. He commissioned George T. Marsh to create the formal **Japanese Garden** beside the Spreckels mansion (now the **Glorietta Bay Inn**) on Glorietta Bay. Hotel guests rode in rickshaws pulled by Japanese workers along the ocean and bay to the garden on the edge of Coronado's first golf course. The number of guests touring the garden increased considerably when construction was completed on Spreckels' most imaginative creation—Tent City. Located south of the hotel on the Silver Strand, this outdoor resort consisted of elaborate red-and-white striped tents with wooden floors, furnished in styles from barracks-basic to luxurious. Some tents had separate small cook tents; washtubs for dirty dishes and laundry were provided on every block. Over the years, Tent City grew until it encompassed Main Street, an indoor swimming pool, dance pavilion, carousel, bowling alley, and bandstand. Even Coronado

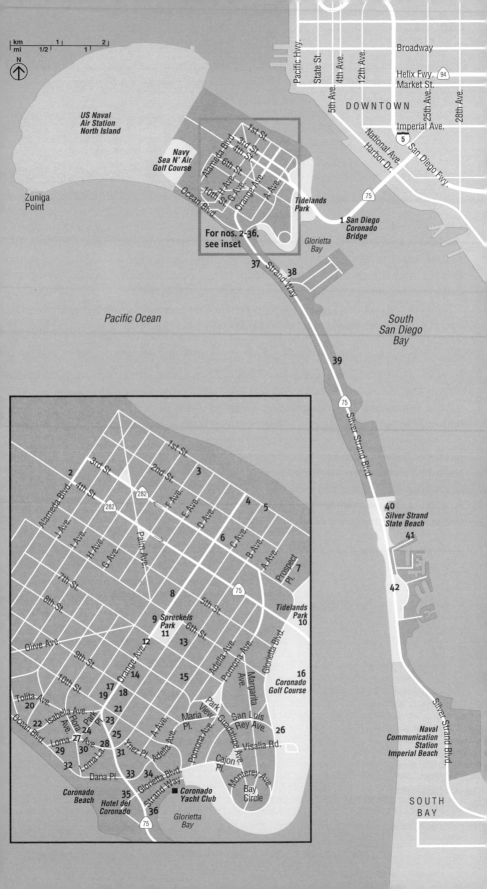

residents closed down their homes for 1 or 2 weeks during the summer months to spend their vacations at Tent City. When J.D. Spreckels died in 1926, his San Francisco–based family sold most of his Coronado properties except for the Hotel Del. Tent City was demolished in 1939. The hotel continued to be a glorious—though somewhat tarnished—resort, and the city kept growing.

In the meantime, the military was becoming an ever more visible presence on **North Island**, which was separated from Coronado by the **Spanish Bight**, a narrow body of water. In 1914 the US Marines set up their first camp on North Island. When the US entered World War I in 1917, the War Department took control of the 1,232-acre island for the army and navy. The naval air station officially began operations on 8 November 1917 and has been in control of North Island ever since (the army left in 1940), contributing greatly to the population and character of Coronado. The navy filled in the Spanish Bight in 1944, giving the base more space and further linking the city to the military. Another navy base for amphibious training was established during World War II, thus sandwiching Coronado between military installations.

Perhaps the single most important event for Coronado in the 20th century was the opening of the **San Diego–Coronado Bridge** in 1969. The city was no longer immune from the horrors of traffic, pollution, and noise, but residents have continued to tenaciously protect their peaceful paradise, restricting tour buses and traffic as much as possible. In the past few decades, the Hotel Del has undergone major renovations, and the city has completed an ambitious redevelopment project that includes a new police station, elementary school, and civic center. Several beloved landmarks have been destroyed by development; others have been lovingly restored. Toll collectors stopped gathering dollars at the bridge in July 2002—yet another controversial move. Some locals feel the toll deters swarms of lookie-loos on their streets. The city hall, recreation center, and a dinner theater on Glorietta Bay will soon be replaced with a large recreation center. At press time, the design had not been finalized, and construction was scheduled to begin in 2003. Coronadans will always have an opinion about what happens in their community—nothing gets done capriciously.

---

1 SAN DIEGO–CORONADO BRIDGE

The views both of and from this 2.13-mile-long bridge are staggering, as is the drive across—especially when there's a strong wind. At its highest point, the bridge arches 246 feet above the San Diego Bay, framing sailboats, freighters, and submarines in the water and the skylines of both downtown and Coronado on the horizon. When the bridge opened in 1969, some islanders thought it was a horrifying blight; others, a blessing—a sign on the **Hotel del Coronado** said "At Last." But all knew it had changed their small-town lives forever. On 2 August 1969, California governor Ronald Reagan gave the dedication speech. Hundreds of runners and bicyclists inaugurated the bridge with a throbbing pulse of energy that tested its earthquake readiness. At 12:01AM on 3 August 1969, cars started rolling in, paying 60 cents each way and wiping the bridge debt clean in less than 20 years. The bridge became toll-free in July 2002. Be forewarned that traffic flows speedily along this asphalt arch; first-time drivers will be hard-pressed to get a glimpse of the side views. ♦ Hwy 75 from downtown San Diego to Fourth St, Coronado

2 NORTH ISLAND

This area was originally an island, separated from Coronado by the Spanish Bight—a narrow body of water that in the 1940s was filled in with sand and mud dredged from the bay. Early aviators used the area as a landing strip, and it was the home of the US's first military aviation school. The US Navy took over the island shortly after World War I broke out, and today the **North Island Naval Air**

Station is an accepted neighbor to the small community; many of Coronado's residents, in fact, are naval retirees. The base is closed to the public. ♦ Fourth St (at Alameda Blvd)

3 JESSOP HOUSE

One of the earliest homes on this side of the city, this house was built in 1901 for Joseph Jessop, founder of **Jessop Jewelers**, the first jewelry business in San Diego. The Colonial Revival architecture is patterned after Jessop's old family home in England. It's a private residence. ♦ 822 First St (between E and F Aves)

4 ZAZEN

Owner Kate Stromberger displays the work of talented designers who create hand-dyed silk dresses, handwoven wraps, and gorgeous jewelry and accessories. ♦ M-Sa or by appointment. 1110 First St (between C and Orange Aves). 435.4780 ♿

4 TARTINE

★$ Roasted eggplant, red peppers, and goat cheese on panini is just one reason to stop here for lunch. Another is the brie and ham on a fresh baguette. Or perhaps you'll be tempted by the salad with smoked salmon and shaved fennel. The high-ceilinged dining room feels spacious and comfortable, and you can see the water from some of the sidewalk tables. ♦ European ♦ Daily, breakfast, lunch, and dinner. 1106 First St (between C and Orange Aves). 435.4323 ♿

5 FERRY LANDING MARKETPLACE

The most enjoyable way to reach Coronado from downtown is the traditional route—aboard a ferry. This modern complex, designed by **Delawie, Britton and Wilkes**, houses not only the ferry pier but commercial enterprises as well. It looks like a Victorian–New England–Old California fishing village, with restaurants, shops, and visitor services clustered under red peaks that call to mind the profile of the **Hotel Del**. An excellent bike path runs south to the **Silver Strand** from the ferry landing under the bridge. A farmers' market is held here every Tuesday evening. ♦ Daily. 1201 First St (between B and C Aves). 435.8895 ♿

Within the Ferry Landing Marketplace:

SAN DIEGO FERRY

From the opening of the Coronado Bridge in 1969 until its debt was paid off almost 2 decades later, this ferry to downtown did not operate. Today it carries commuters, bicyclists, and sightseers (but no cars) back and forth across the bay. ♦ From Coronado daily, on the half hour, 9:30AM-9:30PM; from downtown daily, on the hour, 10AM-9PM. 234.4111

BIKES & BEYOND

Rent a beach cruiser, tandem bike, four-wheel quadricycle seating four, or a pair of in-line skates at this shop and peaceably cruise Coronado's back streets. Customers get a map of suggested bike routes, as well as helmets and locks. Another option is to take a bike on the ferry to downtown and cruise the waterfront there. ♦ Daily. 435.7180

PEOHE'S

★★$$$$ Though the décor resembles something out of Disneyland's Pirates of the Caribbean—lush tropical foliage, trickling waterfalls, and curved bridges—the view of the bay and downtown skyline from this dining spot is undoubtedly the best on the island. Fresh Hawaiian seafood with a tropical flair is the specialty here—try halibut with bananas and macadamia nuts, and the wok-fried whole bass. Many diners have a hard time resisting the crispy coconut shrimp, which you can order as an entrée or in the bar with the requisite mai tai. Don't miss the sinfully rich macadamia-nut ice cream with warm bittersweet-chocolate sauce. ♦ Seafood ♦ M-Sa, lunch and dinner; Su, brunch and dinner. Reservations recommended. 437.4474 ♿

IL FORNAIO

★$$$ The setting is gorgeous but the food unpredictable at this large Italian eatery. Some say the cappuccino is the best you can find anywhere, and the bread and pastries are always divine. And the entrées—pastas, seafood, veal—are sometimes exceptional. The real draw is the terrace seating with an unobstructed view of downtown across the water. ♦ Italian ♦ M-Sa, lunch and dinner; Su, brunch and dinner. 437.4911 ♿ www.ilfornaio.com

Restaurants/Clubs: Red | Hotels: Purple | Shops: Orange | Outdoors/Parks: Green | Sights/Culture: Blue

61

TREKS AND TOURS

Coronado's beauty inspires residents to support all sorts of options designed to ensure that visitors thoroughly appreciate their city. Choose one or all of the following touring possibilities to get a bird's-eye view of the peninsula.

The **Coronado Shuttle** (233.3004), actually the No. 904 bus, is an electric shuttle bus that runs from the **Ferry Landing** through downtown, along **Orange Avenue**—passing the **Hotel Del**—and down the **Silver Strand.** It operates daily every half hour between 9:30AM and 5:30PM.

Coronado Touring (435.5993) features local Nancy Cobb, who leads a 1.5-hour walking tour of Coronado's historic sites. The excursion stops at the **Glorietta Bay Inn,** Hotel Del, and **Star Park,** and along **Ocean Boulevard** and **Orange Avenue,** and is filled with juicy tidbits of gossip and local lore. Tours (admission charged) depart Tuesdays, Thursdays, and Saturdays at 11AM from the Glorietta Bay Inn.

The **Museum of Art and History** (435.7242) offers a Promenade Through the Past walking tour that meanders past many of the finest Craftsman, Victorian, and Spanish Colonial homes in town—a must for architecture buffs. Tours (admission charged) depart from the museum at 2PM on Wednesdays and 10:30AM on Fridays. A local arborist leads the Coronado Tree Tour (435.1764), a 90-minute tour of **Spreckels Park** on Saturdays at 9AM; meet at the park's gazebo.

6 BEST WESTERN SUITES HOTEL

$$ Chain hotels are usually verboten in Coronado, but this hostelry manages to fit in comfortably, thanks to its sloping and curved red shingled roofs à la the **Hotel Del**, convenient location at the entrance to Orange Avenue from the Coronado Bridge, and hidden enclosed parking. The color scheme is muted blue and mauve, with dormer windows acting like skylights to bring the sunshine in. All 63 rooms have refrigerators and microwaves, and an outdoor heated swimming pool is perfect any day of the year. Continental breakfast is served in the lobby, but there's no restaurant. It's a good choice for those seeking dependability, accessibility, and reasonable rates. ♦ 275 Orange Ave (at Third St). 437.1666, 800/528.1234; fax 437.0188

7 CORONADO ISLAND MARRIOTT RESORT

$$$$ Designed in 1986 by **Mosher, Drew, Watson & Ferguson** and approved by Coronadans who had looked at several other models, the hotel's buildings are subtle and unobtrusive. Three-story, pale gray structures surround gorgeous lagoons and tropical gardens that meander over 16 acres along the waterfront facing downtown. Golden koi drift in peaceful streams, and the sounds of waterfalls and gurgling geysers hum in the air.

The 300 rooms (including suites and villas) have a French Provincial motif, with such luxurious amenities as soft terry robes; extra-large bathrooms (with extra-large tubs); and phones by the beds, on writing tables, and in the bathrooms. Further pampering takes place in the spa, where guests indulge in facials, massages, hydrotherapy baths, and the like. For athletic types, there's state-of-the-art fitness equipment, six tennis courts, and a 25-meter heated lap pool (in addition to two other pools). ♦ 2000 Second St (at Prospect Pl). 435.3000, 800/228.9290; fax 435.4183. ♦ www.marriott.com

8 CROWN CITY INN

$$ This inn stands out for its sensible, light-filled rooms equipped with writing tables, coffeemakers, microwaves, and refrigerators. The 33 guest rooms are decorated in light pastels with bleached wood furnishings; there's free underground parking and an in-house laundromat. The **Crown City Bistro** is decorated in pink and green, with ceiling fans reminiscent of *Casablanca*, and is open for breakfast, lunch, and dinner. ♦ 520 Orange Ave (at Fifth St). 435.3116; bistro, 435.3678, 800/422.1173; fax 435.6750

9 CORONADO LIBRARY

J.D. Spreckels hit his stride around 1907, funding the construction of significant buildings in San Diego—from the **Organ Pavilion** in **Balboa Park** to the **Spreckels Theater** downtown. The library trustees on Coronado took note of his prodigious output (including a home on Ocean Boulevard) and asked Spreckels to fund a Coronado library. He agreed and in 1909 commissioned his favored architect, **Harrison Albright,** to design a reinforced concrete Grecian temple with a storage basement and classical columns inside and outside the front door.

When **Homer Delawie** redesigned and expanded the building in 1974, he incorporated the original building within the new, adding two inner courtyards and a community meeting room. Take note of the engraved names of famed thinkers—Byron, Dante, and Chaucer—near the ceiling. Two 60-foot-high star pines and two rose gardens frame the library's entrance. The library was being enlarged again in 2002 but was to remain open during construction. Visitors can get a temporary library card if they can show a similar card from their hometown. The video selection is huge and a good resource for families on extended stays in town. ◆ Daily. 640 Orange Ave (between Seventh and Sixth Sts). 522.7390

10 TIDELANDS PARK

This wildly popular 22-acre park under the northwest side of the bridge has four athletic fields, a children's play area, a skateboard park, a beach on San Diego Bay, a wide-angle view of downtown, clusters of picnic tables, and rest rooms. Originally the old ferry landing area, it was turned into a park in the early 1980s as part of the development of this waterfront land. ◆ Glorietta Blvd (at Fourth St). 522.7342

11 SPRECKELS PARK

J.D. Spreckels donated this 8-acre piece of land to Coronado in 1909. Originally known as **East-West Plaza**, the park was renamed in honor of Spreckels in 1927, a year after his death. The result was a town square complete with a bandstand that remains the island's and city's social center. The park is a popular spot most weekends, with kites flying over family picnics. Art shows are held here the first and third Sunday of the month between June and September, featuring fine art by San Diegans. Summer band concerts are a hometown tradition and occasionally feature local musicians who've made it to the big time. ◆ Bounded by C and Orange Aves and by Seventh and Sixth Sts

12 ORANGE AVENUE

Coronado's main boulevard is named for the orange trees that originally lined its wide median strip. Jackrabbits devoured the orange trees in no time, but the name stuck. In the late 1940s and early 1950s, perfectly formed cedar trees were planted along the median, each with a plaque commemorating the donor's loved ones. Flower gardens line the median beneath the trees and are lovingly tended by volunteers. This strip of trees is lit with Christmas lights for much of December and leads to the city's main Christmas tree in a small green called **Rotary Park** at the intersection of Park Place and **Orange Avenue**. The median becomes a casual reviewing stand during the annual Fourth of July parade, when families with generations of local history in their genes stake out their traditional patch of grass for the day. ◆ From Tenth to First Sts

13 SACRED HEART CHURCH

One of Coronado's most visible examples of **Irving Gill**'s work is this simple and graceful church, designed in 1920. An enhanced version of a Mission-style tower is topped with a blue mosaic tile dome and a gilded cross. Thin panels of stained-glass windows recessed in arches depict the Last Supper, the disciples, and the Virgin Mary. The walls are lined with ceramic dioramas of the birth of Christ and other events. ◆ 672 B Ave (between Seventh and Sixth Sts). 435.3167

14 NIGHT & DAY CAFE

★$ Frank Sinatra croons "My Way" on the jukebox (when it's working) as the short-order cook slides plates piled with hash browns and eggs along the counter. Easily the least expensive and most casual of Coronado's eateries, this is the place to come for inexpensive burgers, meat-loaf sandwiches, and homemade chili. ◆ American ◆ Daily, 24 hours. 847 Orange Ave (between Ninth and Eighth Sts). 435.9776

In true small-town fashion, Coronadans turn out in droves for parades and community celebrations. Among the best gatherings are the St. Patrick's Day Parade, held the weekend before March 17; the Flower Show in April; and Concerts in the Park, held in Spreckels Park on Sundays at 6PM between June and September. But the city's civic pride comes together full force on the Fourth of July. Coronado has hosted one of San Diego's biggest parades since 1948, and it's always a grand event. The military presence in the neighborhood adds a unique touch—tanks roll along Orange Avenue and helicopters swoop overhead. The weekend-long celebration includes a rough-water swim, 15-kilometer run, an art show and concert in Spreckels Park, and a navy air and sea demonstration followed by fireworks at Glorietta Bay. Things slow down until December, when the whole city turns out once again for the Christmas Parade and tree lighting early in the month.

Restaurants/Clubs: Red | Hotels: Purple | Shops: Orange | Outdoors/Parks: Green | Sights/Culture: Blue

15 STEPHENS-TERRY HOUSE

The epitome of Tudor splendor, this manse has a massive chimney, a spotted roof of red and green tiles, and several A-frame dormer windows, topped by what looks like a gun tower or turret. The house was originally designed by **Hebbard & Gill** in 1898 and was remodeled between 1926 and 1930. It's a private residence. ♦ 711 A Ave (at Seventh St)

16 CORONADO GOLF COURSE

Like many of San Diego's waterfront attractions, this golf course actually stands where the waters of the San Diego Bay once bordered Glorietta Boulevard. The course was created from tons of dirt dredged from the bay, plus topsoil from along the strand, all molded into a 200-acre strip of emerald lawns stretching from the old navy housing lots on the north side of the bridge to the yacht club on Glorietta Bay. Now golfers can look toward the office towers of downtown as they enjoy their weekday games on the 18-hole course designed by Jack Daray in 1955. The clubhouse restaurant has an awesome view of the water and downtown and serves inexpensive sandwiches and salads. It's open to the public and is an undiscovered gem for casual dining. The adjacent **Coronado Tennis Center** has courts open to the public. ♦ Greens fee. Daily, 6AM-6PM. 2000 Visalia Rd (at Glorietta Blvd). 435.3121

17 PRIMAVERA RISTORANTE

★★$$$ Superb Northern Italian cuisine is served inside this elegant, split-level dining room. Although all of the dishes are excellent, you won't go wrong with the *scampi diavolo* (shrimp in a spicy tomato sauce); veal stuffed with prosciutto, cheese, and mushrooms; or grilled lamb chops. For dessert, the tiramisù stands out among the very best. ♦ Northern Italian ♦ M-F, lunch and dinner; Sa-Su, dinner. Reservations recommended. 932 Orange Ave (between 10th and Ninth Sts). 435.0454

17 PRIMAVERA PASTRY CAFFÉ

★★$ Formerly **Anderson's Bakery**, this place owned by the daughter of the proprietor of **Primavera Ristorante** is one of the most popular breakfast spots in the city. Inside, the bright-white walls are decorated with green ivy stencils, and the sidewalk café allows diners to people watch while enjoying the excellent omelettes and sandwiches. Locals especially rave about the Yacht Club croissant, stuffed with yellowfin tuna salad. ♦ Bakery/deli ♦ M-Sa, 6:30AM-6PM; Su, 7:30AM-6PM. 956 Orange Ave (between 10th and Ninth Sts). 435.4191

18 CHRIST EPISCOPAL CHURCH

Hand-hewn granite gives a mountain-lodge feel to this Gothic A-frame church designed by **James Reid** in 1894. The blue and purple floral-patterned Tiffany windows took 4 years to complete. ♦ 1028 Ninth St (between C and Orange Aves). 435.4561

19 STRETCH'S CAFE

★$ This long, narrow eatery seems bright and fresh thanks to yellow paint, several healthy trailing plants, a white trellis used as wainscoting, and grass-green tablecloths. There's no meat on the menu, just plenty of fresh, healthful selections, including spinach and sprout salads, melted cheese on seven-grain bread, and baked potatoes stuffed with everything from butter and sour cream to broccoli. ♦ Vegetarian ♦ Daily, breakfast, lunch, and dinner. 943 Orange Ave (between 10th and Ninth Sts). 435.8886

20 REW-SHARP ESTATE

A chest-high concrete wall surrounds an entire block, marking the original boundaries of the 1919 estate built for George Rew, president of Calumet Baking Powder Company. The identity of the original architect is unknown, but there are elements of the Spanish-Moorish designs being used at that time in **Balboa Park**. The front door of the house is framed by ornate molded pilasters; the original façade was covered in concrete mixed with pebbles, giving a rough texture to the walls. The mansion was purchased in 1926 by the wealthy T.E. Sharp; **Sharp Hospital** in San Diego is named for his son. The estate was subdivided over the years (the wall has been cut in sections to make way for driveways), but the main house is still quite impressive. It is a private residence. ♦ 1124 F Ave (between Ocean Blvd and Tolita Ave)

21 GRAHAM MEMORIAL PRESBYTERIAN CHURCH

Elisha Babcock gave architect **James Reid** little time to recover from the construction of the **Hotel Del** and commissioned him to design several other buildings, including this Victorian-Gothic church. Opened in 1890, the structure was named in honor of the parents of his wife, Isabella. Green shingles cover the pointed steeple in picturesque contrast to the white and yellow fish-scale shingles on the façade. The massive gray Victorian house next door, used as the church's offices, was built in 1887 for C.T. Hinde of the Spreckels Company; in 1894, Hinde had the **Christ Episcopal Church** across the street constructed in memory of his daughter. ♦ 975 C Ave (between 10th and Ninth Sts). 435.6860

21 Moo Time Creamery

★$ A life-size Elvis and a full-grown cow guard the door to this funky ice-cream parlor. If you miss the statues, look for the bold blue-neon sign atop the building. Inside is some of the best ice cream you'll ever taste. Waffle irons give off the heady, sugary scent of cones in the making, and rows of glass jars display potential mixings. Pick your flavor (the dark chocolate-orange is divine) and a few tasty tidbits—nuts, crushed cookies, even gummy worms. The counter attendants will scoop your ice cream onto a marble slab, mix your blend, and fill a cone before your lusting eyes. Don't miss it. ♦ Ice-cream parlor ♦ Su-Th, 11AM-10PM; F-Sa, 11AM-11PM. 1025 Orange Ave (between 10th and 9th Sts). 522.6890 ﹠

22 Baby Del

This miniature version of the **Hotel Del** was built in 1887 in southeast San Diego and rescued in 1983 by historic preservationist Chris Mortenson (who was responsible for much of the **Gaslamp Quarter**'s redevelopment in downtown). Mortenson had the home moved to Coronado by barge and restored the pale gray Queen Anne house to its current beauty. It's not open to the public. ♦ 1410 Isabella Ave (at Ocean Blvd)

23 Bay Books

Plan to spend some time at this excellent shop, browsing the shelves and perusing international newspapers and magazines. The clerks post written reviews beside their favorite books, the better to help you choose even more purchases. ♦ M-Sa, 8AM-8PM; Su, 8AM-6PM. 1029 Orange Ave (between C Ave and 10th St). 435.0070

24 Coronado Village Inn

$ This three-story European-style inn from the 1930s stands on the site of the **Blue Lantern Cafe**, the **Hotel Del**'s biggest restaurant

competition in the 1920s. The original café building was moved from the site in 1926, and the square brick and stucco **Blue Lantern Inn** was built in its place. Although the 15 guest rooms have been renovated and modernized, an Old World feel remains, with antique dressers and armoires, incredibly tiny bathrooms, and cushy canopy beds. All rooms have TVs, but none have phones (there's a pay phone in the lobby). Guests have use of the kitchen, where a continental breakfast is served free daily. ♦ 1017 Park Pl (between Flora and Isabella Aves). 435.9318

25 McP's Irish Pub

★$ The Guinness flows like water at this lively neighborhood pub. Patrons are a fun and festive lot who enjoy good ale and hearty grub. It's the only place in town serving mulligan stew and corned beef and cabbage. ♦ Irish pub ♦ Daily, 11AM-2AM; food served until 9PM. 1107 Orange Ave (between B and C Aves). 435.5280

26 Robert House

This simple off-white adobe home designed by **William Templeton Johnson** in 1916 looks like it belongs in Santa Fe rather than facing San Diego Bay. It is tucked behind ancient succulents (including a rare dragon tree) planted by **Balboa Park** landscape designer Kate Sessions. It is a private residence. ♦ 1000 Glorietta Blvd (at San Luis Rey Ave)

27 Star Park

One of the prettiest lawns in all of Coronado is this half-acre in the center of Star Park Circle, where several small residential streets converge. Another J.D. Spreckels donation, the circle is framed by enchanting bungalows with gorgeous flowerbeds. Years ago, the ocean was visible from the little park, but the view disappeared as mansions rose on Ocean Boulevard and the surrounding streets. The park is particularly enjoyable when the magnolias blossom in late spring. ♦ At Loma Ave, Flora Ave, and Park Pl

28 Chez Loma

★★★★$$$$ A more romantic dining spot than this converted 1890 Victorian house

can't be found in Coronado. The inside dining room is filled with antiques and subdued candlelight; the enclosed sidewalk terrace gives the feeling of a private garden, with a few tables set amid vines and potted plants. From the fine selection of cuisine, savor the filet mignon with black truffle jus (an outstanding dish), the salmon with roasted horseradish crust, or the house specialty—roasted duckling with cherry, burnt orange, and green-peppercorn sauce. Save room for the heavenly gingerbread cake with **Moo Time**'s vanilla-bean ice cream. Take your time. Dinner here is a sublime experience. The chef has a wonderful wine-pairing menu featuring foie gras and rack of venison. Prixe-fix menus and early-bird specials make the restaurant a possible choice for those on a budget. ◆ Continental ◆ M-Sa, dinner; Su, brunch and dinner. Reservations recommended. 1132 Loma Ave (at Orange Ave). 435.0661

28 MUSEUM OF ART AND HISTORY

Volunteers worked for many years to create this fascinating museum run by the Coronado Historical Association. The neoclassical **Bank of Commerce** building, which sits on a V-shaped corner by Rotary Park, was the island's first bank when it opened in 1910. It now holds four exhibit spaces with permanent exhibits on the history of the island and the navy's presence there. The photos of **Tent City** are especially fascinating, and traveling exhibits have included shows on the history of surfing and poster images from World War II. The museum has a gift shop and the **Tent City Café**, a good spot for coffee or a light lunch. ◆ Donation suggested. Daily. 1100 Orange Ave (at Loma Ave). 435.7242

Within the museum:

CORONADO VISITOR CENTER

Helpful clerks at the desk beside the front door assist tourists with maps, directions, brochures, and tips on what to do while on the island. ◆ Daily. 437.8788

When the city began reconstructing the sidewalks along Orange Avenue in 2001, workers discovered 100-year-old stamps left in the concrete by the original contractor. The current workers cut out the old stamps and embedded them in the new sidewalks.

There are 19 public tennis courts on Coronado, including eight courts at 150-1 Glorietta Boulevard, six by the Coronado Library, and five at Coronado Cays. Courts are open between sunrise and 6PM. For information, call 435.1616.

28 EMERALD CITY SURF 'N SPORT

The hottest brands and styles of beach gear are arrayed under neon-bright surfing posters, surfboards, and skateboards. Wet suits, bathing suits, and T-shirts in the hippest styles and colors tempt even young-sters to cash out their allowance savings. ◆ Daily. 1118 Orange Ave (at B Ave). 435.6677

28 SPRECKELS BUILDING

In 1916 John D. Spreckels declared that Coronado needed only two more institutions to make it a complete city—a bank and a theater. He commissioned **Harrison Albright** to design a block-long structure to house both, as well as several shops and residences. The resulting neoclassical edifice was one of Coronado's finest until it gradually fell into disrepair over the decades. Entrepreneur Paul Swerdlove bought the building in 1992 and restored the original façade. The following year, the **Lamb's Players** signed a lease on the old theater and remodeled it to the tune of $2.5 million. Trendy cafés and boutiques along the block have established it once again as a centerpiece of life in "The Village." ◆ Orange Ave (between B and C Aves)

Within the Spreckels Building:

CAFE 1134

★$ This sleek coffeehouse-café-gallery serves salads, sandwiches, and coffee drinks in a stark setting. Grab a seat at the sidewalk tables for a great street scene. ◆ Café ◆ Daily. 1134 Orange Ave (between B and C Aves). 437.1134 ఉ

LAMB'S PLAYERS THEATRE

J.D. Spreckels' original **Silver Strand Theatre** opened in 1917 with a performance by Madame Ernestine Schumann-Heink, the most famous contralto of her day. In the 1930s it became a movie house, called the **Coronado Theatre**, which lasted until 1952 when more modern theaters with "refrigerated air" were in vogue. The lobby became a retail space and the theater remained dark until restoration began in 1993. Architect **Douglas Whitmore** found that most of the original details had been removed, including the seven Tiffany glass skylights. He managed to replicate the ornate columns and capitals from the original design and created an intimate 340-seat auditorium for the **Lamb's Players**, a nonprofit theater group. The theater reopened in 1994, and plays are scheduled throughout the year. ◆ Admission. 1142 Orange Ave (between B and C Aves). 437.0600. ఉ www.lambsplayers.org

IN GOOD TASTE

Looking for the perfect hostess gift? Or maybe a special treat to snack on in your room? This is your place. The shelves are stocked with gourmet cookies, crackers, teas, and coffees; the display case presents a tempting array of cheese tortes; and the chocolates are to die for. ♦ Daily. 1146 Orange Ave (between B and C Aves). 435.8356

PLUMS

Picture frames, cookbooks, stuffed animals, jewelry—there are enough trinkets and treasures in this little shop to satisfy the pickiest shopper. ♦ Daily. 1158 Orange Ave (between B and C Aves). 435.5542

RHINOCEROS Cafe & Grille

RHINOCEROS CAFE & GRILL

★★$$ Floor-to-ceiling windows make this white-on-white café a bright and cheery place to dine on huge salads, cioppino, shrimp with lobster cream, and home-style meat-loaf sandwiches. Grab a table by the windows and watch the street scene. ♦ Daily, lunch and dinner. 1166 Orange Ave. 435.2121

29 CLAUS SPRECKELS HOUSE

J.D. Spreckels's first Coronado home was this 1908 beach cottage designed by **Harrison Albright**. Spreckels subsequently gave the house to his son Claus as a wedding gift. The cottage is nearly hidden by tall eugenia bushes, but you can get a glimpse of it from across the street. It is a private residence. ♦ 1043 Ocean Blvd (between Loma Ave and Ocean Blvd)

29 CROWN MANOR

This English-Tudor estate is a modest home with *only* 17 bedrooms and 13 baths semi-hidden behind a wall. The home was originally designed in 1901 by **Hebbard & Gill** for Bartlett Richards, a Nebraska cattleman and banker. In 1913 Richards's widow sold the home to Walter and Florence Dupee of Chicago, who commissioned **Frederick Roehrig** to add two wings to the house in 1914, increasing its size to 20,000 square feet. Walter Dupee was instrumental in creating both the **Coronado Country Club** and the **Coronado Beach Polo Club**, which became world renowned. The house gained national notoriety when President Bill Clinton and his family vacationed here in the middle of Republican territory. It is a private residence. ♦ 1015 Ocean Blvd (between Loma La and Loma Ave)

30 LEMECHE-MEADE HOUSE

The pale yellow bungalow with blue shutters and window boxes to the right facing **Star Park** was a favorite retreat for L. Frank Baum, author of *The Wizard of Oz*. The house was built in 1896, and Baum wintered there for several years, completing several books in what must have been a serene and inspirational hideaway. The house is a private residence. ♦ 1101 Star Park Circle (between Loma and Flora Aves)

31 LA AVENIDA INN

$$ A gray-and-purple awning marks the entryway to this 29-room, motellike establishment on the former site of **La Avenida Cafe**, once one of Coronado's most beloved landmarks. All the guestrooms have king- or queen-size beds, and nonsmoking rooms are available. There's no restaurant, but complimentary coffee is served in the lobby. A small swimming pool provides refreshment on hot days. ♦ 1315 Orange Ave (at B Ave). 435.3191, 800/437.0162; fax 435.5024 ♿

32 OCEAN BOULEVARD AND SEAWALL

From the beginning, Ocean Boulevard was the most desirable address in Coronado, and lavish mansions were the preferred type of residence. When a severe storm threatened the homes in 1905, boulevard residents voted in a $145,000 bond issue to finance building a seawall. Spreckels, the railroad magnate, built a rock foundation in front of the **Hotel Del** to extend the **Belt Line Railroad**'s tracks toward the boulevard, then hauled some 67 tons of rock from the Sweetwater Valley to

---

Restaurants/Clubs: **Red** | Hotels: **Purple** | Shops: **Orange** | Outdoors/Parks: **Green** | Sights/Culture: **Blue**

construct the wall. The rocks did minimize storm damage for a while, but eventually the rocks themselves were used by the forces of nature as weapons when fierce tides and winds tossed the boulders onto the boulevard. The seawall was reinforced in 1912, and again several times since. A long and deep beach was eventually created between the seawall and the sea, which kept the waves from beating directly on the wall and boulevard. Today, sand dunes topped with succulents help hold the water at bay, making the beach one of the most scenic in the county, and several fire rings line the beach's north end. The city installed a 145-foot-long pathway made of recycled rubber for wheelchair access to the beach.

Across the street is **Sunset Park**, a popular spot for volleyball games. There is a second entrance to North Island here; just inside the gate (where a sign says "patrolled by military working dog teams") is the **North Island Naval Air Station**'s golf course. ♦ Ocean Blvd (between Churchill Pl and Ocean Dr) ♿

33 BRIGANTINE

★★$$ Locals swear by the juicy, thick burgers, crisp fish and chips, and gigantic Cobb salads at this casual restaurant, where cozy booths line the walls. Salty types flock to the dark, nautical bar for spirits and boat talk. The grilled fish is always good, and the swordfish marinated in soy, dijon mustard, and garlic is superb. The Sunday-to-Thursday early-bird dinners are a great deal. ♦ Steak/seafood ♦ M-F, lunch and dinner; Sa-Su, dinner. 1333 Orange Ave (between Adella and B Aves). 435.4166

33 EL CORDOVA HOTEL

$$ Character and charm make this rambling old hacienda a great choice for those who want casual comfort and a homelike setting. The original building was Elisha Babcock's home, built in 1902; the other Spanish-style buildings were added in the 1930s. Wide stairways are lined with Mexican tiles; wrought-iron balconies face a quiet stretch of Orange Avenue, and the pool and gardens are tucked beneath ancient bird of paradise plants. The peach stucco and green trim on the hotel's exterior are showing their age, and the furnishings in the 39 rooms are well worn, but some accommodations have kitchenettes

and living rooms where you can set up housekeeping by the day, week, or month. ♦ 1351 Orange Ave (at Adella Ave). 435.4131; fax 435.0632

Within El Cordova Hotel:

MIGUEL'S COCINA

★★$ One of the most popular restaurants in Coronado is this courtyard patio covered with latticework and *palapas* (thatch-roof huts). The waitresses wear colorful costumes, Mexican ballads play in the background, and a festive attitude prevails among the clientele. Like most old-line Mexican restaurants, this place has its own secret preparations for all the standard fare; good choices are the *carnitas* (marinated pork served with tortillas), fish tacos, and *chiles rellenos* (stuffed peppers). Count on waiting for a table on weekend nights. ♦ Mexican ♦ M-Sa, lunch and dinner; Su, brunch and dinner. 1339 Orange Ave (at Adella Ave). 437.4237

33 ADELLA PLAZA

A tiled fountain splashes in the middle of this small plaza lined with benches and palms. Look for the plaque on the wall commemorating one of Coronado's proudest achievements. In 2000, the city was given a Great American Main Street Award by the National Trust for Historic Preservation. The award is prestigious and much coveted. Orange Avenue, with its gardens and carefully restored historic buildings, was deemed worthy by a panel of noted architects and city planners. ♦ Adella Ave (at Orange Ave)

34 GLORIETTA BAY INN

$$ When sugar baron J.D. Spreckels moved to Coronado, he commandeered an entire block above Glorietta Bay (where his yacht could be safely berthed) and commissioned **Harrison Albright** in 1908 to build a mansion that suited his position within the community. A marble-and-brass staircase with leather handrails leads from the hotel's lobby to the 11 guestrooms furnished with antiques. Be sure to take a look at the music room, added to the mansion in 1912 to house Spreckels's Aeolian organ and its 2,000 pipes. Brass and

---

Coronado's strange configuration is due in part to **Palm and Olive Avenues**, two 100-foot-wide boulevards (planted, of course, with palm and olive trees) running diagonally from the peninsula's northwest and southwest corners to a central point in Spreckels Park.

copper doors were installed in the long oval room, along with indirect lighting behind handmade curved plaster moldings next to the ceiling. Newspaper magnate Ira Copley bought the house in 1926; when he died in 1949, his family sold the entire block for $90,000. Several two-story buildings were built on the grounds in later years and now are tucked amid mature tree ferns and palms. The variety of rooms, from low-priced but comfortable standards to delightful mansion suites, makes this a good choice for all types of visitors. Some units have kitchenettes and separate bedrooms. There's no restaurant, but guests are served a complimentary continental breakfast in the Music Room, along with warm drinks and gingersnaps in the afternoon. The hotel has a warm, friendly feeling; it has received many awards for its service. Perhaps that's why many guests return annually. ♦ 1630 Glorietta Blvd (between Orange Ave and Ynez Pl). 435.3101, 800/283.9383; fax 435.6182. & www.gloriettabayinn.com

35 HOTEL DEL CORONADO

$$$$ The oldest (completed in 1888) Pacific Coast resort from Alaska to Acapulco, this renowned, celebrated, and venerated hotel is the place to live out aristocratic fantasies. Start in the regal lobby, a handsome room of polished dark Illinois oak and Honduran mahogany that feels like the inside of an English millionaire's country estate. The lobby was originally used primarily by men registering their families at the front desk and dragging in their catches from hunting and fishing trips around the barren island. The women used a separate entrance and lobby, freshening up before riding one of three birdcage electric elevators to their rooms.

Elisha Babcock and H.L. Story were nothing short of visionaries when they conceived of building an oceanfront resort so spectacular that even jaded Easterners would be drawn west by its grandeur and style. Architects **James** and **Merritt Reid** designed this Queen Anne castle, working with a general vision, conceptual drawings, and a generous amount of flexibility, rather than specific plans. Chinese laborers and skilled craftsmen of varied nationalities were brought in from San Francisco, and hundreds of thousands of feet of redwood, fir, cedar, hemlock, pine, and oak trees were shipped in to build the largest all-wood structure in the country. Advanced sprinkler systems were installed throughout the hotel, but to this day there hasn't been a fire. A 200-foot-long tunnel was dug to install water, steam, gas, and electrical power lines that led to a separate powerhouse and

laundry. An estimated two million red shingles cover the peaked roofs, dormers, and towers. Perhaps the building's most spectacular feature at the time was its use of electricity. A cable was run underneath the bay from San Diego during construction, furnishing the current for the lights that illuminated the site for the night crews. When the hotel opened, each bedroom had an electric light, a novelty at the time.

A formal opening was held in February 1888, a mere 11 months after construction began. The entire project cost $1 million, and J.D. Spreckels repeatedly rescued Babcock and Story from financial ruin in the hotel's early years; by the time he moved from San Francisco to San Diego in 1906, he had taken over, with Babcock working as an employee. The hotel flourished through the early Spreckels years, much aided by the owner's investments in **Tent City** and the railroad lines that brought a steady flow of guests. Although the Great Depression, World War II, and the next few owners all left their mark, the hotel remained a star (though sometimes a tarnished one)—attracting luminaries and celebrities who recorded the hotel's charms in letters, books, and films. *Some Like It Hot*, starring Marilyn Monroe, Jack Lemmon, and Tony Curtis and directed by Billy Wilder, was filmed here in 1958.

In 1963, the Hotel Del Corporation purchased the property and spent the next 20 years and $80 million restoring the main building's structural and mechanical supports. The addition of a seven-floor tower created a disgruntled stir among longtime Coronado residents. But many of the hotel's original features, including the gazebo in the garden (which still contains palms planted by landscaper Kate Sessions in 1888) and the porte cochere at the entrance were restored. Another $55 million major restoration was completed in 2001. The unsightly tennis courts that once stood in the main hotel's courtyard have been torn down and replaced with the lovely Windsor Lawn—an idyllic wedding setting. A full-service spa was added to the hotel, and the restaurants were remodeled and updated. The best addition is the **Babcock & Story Bar**, a comfortable lounge with views of the sea, live music, and excellent signature margaritas and tapas.

The hotel initially had 399 guestrooms and 75 bathrooms (the largest number of indoor toilets anywhere in the country at that time). Today, each of the 381 rooms in the original building has a private bath, and the configurations formed by these additions make for some strangely shaped rooms. Another quirk: Rubbernecking is a must in some ocean-view rooms. There are also 293 rooms in the more modern tower with great ocean and bay views. Other assets include two swimming pools above a pristine beach, six tennis courts, several galleries and boutiques, four restaurants, and two bars. ♦ 1500 Orange Ave (between Ave del Sol and Ocean Blvd). Reservations, 435.6611, 800/468.3533; fax 522.8262. &. www.hoteldel.com

Within the Hotel del Coronado:

CROWN ROOM

★★★$$ Don't miss Sunday brunch in this majestic dining room with the second-largest unsupported domed ceiling in the US (the first is the Mormon Tabernacle in Salt Lake City). L. Frank Baum, author of The Wizard of Oz, designed the room's original crown chandeliers, which have since been replaced. On Sunday mornings, hundreds of diners line up at long tables filled with salads, entrées, and sinful desserts, lingering for hours, listening to harp music over the din of happy chatter. Some find the brunch to be overpriced and overcrowded, but it still holds a special charm for first-timers. Weekday meals are far more sedate. ♦ American ♦ M-Sa, breakfast, lunch, and dinner; Su, brunch and dinner. Reservations recommended for brunch. 522.8496

PRINCE OF WALES GRILL

★★★★$$$$ Formerly stuffy and dark, this elegant restaurant has been completely remodeled with floor-to-ceiling windows facing the ocean and a silver, white, and taupe color scheme. The menu has been updated as well, with California lobster flash-seared and served with a lemongrass broth and the grill's dependable New York steak now served with violet mustard sauce and confit potatoes; the

Residents take Coronado's April Flower Show very seriously. Gardeners set to work on their front yards weeks in advance, planting hollyhocks, delphiniums, foxgloves, and sweet peas in preparation for the annual competition. The show includes a weekend-long celebration in Spreckels Park, with exhibits by local gardeners, an excellent book fair, and an auto show.

One of Coronado's most treasured artworks was rescued from the dilapidated La Avenida Cafe before the restaurant closed and was restored to its original splendor. *El Día del Mercado*, painted by muralist Alfredo Ramos Martínez in 1938, was found covered in grease and nicotine stains, with holes drilled in it for light-switch plates. If all goes according to plan, it will hang in the library after the building is renovated.

wild boar and Sonoma squab are both palate pleasers. Complete with a pianist playing soft jazz in the background, this place offers an elegant and romantic dining experience. ♦ American ♦ Daily, dinner. Reservations recommended. 522.8818

36 THE BOATHOUSE

★$$$ The **Hotel Del**'s original boathouse was designed by **James** and **Merritt Reid** and built in 1887 by Chinese laborers practicing the skills they later used so impressively in constructing the hotel. The building, on the edge of Glorietta Bay, is a fantastical miniature of the hotel, with red-shingle turrets and gables and peaks poking out from the white wooden façade. A bathhouse was once connected to the boathouse, providing heated dressing rooms and bathing suits rented for 35 cents. In the summers of 1903 and 1904, biologist William E. Ritter from the laboratory of the University of California at Berkeley studied the marine life of Glorietta Bay here. Ritter attracted the attention of wealthy San Diegans like J.D. Spreckels, William Marston (the force behind much of **Balboa Park**), and the Scripps family, who later provided him with the beginnings of La Jolla's famed **Scripps Institution of Oceanography**. The boathouse also served as the headquarters for three different yacht clubs and has housed several restaurants. The current tenant opened in 2001 and serves standard steakhouse fare. ♦ Seafood/steak ♦ Daily, dinner. Reservations recommended. 1701 Strand Way (at Glorietta Blvd). 435.0155

37 THE SHORES

As if the bridge weren't enough of a shock to Coronado's tranquillity, these glaring 15-story concrete and steel condo towers, designed by **Krisle & Shapiro**, began poking up from the sands south of the **Hotel Del** in 1971. Now there are 10 buildings on 35 acres bordered by a 2,100-foot-long seawall. The community reacted by creating a 40-foot, three-story limit on all future buildings. Units in the 10 towers are available for rent on a monthly basis. These are private residences. ♦ Ave de las Arenas (at Orange Ave). 435.6238

38 CORONADO BOAT RENTALS

Sailboats, motorboats, Windsurfers, and canoes are all available at this spot by **Glorietta Bay Park**, where boaters line up early on weekend mornings to launch their vessels from the public ramp. ♦ M-Sa. 1715 Strand Way (between Aves Lunar and del Sol). 437.1514

39 NAVAL AMPHIBIOUS BASE

Swarms of Navy SEALs practice their maneuvers at this amphib base, established during World War II, storming the beaches at the north end of the Silver Strand. ♦ North end of Silver Strand

40 SILVER STRAND STATE BEACH

This spectacularly wild and windswept beach became a state park in 1932 and is still one of the best beaches in the county for surf fishing and clam digging. There's a campground for recreational vehicles, four parking lots, public rest rooms, showers, and fire rings. ♦ Camping fee. Daily, 8AM-7PM. Silver Strand Blvd (at Coronado Bay Rd). 435.5184

41 LOEWS CORONADO BAY RESORT

$$$$ It's hard to imagine that into the 1990s there was still a 15-acre undeveloped peninsula on the **Silver Strand**. Then Loews corporation hired architect **C.W. Kim** to design a 440-room resort and 80-slip marina. It sits on Crown Isle just north of the **Coronado Cays** and is surrounded on three sides by water with views of the bridge, downtown, and the marina. All spacious, soothing rooms and suites feature waterfront views and private balconies. The bayside villas are especially enchanting, with their private decks right over the water. A spectacular spa (the largest on the island) was scheduled to open in early 2003. The **Kid's Camp** is open year-round and on Friday and Saturday evenings in summer—a major plus for parents who want a romantic interlude at one of the hotel's fabulous restaurants or a sunset cruise in a gondola. Other pluses include a fitness center, five tennis courts, three swimming pools, and a fascinating herb garden. Locals pack the **Market Café** during Sunday brunch—a culinary festival of fresh seafood, carved meats, unusual salads, and to-die-for desserts. Shops include **R.R.R.'s Market**, with its irresistible selection of gourmet foods, beachwear, straw hats, and kids' toys. The **Loews** is a bit removed from downtown Coronado, which makes it an idyllic hideaway. There's a shuttle to downtown San Diego if you must leave the property. ♦ 4000 Coronado Bay Rd (at Silver Strand Blvd). 424.4000, 800/235.6397; fax 424.4400. ♿ www.loewshotels.com

Within the Loews Coronado Bay Resort:

AZZURA POINT

★★★★$$$$ A wide, sweeping staircase leads to this elegant second-story dining room with windows looking out to the bay and central Coronado. Venetian-style chandeliers, suede and silk draperies, chenille seat coverings, and unusual leopard-patterned tabletops give the room an exotic, elegant, and comfortable ambiance. The California French menu is filled with unusual delights, including a fabulous grilled swordfish with foie gras, sautéed pheasant, and venison loin wrapped in bacon. Be sure to save room for the sublime Valrhona milk chocolate mousse with passion fruit. ♦ Seafood ♦ Daily, dinner. Reservations recommended. 424.4477

42 CORONADO CAYS

One of the most exclusive residential communities in Coronado is built on the site of the **Hog Ranch**, one of the most heavily disputed plots of land on **Silver Strand**. The ranch was in its prime during the days of **Tent City**, when the garbage from that resort served as bountiful fodder for the livestock on this ranch 4 miles south of the resort. The Riis family operated the farm, and when it was washed out by a high tide in 1916, they moved their operation to the mainland. Coronadans continued to dump their junk on the property, and the *Coronado Journal* reported at one point that "the Navy never disposed of anything smaller than a used battleship there." In 1954, the city council designated the area off-limits for dumping, the navy announced the land would not be needed for military purposes, and the controversy began over **Rancho Carrillo** (as the Hog Ranch became known). Fourteen years later the Atlantic Richfield Company purchased the land for $4 million and built **Coronado Cays**, a 1,500-unit residential community. The development is home to Hollywood stars, retired navy officers, and others seeking a private hideaway. These are private residences. ♦ Silver Strand Blvd (at Coronado Cays Blvd)

Restaurants/Clubs: Red | **Hotels: Purple** | **Shops: Orange** | **Outdoors/Parks: Green** | **Sights/Culture: Blue**

UPTOWN

A cluster of centuries-old suburbs and villages, each with its own character, uptown includes the communities of **Little Italy**, **Middletown**, **Mission Hills**, **Hillcrest**, and segments once considered to be downtown. It borders **Balboa Park**, the city's urban treasure, and **Mission Valley**, where cattle ranges have given way to shopping malls. A wide variety of people populate the area: middle-class families, upper-class dynasties, ethnic minorities, gays and lesbians, and up-and-coming singles.

Near downtown on **India Street**, Italian immigrants feel at home among family and friends in Little Italy, where the church is the center of the community. Middletown began as a suburb that grew up between San Diego's original center, known today as **Old Town**, and the current downtown, which was called **New Town** (or **Horton's Folly**) at the turn of the 19th century. Nowadays it's an intersection of highways and byways, with hidden neighborhoods wedged between main thoroughfares. There are some great old houses and cottages loaded with character and charm along its back streets, boasting very attractive rents. Artsy types have always gravitated to these secluded wooden homes overgrown with vines and gathered on India Street, in one-of-a-kind coffeehouses and cafés.

High-society settlers in the late 1800s headed straight to Mission Hills after hearing steamship captain Henry James Johnson vividly describe the hillside's beauty and his 65 acres of land overlooking **San Diego Bay**. Quite the salesman, the captain was successful in quickly selling parcels to these pioneers. As the city grew, the canyons and parklands of Mission Hills remained relatively natural and wild, with coyotes, owls, and white deer browsing behind palatial estates housing wealthy families whose surnames were synonymous with San Diego history. It's a place where all of San Diego's leading architects have built residences: This is **Irving Gill** country, with plenty of examples of works by **William Templeton Johnson**, **Richard Requa**, **Sam Hamill**, the **Quayle Brothers**, **John Lloyd Wright**, and **Homer Delawie** as well. Architectural styles range from Italian Renaissance to Mission Revival, Spanish Colonial, Moorish, Craftsman, and Victorian. The neighborhood still holds the prestige of old, with streets named after local judges and financiers, and homes in the grandest Spanish hacienda style bordering the rolling lawns of the original presidio and Old Town. In the spring, when the jacarandas bloom, entire neighborhoods are shrouded in a purple haze. It's no wonder Kate Sessions, **Balboa Park's** first gardener, chose to build her 1912 home here.

Hillcrest was also a desirable address when downtown was in its nascent prime and bankers and bureaucrats erected their mansions looking down upon the center city. Only those with horse-drawn carriages could afford to live atop the steep incline of **Fifth Avenue**. Exclusivity was established as early as 1907, when developer William Wesley Whitson purchased 40 acres for $115,000 and began selling lots. *For profit or for comfort buy in a restricted tract*, read his ads. *If you buy now your investment may double before your second payment is due.*

In the 1920s, Hillcrest was the city's first suburb, complete with trolley stop, movie theaters, restaurants, and parks. In 1940, local merchants were so proud of their thriving commercial district that they mounted a giant sign boldly emblazoned with the name *Hillcrest* atop two tall wooden posts and stretched it across Fifth Avenue at **University Avenue**. Eventually the posts were replaced with cement pillars, but in the 1960s, when residents began to move to more peaceful suburbs, business declined. The sign fell into disrepair and was removed.

In the 1980s, a new wave of yuppified gays, lesbians, and straights took interest in the cottages built during Whitson's time, and Hillcrest's charms were restored. The subsequent gentrification has driven away many of Hillcrest's landmark old-time businesses as a result of spiraling rents and the proliferation of minimalls. Yet excellent restaurants and cafés abound, and despite all its modern urban trappings, Hillcrest has retained its neighborly feeling.

Hillcrest is most broadly bounded by **Washington** and **Laurel Streets** and by **Park Boulevard** and **First Avenue**. It borders **Balboa Park** and is home to many of the city's grandest churches, synagogues, homes, and hospitals. Many of the area's old Victorian homes are headquarters for medical clinics and social services agencies. The avenues on the south side of Hillcrest are a veritable museum of San Diego's architectural styles, with homes designed by the same architects as in Mission Hills. The hill sloping toward downtown has alternately been called **Bankers Hill** and **Pill Hill** (in reference to the many doctors in residence). Outstandingly renovated Victorian homes, many from the late 1800s, now house small inns, attorneys' and doctors' offices, and the offspring of some of San Diego's founding families.

Until the building of the **Uptown District**—a 14-acre complex of condos, cafés, and shops—was completed in 1989, Hillcrest's eastern edge was an area filled with discount warehouses and transvestite bars. A far smaller complex, **Village Hillcrest**, revived the corner of Fifth Avenue and Washington Street, although today some of the storefronts are empty and the multiplex theater, showing many art films, is the biggest draw. With these two additions, the area is definitely on the upswing, and the development craze seems to have slowed down—at least for now.

---

1 ADAMS AVENUE GRILL

★$$ A fun restaurant with locally made art on the walls, this is a place you can take your parents, your boss, a date, or your friends. Interesting soups (try the fabulous carrot-ginger) and weekly specials (such as eggplant parmesan or stuffed red peppers) keep the faithful regulars from getting bored. There's a wide variety of tastes, from spicy Asian dishes to American comfort foods. ◆ American/eclectic ◆ Sa-Su, breakfast; lunch and dinner daily. Dinner reservations recom-mended. 2201 Adams Ave (at Mississippi St). 298.8440 &

2 EL ZARAPE

★★$ Locals depend on this neighborhood fast-food restaurant for delicious Mexican food at good prices and in large portions. The menu offers lots of seafood—try the fabulous shrimp burritos. Vegetarians can ask for many of the same dishes to be made without meat. ◆ Daily. 4642 Park Blvd (between Madison and Adams Aves). 692.1652

THE BEST

Bill Keller

Co-owner, Le Travel Store

After decades of dumb growth (malls, sprawl, and urban decay), vitality has returned to San Diego's urban core. **Downtown** has become a lively pedestrian community, more like a European city with dense housing, outdoor cafés, excellent restaurants, and a sense of pride. For natives like myself, it's astonishing to see downtown become the city's hottest residential district—condos from the low $300's to over $1 million. Cranes and construction everywhere!

My neighborhood is the center of activity. The **Gaslamp Quarter** stretches eight blocks from the **Convention Center** up Fourth, Fifth and Sixth Avenues to Broadway. At midday on weekdays, office workers pour into the **Gaslamp** from the north. Conventioneers come up from the south by day. At night, they come from the surrounding hotels. Downtown residents come in from the east and west. On Friday and Saturday nights, people from the suburbs and day-trippers from L.A. come for dinner. At 10PM, a younger club crowd takes over and keeps growing past midnight. On the weekend, shoppers frequent the boutiques and unique stores.

City leaders, architects, and developers all deserve enormous credit for redevelopment in San Diego. But—excuse my bias—it's the skill and creativity of business owners that bring life into a neighborhood. Our exuberant diversity comes from thousands of customers patronizing the stores, restaurants, and clubs. A few entrepreneurs deserve special attention.

Starting in 1985, Ingrid Croce (widow of Jim and mother of A.J.) created a restaurant, jazz bar, and club in the still-seedy neighborhood. With great energy and perseverance, she created a landmark at Fifth and F.

Then came the Italian invasion. One block south, Alessandro Minutella and Vincenzo Lo Verso opened the popular **Osteria Panevino**, followed by **Trattoria Portobello** on Fourth Avenue and **Greystone Steakhouse** on Fifth. Now there are more than a dozen Italian restaurants in the Gaslamp. David and Leslie Cohn have set the standard for dining in San Diego. They have created six unique restaurants—**Blue Point Coastal Cuisine** and **Dakota** on Fifth Avenue in the Gaslamp, plus the **Prado** in **Balboa Park**, **Corvette** and **Kemo Sabe** in **Hillcrest**, and **Indigo Grill** in **Little Italy**.

I'm personally grateful to all the restaurants offering a superb lunch at a modest price. My Fourth Avenue favorites are **Sanban**, the busy Japanese restaurant near E Street; **Bandar**, the marvelous Persian place near F Street; and the **Cheese Shop**, everyone's favorite deli near G St. On Fifth Avenue, I suggest **Sadaf**, the other excellent Persian restaurant near E Street; **Royal Thai** on the corner at Island; and **Cafe 222** at Second and Island.

Home to over seventy stores, the Gaslamp is growing into an urban shopping district. Be sure to stop into the venerable **San Diego Hardware** on Fifth. Galleries and import shops are concentrated between G Street and Island. Be sure to see **Golden Pacific**, the **Paperie**, **Kita Ceramics**, **Robson Gallery**, **Elephant Trunk**, and **Galeria del Sol**.

As the smart growth movement sweeps the US, downtown San Diego is proving that you can have increased residential density and an improved quality of life. On the other hand, I'm writing this essay on a February afternoon. It's 75 degrees in the Gaslamp. The neighborhood is packed; people are strolling or lounging in outdoor cafés. This was a smart place to build a city!

2 BOURBON STREET

The crowd at this New Orleans–style bar is diverse, attracting young and old, straights, gays, and lesbians. Several contiguous homes have been opened up and revamped to make this super-fun bar feel like home. Smokers congregate around the fountain on the open back patio. The bar itself is dark and seductive; one corner has a piano where Barbra Streisand wannabees sing heartfelt songs in competition most nights for prizes and the acclaim of their peers. ♦ M-F, 2PM-12AM; Sa, 11AM-12AM; Su, 9AM-12AM. 4612 Park Blvd (between Madison and Adams Aves). 291.4043 &

3 TWIGGS COFFEE SHOP

★★$ The owners of this popular coffee spot live in the neighborhood and are a real part of the community. Adjoining the comfortable neighborhood café is the **Green Room**, a performance space used for music, poetry readings, and AA meetings. Clients line up prior to these events to order excellent coffee, homemade pastries, cookies, and pies (made in **Twiggs**'s own bakery across the street). You can order salads and sandwiches as well, and sit on the living room furniture, at tables and chairs, or outside along one of the more attractive stretches of Park Boulevard. ♦ Daily. No credit cards. 4590 Park Blvd (at Madison Ave). 296.0616

4 BUDDHA'S LIGHT

Located in the revitalized area of Park Boulevard near the beginning of Adams Avenue, this very Zen book shop sells books on religion and spirituality. Likewise, you'll find yoga magazines and some gift items, mainly

Restaurants/Clubs: Red | Hotels: Purple | Shops: Orange | Outdoors/Parks: Green | Sights/Culture: Blue

statues of Buddha. ♦ 4538 Park Blvd (at Monroe Ave). 298.1248

5 FRANCIS PARKER SCHOOL

Architect **William Templeton Johnson**, who shaped much of the physical appearance of San Diego in the early 1900s, also contributed to its spirit by founding and designing this independent, private school that remains prestigious today. The school is named for Colonel Parker, a prescient educator who espoused independent thinking and individual instruction. As was his forte, Johnson designed the school in 1913 in the Spanish-Colonial style with classrooms opening onto canyons, courtyards, and porches. It's not open to the public ♦ 4201 Randolph St (between Montecito Way and Arbor Dr)

6 KATE O. SESSIONS HOUSE

William Templeton Johnson is said to have designed this home in 1912 for **Kate Sessions**. The neoclassical stucco-and-brick rectangle at the edge of a canyon has been rescued after some years of neglect. The wood-framed arch windows and perforated brick parapets have remained the same since 1912. Not as inspired as it was under the green thumb of its original owner, the front garden today sports daylilies, heavenly bamboo, and impatiens as well as more pedestrian pink oleander and purple trailing lantana. ♦ 4161 Lark St (between Montecito Way and Arbor Dr)

7 MISSION HILLS NURSERY

California and Iceland poppies bob above midnight blue lobelia and snow white alyssum in the flower bed bordering the nursery yards where **Kate Sessions** sold the palms and junipers that now tower above Mission Hills estates. Sessions opened this nursery in 1910 when she was forced to leave her planting grounds at **Balboa Park**

The city of San Diego's motto is "America's Finest City," which some might think is a bit pretentious for a place with such a laid-back clime.

The average annual salary of a San Diegan is close to $40,000.

Kate Sessions's advertising slogan for her nursery in Mission Hills was "Never plant a $5 tree in a 50¢ hole."

Newspaper baron E.W. Scripps called San Diego "a busted, broken-down boom town" when he arrived in 1890. Then again, he called his autobiography *Damned Old Crank.*

---

to make way for the 1915 exposition. She was San Diego's leading horticulturist between the 1870s and the 1930s, greatly influencing and creating the landscape of today's San Diego. When she moved to Mission Hills in 1903, the canyons and hayfields were undisturbed, with a view west to the bay and east over Mission Valley. During her stay, she persuaded builders to follow the land's natural curves instead of subdividing the hills into square lots. Within 10 years, she felt the neighborhood had become too crowded for her acres of seedlings, and she began amassing land in Pacific Beach. Gradually, her assistant, Giuseppe Antonicelli, took over the nursery, then turned it over to his son Frank, who sold it in 1989. As in Sessions's days, the nursery is a botanical garden filled with the ordinary and odd plants that flourish in San Diego. One yard is filled with healthy perennials, another with trees and vines. There's a room with gardening books and another with moist and shady with ferns. Get your housewarming gifts here. ♦ Daily. 1525 Fort Stockton Dr (between Randolph and Palmetto Sts). 295.2808

8 2055 SUNSET BLVD

This Italianate mansion designed by **Robert S. Raymond** in 1921 is a great example of the grandeur and elegance of early Mission Hills. Though the gray-blue trim against beige walls seems too modern for the imposing façade, the wide, sweeping lawns are a reminder of the vast spaces available for private homes back when few streets etched through the hills. This is a private residence. ♦ Between Couts and Witherby Sts

9 MISSION HILLS PIONEER PARK

Children playing at this neighborhood park might become wide-eyed if they heard of its origins. The park was once the **Calvary Cemetery**, founded in 1874 with 5 acres of burial grounds for Catholics and 5 for Protestants. About 2,000 San Diegans were interred here, including many of the city's original pioneers; the last burial took place in 1960. In the early 1970s, Mission Hills residents closed the cemetery and turned the land into a park, which opened on 11 December 1977. About 40 tombstones large and small are clustered together at one corner of the park, and there is a rusty plaque listing the names of all those known to be buried beneath the immaculate lawns where the living play Frisbee and touch football. Facilities include playground equipment, rest rooms, and tennis courts. ♦ Washington Pl (at Randolph St)

10 PAPYRUS

This secondhand store boasts first-class finds among the rhinestone brooches, satin dressing gowns, and wicker lounge chairs. ♦ W-Sa. 116 W Washington St (between First Ave and Front St). 298.9291

11 SOMMERSET SUITES HOTEL

$$$ All 80 units at this hotel have full kitchens with microwave, dishwasher, and toaster and comfortable living rooms and bedrooms. This building has the ambiance of an apartment complex for instant transplants, with all the necessities (alarm clocks, coffeemakers, etc.). There's no restaurant, but a complimentary continental breakfast is served in a pleasant dining room. The second-floor pool is surrounded by tropical plants. Ask for a room away from the traffic on Washington Street. ♦ 606 Washington St (between Fifth and Fourth Aves). 692.5200. 800/962.9665; fax 692.5299. ♿ www.sommersetsuites.com

12 PARALLEL 33

★★$$$$ It's hard to categorize this eclectic gourmet fusion food restaurant, where decorations of woven baskets and tall reeds are enhanced by subdued lighting. The concept is food from regions and countries that border parallel 33, including California, Morocco, Lebanon, and the world's earliest breadbasket—the Tigris-Euphrates river valley. Enticing appetizers and salads lead to sharing of plates; the main dishes are less alluring, somehow, although the udon noodles with spinach, eggplant, Kalamáta olives, dried tomatoes, and feta is a definite go. For dessert there's a wonderful date cake. ♦ Fusion ♦ Daily, dinner. 741 W Washington St (at Falcon St). 260.0033 ♿

13 BRONX PIZZA

★$ Choices are refreshingly limited at this bustling New York–style pizza parlor decorated with decades of prizefight photos and the standard red-and-white-checked tablecloths. Order an 18-inch pie or a slice, with spinach and ricotta cheese, eggplant and roasted red peppers, or more traditional sausage and pepperoni. Homemade calzone is available; no salad or beer, but you can bring the latter to drink on the premises. ♦ Italian ♦ Daily. No credit cards accepted. 111 Washington Street (at First Ave). 291.3341 ♿

14 VILLAGE HILLCREST

Hillcrest took on an upscale look when this mixed-use development opened in 1991. The buildings—with walls painted in various hues of wheat, gold ochre, rust, greens, and pinks—comprise an entire city block and house retail shops, restaurants, studio apartments, offices, and a theater complex. The underground parking lot is a major plus in this congested area. ♦ Bounded by Sixth and Fifth Aves and by University Ave and Washington St. 296.4051 ♿

Within Village Hillcrest:

PIZZA NOVA

★★$$ Hungry for something quintessentially California? Try the Thai shrimp pesto pizza or tequila-chicken atop spinach fettuccine with jalapeño cream sauce at this trendy, casual bistro. The salads are outstanding and can be a full meal unto themselves. If you're dining with a partner, order a salad and a pizza and you'll have leftovers to take home. There's a nice variety of outdoor and indoor seating areas, with very comfortable booths in the main restaurant. ♦ Italian ♦ Daily, lunch and dinner. 3955 Fifth Ave (between University Ave and Washington St). 296.6682 ♿

14 LANDMARK'S HILLCREST CINEMAS

The latest art and foreign films are featured at this five-plex movie house. Though this theater may lack the charm of its older siblings, the now-defunct **Guild** and **Park**, it's infinitely more comfortable and plush. The roomy seats have holders for drinks and popcorn, onto which real butter, not "golden flavoring," is drizzled. ♦ Admission. Daily. 3965 Fifth Ave (between University Ave and Washington St). 299.2100 ♿

Restaurants/Clubs: Red | Hotels: Purple | Shops: Orange | Outdoors/Parks: Green | Sights/Culture: Blue

14 KAZUMI SUSHI

★★★$$ Owner and head chef Kazumi supervises the bustling crew of his tiny, unpretentious, and totally dependable neighborhood sushi bar. In addition to well-rendered classics like tempura and sashimi are such inspired creations as a puff pastry of scallops and fish topped with a creamy ponzu sauce. ◆ Tu-F, lunch; Tu-Su, dinner. 3975 Fifth Ave (between University Ave and Washington St.). 682.4054

15 UPTOWN DISTRICT

Lorimer-Case designed the eastern section of this massive development to house 320 apartments, town houses, and condos; and the **SGPA** group drew up plans in a variety of styles for the commercial buildings that fill the western section. Some of the shops in the commercial area look like mining-town banks; others have Mission-style arches and Spanish wrought-iron gates. In the residential part, balconies face inner courtyards and pathways lead from the parking lots past fountains and flower gardens. When it opened in 1990, the development seemed like an overwhelming intrusion into the neighborhood; now it's become an integral part of Hillcrest and a model for integrated housing and business development. ◆ Bounded by University Ave and Washington St and by Richmond St and 10th Ave

Within the Uptown District:

RALPH'S

Park in the underground lot, grab a shopping cart, and ride the rubberized ramp up to this store, then try to resist the dazzling display of state-of-the-art grocery merchandising (and the social "meet" market). ◆ Daily, 24 hours. 1030 University Ave (between Vermont St and 10th Ave). 298.2931 ♿

LAGUNA TRENDS

Fans of greeting-card artist Mary Engelbreit find a heartwarming selection of artists' calendars, stationery, memo pads, and cookie tins; chocoholics crave the shop's pecan brags—a Texas-style and Texas-size turtle loaded with caramel and nuts. It's the perfect place to find a gift for someone who has everything, or to get personalized stationery or printed invitations. ◆ Daily. 1080 University Ave (between Vermont St and 10th Ave). 298.2555

16 FARMERS MARKET

Held every Sunday at the impersonal venue of the Department of Motor Vehicles building off Washington Street, the **Farmers Market** is a fun place to shop for fresh flowers, baked goods, and Kalamáta olives as well as pesticide-free fruits and vegetables. ◆ Su,

9AM-noon. 3960 Normal St (between Blaine St and Lincoln Ave). 299.3330

17 CHILANGO'S MEXICO CITY GRILL

★★★$ This tiny, unobtrusive storefront eatery is the last place you'd expect to find authentic regional Mexican cuisine, yet some of the best in the city is made here. Specialties include *huaraches* (soft, thick, sandal-shaped corn patties topped with savory chicken or pork), burritos stuffed with *pollo pibil* (chicken marinated in tangy orange juice and spices), and quesadillas with *adobado* (pork in a red chili sauce). There are plenty of vegetarian selections and wonderful spicy soups. When it's available, the chicken with *mole poblano* sauce (a mix of bitter chocolate and spices) is excellent. Consider getting your meal to go—there's limited seating. ◆ Mexican ◆ Tu-Su, breakfast, lunch, and dinner. 142 University Ave (between Third and First Aves). 294.8646

18 BREAD & CIE

Hungry customers can't resist the aroma of this cavernous bakery's extraordinary breads that are made in the open kitchen throughout the day. Try the anise and fig loaf or the black-olive loaf. Unusual sandwiches abound: There's tuna with capers, walnuts, and basil piled on a crusty baguette; turkey breast with hot-pepper cheese on rosemary bread; and imported mozzarella layered with roasted peppers and red onions and served on foccacia. If you can't wait until you get home to devour these delicacies, sit indoors under the original art lining the walls or outside on the shaded open patio. ◆ Daily. No credit cards accepted. 350 University Ave (between Fourth and Third Aves). 683.9322 ♿

19 THE CORVETTE DINER, BAR & GRILL

★$$ Noise, fun, and general pandemonium reign amid 1950s décor at this eatery—a neon Statue of Liberty, a genuine yellow Corvette, and a soda fountain with soda jerks.

Ponytailed waitresses sling hash, meat loaf and gravy, chicken-fried steak, and good-natured barbs at the temporarily infantile crowd. If you're not driving, try the Jell-O shooters flavored with peach schnapps and mai tai mix—they pack a powerful wallop. This may be the only burger joint in town with valet parking. ♦ American ♦ Daily, lunch and dinner. 3946 Fifth Ave (between University Ave and Washington St). 542.1001 ♿

19 KEMO SABE

★★$$$ Small, modern, and noisy, **Kemo Sabe** is distinguished by the luscious and sometimes outrageous look of dishes prepared by chef Deborah Scott. Portions are large, but because of the stylish presentation, the Asian-fusion dishes beg to be eaten in rather than taken home. It's best, therefore, not to order too many appetizers or side dishes. The bar bustles with those cruising for a night out, quaffing the wide variety of martinis. Like much of the food, the jalapeño martini is fiery hot. ♦ Fusion ♦ Daily, dinner. Reservations recommended. 3958 Fifth Ave (between University Ave and Washington St). 220.6802 ♿

20 500 UNIVERSITY AVE

Security Commercial and Savings Bank built this ornate antebellum-style neoclassical box of a building with third-floor balconies and hand-painted ceiling murals in 1927. Between stints as a branch for various banks, the edifice was a mental health facility and senior center. In 1960, a modern false façade completely covered the curlicues and sculpted moldings, supposedly giving the bank's customers a sense of future prosperity. FarWest Savings bought the building and land in 1976 and hired architects **M. Wayne Donaldson** and **Mark Lyon** to oversee its restoration in 1987. The bank closed a few years later, and the building has held several tenants. ♦ 500 University Ave (between Sixth and Fifth Aves)

21 BABETTE SCHWARTZ, THE STORE

Named for and owned by a celebrated local drag queen, this emporium of pop-culture kitsch purveys everything from "Nunzillas" (wind-up nuns shooting sparks from the mouth) to "trailer trash Barbies" to Day of the Dead miniatures and an assortment of Virgin of Guadalupe candles. Don't miss the wacky selection of greeting cards. ♦ Daily, 11AM-9PM. 421 University Ave (between Fifth and Fourth Aves). 220.7048

COLUMN ONE

21 COLUMN ONE

This fabulous shop has everything one needs for a beautiful garden—except the plants. There are sculpted stone statues, cement benches, and cherubs and saints in a variety of materials. Wandering among the fountains and waterfalls and smattering of ethnic, outdoor-oriented bric-a-brac serves both to relieve the stress of shopping elsewhere and to give you terrific ideas for improving your patio or backyard. Delivery is available at extra cost. ♦ Daily. 401 University (between Fifth and Fourth Aves). 299.9074

22 KAHN BUILDING

One of the oldest commercial buildings in Hillcrest (constructed in 1928), this structure is highlighted by an elaborate sculpted mural of giant fruits along the building's upper edges. The mural and other decorations were covered with stucco for many years, but when plans to demolish it were made public, Hillcrest residents resorted to furtive guerrilla tactics and began chipping the stucco off the ornamental panels. The building was saved and remodeled and became the **City Deli**, a mediocre restaurant and bakery that's an okay place to come as a last resort at midnight. The building's most remarkable aspect, its bas-relief fruit mural in reds, yellows, and greens, could benefit from a touch-up. ♦ 535 University Ave (between Sixth and Fifth Aves) ♿

22 WEAR IT AGAIN SAM

Looking for just the right gown for that black-tie affair? Try this vintage-clothing shop's collection of capes and beaded and bangled evening dresses. The farther back in the shop you go, the farther back in time, finally reaching the 19th century. There's a good selection of men's clothing at the front of the store; for women, you'll find shoes, hats, handbags, jewelry, and even old-fashioned bathing suits and halter tops in season. ♦ Daily. 3823 Fifth Ave (between Robinson and University Aves). 299.0185

Restaurants/Clubs: Red | Hotels: Purple | Shops: Orange | Outdoors/Parks: Green | Sights/Culture: Blue

22 TASTE OF SZECHUAN

★$ Good food preempts mediocre mauve décor at this laid-back Hillcrest eatery in a university-street strip mall. If the color scheme is mismatched, at least the leatherette booths are comfortable. Maybe this is why the restaurant seems even more popular for take-out than for sit-down dining. The food, however, is quite tasty. The salt-and-pepper chicken is predictably salty, bone dry, and light as popcorn; it is served with white rice only. Go at lunch for the inexpensive combos, which include a reasonably priced entrée plus soup, egg roll or fried chicken wing, rice, and tea. ◆ Chinese ◆ Daily, lunch and dinner. 670 University Ave (at Sixth Ave). 291.3341

23 POMEGRANATE

An interesting and reasonably priced mix of practical yet fashionable furnishings shed light on the Hillcrest lifestyle. In living, dining, and sleeping sections are sofas, tables, and beds along with lamps, vases, frames, and other pleasing accessories that are modern but somehow classic as well. In the bedroom area are books on how to teach yourself to dream; in the living room are a stack of books titled *The 100 Simple Secrets of Happy People.* ◆ 1037 University Ave (between Vermont St and Tenth Ave). 291.0999; fax 291.8844

23 ACE HARDWARE

Here you'll find every kind of household item: from turkey basters to tea lights, potting soil and plant food to rat poison, and more. It's a fun, modern, well-organized hardware store in the heart of the uptown shopping district. ◆ 1007 University Ave (between Vermont St and Tenth Ave). 291.5988

23 METROPOLIS

Everything sold here is plush and warm; there's really nothing that's stark, terribly modern, or uncomfortable. Lots of sales associates are available to massage your dream schemes and arrange custom orders of furniture, sofas, and chairs. The store specializes in mahogany and leather furnishings. ◆ 1003 University Ave (between Vermont St and Tenth Ave). 220.0632

24 MONTANA'S AMERICAN GRILL

★★★$$ Owned by chef-turned-restaurateur Tony Bensel and his wife and partner Mary Williams, this sleek, high-tech dining spot is a true meat-lover's paradise. The menu covers specialties of the western states, mixing California, Southwestern, and Texas (steaks, barbecue) cuisine. It is *the* place to go for slabs of barbecued ribs—they are meaty, tangy, and served in huge portions. The side dishes are never boring—for example, black beans and grilled chilies stuffed with cheese. Those who want to save money or just get an early start on the evening will benefit from early dinner specials of salads and sandwiches (4:30-6:30) and happy hour specials (5-6:30), when you can also get an array of tempting appetizers. ◆ American ◆ M-F, lunch and dinner; Sa-Su, dinner. Reservations recommended for dinner. 1421 University Ave (at Normal St). 297.0722. ♿ www.montanasgrill.com

24 ICHIBAN

★★$ This Japanese eatery, with tiny tables packed together on the sidewalk and in the minuscule dining room, is eternally crowded. But the food is good, cheap, and abundant, with no frills. The sushi and sashimi are as fresh as they can possibly be; also available are bountiful portions of sesame or teriyaki chicken. Although the sidewalk patio has been expanded to accommodate the constant flow of foot traffic, it's still crowded. If seating is a problem, get your sushi to go and sit on a bench at the **Uptown District** across the street. ◆ Japanese ◆ Daily, lunch and dinner. No credit cards accepted. 1449 University Ave (at Normal St). 299.7203

25 NEALE STREET

The canyons north of Washington Street are a backdrop for a mélange of architectural styles. One such example is the house at **1820** built in 1949 by **John Lloyd Wright**, the son of famed architect **Frank Lloyd Wright**. A low, wide wood-shingle roof shades and shelters the house like a Japanese pagoda, and a window corner looks into and across the canyon. At **1833**, architect **Homer Delawie** perched his narrow, rectangular wood home on the side of a canyon in 1963, blending the structure in naturally with the brown dirt, rocks, and eucalyptus trees. Delawie even created a living-room garden space, integrating an old California pepper tree that had been growing on the lot. These are both private residences. ◆ Between Keating and Pringle Sts

According to the US Census Bureau, California has the highest percentage of foreign-language-speaking residents in the US. Overall, San Diego ranks 14th in percentage of residents who speak a foreign language at home, at 38.9%.

Though the Portuguese community is largely credited with establishing San Diego's fishing industry, the Chinese actually preceded them, filling San Diego Harbor with their junks and living in Chinatown, now a part of the Gaslamp Quarter.

26 OFF THE RECORD

When this old-time commercial building was remodeled in 1988, carpenters uncovered massive sky-lights, now open to view above a wrought-iron grate. The structure housed a pharmacy in the 1950s; now posters advertising albums from Nirvana and Radiohead to P.J. Harvey cover the walls of this raucous shop. It's known for its collection of used and out-of-print record-ings that come in vinyl, CD, and tape. ♦ M-Sa, 10AM-9PM. 3849 Fifth Ave (between Robinson and University Aves). 298.4755

27 THE FLAME

♀ The original **Garden of Allah** restaurant in this Egyptian-Revival building was gutted by a fire in 1954. Its owner, Wilson A. Pickney, admired the International style of other build-ings in his neighborhood and had architect **Richard George Wheeler** incorporate elements of this style in the 1955 remodeling. Pickney's new restaurant was named after the fire that had destroyed the first, and he erected a neon sign that still flashes at night. Today it is a lesbian bar that endures the trends of the times and always draws a following. ♦ Daily, 5PM-2AM. 3780 Park Blvd (between Robinson and University Aves). 295.4163

28 CAFE ON PARK

★★★$ Bleached-wood tables and stark-cement walls hung with paintings by local artists complement this eatery's creative cooking and credible cost. Breakfast (served until 3PM) runs the gamut from rosemary-scented turkey hash and eggs to gargantuan bowls of Cap'n Crunch. Linger over a giant jelly jar of iced tea and a grilled ham-and-brie sandwich while people watching along Park Boulevard. Lunch options overwhelm, and dinner is among the best deals in town. ♦ American ♦ M, Su, breakfast and lunch; Tu-Sa, breakfast, lunch, and dinner. You can also sit at the bar to eat or have a drink. 3831 Park Blvd (between Robinson and University Aves). 293.7275 &

28 MY BEAUTIFUL DOG-O-MAT

Three large washtubs for bathing dogs and a boutique of all things canine are available at this do-it-yourself dog wash. Even if you don't have a pet, it's worth checking out. Cats are also welcome. ♦ Daily. 3789 Park Blvd (between Robinson and University Aves). 295.6140

29 BUSALACCHI'S

★★★$$$ Chef Santo Tarantino bursts from the kitchen to perform with an operatic flair whenever head chef and owner Joe Busalacchi gives him a break. Diners feel at home here: It's a restored two-story Victorian house with a lively bar. Even dieters can't resist the pastas and cheese-stuffed calamari, though the chef will also prepare a low-fat sauce with fresh tomatoes, basil, and garlic. Other highlights include gnocchi with clam sauce and *pasta con fagioli* (a hearty vegetable-and-bean soup). The large, enclosed sidewalk patio is ideal for a leisurely lunch. ♦ Italian ♦ M-F, lunch and dinner; Sa-Su, dinner. Reservations recom-mended. 3683 Fifth Ave (between Pennsylvania and Robinson Aves). 298.0119 &

30 BUFFALO BREATH

Ali Baba? Check. Sexy Mrs. Santa? Check. Admiral Nelson? You bet. The San Diego location of the national chain is the place to indulge your clothing-related fantasies. The store boasts 25,000 costumes, most for sale or rent, in sizes small through extra large. It's helpful that many outfits are accessorized; the caveman and -woman come with large plastic clubs; the Marie Antoinette, with a wig and necklace in addition to an impressive dress made of miles of material. The least expensive rental is $45 per day; "Scrappy," the 8-foot rubberized robot costume, isn't for sale, but you can rent it for $500 per day. ♦ M-Sa, 2050 Hancock St (between Washington St and Witherby Ave). 297.1175

31 YOSHINO

★★★$ Only the freshest translucent yellowfin tuna slices are used for sashimi in this outstanding dining spot, where the sesame chicken also gets a high score. In a bow to current tastes, the owners finally added sushi to the menu. But they've done little else to update the place. The ambiance is coffee-shop plain, with slick, Formica-topped tables that are slightly askew, sometimes causing teacups to slide around. The beyond-efficient waitresses keep the lunchtime crowd of attorneys, accountants, and carpenters moving at a brisk pace. Dinner is a bit less popular, so the lines for a table are somewhat shorter. ♦ Japanese ♦ Tu-F, lunch; Tu-Su, dinner. 1790 W Washington St (at India St). 295.2232 &

32 INDIA STREET

When hunger strikes, head for the intersection of India and Washington Streets, where a line-up of inexpensive restaurants and take-out

---

Restaurants/Clubs: Red | Hotels: Purple | Shops: Orange | Outdoors/Parks: Green | Sights/Culture: Blue

stands survives changing taste trends. When **Raoul Marquis** bought the southeast corner of India Street at Washington in the 1970s, he put out a sign calling the cluster of houses and shops the **India Street Art Colony**. **Marquis** was a lawyer, architect, sculptor, and Renaissance man and wanted to surround himself with like-minded talents. The now-defunct **India Street Poets Theater** was formed and the annual jazz festival was a riot of eclectic creativity. Rickety wooden stairs led up a small hill to small shops, where newly immigrated Hmong artisans from Cambodia found a lucrative outlet for their needlework. Gradually, the shops became burger stops, and the poets, playwrights, and painters moved on. Still, the corner never gave way to tacky take-out places and strip malls. Instead, one-of-a-kind restaurants opened, trying to capture the India Street character. Some failed miserably; others have survived and thrived. At times, it seems like the artists' colony could be revived, with the help of an appropriate gathering spot. The neighborhood's quiet back streets and canyons still attract writers, architects, and transients; if you're a patient driver, wander the hillside's network of one-way alleys and streets between India and Goldfinch Streets on the south side of Washington Street and note how the homes become more extravagant as the harbor view becomes more distinct. ◆ At Washington St

33 SHAKESPEARE PUB & GRILLE

★$ Order a pint of Abbott Ale and a plate of fish and chips (or bangers and mash) and grab a table on the sun-dappled patio of this airy, authentic English pub. The gregarious owners, known simply as Paul and Frasier, formerly tended the taps at **Princess of Wales** down the street (see page 87). ◆ Pub ◆ Daily, lunch and dinner. 3701 India St (between Winder and Andrews Sts). 299.0230

33 SAFFRON

★★$ Owner Su-Mei Yu grew up in Bangkok and missed the grilled chicken she used to buy at ramshackle huts by the Thai city's boxing arena. Now Yu and a slew of clerks and cooks serve up fragrant marinated chicken with peanut sauce and jasmine rice from a tiny, tidy storefront. She's added a noodle and satay shop next door and expanded the menu so even regulars can discover new favorites. ◆ Thai ◆ M-Sa, lunch and dinner; Su, lunch. 3731B India St (between Winder and Andrews Sts). 574.0177

33 GELATO VERO CAFFÈ

★★$ There is a steady lineup of Vespas next to the sidewalk tables at this popular café, where flaky *palmiers* (puff pastry cookies), giant blueberry scones, espresso drinks, and sublime gelati are the main draws. ◆ Coffeehouse ◆ Daily. 3753 India St (at Washington St). 295.9269

34 CHEZ ODETTE

★★$ Office workers swamp this tiny deli at lunchtime, craving tuna sandwiches with capers, fresh celery root salad, hearty *boeuf bourguignon* (beef stew), or a few Belgian chocolates. Arrive early and claim one of the few tables, then watch the steady stream of regulars. Busy workers can also stage gourmet repasts at home with one of the eatery's elegant dinners to go. ◆ French/deli ◆ M-F, breakfast and lunch. No credit cards accepted. 3614 Fifth Ave (between Brookes and Pennsylvania Aves). 299.1000 ☼

34 HASH HOUSE-A-GO-GO

★★$ Award-winning breakfasts are the main draw, but late breakfasts also allure, with scrambled eggs garnished with roasted rosemary and garlic. For lunch, try the sloppy joe, roasted chicken, or a meat-loaf sandwich with a side of cucumber salad or french fries. For dinner, there's rib eye, salmon with goat cheese, or rack of lamb, each with baked potato and appropriate side dishes. If you haven't guessed it already, this is quintessential American cuisine. ◆ Daily. 3628 Fifth Ave (between Brookes and Pennsylvania Aves). 298.4646

35 MIXX

★★$$$ Regular customers of this eclectic dinner restaurant find it difficult to venture far from their favorite dishes, although it's hard to go wrong no matter what you choose. The popular eatery successfully embraces Vietnamese, French, Mediterranean, and California cuisines, among others. For a healthy meal, choose the burnt walnut and gorgonzola salad on a bowl of mixed greens. There's no pressure to finish up and go, whether you're on the pretty back patio, in the second-floor dining room, or in the front room listening to local musicians. The walls showcase local artists' work as well, providing topics of conversation for awkward first dates. ♦ Daily, dinner. 3671 Fifth Av (between Brookes and Pennsylvania Aves). 299.6499 ♿

36 MISSION BREWERY PLAZA

Early San Diego's German community included brewmasters from across the Atlantic who quickly responded to the immigrants' thirst for home-style beers. In 1912, August Lang, president of Bay City Brewing Company, hired the premier brewery architect of the time, **Richard Griesser**, to build a Mission-Revival–style brewery by San Diego Bay. Mission Brewing Company opened in 1913, producing Old Mission and Wurzberger beers using imported Bavarian hops and San Diego water (considered superior at the time). The burgeoning Temperance Union and wartime animosity toward Germans began to affect business; a new nonalcoholic beer, Hopski, did little to attract more customers, and the brewery closed in 1918–2 years before Prohibition.

The brewery served as a seaweed-processing plant for American Agar from 1923 until the company relocated to Spain in 1987. Later that decade, developer Mike Foote took interest in the site at the foot of Mission Hills, overlooking the airport and bay. He originally planned to raze the brick building but gradually became entranced by the idea of restoring and reopening the brewery. A successful ballot initiative exempted the building from coastal height limitations, and the original 80-foot brick chimney, tile roof, and cupola were restored in 1989 by architect **Jim Galvin** and topped by a 140-pound welded copper weather vane made by sculptor Robert Feeley. The brewery was added to the National Register of Historic Places in 1989. Today, in addition to the brewery, low-rise office suites and commercial spaces—following the original brick and wood design—make up this plaza. Don't come expecting a cold one, however; there's no pub on the premises. ♦ 1751 Hancock St (between Washington and Keating Sts).

El Indio
Catering

37 EL INDIO

★★$ Ralph Pesqueria Jr. followed his father's example and kept this over-50-year-old Mexican take-out stand simple and straightforward, though he did add an indoor dining area with booths and Southwestern décor. On sunny days, snag a picnic table on the patch of pavement across the street. Best bets include giant quesadillas stuffed with cheese and guacamole, *taquitos* (deep-fried rolled tacos) with shredded beef, homemade tamales, and *carnitas* (marinated pork served with tortillas, rice, and beans). This place's legendary chips and salsa are often flown to homesick pols in Sacramento and Washington, DC, and can be found at even the swankiest La Jolla parties. ♦ Mexican ♦ Daily, breakfast, lunch, and dinner. 3695 India St (between Chalmers and Winder Sts). 299.0333 ♿

The Hillcrest Inn

38 THE HILLCREST INN

$ Gay travelers from all over the world find their way to this 45-room hotel across from **Balboa Park**. Guest rooms are plain and somewhat worn but have refrigerators and microwaves and either a double or two twin beds. There's a sundeck and hot tub on the back patio. This hotel's best recommendation is its location close to the action on Fifth Avenue. ♦ 3754 Fifth Ave (between Walnut St and Brookes Ave). 293.7078, 800.258.2280

39 3500 BLOCK OF SEVENTH AVENUE

Bordered on three sides by **Balboa Park**, this block was one of San Diego's most exclusive neighborhoods in the early 1900s when **Irving Gill** and **W.S. Hebbard** designed homes for a number of San Diego's prestigious residents. Alice Lee and Katherine Teats, two avid supporters of Gill's work, commissioned three cottages clustered around a common garden designed by **Kate Sessions** in 1906. The two women lived in neighboring houses and shared their gardens with the neighbors; today the cottages are nearly overgrown with ivy, and the Kate Sessions garden is off-limits to the public. Across the street at **3565** and **3575** are two brick houses from Gill's New England stage that have been significantly altered. The Gill house at **3526** demonstrates yet another style, with its break from the boxes and cubes of the other houses to a multiwing, multifloor style. The **George White Marston Residence** at **3525** has been restored by the San Diego Historical Society as a part of Balboa Park (see page 14). Together, this collection of houses represents a mini-museum of Gill's early work. These are all private residences. ♦ From Upas St to Pennsylvania Ave

---

Restaurants/Clubs: Red | Hotels: Purple | Shops: Orange | Outdoors/Parks: Green | Sights/Culture: Blue

40 ALBATROSS CANYON COTTAGES

The master plan for development along the edge of Albatross Canyon included eight homes to be designed by **Irving Gill**. Four cottages, at **3407**, **3415**, **3367**, and **3353 Albatross Street**, were completed between 1905 and 1912 and still stand today; the others were never put up. The wood-frame stuccoed cottages were built as rental units for Alice Lee and Katherine Teats and have similar arched entrances and windows, simple lines, and abundant landscaping. They have all been restored with the traditional Gill colors of beige stucco with green, gray, and brown trim. Large hedges screen the last home on the block, **3353**, from view. Across the street are lovely vintage homes with leaded glass windows; this is a great neighborhood for a walk. These are private residences. ♦ At Upas St

41 SELF-REALIZATION FELLOWSHIP

Irving Gill designed this white Mission-style building in 1908 for the **Bishop's Day School**. Today it houses the **Self-Realization Fellowship**, whose members often gather on the wide green lawns in front of the building's arched windows, or within the simple meditation garden overlooking San Diego Bay. ♦ 3068 First Ave (between Spruce and Thorn Sts). 295.0170

42 SPRUCE STREET FOOTBRIDGE

Children love running across this 375-foot-long suspension bridge over a deep, forested canyon. The bridge was originally built in 1912 by **Edwin M. Capps** to give residents on the east side of the canyon access to the trolley running to Hillcrest from downtown. ♦ Between Front and Brant Sts

43 435 WEST SPRUCE STREET

Three massive retaining walls shelter the elaborate gardens—and the view—of this 1913 Mediterranean villa, which has been called the finest local example of **Richard Requa**'s work. Construction lasted for more than a year— understandable, given the many stacked levels of gardens and living space. The house is a private residence. ♦ At Curlew St

44 407 WEST SPRUCE STREET

William Templeton Johnson designed this sandstone-colored Mediterranean house in 1928. In 1991, **Mark Tarasuck** oversaw the house's remodeling and expansion, with a fanciful eye toward the original design. The addition includes molded concrete windows in the Moorish design favored by Johnson. It is a private residence. ♦ At Brant St

45 3162 SECOND AVENUE

Carleton Winslow designed this Mediterranean mansion in 1915 for Hortense Couter, a singer and cultural maven who was a member of the Wednesday Club and sponsored appearances by symphonies and opera companies in San Diego. This off-white building with gray trim around the arched windows has an imposing appearance and provides a sense of gentility. The ancient pines in the front yard are loaded with pinecones in the spring. The house is a private residence. ♦ Between Redwood and Spruce Sts

46 JIMMY CARTER'S CAFÉ

★$ You can get hearty portions of standard American bacon and eggs here, or something a bit more exotic from the Mexican and Indian menus. This eclectic, unpretentious café is a neighborhood favorite, especially for breakfast. Count on standing in line on weekend mornings. ♦ American ♦ Daily, breakfast, lunch, and dinner. 3172 Fifth Ave (at Spruce St). 295.2070

47 PARK MANOR SUITES

$$ Actors appearing at the Old Globe frequent this all-suites hotel in an attractive brick building across from **Balboa Park**. The ambiance is that of an old European hostelry, which means it's low on California glitz but high on coziness and charm. Accommodations include studios and one- and two-bedroom suites with kitchenettes, some with views of the park. Rates include a complimentary continental breakfast. Check out the view from the terrace at the **Top of the Park** bar atop the hotel—on a clear day you can see the Coronado Bridge. The **Inn at the Park** restaurant serves continental cuisine. ♦ 525 Spruce St (between Sixth and Fifth Aves). 291.0999 or 800.874.2649; fax 291.8844. www.parkmanorsuites.com

48 QUINCE STREET BRIDGE

When the city planned to close this 236-foot-long wood-trestle bridge in the late 1980s, neighbors were aghast. **George A. d'Hemecourt** designed the bridge in 1905 so residents could cross a deep canyon filled with palms and eucalyptus to reach a trolley stop. More recently, walkers, joggers, and nature lovers had found the bridge a quick and scenic shortcut across the canyon. Their protests convinced the city to refurbish and reopen the bridge, where neighbors once again can run. ♦ Quince St (between Fourth and Third Aves)

49 VEGETARIAN ZONE

★★$ The clientele is beyond healthy at this vegetarian eatery, looking robust and permanently tanned as they dine on tofu burgers and carrot juice in the outdoor patio. Craving Asian? Have *kaddu patra*: spicy sweet pastries filled with pumpkin and mango. Feeling righteous? Have a big chef salad with cheese, guacamole, and a variety of toasted nuts. This is healthy veggie food with style—it tastes spicy, flavorful, and downright delicious. To drink, there are hot and cold herbal teas, smoothies, beer, and wine. The adjoining shop sells tabbouleh to go, New Age cassettes, and health sandals that massage your feet as you walk. ◆ Vegetarian ◆ M-F, lunch and dinner; Sa-Su, breakfast, lunch, and dinner. 2949 Fifth Ave (between Palm and Quince Sts). 298.7302 ⅃

49 EXTRAORDINARY DESSERTS

★★★$ One of the top pastry chefs in town, Karen Krasne, graduated from Le Cordon Bleu in Paris, and opened this wonderful bakeshop. Supremely exquisite desserts—white chocolate linzertorte, *truffe framboise* (raspberry truffle), toasted macadamia caramel cheesecake—are displayed on a sleek granite counter. Browsers are encouraged to relax with a cup of Kona coffee (ground fresh for each customer) at the counter or one of the coveted tables. Krasne approaches her work with an artistic eye, shaping macaroons into pyramids, weaving ribbons and flowers around her cakes. It's the perfect place to buy a cake to go with a fabulous feast or indulge a craving for sweets on the spot. ◆ Bakery ◆ M-Th, 8:30AM-11PM; F-Sa, 8:30AM-midnight; Su, 2–11PM. No credit cards accepted. 2929 Fifth Ave (between Palm and Quince Sts). 294.7001

50 KEATING HOUSE

$$ Nestled on a quiet residential street, this bed-and-breakfast in a historic 1888 Victorian home offers nine comfortable rooms; all have a private bath, but only some have a bathtub. If you're at all tall or of ample girth, ask for the room with the largest bed—most seem tiny by today's standards. The newer **Butler's Cottage** next to the main house has two rooms, each with a private bath. A full breakfast is served each morning, and there's always a bottle of tawny port on the sidebar for a pre- or postprandial drink. Smoking is not allowed inside the house. ◆ 2331 Second Ave (between Laurel and Maple Sts). 239.8585, 800/995.8644

51 BERTRAND AT MISTER A'S

★★$$$ High atop the **Fifth Avenue Financial Center**, this is the best place for a heart-stopping view of downtown San Diego and jets passing by the 12th-story windows as they approach **Lindbergh Field**. San Diego's old guard lost its longtime gathering place for martinis and Manhattans when the legendary **Mr. A's** closed in February 2000. Tournedos of beef, chateaubriand, and cherries jubilee were replaced with contemporary American cuisine with Mediterranean inspiration when it reopened in 2001. However, the restaurant maintains its traditionally lavish display of Christmas lights wrapping the building between Thanksgiving and New Year's—a good time to stop by for cocktails or to drink in the view. ◆ Eclectic ◆ M-F, lunch and dinner; Sa-Su, dinner. Reservations recommended. 2550 Fifth Ave (between Laurel and Maple Sts). 239.1377

52 THE CASBAH

The multiple small rooms of this super-cool club impart a tunnel-like feeling that is right on for viewing alternative showcase bands. There's a game room with a pool table and an outdoor patio for smokers, but most people come for the excellent bands—six or seven nights a week—and the low cover charge, usually $10 tops. ◆ Daily, 8:30PM-2AM. 2501 Kettner Blvd (at Laurel St). 232.5957. www.thecasbah.com

53 LONG-WATERMAN HOUSE

This astounding example of Queen Anne-Victorian eccentricity features bay and dormer windows, gables, and towers protruding from all sides and an intricate original latticework porch railing that curves around the side of the house. The house was originally designed by **D.P. Benson** in 1889 for John Long, a lumberman in Colorado who supplied much of the veneers used throughout the interior. California Governor Robert Waterman purchased it in 1893, and the house was the center of social and cultural life at the turn of the 19th century. The building, which has been faithfully preserved, now has a subdued gray, cream, and green color scheme and houses private offices. ◆ 2408 First Ave (between Juniper and Kalmia Sts)

54 HOB NOB HILL

★★$ One of the most popular hangouts in town since 1944 when it opened as a 14-stool lunch counter named **Juniper Cafe**, this place still offers a down-home menu and ambiance. It's frequented by some of San

Long-Waterman House

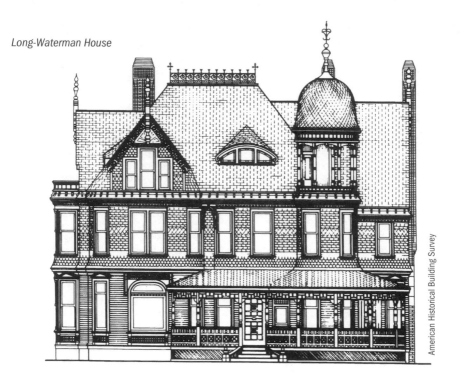

American Historical Building Survey

Diego's most prominent politicians, doctors, attorneys, and accountants, who conduct their power-breakfast deals over beef hash and eggs, oatmeal with pecans, or sunny-side-up eggs with thick slices of hickory-smoked bacon. Breakfast (served all day) is the best meal here, but such rib-sticking repasts as fried chicken; roast leg of lamb or pork with vegetables, potatoes, gravy, and bread; and hot turkey sandwiches drenched in gravy are also quite pleasing. Multiple-generation families assemble here for a traditional Sunday dinner, and the waitresses (some of whom have been here for decades) know them all by name. ♦ American ♦ Daily, breakfast, lunch, and dinner. 2271 First Ave (at Juniper St). 239.8176

55 FIFTH & HAWTHORN RESTAURANT

★★$$$ Owners David Witt and Ed Nickelson honed their skills at **Cafe Pacifica** in Old Town, and the menu reflects their training. There's an emphasis on fresh fish, including ahi, sea bass, and swordfish—all simply prepared with unusual garnishes. Theatergoers are offered a one-course dinner with choice of several entrées—fast service ensured. Those not in a rush might choose the "wine dinner," which includes a decent vintage along with shared appetizer, soup or salad, entrée, and shared dessert; the crème

brûlée is recommended. ♦ Seafood ♦ M-F, lunch and dinner; Sa-Su, dinner. Reservations recommended. 515 Hawthorn St (between Sixth and Fifth Aves). 544.0940

56 ASSENTI'S PASTA

The smell of fresh basil and pungent garlic permeates the air at this small Italian market known countywide for its fresh, homemade pasta and sauces (many local *ristoranti* buy their pasta here). Pasta of every shape and flavor is made fresh daily and is available by the pound. The freezer is stocked with an assortment of delicious and inexpensive pasta dinners packaged in family-size pans or individual portions ready for the microwave. Try the lemon-basil angel-hair with pesto. ♦ M-Sa. 2044 India St (between Grape and Hawthorn Sts). 239.5117

56 BOOMERANG

People flock to this shop for the "midcentury modern" designs of the 1940s through 1960s. Choose from a variety of furnishings—from kidney-shaped couches to orange vinyl bar stools—and the requisite collection of dinnerware from these periods, including Tickled Pink. Reissues from masters of the period such as Herman Miller and Akari are also available. ♦ M-Sa. 2040 India St (between Grape and Hawthorn Sts). 239.2040

57 FILIPPI'S PIZZA GROTTO

★★★$ San Diego's original pizzeria (ca. 1949) is still one of the most popular pizza parlors in the city. The aromas of garlic and olive oil pervade the crowded dining quarters decorated with giant salamis dangling from the ceiling, red-checkered tablecloths, a few phony grape arbors, and dim lighting to

hide the flaws of age. Although spaghetti, ravioli, fettuccine, and the like are on the menu, for a true experience, order a jug of Chianti and a thick-crusted pizza with extra cheese, anchovies, ripe olives, and pepperoni (though you can choose a tamer combo if you like). Everything on the menu—plus deli meats, cheese, virgin olive oil, and fresh-baked Italian cookies—is available at the front take-out counter. ♦ Italian ♦ Daily, lunch and dinner. 1747 India St (between Date and Fir Sts). 232.5095

58 LA PENSIONE HOTEL

$ Budget travelers who don't mind being away from the beach are in luck at this stylish hotel in the heart of Little Italy. The 81 rooms are small, but with sunlight beaming in the window-filled space and the high ceilings, you won't even notice. Each guest room has double or twin beds, colorful Kandinsky prints on the walls, and a small kitchenette with microwave, sink, and refrigerator. The shady courtyard adjacent to the lobby is secluded and peaceful. Several great Italian restaurants in the neighborhood will fill all your dining needs. Downtown is within easy walking distance, and there is a trolley stop nearby. ♦ 606 W Date St (at India St). 236.8000, 800/232.4683; fax 236.8088 &

59 PRINCESS OF WALES

★★$ A great watering hole for mugs of Guinness or Black-and-Tans, or Scotch eggs and chips. Old photos of Princess Di are featured prominently on the walls; regulars play darts, watch golf on TV, or belly up to the shiny wood bar with brass beer taps. Traditional pub décor is lightened by open front windows, swirling ceiling fans, and California's no-smoking ordinance. ♦ Pub ♦ Daily, lunch and dinner. 1665 India St (at Date St). 702.3021

59 SOLUNTO BAKING COMPANY

If you eat in any Italian restaurant in San Diego or just order a submarine sandwich from a deli, chances are you'll be served the crusty, melt-in-your-mouth bread made at this institution. Even the French cafés are known to buy their baguettes here. Stop by for a loaf or for one of the flaky, fruit-filled breakfast pastries, light-as-air doughnuts and crullers, or Florentine cookies coated with bittersweet chocolate. For further sustenance, consider a serving of spicy eggplant parmesan, sausage sandwich dripping with sauce, or salami sub lathered in vinegar and oil. There are tables in front of the deli counter for those who can't wait, but most customers get their goodies to go. ♦ M-Sa. 1643 India St (between Cedar and Date Sts). 233.3506 &

Old Town is said to attract more visitors than any other sight in San Diego, with four million to five million visitors per year passing through the **Old Town San Diego State Historic Park**. It's the only place in the city where you can steep yourself in local history, a fact perceived by its savvy merchants and restaurateurs, who have fostered an air of festivity, color, and music in the neighborhood. Tourists and locals stroll about cheerfully, browsing through the one-of-a-kind shops, stopping for a leisurely margarita, and munching on salsa and chips. Parking is free and abundant except in the busiest of seasons; tour and city buses make regular stops here, as does the **San Diego Trolley**. It's easy to ditch your vehicle and make foot power your mode of transportation here. But you'll need to get back into your car to make it up **Presidio Hill**, the site of San Diego's first fort in the 1700s. The view west, beyond civilization to the ocean and bays, and east over Mission Valley to the **Cuyamaca Mountains**, is outstanding, especially on a clear day.

Mission Valley, ranging east along the **San Diego River**, is a tribute to the automobile and to a more modern style of prosperity. Its main street, aptly named **Hotel Circle**, is

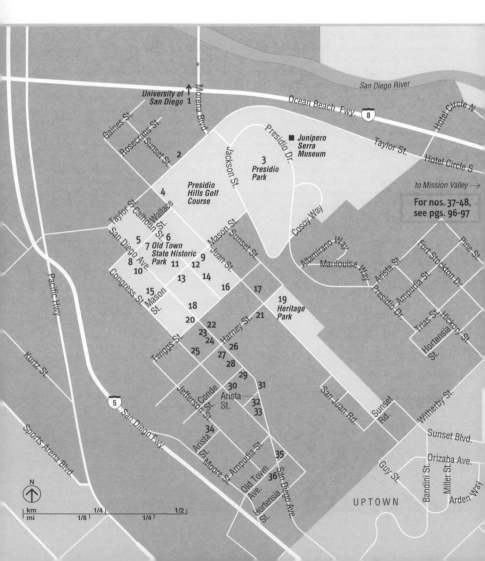

lined with convenient places to stay. Every major freeway in town hits the valley at some point—see those terrifying overpasses swooping through the sky? The frontage roads on this stretch of the freeway are packed with shopping centers, restaurants, and chain hotels. The Blue Line of the San Diego Trolley goes from Old Town through the valley to **Qualcomm Stadium**. Condo and townhouse complexes, modern shopping plazas, and trendy restaurants are cropping up along the north side of the river, once the most fertile cattle-raising area in the county.

OLD TOWN

1 UNIVERSITY OF SAN DIEGO

The white Spanish tower and sky-blue tile dome on the hills above I-5 crown the **Immaculata Church** at the **University of San Diego** (USD), one of the most beautiful campuses in the county. The independent Catholic university began as the **San Diego College for Women** in 1949 and was modeled after the University of Alcalá de Henares near Madrid in the Spanish Renaissance style. The first building for the **Women's College** included a chapel (now called **Founders' Chapel**), lavishly decorated with a white Botticino marble altar from Italy, gold leaf gilding on the interior architectural details, 14 stained-glass windows, and a rose marble floor. Weddings are booked back-to-back here on most weekends, as well as at the Immaculata Church, which stands like a grand cathedral at the heart of the campus. *Our Lady of Grace*, a statue by artist Chris Mueller, stands atop the dome—no small feat, because the cast-stone prayerful Virgin weighs about 4.5 tons and stands 11 feet high. All the buildings added to the campus (called **Alcalá Park**) have complemented the original style, creating a picturesque setting. USD's students, some of whom live above their classrooms in historical landmark buildings, are attracted by the school's reputation of excellence in law, nursing, and business administration, as well as its natural setting. ♦ 5998 Alcalá Park (at Linda Vista Rd). 260.4000

2 PADRE TRAIL INN

$$ Recently remodeled to replace the previous 1950s motel décor, the rooms are now brighter and more inviting—and still the cheapest rooms within walking distance from Old Town's shops and restaurants. The motel has 100 rooms, a pool (not heated), and a restaurant open only for breakfast. It's a viable option for those wishing to spend the big bucks on other things. ♦ 4200 Taylor St (between Juan St and Morena Blvd). 297.3291 ♿

3 PRESIDIO PARK

There's no better vantage point from which to see the contrast between old and new San Diego than atop **Presidio Hill**. The view encompasses much of the county, and you can easily imagine how spectacular it was before smog and commerce took over. To the west lie Mission and San Diego Bays and the Pacific Ocean. To the east, freeways carve into the canyons of Mission Valley, sending a ribbon of traffic toward the Cuyamaca Mountains. Within the park, the frenzy of civilization seems remote. It's easy to see why early settlers chose to live here.

Padre Junípero Serra founded the first Franciscan mission in Alta California (as opposed to Baja California, which is in Mexico) on 16 July 1769, beside the first Spanish fort on Presidio Hill. The soldiers, who thoroughly abused the local Kumeyaay tribe, made poor neighbors, and the mission was moved farther east in Mission Valley in 1774. (In 1775, the Kumeyaay destroyed the new mission, but it was rebuilt and remains in Mission Valley.) The Mexican flag appeared above the hill in 1824; the US flag replaced it in 1847.

At the turn of the 20th century, merchant and philanthropist George White Marston purchased the land for **Presidio Park** piece by piece, spending more than $392,000 over a span of 22 years. In 1929 he presented the park and its historical landmarks to the city as a gift. Architect **William Templeton Johnson** set to work on the **Junípero Serra Museum**; landscape architect John Nolen plotted long swaths of green grass down the hillsides and planted several secluded groves of eucalyptus and pine trees. Sculptor Arthur Putnam cast the *Indian* and the *Padre* in bronze; a bronze cannon, *El Jupiter*, marks the spot where the US flag first flew. Presidio Park is one of San Diego's overlooked treasures. It is an outpost of natural gentility, a lovely setting for an

---

Restaurants/Clubs: Red | **Hotels: Purple** | Shops: Orange | **Outdoors/Parks: Green** | Sights/Culture: Blue

afternoon garden wedding. The palatial homes of Mission Hills overlook its sloping lawns and miniforests of pines and oaks. ♦ Bounded by Harney and Taylor Sts and by Jackson St and Hotel Cir S

Within Presidio Park:

JUNÍPERO SERRA MUSEUM

Architect **William Templeton Johnson** paid full tribute to San Diego's heritage in this reinforced concrete Spanish-Colonial mission with its red-tile roofs, white stucco arches, colonial windows, and narrow, shaded passageways. The museum contains Father Serra's records and vestments; a cross outside the building was made from adobe bricks from the remains of the original mission. Archaeological finds from excavation of the presidio are on display in the *Treasures Uncovered* exhibit. ♦ Admission. Tu-Su. 2727 Presidio Dr (at Taylor St). 297.3258

FORT STOCKTON MEMORIAL

When Mexico lost the battle for **Presidio Hill** in 1846, US soldiers renamed the hill **Fort Stockton** for Robert Stockton, commander of the American Pacific Squadron. Later that year, Stockton and his men built walls from sand and dirt, mounted 12 guns, and dug a moat. The fort no longer exists, but a flagpole, bronze statues, and several monuments mark the site. ♦ Jackson St (on south side of park)

4 LA PIÑATA

★$ This veteran dining spot has offered decades of service to families who enjoy the peaceful patio, peach margaritas, and lobster with tortillas, rice, and beans. ♦ Mexican ♦ Daily lunch and dinner. 2836 Juan St (between Wallace and Taylor Sts). 297.1631

5 ROBINSON-ROSE HOUSE AND VISITORS' CENTER

The park offices and visitors' center are located in this building. It was built around 1853 and has housed law offices, railroad headquarters, and a newspaper office. Park rangers cheerfully dispense up-to-the-minute information from the 19th-century house, and a few books on Old Town are for sale. Public rest rooms, pay phones, and parking are all available here. Take time to visit the rooms that have been restored and outfitted with period furnishings. The **Silvas-McCoy House**, adjacent to the visitors' center, is currently undergoing restoration. It was built in 1869 by James McCoy, a wealthy Irish immigrant who served as San Diego's sheriff and state senator. ♦ Free. Daily; guided tours of the park depart at 11AM and 2PM. 4002 Wallace St (between San Diego Ave and Calhoun St). 220.5422

6 BAZAAR DEL MUNDO

For many visitors, this *is* Old Town—the blooming hibiscus, the mariachis and margaritas, the crush of people who wander from shop to shop, past caged macaws and parrots. It's all the brainchild of interior designer Diane Powers, who recognized the value of a rundown hotel in an overgrown courtyard in the **Old Town State Historic Park**. In 1971, she leased a large section of the historic park from the state, including the 1824 wood and adobe home where Governor Pío Pico lived as a child. The house had eight entrances facing a central courtyard and was the center of society in the burgeoning community of early San Diego. In the 1940s the house had become the **Pico Motor Lodge**, and when Powers took over the property, she made it the focal point for her **Bazaar del Mundo**. The bazaar is a splash of vivid colors—hot pink, orange, and purple predominate—with 16 specialty shops and 5 restaurants surrounding a lush courtyard where folkloric dancers appear in a central gazebo on weekend afternoons. ♦ All shops open daily, 10AM-9PM. 2754 Calhoun St (at Wallace St). 296.3161 &

Within the Bazaar del Mundo:

DESIGN CENTER ACCESSORIES

Napkins and table runners in vivid Guatemalan fabrics, glassware and dishes from Italy and Mexico, and all sorts of clever kitchen gadgets are available here. ♦ 296.3161

THE GALLERY

This shop features jewelry by Native American Indian and Latin American artisans. ♦ 296.3161

THE GUATEMALA SHOP

Here you'll find dresses, vests, and jackets made from gorgeous Guatemalan tapestries, as well as woven purses and shawls and a good selection of fabrics. ♦ 296.3161

LIBROS BOOKSTORE

This bookstore's stock consists of a small but fascinating selection of books (some in Spanish) on Latin America, psychology, and philosophy. There's also a great assortment of contemporary fiction, children's books, and greeting cards. ♦ 299.1139

CASA DE PICO

★★$ The Pico family's home is now a festive restaurant where diners wait in long, winding lines for a table in the courtyard. Take turns holding your place in line and browsing through the shops, but keep an eye on your lineholder, because your party will not be seated until all members are present. The quality of the food is erratic and tends to slip during peak tourist seasons, but locals and guests enjoy the experience (aided by boda-cious *bebidas*, or beverages). Stick with the chimichangas, enchiladas, burritos, and tacos and try a sweet *buñuelo* for dessert. ♦ Mexican ♦ Daily, lunch and dinner. 296.3267

ARTES DE MEXICO

The arts of Mexico for sale here include wooden animals and pottery dolls from Oaxaca, lacquered trays from Guerrero, silver jewelry from Taxco, and pottery from Puebla. ♦ 296.3266

ARIANA

Wildly colorful and exotic women's clothing and accessories are featured in this attractive boutique. ♦ 296.4989

GEPPETTO'S

This fabulous toy store sells inexpensive games and gadgets as well as wildly expensive stuffed animals, clothing, and toys. ♦ Daily, 10AM-9PM. 291.4606

LA PANADERIA

Mexican treats, including *churros* (sweet dough deep-fried and rolled in sugar) and *dulces* (candies made from caramel paste, mango jelly, and nuts). ♦ Daily, 10AM-9PM. 296.3161

7 OLD TOWN STATE HISTORIC PARK

A cluster of buildings and 13 acres of land that formed the center of early San Diego became a state historic park in 1968. Architects **Delawie, Macy & Henderson** were consulted to help create a master plan for the complete restoration of Old Town. Archaeologist Ray Brandes excavated sections of the park to determine the exact location and dimensions of former buildings. Restored structures, most from the mid-1800s, include several adobe and wood houses and stores. Cars are banned from the park, allowing pedestrians to wander and

congregate on park benches beside the central lawn, where art shows are often held. Take a self-guided walking tour of the park's historic buildings; they're all set around the park lawn. ♦ Bounded by Twiggs and Wallace Sts and by Congress and Juan Sts. 220.5422 ⬠

8 LA CASA DE MACHADO Y SILVAS

The Silvas and Machado families lived in this house for over 100 years. The kitchen and dining room have been converted to a minimuseum, set up as they would have been had the family been about to dine, with authentic tableware and foods in the kitchen. A walk through the kitchen takes you to the herb garden. There are periodic demonstrations of the arts of making traditional corn-husk dolls and tortillas. ♦ Free. Daily. San Diego Ave (between Mason and Wallace Sts). No phone

9 BLACK HAWK SMITHY & STABLE

J.B. Hinton began blacksmithing here in the 1860s. Today the smithy has been restored and vintage blacksmithing techniques are demonstrated. ♦ Free. W, Sa, 10AM-2PM. Mason St (between Calhoun and Juan Sts). No phone

10 RACINE & LARAMIE

The aroma of pipe tobacco pervades the air in this reconstruction of San Diego's first tobacco shop, an 1830s store-turned-saloon, which burned down in 1872. The wooden boxes of custom cigars are a good gift for a discerning smoker; antiques lovers should check out the items in the glass-and-wood display cabinets. ♦ Daily. 2737 San Diego Ave (between Mason and Wallace Sts). 291.7833

11 OLD TOWN PLAZA

Also called **California Plaza** and **Plaza de las Armas**, the town green is marked by a flagpole at the site where the American flag was first raised here in 1846. Art shows are sometimes held here. ♦ Bounded by Mason and Wallace Sts and by San Diego Ave and Calhoun St

12 CASA DE BANDINI

★★$ This classic Spanish hacienda was built in 1829 for Old Town's wealthiest resident, Peruvian Juan Bandini, and later purchased by stagecoach entrepreneur Albert Seeley, who turned it into the **Cosmopolitan Hotel**. Interior designer Diane Powers has renovated the hacienda and created a gorgeous restaurant featuring an enormous enclosed patio with whitewashed

---

Restaurants/Clubs: Red | **Hotels: Purple** | Shops: Orange | **Outdoors/Parks: Green** | Sights/Culture: Blue

walls and iron gates, flowers blooming around bubbling fountains, green-striped umbrellas shading patio tables, and portable heaters to make the courtyard suitable for year-round outdoor dining. Indoor dining rooms are decorated with folk art and tapestries, and drinks are sometimes served on the upstairs balconies overlooking Old Town. The menu features Mexican specialties, including a fragrant *sopa Azteca* laced with cheese and fried tortilla strips and *enchiladas de Tlaquepaque* covered with chili verde sauce and cheese. The quality of the food is unpredictable, though portions are always generous. ♦ Mexican ♦ Daily, breakfast, lunch, and dinner. 2754 Calhoun St (at Mason St). 297.8211

13 La Casa de Estudillo

This beautifully restored adobe was once the home of *Capitán* José María Estudillo, a retired fort commander, during California's Mexican period. The house was first restored under the direction of architect **Hazel Waterman** in 1910; the state restored the home again in 1969 for San Diego's bicentennial. The house is furnished with items representative of the 16th through 20th centuries with assistance from the National Society of Colonial Dames of America. ♦ Free. Daily. Mason St (between San Diego Ave and Calhoun St). 220.5426

14 Seeley Stables

The original terminal of the **Seeley and Wright Stage Line**, which was conveniently located next door to old San Diego's largest hotel, now houses the **Roscoe Hazard Museum**, a collection of stagecoaches and other horse-drawn vehicles, saddles, and Western artifacts. A 20-minute film on early San Diego history is shown throughout the day. ♦ Free. Daily. Calhoun St (between Twiggs and Mason Sts). 220.5427

15 Mason Street School

This classic one-room schoolhouse displays artifacts such as students' and teachers' desks and textbooks. Read the comments of its teachers, including those of Mary Chase Walker, who arrived from Massachusetts in 1865 and said of her new hometown: "Of all the dilapidated, miserable-looking places, this is the worst." She later married the president of the school board. ♦ Free. Daily. Mason St (between Congress St and San Diego Ave). 297.1183

16 The Theatre in Old Town

An eclectic selection of musicals, plays, and historical vignettes are staged in this theater, which looks like a barn yet has only 244 seats. Recent shows have included *Shear Madness* and *Forever Plaid* (so popu-

lar that it ran for 4 years). Nearby are large parking lots, where tour buses drop off and pick up passengers. ♦ Admission. 4040 Twiggs St (between Calhoun and Juan Sts). 688.2494 &

17 Mormon Battalion Memorial Visitors Center

The center is staffed by Mormon volunteers from various countries who devote their time to educating their guests about how Mormons contributed to the settling of Old Town. ♦ Daily. 2510 Juan St (between Harney and Twiggs Sts). 298.3317

18 San Diego Union Newspaper Historical Building

This restored wood-frame structure was built in Maine in 1851, then shipped around Cape Horn. The first edition of the *San Diego Union* (still San Diego's daily newspaper) came off the presses here in 1868. Visitors can see the original printing presses. ♦ Free. Daily. San Diego Ave (between Twiggs and Mason Sts)

19 Heritage Park

Some of San Diego's most precious historic Victorian houses line the cobblestone walks of this 7.8-acre park, operated by San Diego County. The concept of creating a park where historic houses slated for destruction could be preserved was born at meetings of a group of nostalgia buffs, led by San Diego artist Robert Miles Parker, who began the Save Our Heritage Organization (SOHO). Saved from demolition in other parts of the city, several grand Victorian homes and a temple have been moved to the park and restored and now contain offices, shops, and a bed-and-breakfast. ♦ Bounded by Sunset Rd and Harney and Juan Sts. For information, call the San Diego Parks and Recreation Department, 858/565.3600

Within Heritage Park:

Sherman-Gilbert House

This 20-room house was designed by **Comstock & Trotsche** in 1887 in the Stick-Eastlake style and named after Charles Eastlake, English author and furniture designer. The style's distinctive applied stick-, lattice-, and scrollwork are evident in the bright white trim and the peaked widow's walk. The Gilbert family purchased the house in 1897, and sisters Bess and Gertrude, active in the arts, hosted many soirées for famous guests, including the Von Trapp Family Singers and Yehudi Menuhin, until Bess died in 1965. The house originally was on the edge of downtown; in 1940, the widow's walk was removed because it obstructed the flight path to Lindbergh Field. The house was moved to **Heritage Park** in

1971 and lovingly restored, with the widow's walk intact once again. ◆ Free. Daily. Heritage Park Row (between Sunset Rd and Harney St)

HERITAGE PARK BED & BREAKFAST INN

$$ The Queen Anne–style Christian House, built in 1889 by merchant Harfield Timberlane Christian, now houses this peaceful, picturesque inn, easily the most charming hostelry in Old Town. The nine bedchambers (all with private baths) are appointed with period antiques, finished wood floors, and Oriental rugs. Modern amenities include meeting facilities with fax, computer, and audiovisual equipment; Old World touches include fireplaces and afternoon tea. Airport and train station shuttle service is available. Breakfast is included, and candlelight dinners can be arranged with 24-hour notice. ◆ 2470 Heritage Park Row (between Sunset Rd and Harney St). 299.6832, 800/995.2470; fax 299.9465 &

BUSHYHEAD HOUSE

Edward Wilkerson Bushyhead was an early San Diego sheriff and a founder of the *San Diego Union*. He built this Italianate-style Victorian in 1887 in the same fashionable downtown neighborhood as the Sherman-Gilbert house; in the 1920s, it became a rental unit, then deteriorated over the next 50 years. In 1978, SOHO moved the house to the park and restored it. Today it is part of the Heritage Park Bed & Breakfast Inn, with three rooms available to guests. ◆ 2460 Heritage Park Row (between Sunset Rd and Harney St). 299.6832, 800/995.2470; fax 299.9465 &

TEMPLE BETH ISRAEL

This odd, Victorian-eclectic-style building was the first synagogue in Southern California and was used for the first time on Rosh Hashanah eve, 25 September 1889. The interior has been restored as a community hall available for rent to the public. ◆ Open during events only. 2455 Heritage Park Row (between Sunset Rd and Harney St)

20 DODSON'S CORNER

When Old Town was first reconstructed, this shopping complex was named **Squibob Square** after Lieutenant George H. Derby, a famed humorist who used the pen name Squibob. The square's wooden buildings, reproductions of typical stores from the 1800s, were destroyed for an archaeological dig in the early 1990s; the dig didn't turn up much, and the stores were restored once again. ◆ Daily; 2611 San Diego Ave (between Twiggs and Mason Sts). 293.4884

21 BEST WESTERN HACIENDA SUITES–OLD TOWN

$$ The original tenant of this hilltop compound was a highly unsuccessful shopping center, and it seemed the hacienda-style buildings and terraced patios would be destroyed. But crafty developers envisioned hotel rooms where knickknack shops once stood, and spent a year renovating and expanding the complex into a very successful, charming, all-suites hotel overlooking Old Town. The 169 large, high-ceilinged rooms are spread over several levels, with fountains bubbling on brick patios, wooden balconies looking out to the street, and rustic wood furnishings imported from Mexico. The rooms have VCRs and kitchenettes with microwaves, coffeemakers, and refrigerators. There's plenty of room for children to roam, but anyone who has trouble climbing stairs and hills might be unhappy here. ◆ 4041 Harney St (between San Diego Ave and Juan St). 298.4707, 800/888.1991; fax 298.4771

Restaurants/Clubs: Red | Hotels: Purple | Shops: Orange | Outdoors/Parks: Green | Sights/Culture: Blue

22 IMMACULATE CONCEPTION CHURCH

Just as construction of this Catholic church was underway, Alonzo Horton began building his New Town, and Old Town's good fortunes ceased. The cornerstone of the church was laid in 1868, but it wasn't dedicated until 1919 and was finally completed in 1937. ◆ 2540 San Diego Ave (between Harney and Twiggs Sts). 295.4148

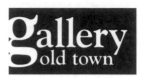

23 GALLERY OLD TOWN

Some of our favorites and some rare and previously unreleased images from *Life*'s top photojournalists are for sale in this small gallery. Hand-signed photographs by Margaret Bourke-White, Alfred Eisenstaedt, and Joe Rosenthal are framed and ready to be hung on your wall. ◆ 2513 San Diego Ave (between Harney and Twiggs Sts). 296.7877

24 CHUCK JONES STUDIO GALLERY

Showcasing the animation art of one of Warner Bros.' former (and most famous) artists, this large gallery is home to the like-nesses of Bugs Bunny, Daffy Duck, and Wile E. Coyote, as well as fine art drawings by the artist. ◆ M-W, Su, 10AM-6PM; Th-Sa, 10AM-8PM. 2501 San Diego Ave (between Harney and Twiggs Sts). 294.9880

The San Diego–Los Angeles Stage Line made the trip from Old Town's Seeley Stable to Los Angeles in 24 hours—a drive that takes 3 hours today.

San Diego's Mexican heritage is celebrated every Christmas in Old Town with the evening luminaria procession, with children bearing lit candles and singing Christmas carols in Spanish.

A monument in Presidio Park honors the burial site of the beloved white deer that lived on the hillside below Mission Hills and above Mission Valley as it underwent development in the 1960s and 1970s. Park regulars and neighbors cherished the white deer and shuddered with horror when she would wander down to I-8 and get caught in the traffic. In 1975, when the freeway proved too great a risk for the deer, she was shot with a tranquilizer and unexpectedly died.

25 ENCHANTED WOODS OF OLD TOWN

This friendly boutique is crowded with all of those things you didn't know you needed until you saw them: winged pigs, giant carousel horses, and lovely pastel-painted wood-frame mirrors. Tucked among the truckloads of Balinese imports are Guatemalan hammocks and sequined dresses from India. There are many inexpensive yet charming baubles to take home to the kid who's watering your lawn or feeding the fish. ◆ M-Th, Su, 1PM-10PM; F-Sa, 1PM-11PM. 2533 Congress St (between Harney and Twiggs Sts). 296.9663

26 WHALEY HOUSE

Thomas Whaley, entrepreneur, merchant, and pillar of the community, came from a family with ancestors at the Battle of Hastings and the Boston Tea Party. His 1856 Old Town home was a solid two-story brick mansion, now completely restored and authentically furnished. The house served for a time as a theater and in 1869 became the **County Courthouse**. The last Whaley to live in the house was Corinne Lillian, youngest of the Whaleys' six children, who died in 1959 at the age of 89. The house's four resident spirits—Mr. and Mrs. Whaley, a young girl, and Jim Robinson (who was hanged near the house)—have been featured in television shows and books and are said to favor dreary cold days near Christmas. The ghosts are a hit with schoolkids—over 10,000 visit the house each year. ◆ Admission. Closed Tu. 2482 San Diego Ave (between Conde and Harney Sts). 297.7511

27 OLD TOWN MEXICAN CAFE AND CANTINA

★★★$ Perhaps the most popular Mexican restaurant in San Diego, this eatery wins all the best restaurant surveys. It's famous for *carnitas* (marinated pork) served with tortillas fresh from the grill, beans and rice, and a tray of condiments including cilantro, onions, and guacamole. Breakfast hangover cures (served all day) include an egg-and-*chorizo* taco and saucy *chilaquiles* (fried tortilla strips in red sauce) with fried eggs. The restaurant keeps expanding to outdoor patios and more dining rooms, but that never seems to shorten the lines of patrons waiting for tables. ◆ Mexican ◆ Daily, breakfast, lunch, and dinner. 2489 San Diego Ave (between Conde and Harney Sts). 297.4330

28 THE SILVER DESIGNER

This is the best shop in a small plaza called the Old Town Esplanade. The exquisite silver jewelry here is designed in Taxco, Mexico, by owner George Martinez. ◆ Daily, noon-8PM.

2461 San Diego Ave, suite 105 (between Conde and Harney Sts). 298.8255

29 APACHE INDIAN ARTS GALLERY

Navajo, Zuni, Hopi, and Santo Domingo Indian art, kachina dolls, rugs, and the requisite moccasins are all for sale here. ♦ Daily, 10AM-8PM. 2425 San Diego Ave (between Arista and Conde Sts). 296.9226

30 OLD ADOBE CHAPEL

Dedicated as a chapel in 1858, this small adobe house served as the **Immaculate Conception Church** in Old Town for far longer than expected, because it took over 60 years to build the current church. It is now listed as a California state historical landmark. ♦ Conde St (between Congress St and San Diego Ave)

31 THE BRIGANTINE

★★$$ Remodeled in 1997, this joint pulses after work with San Diegans celebrating the end of the work day and quaffing oyster shooters. Mondays are particularly boisterous, as happy hour extends until closing time. On the outdoor patio, canned music nullifies the noise of passing traffic, and a potbellied stove takes the chill out of San Diego evenings. Seafood, pastas, chicken, and steaks are all fresh and flavorful; less expensive items include the excellent burger and crab and shrimp salad on sourdough. The Sunday brunch (not a buffet) includes unlimited champagne. ♦ American ♦ M-Sa, lunch and dinner; Su, brunch and dinner. 2444 San Diego Av (at Conde St). 298.9840 ᕈ. Also at 2725 Shelter Island Dr, Point Loma. 224.2871; 1333 Orange Ave (between B and Adella Aves), Coronado. 435.4166; 3263 Camino del Mar (at Via de la Valle), Del Mar. 858/481.1166

31 CAFE PACIFICA

★★★★$$$ The sleek white dining rooms have twinkling white lights, murals on the walls, and plenty of mirrors for studying the who's-who crowd. The café was the first venture for the now-revered dining duo of Kipp Downing and Deacon Brown. Offerings include excellent fresh seafood, including Hawaiian ahi with shiitake mushrooms and ginger butter, spicy garlic seafood over fettuccine, and mustard catfish. Long-time general manager Frank Busic bought Cafe Pacifica in 2001 and has since introduced live abalone, farm-grown in Ensenada, Mexico, to the menu. There are two presentations, abalone piccata, served with lemon, butter, and white wine, or herb-crusted abalone with panko bread crumbs. Be sure to call ahead for avail-

ability. The crème brûlée is a must, especially when topped with fresh raspberries. ♦ Seafood ♦ Daily, dinner only. Reservations recommended. 2414 San Diego Ave (between Arista and Conde Sts). 291.6666

31 EL CAMPO SANTO

The Sacred Field was Old Town's original cemetery. Many of San Diego's original settlers are buried here behind an adobe wall. ♦ San Diego Ave (between Arista and Conde Sts)

32 JACK AND GIULIO'S ITALIAN RESTAURANT

★★★$$ This father-and-son team brings decades of restaurant experience to Old Town (Giulio's **Pacific Beach** restaurant was an institution until it closed a few years ago). The atmosphere is open and light, with bright red leatherette booths along one wall and an umbrella-shaded patio out front. Most often requested are *scampi alla Giulio*, butterfly shrimp sautéed with mushrooms and garlic, and the *tortelloni verdi*, home-made spinach pasta stuffed with spinach and cheese topped with porcini mushroom sauce. There is a full bar with both California and Italian wines available. ♦ Italian ♦ Daily, lunch and dinner. 2391 San Diego Ave (at Arista St). 294.2074 ᕈ

33 BASIC BROWN BEAR FACTORY

A kid and a teddy bear—a timeless bond. Add to that a child's curiosity about how things are made, and you have a winning combination. Children of all ages will delight in creating their own teddy bear by selecting an unstuffed bear (brown bruin or white?), stuffing it themselves, then giving it an "air bath" and accessorizing it with a jacket, hat, or ribbons to get their own cuddly creature. Birthday parties are also available by prior arrangement. ♦ Daily. 2375 San Diego Ave (at Arista St). 497.1177. ᕈ www.basicbrownbear.com

34 HOLIDAY INN OLD TOWN

$$ The first hotel on this site was far more elegant, and less convenient, than the current one. The **Gila House Hotel**, built by Juan Bandini in 1850, was the center of old San Diego's social life and looked out to the bay where steamships brought new pioneers to town. Today's incarnation overlooks I-5—which makes it easily accessible. Ask for a room away from the freeway, facing into the courtyard. The sights of Old Town are within reasonable walking distance, and the hotel is popular for medium-size group meetings. The 171 rooms and suites are pleasantly comfortable; suites have wet bars,

---

Restaurants/Clubs: Red | Hotels: Purple | Shops: Orange | Outdoors/Parks: Green | Sights/Culture: Blue

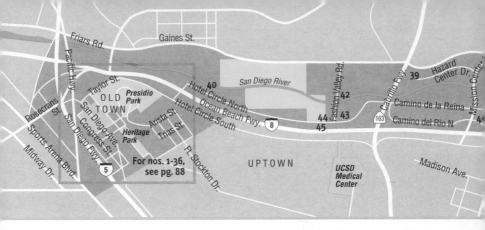

microwaves, hair dryers, and refrigerators. The shaded pool and spa are heated, and there's a complimentary continental breakfast as well as full-day service in the restaurant. Other amenities included covered, enclosed parking and shuttle-bus service to the airport and train station. ♦ 2435 Jefferson St (at Arista St). 260.8500, 800/255.3544; fax 297.2078 &

35 EL AGAVE RESTAURANT AND TEQUILERIA

★★★$$ Often touted as the most authentic regional Mexican food to be found in San Diego, **El Agave** has a varied menu and even more extensive tequila listing. With over 600 different types of tequila ranging in price from a few dollars to over $100 for a single shot, the proprietors here will tell you that they offer more selections than any other restaurant in the country. Seafood, beef, and chicken dishes are prepared as they are in Mexico. If you have never tried *mole* (pronounced "MO-lay"), this may be the place to take the plunge. A spicy, unique sauce prepared with everything from chilies to chocolate, El Agave features six different kinds, usually served over chicken or pork. The cozy dining room is located upstairs. ♦ Mexican ♦ Daily, lunch and dinner. 2304 San Diego Ave (at Old Town Ave). 220.0692

36 RAMADA LIMITED

$$ The peaceful peach-and-pink rooms are clustered around a winding walkway and courtyard, with bubbling fountains and tall palms. Pseudo-antique armoires and floral quilted spreads give an old-fashioned feel to the 125 rooms and suites, whereas microwaves, refrigerators, and coffeemakers offer modern convenience. The long, three-story buildings and gated pool area create a motellike appearance, but the parking is underground and free. Old Town's shops and restaurants are just west of the hotel, and the entrance to I-5 is a block west. ♦ 3900 Old Town Ave (between Jefferson St and San Diego Ave). 299.7400, 888/298.2054; fax 299.1619 &

MISSION VALLEY

37 QUALCOMM STADIUM

Upgraded in 1997 to the tune of $78 million, the 71,500-seat stadium is home to the **San Diego Padres**, **Chargers**, and **San Diego State Aztecs**. The stadium was built in 1967 (designed by **Hope Consulting**). It's also the venue for major rock concerts. The **Super Bowl** was held here in 1998; Denver beat Green Bay 31 to 21. ♦ 9449 Friars Rd (between Hwy 15 and Stadium Way). 525.8282

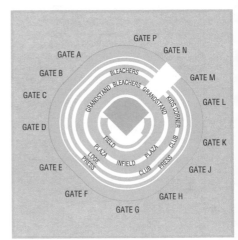

38 MISSION BASILICA SAN DIEGO DE ALCALÁ

The first Franciscan mission in California was the **Mission San Diego de Alcalá**, established by Padre Junípero Serra in 1769 on **Presidio Hill** overlooking Mission Valley and Old Town. The mission was moved 6 miles upriver to this location in 1773, then nearly destroyed in an Indian uprising in 1775. But by the early 1830s the mission was firmly established and the Native Americans were either converted

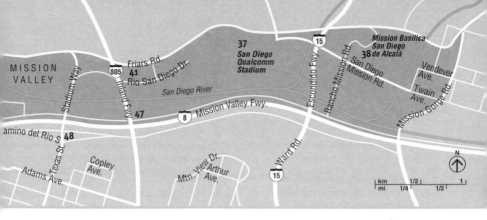

or displaced. The mission was restored in 1931. The church is a simple, small wooden chapel with little adornment. The **Father Luis Jayme Museum** at the mission is the only permanent interfaith ecclesiastical art museum in Southern California and includes original mission records, liturgical robes, books, and relics. The museum was named after Father Jayme, a Franciscan missionary who was martyred by the Kumeyaay during the 1775 uprising. ♦ Admission to tour buildings and grounds. Daily. San Diego Mission Rd (between Mission Gorge and Rancho Mission Rds). 281.8449

39 HAZARD CENTER

The focus of Mission Valley moved east along the river to this $200 million, 42-acre development, designed by **Arechaederra/Hong/Treiman** and **SPGA** in 1990. The complex includes a high-rise hotel, office tower, shopping/dining area, movie theaters, and a park along the northern banks of the San Diego River. A paved sidewalk runs along the river bank, a perfect place to unwind and stretch your legs. ♦ Hazard Center Dr (between Camino de la Reina and Friars Rd). 497.2674

Within Hazard Center:

TROPHY'S SPORTS GRILL

★★$ The name says it all. Sports fans are happy here watching games on wide-screen TVs while devouring stone-fired pizzas, mesquite-grilled burgers, and bountiful salads and sandwiches. The food is good, the crowd friendly and lively, and the setting family-oriented, with a separate menu for children. ♦ American ♦ M-Sa, lunch and dinner; Su, brunch and dinner. 7510 Hazard Center Dr (between Camino de la Reina and Friars Rd). 296.9600 &

PREGO RISTORANTE

★★$$ This Italian restaurant is an offshoot of a San Francisco–based chain. The style is loud, trendy, and chic, with a bustling Italian market atmosphere and an exhibition kitchen that turns out nice gourmet pizzas—the one with smoked mozzarella, grilled eggplant, basil, and tomato is especially good. Also on our list are the Italian sausage with polenta, spinach, and roasted peppers, and the lasagnette al pesto—lasagna with basil, pine nuts, and parmesan. ♦ Italian ♦ M-F, lunch and dinner; Sa-Su, dinner. Reservations suggested. 1370 Frazee Rd (between Hazard Center Dr and Friars Rd). 294.4700 &

DOUBLETREE HOTEL

$$ It's just a 15-minute walk from the **Mission Valley Center** (see page 98) but worlds away from the noise and traffic on the freeway. This 300-room hotel, built in 1990 and owned by Doubletree since 1997, is favored by business travelers who appreciate ample work space and PC data ports in their rooms, a spacious dining room for doing lunch, and easy freeway access. Other amenities include a health club with fitness center, two tennis courts, an indoor lap pool, and an outdoor pool. Another plus is the hotel's proximity to the **Hazard Center**'s shops, movie theaters, and restaurants. ♦ 7450 Hazard Center Dr (between Camino de la Reina and Friars Rd). 297.5466, 800/547.8010; fax 688.4088 &

Restaurants/Clubs: Red | Hotels: Purple | Shops: Orange | Outdoors/Parks: Green | Sights/Culture: Blue

40 RED LION HANALEI HOTEL

$$ Of the dozens of hotels lining I-8 in Mission Valley, this one stands out—both as a curiosity and a decent hostelry. The Polynesian tropics theme has remained much the same since the hotel opened in the 1960s, so the palms and flowering shrubs have matured, giving the courtyard pool area a soothing Hawaiian ambiance. The 416 rooms are pretty standard fare, but the location is great for hopping on a freeway to anywhere in the county. Facilities include several restaurants and lounges, a business center, and a small fitness center. ♦ 2270 Hotel Cir N (between Fashion Valley Rd and Taylor St). 297.1101, 800/882.0858; fax 297.6049

41 SAN DIEGO MARRIOTT MISSION VALLEY

$$$ This elegant hotel, with an abundance of marble and granite, claims to be the accommodation closest to **Qualcomm Stadium** (see page 96), making it an obvious choice for pro-team players, musicians, and other celebrities appearing for games and concerts. The Modernist pool area with sleek waterfalls and plenty of lounging space is the gathering spot for visiting celebs. The 350 rooms have dusty-rose couches and king-size beds, and a great selection of toiletries in the bath. The restaurant is open for all meals. ♦ 8757 Rio San Diego Dr (between I-8 and Stadium Way). 692.3800, 800/842.5329, 800/228.9290; fax 692.0769

42 FASHION VALLEY CENTER

Opened in 1969, when malls were just hitting their forward stride, this compound offered direct competition for **Mission Valley Center** and formed a shopping combo that would make Mission Valley the retail—as well as the geographic—heart of the county. It boasts **Neiman Marcus**, **Nordstrom**, and **Macy's**; 148 specialty shops, and several restaurants and theaters. ♦ Daily. Fashion Valley Rd (between Hotel Circle N and Friars Rd). 297.3381

43 TOWN AND COUNTRY HOTEL

$$ Restaurateur Charles H. Brown built this hotel in the 1950s amid dairy farms in the bucolic river valley. Brown's vision of Mission Valley as a center of commerce became reality in the next 2 decades, and in 1970 the **Town and Country Convention Center** opened beside the hotel. Today the 40-acre resort includes 1,000 rooms and suites in high-rise towers and ranch-style bungalows, five restaurants, five bars, four pools, and all the services necessary to keep travelers and conventioneers content. The compound seems outdated, especially when compared to San Diego's new downtown convention center and hotels, but it attracts a considerable number of midsize conventions on everything from aerobics to Zen. Business travelers appreciate the phones and desks by the beds, the proximity to all major freeways, and the variety of restaurants on the grounds. Check out the archway of 20-foot-high palms at the entranceway. ♦ 500 Hotel Cir N (between Camino de la Reina and Fashion Valley Rd). 291.7131, 800/854.2608; fax 291.3584 ♿

44 HANDLERY HOTEL & RESORT

$$ Built in 1956 by the Handlerys, this 222-room hotel was called the **Stardust** at one point but has reverted once again to the family name. With its close proximity to the **San Diego Zoo** and **Sea World**, as well as baby-sitting services and a playground, it's a popular choice with families. The adults will want to check out the **Swim & Tennis Club** (with three swimming pools and eight lighted tennis courts) and the fitness center. The **Riverwalk Golf Course**, a 27-hole championship course, recently renovated and reopened in 1998, is adjacent to the hotel. ♦ 950 Hotel Cir N (between Hwy 163 and I-5). 298.0511, 800/676.6567. www.handlery.com

45 ADAM'S STEAK 'N' EGGS AND ALBIE'S BEEF INN

★★★$ These tandem restaurants in front of the **Travel Lodge Mission Valley** are traditional local favorites for hearty no-nonsense food. **Adam's** has a mountain lodge décor and is open only for breakfast—superb steak and eggs, corn fritters with honey butter, *carne asada* (grilled beef) with eggs, beans and tortillas, grits and home fries, and outrageous waffle concoctions. **Albie's** is a classic steak house—dark and woodsy, with red leather booths. Try the top sirloin, New York steak, or the chicken-fried steak with mashed potatoes and gravy. ♦ American ♦ Adam's: daily, breakfast. Albie's: M-F, lunch and dinner; Sa, dinner. 1201 Hotel Cir S (between Hwy 163 and I-5). 291.1103 ♿

46 WESTFIELD SHOPPINGTOWN MISSION VALLEY CENTER

Mission Valley seemed the likely location for San Diego's first modern mall, which became the cornerstone for the valley's transformation from farming to commerce in 1961. The center was remodeled in 1995 and now has a

20-theater movie complex, several mainstream stores—the **Robinson's-May Company** and **Bed Bath & Beyond**—plus 100 specialty stores including **Macy's Home & Furniture**, **B. Dalton**, **Ann Taylor**, and **Mrs. Fields Cookies**, ♦ Daily. Mission Center Rd (between Camino del Rio N and Friars Rd). 296.6375

Within Mission Valley Center:

Established 1982

SEAU'S THE RESTAURANT

★★$$ Owned by the San Diego Chargers' hometown hero, linebacker Junior Seau, this huge restaurant boasts 57 television monitors, with the daddy of them all, an 11 × 14–foot projection screen suspended from the 30-foot-high ceiling. The menu encompasses classic American grill fare (pizzas, pasta, steaks, and burgers) with a few of "Mama Seau's" Samoan-style recipes thrown in as well. This isn't the place to come for a quiet lunch, but it is a fun place to enjoy good food and maybe catch a glimpse of your favorite sports star. ♦ American ♦ Daily. 1640 Camino del Rio North (at Mission Center Rd). 291.7328 &

47 DAVE & BUSTER'S

★★$$ For all you kids masquerading in grown-up bodies, **Dave & Buster's** is the playground for you. This place is gigantic,

with 48,000 square feet devoted to an astonishing array of state-of-the-art video games and simulators. The pool tables are top-notch and custom-made, as are the shuffleboard tables. The front of the building houses the restaurant, with a turn-of-the-19th-century feel with lots of stained glass and dark wood. Seafood, chicken, and salads are tastefully prepared, with an enticing dessert selection offering key lime pie and triple chocolate cake. The bar has two banks of elevated televisions with continuous sports coverage, though you may be too busy playing games yourself to watch. ♦ American ♦ 2931 Camino del Rio North (at the I-805-I-8 interchange). 280.7115 &

48 BULLY'S

★★★$$ Hungry for real beef? Then this is your place: It's legendary for its thick prime rib served with baked potato, crisp iceberg-lettuce salad with chunky blue cheese dressing, and plenty of spicy horseradish. The steaks are good, as are the chicken and seafood dishes, but it's the prime rib that keeps the place filled. The red leather booths are the best seats, but the place gets so busy on weekend nights you'll be happy with a table in the center of the dimly lit dining room. Early-bird dinners, served nightly (4:30–5:30PM), are a great bargain. There's a large round table at the end of the bar for single diners. ♦ American ♦ Daily. 2401 Camino del Rio S (at Texas St). 291.2665 &

POINT LOMA/ HARBOR ISLAND/ SHELTER ISLAND

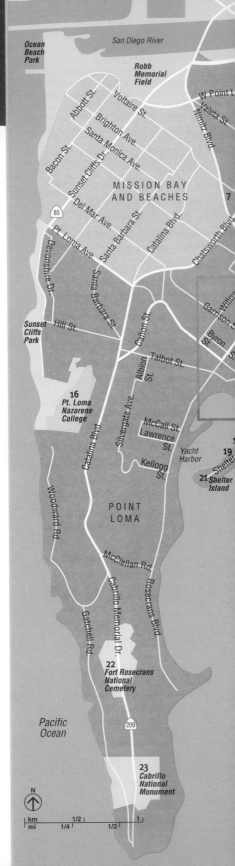

Point Loma may be the most beautiful spot in San Diego (with the possible exception of the more refined La Jolla). Pines and junipers twist and bend in the stiff winds atop the point's treacherous cliffs, jutting 500 feet above sea level. Handsome homes and gardens rise proudly behind protective hedges on twisting streets named for authors from Byron to Zola. **Fort Rosecrans**, a 71-acre garden with bright white tombstones, guards the point's southern end like a silent sentinel protecting the sloping hillsides from encroachment. At the tip, **Cabrillo National Monument**, where Juan Rodríguez Cabrillo landed in 1542, perches above the waves, offering rugged nature, nautical vessels, gray whales, and spectacular views. As befits Point Loma's seafaring history, the US Navy and the Marine Corps have commandeered much of the land with large compounds that include the **Marine Recruit Depot**, the **Fleet Anti-Sub Warfare School**, and the **Naval Ocean Systems Center**.

Various settlers were determined to bring Point Loma fame and financial gain. Nineteenth-century residents lived in shacks made of cowhides while they operated lucrative tanneries and tallow-rendering businesses. Chinese immigrants anchored their junks along the point's shores, beginning the fishing industry that would be passed on to the Italians and then the Portuguese, whose descendants still dock their boats in Point Loma's marinas.

Point Loma was also the home of the colorful Madame Katherine Tingley, a dedicated theosophist. Madame Tingley created a commune named **Lomaland**, which caused quite a stir from 1897 to

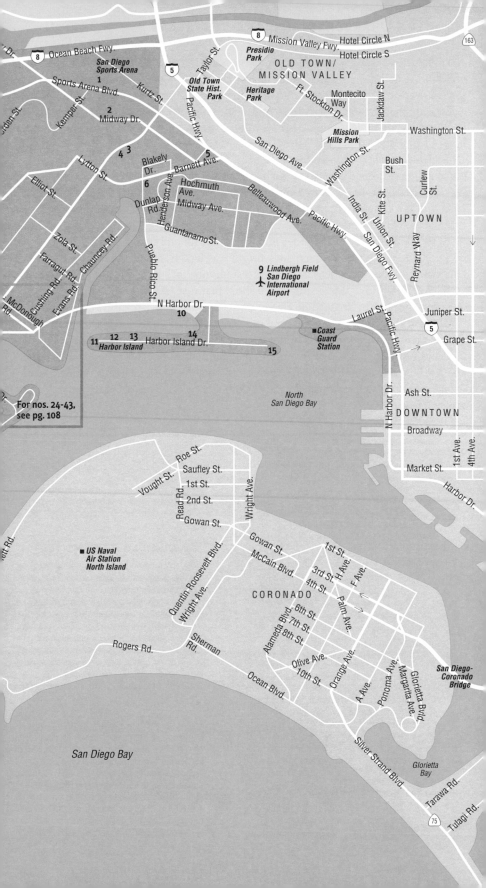

1942. Residents sought divine wisdom through the study of comparative religion, philosophy, literature, theater, and art. By the 1930s, however, spiritualism was on a steady decline and the community began to fall apart. Treasured buildings were destroyed, and the lands passed through a series of owners until taken over by **Point Loma Nazarene College,** which has its administration offices in one of the remaining houses from Madame Tingley's utopia.

The point's neighbors are not as naturally and historically endowed. Two of the most popular spots—Harbor Island and Shelter Island—were both created from landfill. Both have become picturesque tourist enclaves, where hotels, restaurants, and parks flourish amid lush lawns and majestic palms, and marinas fill the bay with private boats. Nearby is **Lindbergh Field,** San Diego's international airport.

Harbor Island was built from 3.5 million tons of silt and sludge dredged from the **San Diego Bay** to make way for the navy's aircraft carriers. Hotels soon lined the fake island and were eventually joined by a lineup of restaurants, including one in a paddle wheeler.

Shelter Island is a former submerged shoal that rose above the water line as another dumping ground for dredged dirt. Ever since the city built a causeway on top of the landfill in 1950, hotels, boatyards, and restaurants have steadily filled every inch on the shores, facing east to the lights of downtown and west to the palatial estates and steep cliffs of Point Loma. On weekend mornings, hundreds of boats launch for scuba diving and fishing trips along the point or out in the open sea. The island's nautical bent is firmly anchored by the **San Diego Yacht Club** and by San Diego's most venerable boat brokerages and builders.

---

1 **SAN DIEGO SPORTS ARENA**

This outdated eyesore holds too few people (14,200) for a major-league hockey or basketball franchise, and is a dismal place for concerts. Still, it's the biggest indoor venue in town, so music lovers have to put up with the nosebleed seats and lousy acoustics for now. The arena is best used for ice shows, volleyball tournaments, and exhibition games. The parking lot is used for a giant swap meet on Saturday and Sunday during daylight hours. ♦ Box office: daily. 3500 Sports Arena Blvd (between Rosecrans and Kurtz Sts). Office, 225.9813; recorded information, 224.4176

2 **FAIROUZ**

★★$ Owner Ibrahim Al-Nashashibi, a native of Jerusalem, was an attorney in Kuwait before coming to San Diego and opening this restaurant; he has since brought in many family members to help run it. The food is consistently good and inexpensive, especially the excellent hummus, falafel, and stuffed grape leaves. The combination plates—big enough to split—offer generous samplings of many dishes. There's a bountiful, inexpensive vegetarian lunch buffet, and the dinner menu has been expanded to include chicken, beef, and lamb dishes. ♦ Middle Eastern ♦ Daily, lunch and dinner. 3166 Midway Dr (near Rosecrans St). 225.0308

3 **PANNIKIN COFFEE AND TEA**

★$ There's a good array of pricey cakes, muffins, desserts, soups, salads, chicken curry, and quiches to accompany the standard espresso coffee drinks. Patrons scrunch into movie-house seats rescued from the **Loma Theater** and dangle their feet from high bar stools. There's a small shop with an excellent selection of coffees, teas, and wonderful accoutrements. ♦ Coffeehouse ♦ Daily, 7AM-11PM. 3145 Rosecrans St (between Rosecrans Pl and N Evergreen St). 224.2891 &

4 **BOOKSTAR**

Movie lovers moaned in unison at the passing of the 1945 **Loma Theater,** one of the last big screens in town. Just when it seemed the theater would certainly be torn down to make space for a new strip mall, the **Bookstar** chain bought the building and commissioned **Alamo Architects** to refurbish it. The restored tail-fin marquee touts the latest best-sellers, whereas the old silver screen is the backdrop

BIRD'S-EYE VIEWS

The **San Diego Bay** area is known for its sweeping vistas. Here are several of the very best:

* **Coronado Bridge**
* The top of the 70-foot dip on the **Giant Dipper** roller coaster in **Belmont Park**
* Landing at **Lindbergh Field**
* Hot-air balloons over **Del Mar**
* **Sea World Tower**
* The **Skyfari** ride at the **San Diego Zoo**
* **Cabrillo Monument**

* **Mr. A's** restaurant
* **Fort Rosecrans Cemetery**
* **Salk Institute**
* **Mount Soledad**
* **Palomar Observatory**
* **Mount Helix**
* **County Administration Building cafeteria**

for an impressive newsstand. ♦ Daily, 9AM-11PM. 3150 Rosecrans Pl (between Barnett Ave and N Evergreen St). 225.0465 ♿

5 US MARINE CORPS RECRUIT DEPOT

During the military's boom years, thousands of recruits passed through here so quickly that graduations were held every Friday morning. The compound, originally designed in 1920 by **Balboa Park**'s master architect **Bertram Goodhue**, contains several Spanish-style buildings with red-tile roofs and classic archways. Stuccoed in a soft gold color, these buildings seem almost to glow in the sunlight. The corps museum on the grounds is open for docent-led tours by appointment. ♦ South Pacific Hwy (between Barnett Ave and Rosecrans St). Information, 524.4426

6 US NAVAL TRAINING CENTER/LIBERTY STATION

Between 1923 and 1999, the navy used this prime waterfront property adjacent to the airport for training. The City of San Diego now controls the land, which is undergoing an enormous redevelopment project. Overwhelmingly controversial, the **Liberty Station** development is projected to include museums, shops, residences, hotels, and open spaces. The area is currently closed to the public while the navy's barracks and other buildings are destroyed (some historic structures will be preserved). The redevelopment is expected to last at least 10 years. ♦ Main Gate on Rosecrans St, at Lytton St. City of San Diego information, 236.5555

7 HOSTELLING INTERNATIONAL

$ Although not particularly attractive, this Hostelling International affiliate is predictably inexpensive and is a great place to meet national and international travelers. There are six private rooms with double beds, as well as the traditional separate-sex dorms with bunk beds. All rooms have shared baths. Kitchen facilities are available. ♦ No credit cards accepted. 3790 Udall St (at Worden St). 223.4778; fax 223.1883. www.hostelweb.com/sandiego

8 THE VENETIAN

★★$$ Owner Vince Giacalone, who opened this pizza parlor in 1965, now counts on his sons Frank and Joey to help run the business. Many Point Lomans grew up on the **Venetian**'s pizza, which is among the best in town. The secret is a crisp crust—not too thin, not too thick—topped with an unusually spicy sauce. It's great with masses of paper-thin onion slices and fresh tomatoes on top. Takeout is available. ♦ Italian ♦ M-F, lunch and dinner; Sa-Su, dinner. 3663 Voltaire St (between Chatsworth Blvd and Worden St). 223.8197

9 LINDBERGH FIELD SAN DIEGO INTERNATIONAL AIRPORT

When Charles Lindbergh was practicing his moves in the *Spirit of St. Louis* back in 1927, the tidelands along the bay seemed a perfect launching pad. Today they seem an odd use of space for an international airport, with jets roaring over crowded neighborhoods less than 3 miles from downtown. For detailed informa-

Restaurants/Clubs: Red | Hotels: Purple | Shops: Orange | Outdoors/Parks: Green | Sights/Culture: Blue

SEALIFE CALENDAR

San Diego residents are fascinated with the underwater seasons. Many depend on the sea for their livelihoods; many more, for their fun. Anglers, divers, and seafood lovers divide the year by their prey:

* **January through March:** rock cod
* **March through September:** bonita and barracuda

* **Late spring:** yellowtail, bass, and bonita
* **4 July through October:** marlin, albacore, bluefin tuna, and shark

Divers follow these seasons:

* **May through June:** mussels, clams, and other bivalves found along coast are poisonous now

* **October through March:** lobsters are in season

* **December:** squid spawn off **La Jolla** shores

---

tion and a map, see the "Orientation" chapter. ♦ 3707 N Harbor Dr (between Laurel and Pueblo Rico Sts). 686.8095

10 SPANISH LANDING

Ⓟ Take the afternoon off to enjoy a picnic on this beautiful strip of grassy, tree-shaded land overlooking the harbor. The view of sailboats adrift in the bay makes this the perfect spot for harborside walks, though the traffic from North Harbor Drive is distracting. Barbecues, picnic tables, and rest rooms are available. The **Cancer Survivors Park** at the south end of the landing is one of a series in the country donated by Richard Bloch, a two-time cancer survivor. The park, designed to provide encouragement and comfort for those with cancer, includes a waterfall, bronze figurines, and plaques with inspirational messages, all topped by white sails that glow at night. ♦ N Harbor Dr (between Harbor Island Dr and Nimitz Blvd)

11 TOM HAM'S LIGHTHOUSE

$$ This restaurant's working Coast Guard beacon flashes every 5 seconds from a 55-foot cupola, which is an exact replica of the **Old Point Loma Lighthouse** tower. Because the building juts out into the water, the view, if not the food, is terrific, and the interior boasts an extensive collection of California seafaring memorabilia. It's worth a visit, and the seafood and prime rib are better than at most tourist-oriented restaurants. The champagne brunch is a big hit, especially on Easter, Mother's Day, and graduation weekends. ♦ Steak/seafood ♦ M-F, lunch and dinner; Sa, dinner; Su, brunch and dinner. 2150 Harbor Island Dr. 291.9110 &

12 THE BOAT HOUSE

★$$ One of the first businesses on the island, this restaurant has been through several remodelings and still has one of the best views of the bay. The menu features well-prepared seafood and steak; try the halibut with lemon–macadamia nut butter or the chicken Marsala. The island is full of mediocre restaurants; this is one of the better options. ♦ Seafood ♦ Daily, lunch and dinner; Su, brunch. Reservations recommended for dinner and brunch. 2040 Harbor Island Dr. 291.8011 &

12 HARBOR SAILBOATS

This is the place to charter a sailboat (with or without captain) or to sign up for sailing lessons. ♦ Daily. 2040 Harbor Island Dr. 291.9568

13 HILTON SAN DIEGO AIRPORT HARBOR ISLAND

$$ One of the oldest hotels on the island, this isn't flashy and luxurious, but it's a good bargain for lodgings on the water and often has special rate discounts. The lobby and 207 rooms are acceptable but hardly exciting, with a staid hunter-green–and-burgundy color scheme, but the rooms have all the right amenities for business travelers, from coffeemakers to irons to dataports. The restaurant is only fair, but the health club and pool are fine. ♦ 1960 Harbor Island Dr. 219.6700, 800/578.7878; fax 293.0694. & www.sandiegoairport.hilton.com

14 SHERATON SAN DIEGO HOTEL AND MARINA

$$$$ Two hotels in one, the **Sheraton** has 1,050 rooms in its two towers. In the original 700-room **East Tower**, the lobby's ceiling frescoes are lit by a computerized system designed to replicate sky patterns at different times of the day. The rooms here are smaller than in the **West Tower**, but proximity to the recreation facilities is a plus. The West Tower's 350 rooms have separate seating areas, work spaces (if you must), and amenities like terry-cloth robes. All rooms have coffeemakers and hair dryers. The two towers share lavish facilities, including three pools, three tennis courts, a health club and spa, jogging trails, three restaurants, and a marina. Though the airport is actually within walking distance (if you're not hauling luggage), the noise from the jets is not bad. ♦ 1380 Harbor Island Dr. 291.2900, 800/325.3535; fax 692.2363. & www.sheraton.com/sandiegomarina

Within the Sheraton:

ALFIERE

★$$$ Murals, carnival masks, and glass sconces give a Mediterranean feel to this chic bistro in the hotel's west tower. A standout amid the island's eateries, the bistro features a grilled Kobe steak with truffle demiglace, smoked prosciutto–wrapped baby lobster tails, and a sublime dark chocolate soufflé. There's an impressive list of Italian and French wines. ♦ Mediterranean/Italian ♦ Daily, breakfast, lunch, and dinner. 692.2778 &

15 REUBEN E. LEE

★$$ This Mississippi-style paddle wheeler was built specifically as a restaurant. The boat doesn't travel, but landlubbers might still get a bit green around the gills, especially because the windows don't open. Upstairs is the seafood deck, with Southern riverboat décor reminiscent of Disney's Frontierland. Downstairs houses **Jared's**, a beef house. Both levels, with predictable nautical décor, have spectacular views of San Diego Bay and the downtown skyline, breathtaking at sunset with the orange sun reflecting off the mirrored buildings. ♦ Steak/seafood; Tu-Su, dinner; Su, brunch. 880 E Harbor Dr. 291.1880

16 POINT LOMA NAZARENE COLLEGE

You couldn't dream of a better setting for an institute of higher learning than here along Point Loma's ridge, on rugged cliffs above the Pacific. This priceless property, originally built in 1895, housed Madame Katherine Tingley's **Theosophical Institute**; her ghost reportedly haunts the campus. Tingley and her followers opposed the materialism of science and all dogmatic theology. She was also opposed to war, capital punishment, and electric power poles. One of the institute's original buildings, the **Spaulding House**, stands in the middle of the campus, its purple domes (which bear a startling resemblance to red onions) acting as a landmark. It's hard to imagine any studying getting done here, with dorms looking out to sea and tennis courts above the ocean. The view from the campus is breathtaking. ♦ 3900 Lomaland Dr (off Catalina Blvd). 221.2200

17 BAY CLUB HOTEL AND MARINA

$$ This low-rise, wood-shingled resort hotel offers a welcome escape from the predominant tropical theme of other Shelter Island resorts. The rooms at the back of the hotel have balconies looking out to the boats moored at marinas and at gorgeous homes and Point Loma; the rooms at the front look across the way to downtown; and second-floor rooms have views both ways. The 105 rooms and suites have refrigerators and desks, and there's a small pool, spa, and weight room. There's no restaurant, but a full complimentary breakfast buffet is available. Relax on one of the comfortable bamboo couches near the fireplace in the lounge, which overlooks the marina. ♦ 2131 Shelter Island Dr. 224.8888, 800/672.0800; fax 225.1604. www.bayclubhotel.com

18 BEST WESTERN ISLAND PALMS HOTEL

$$ Cozy first-floor marina-view suites and rooms have terraces, but the rooms without

---

Eight weeks after Easter, Point Loma's Portuguese community celebrates the Festa do Espírito Santo, a feast of thanksgiving, which climaxes with a festive parade.

The first lighthouse in the harbor was installed in 1769 and consisted of a pole formed from the tallest tree on the point equipped with a rope to haul a lantern to the top at sunset each day. Tallow candles provided the light.

There once was a canyon on the south side of Point Loma dubbed Hermit's Canyon. A hermit made the canyon his home, planting fig, lemon, and orange trees; carving chairs from sandstone; and making a tub for collecting rainwater.

In the Ice Age, Point Loma was an island.

---

views tend to be small. The 29 suites have kitchenettes, and slips are available in the marina. The sundeck features a whale-shaped pool and whirlpool overlooking the marina. There's a coffee shop that serves light meals all day. The rates for the 97 rooms are among the lowest on the island. ♦ 2051 Shelter Island Dr. 222.0561, 877/484.3725; fax 222.9760. www.islandpalms.com

19 SHELTER POINTE HOTEL & MARINA

$$ Built in 1952 as the Kona Kai, this resort was a Polynesian-style post–World War II honeymooners' dream. It's been revived with more modern Mediterranean architecture and décor. The 237 guestrooms and suites are decorated with bleached wood armoires and desks, king or double beds, and blue floral drapes and spreads. Most have a view of the 516-slip marina or the gardens. The townhouse suites have separate bedrooms and kitchens. Amenities include two swimming pools, two tennis courts, a health spa, and a waterfront restaurant. ♦ 1551 Shelter Island Dr. 221.8000, 800/566.2524; fax 222.9738. www.shelterpointe.com

20 TUNAMAN'S MEMORIAL

This bronze sculpture by F. Vianello of three larger-than-life fishermen casting their lines for yellowfin tuna was erected in 1986. The inscription reads: "Honoring those that built an industry and remembering those that departed this harbor in the sun and did not return." ♦ East side of Shelter Island (south of the fishing pier)

21 YOKOHAMA FRIENDSHIP BELL

Dedicated to San Diego from her sister city in Japan, this 2.5-ton bronze bell was installed at the end of Shelter Island Drive in 1960 as a symbol of eternal friendship. ♦ Southern tip of Shelter Island Dr

21 PACIFIC RIM PARK

Designed by architect **James Hubbel** with architecture students from San Diego's sister cities in China, Mexico, and Russia, this small park is a peaceful setting for surveying the harbor. The park's tiled mosaics flow around a spurting fountain and under an ironwork archway and are meant to represent peace and unity among nations. ♦ Southern tip of Shelter Island Dr

22 FORT ROSECRANS NATIONAL CEMETERY

Seventy-one acres of white headstones flank both sides of Cabrillo Memorial Drive. One of California's five national cemeteries, it has been the burial site for San Diego's military

MUSICAL NIGHTS

Between May and October, the lawn between **Humphrey's** restaurant and the marina fills with folding chairs for intimate nighttime concerts under the stars. Lazy San Diego nights are stirred by such blues players as B.B. King, Buddy Guy, and Ray Charles; such jazz musicians as Al Jarreau, Huey Lewis & the News, and George Benson; and such comedians as Bill Cosby, Dana Carvey, and Jay Leno. Freeloaders catch the show from dinghies and kayaks bobbing in the water by the stage or listen to the amplified music on the lawns outside Humphrey's. Dinner packages include a pre-show meal and guaranteed seating for the concert in rows 2–7. Tickets can be purchased at Humphrey's box office (recorded information, 523.1010; restaurant, 224.3577). Tickets can also be obtained by phone through Ticketmaster (220.8497).

personnel since 1899. A 75-foot obelisk honors 60 men who were killed in the *USS Bennington* boiler explosion of 1905. A stroll along the grounds affords a spectacular and moving view of the San Diego Harbor and beyond. ◆ Daily. Cabrillo Memorial Dr. 553.2084

23 CABRILLO NATIONAL MONUMENT

The most awesome panoramic view in San Diego can be had from a rocky promontory 400 feet above sea level at the tip of Point Loma. From its heights, one can see the Pacific, San Diego Harbor, Coronado, and south to Mexico. The point is a seafarer's delight, a navigational pointer marking the entrance to San Diego Bay and the continental US. In 1542, a Portuguese explorer named Juan Rodríguez Cabrillo sailed into this "closed and very good harbor," anchored inside what is now Ballast Point (formerly known as Fort Guijarros, which translates to "Fort Cobblestones"), and named the bay San Miguel. Spanish explorers and pirates charted the point and the bay; 3 centuries later, the US Navy claimed the point, which now is closed to the public and used as a submarine base.

When President Woodrow Wilson established **Cabrillo National Monument** in 1913, it was half an acre in size, the smallest national monument in the US. President Dwight Eisenhower transferred 80.6 acres from the navy to the National Park system in 1959; ever since, the military and the park have kept the point a relatively undisturbed natural habitat. For a good overview of the continued military presence in San Diego, check out the observation deck behind the gift shop and the charts of military ships and aircraft based along the point and across the bay at the **North Island Naval Air Station**. You too will be able to tell the difference between a carrier and a sub. A small exhibit hall includes a scale model of Cabrillo's sailing ship, the *San Salvador*. Slide shows about the whales and tide pools are presented throughout the day in the auditorium. The park's bookstore and gift shop are worth a visit, especially if you're into local history or nautical stuff. Save your souvenir shopping for here. ◆ Admission; parking fee. Daily. Take Rosecrans St to Cañon St to Catalina Blvd. Proceed on Catalina Blvd, which changes to Cabrillo Memorial Dr, through Naval Ocean Systems Center gates to end of the point. 557.5450

Within Cabrillo National Monument:

CABRILLO STATUE

A statue of Juan Rodríguez Cabrillo was sculpted by Portuguese artist Alvario de Bree in 1904. Through a series of mishaps, it sat in storage until 1942, when California State Senator Ed Fletcher somehow "kidnapped" the statue and had it installed near the harbor. In 1949, the statue was moved to the grounds of **Cabrillo National Monument**, where it weathered the winds until 1988, when a visiting Portuguese admiral commented on its sad condition. A new sandstone statue took its place in 1989. ◆ East of the Visitors' Center

WHALE OVERLOOK

Between December and February, you may see the annual migration of the gray whales as they pass Point Loma on their way from the Bering Sea to the lagoons of Baja, California. The lookout perched above the point's tip has a good vantage point, but the whales are becoming less visible each year as they swim farther from shore to avoid the hordes of whale-watching boats. ◆ West side of the point

---

Restaurants/Clubs: Red | Hotels: Purple | Shops: Orange | Outdoors/Parks: Green | Sights/Culture: Blue

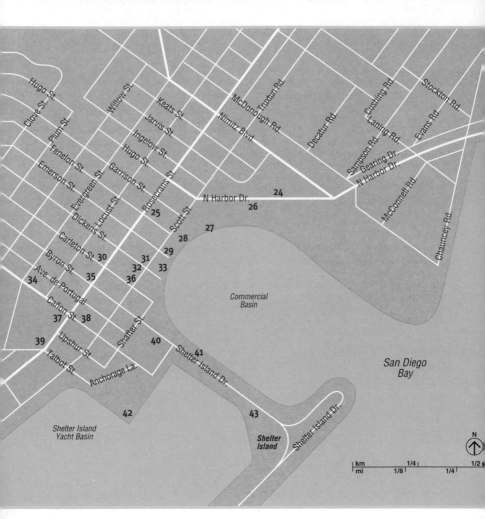

OLD POINT LOMA LIGHTHOUSE

Beaming its beacon a whopping 462 feet above sea level, the original lighthouse served as the southernmost Pacific Coast beacon in the US from 1855 to 1891. Called Star of the Silver Gate, it was designed in Cape Cod style by **Francis Kelly** and **Francis Gibbons**. The lighthouse deteriorated miserably until 1933, when the National Park Service took responsibility for its restoration. You can't actually climb the tower or visit the rooms, but you can peek in. The building is distinctive and beautiful. ◆ Center of the park

BAYSIDE TRAIL

This winding dirt trail curves down the rocky slopes of the point, passing the former hunting and gathering grounds of the Kumeyaay people, who inhabited the shores long before Cabrillo anchored. Take note of the panting hikers headed back uphill and gauge your distance accordingly. A map of the hike with good sketches and descriptions of native plants is available at the ranger-station counter in the gift shop. Wear sturdy shoes when you hike around the cliffs and stay away from the edges, which can crumble with the slightest provocation. ◆ South of the *Cabrillo* statue

TIDE POOLS

The rocky coast of the point's western side harbors a flourishing colony of tide pools. The best time to see the 100 or so different species of marine flora and fauna is during the low tides of fall, winter, and spring. Check the tides in the newspaper or local TV news. Wooden fences and dirt trails lead to several good pools. Watch your footing—those rocks get slippery. ◆ Cabrillo Rd (at Cabrillo Memorial Dr)

24 HOLIDAY INN SAN DIEGO BAYSIDE

$$ This four-story brown-and-white hotel offers marina luxury at inland prices. The basic rooms are decorated in pinks, greens, and blues; reserve a room on the top floor on the south side for a good view of the boats in the bay. The proximity to the airport and marinas makes up for the lack of luxury. The 237 rooms have refrigerators and coffeemakers, and the hotel has a coffee shop, fitness center, and small beach on the bay. Children under 12 eat free when dining with a parent at the inn's Point Loma Grill. ◆ 4875 N Harbor Dr (off Nimitz Blvd). 224.3621, 800/692.8899; fax 224.3629. & www.holinnbayside.com

25 RAMADA LIMITED HARBOR VIEW

$ Popular with fishermen and boaters, this super-clean chain property has only 83 rooms, which means you can usually get a lounge chair by the heated pool. The harbor views are excellent from the top-floor rooms; many have balconies. Microwaves, refrigerators, and coffeemakers in the rooms make the hotel a good choice for those on a budget. The **Captain's Quarters** bar and restaurant ◆ hosts a popular Wednesday-night fish fry. ◆ 1403 Rosecrans St (at Scott St). 225.9461; fax 225.1163. www.the.ramada.com/sandiego07628

26 PIZZA NOVA

★★$ This two-story building with great water views from the upstairs deck is one of a wildly successful chain of gourmet pizza-pasta cafés. Best bets include the tequila chicken fettuccine, roasted garlic shrimp pizza, Oriental chicken salad, and chopped salad with turkey, ham, and cheese. Check local papers for the frequent coupons, and get by inexpensively with the pizza or pasta and salad lunch specials. Delivery is available ◆ Californian ◆ Daily, lunch and dinner. 5120 N Harbor Dr (off Scott St). 226.0268

27 MUNICIPAL SPORTFISHING PIER

Although the majority of San Diego's tourists hop from the **Convention Center** to **Old Town** to the **Zoo**, a special breed heads here. They usually carry coolers and tackle boxes and crash at various budget hotels no more than a block from their boats. They're up at 5AM, stalking tuna, yellowtail, and dorado; stop by in the afternoon for a survey of the day's catch. Several commercial sportfishing boats depart from this pier; most companies also offer whale-watching tours. Parking is at a premium. ◆ Scott St (at the foot of Garrison St). No phone

28 FISHERMAN'S LANDING

A fleet of short- and long-range boats are available for charter or party-boat fishing trips; whale-watching and long-range trips also available. ◆ 2838 Garrison St (at Scott St). 221.8500; recorded information on boats and fish count, 224.1421

29 H&M LANDING

This is one of the largest sportfishing operations in San Diego, with private charters and party boats to the Point Loma kelp beds, the Coronado islands, and San Diego Bay. Also available are long-range trips to Baja, and in the winter, whale-watching trips. ◆ 2803 Emerson St (at Scott St). 222.1144; daily fish count, 224.2800

29 LEE PALM SPORTFISHERS

This outfit's *Red Rooster III*, a 105-foot boat specially outfitted for sportfishing, is one of the most popular among serious anglers. The fishing trips last anywhere from 3 to 21 days. Anglers rave about the crew and the cooks. ◆ 2801 Emerson St (at Scott St). 224.3857. www.redroosterIII.com

30 PT. LOMA CAMERA

If you're into underwater photography, this is the place to check out the latest gear and get straight answers from knowledgeable clerk-shutterbugs. The selection of all types of cameras is excellent, and the staff can often fix small problems without having to send your camera out for costly repairs. ◆ M-Sa. 1310 Rosecrans St (between Carleton and Dickens Sts). 224.2719

31 SEABREEZE LIMITED

This shop caters to every nautical need and whim and is bound to warm the cockles of any old salt's heart. You'll find every type of boating gadget, clothes, trinkets, nautical art, videos, and books. Salespeople are friendly, accommodating, and knowledgeable about the boating life. ◆ Daily. 1254 Scott St (between Carleton and Dickens Sts). 223.8989

Restaurants/Clubs: Red | Hotels: Purple | Shops: Orange | Outdoors/Parks: Green | Sights/Culture: Blue

32 HOOK, LINE & SINKER

Jigs with neon pink tassels for attracting dorado, rods and reels for the mightiest marlin, and all the latest info on the local fishing scene can be picked up here. ◆ Daily. 1224 Scott St (between Carleton and Dickens Sts). 224.1336

33 POINT LOMA SEAFOODS

★★★$ A terrific seafood experience can be had at this take-out seafood café and retail fish market, which is always noisy and jammed. Take a number for your order—a squid or crab-salad sandwich on soft sourdough; seviche still tasting of the sea; fresh albacore with mayonnaise, celery, and red onions; heaping plates of fried shrimp, scallops, fish, and squid with fries and slaw; fresh lemonade; chocolate-chip cookies. Take your food to the enclosed patio or the outdoor tables by the waterfront for a postcard view of the marina. The fish market is the best in town, with the pinkest, freshest selection of local catches and a lavish display of smoked fish and sushi. Offer to bring dinner, then stop here for swordfish (worth its weight in dollars), red snapper, yellowfin tuna, or halibut. Add a loaf or two of savory sourdough, a bottle of wine, and some brownies—and a lemon, of course. Don't miss this place! ◆ Seafood ◆ Daily. 2805 Emerson St (at Scott St). 223.1109

34 ST. AGNES ROMAN CATHOLIC CHURCH

Since 1933, this immaculately kept Spanish-style church in the La Playa area of Point Loma has been the center of San Diego's Portuguese community. The surrounding neighborhood, with perfectly maintained homes and neatly manicured lawns, is still very much alive with Portuguese culture, which has been a part of the city's life since the 1880s, when the first fishermen from the Azores sailed into San Diego Bay. ◆ 1145 Evergreen St (between Cañon St and Ave de Portugal). 223.2200

35 WEST MARINE

This outfit is one of the largest boating retailers in the world. You'll find everything for the boating life here—from clothing and calendars to hats and hardware. ◆ Daily. 1250 Rosecrans St (between Byron and Carleton Sts). 224.8222

36 MIGUEL'S COCINA

★★$ Brightly painted wooden masks and balsa-wood parrots create a party atmosphere in this lively restaurant, although the TV in the bar can be distracting. The menu features Mexican food with a flair for seafood—try the calamari *relleno* (stuffed), topped with jalapeño white sauce. Children and light eaters benefit from the extensive à la carte menu. The pleasant second-floor patio is heated on cool evenings. ◆ Mexican/seafood ◆ M-Sa, lunch and dinner; Su, brunch and dinner. 2912 Shelter Island Dr (between Scott and Rosecrans Sts). 224.2401

37 CON PANE RUSTIC BREADS & CAFE

★$ The lines outside this fragrant bakery don't discourage loyal patrons craving fresh sourdough, whole-grain, and specialty breads. There are tables indoors and out for feasting on sandwiches, or take your lunch to go and eat down by the waterfront. ◆ Coffeehouse/bakery ◆ Daily. 1110 Rosecrans St (at Cañon St). 224.4344

38 OLD VENICE

★★★$ The pizzas are so good at this Point Loma institution that the recipe was part of the deal when the business changed hands in the 1980s. Try the Greek Goddess pizza (with feta cheese and olives) or a veal parmesan sandwich. If you've got a sweet tooth, save room for the "monster cookie," loaded with chocolate chips and pecans and topped with gelato. Ambiance is informal; every table has butcher paper and felt pens to amuse the little ones and their adult companions. Jazz tapes play in the background as patrons unwind over wine and foccacia with fresh pesto, or Magic Mushrooms (mushrooms stuffed with shrimp and crabmeat). Adjacent to the dining room is a cozy bar, with stools along its green marble counter and upholstered chairs by the fireplace. ◆ Italian ◆ M-Sa, lunch and dinner; Su, dinner. 2910 Cañon St (between Scott and Rosecrans Sts). 222.5888

39 LIVING ROOM COFFEEHOUSE

★$ What was once the **Jennings House**, built in 1886, is now a comfy coffeehouse. Sandwiches, soup, quiche, and individual pizzas are served throughout the day for a light lunch or dinner. Thai coffee and Italian sodas bring an exotic touch to the California cuisine. Business bunches up during breakfast and the after-dinner hours; the rest of the day, customers settle in for hours over local newspapers. ◆ Coffeehouse/Californian ◆ Daily. 1018 Rosecrans St (between Talbot and Upshur Sts). 222.6852

40 THE BRIGANTINE

★★$$ Lunch and dinner specials are changed each month but typically offer a selection of seafood and meats, including catch of the day and marinated jumbo shrimp, and fresh veggies, all basted in butter and charbroiled. The décor is nautical, with lots of unfinished wood and shiny black booths for privacy. The bar fills up in late afternoon with deckhands and yacht owners. The Brig Burger is superb. ◆ Seafood/steak ◆ M-Sa, lunch and dinner; Sa-Su, dinner. 2725 Shelter Island Dr (between Anchorage La and Shafter St). 224.2871

41 RED SAILS INN

★$ This old-line waterfront seafood house (since 1935) is a bit musty inside, but it's still a favorite with the locals—particularly the sailors and boaters, who can get pretty boisterous in the bar. Nautical décor with bay windows overlooking a marina, and fast, no-frills service with plastic plates and paper napkins add to the salty atmosphere. Try the good basic omelettes in the morning; later in the day, order some great shrimp or crab Louis, or breaded jumbo shrimp with fries. Head for the waterfront deck with shaded tables on a sunny day. ◆ Seafood ◆ Daily, breakfast, lunch, and dinner. 2614 Shelter Island Dr (near Anchorage La). 223.3030

42 SAN DIEGO YACHT CLUB

The peaked red roof of the clubhouse rises above a seascape of masts and sails. From the water, the building looks cool, inviting, and important, conjuring images of blue blazers, jaunty caps, and ever-so-refined cordiality. When architect **Frederick Liebhardt** designed the building in 1964, he aimed for a classic seaworthy boathouse, not a clubhouse that could be perched at the edge of a golf course. In the end, the building reflected the image of the old **Coronado Boathouse**, which in turn echoes the towers and terraces of the **Hotel del Coronado**. When construction began, the existing house, an old navy barracks, was lifted and set in the parking lot, giving members a built-in reviewing stand for critiquing their emerging home, which

weathered the gusts of opinion with aplomb to become the landmark of sailing in San Diego. Since its inception in 1885, the club has boasted a stellar roster of world-class sailing champions. This is a private club. ◆ 1011 Anchorage La (near Shelter Island Dr). 221.8400

43 HUMPHREY'S HALF MOON INN & SUITES

$$ Take a trip to the islands without leaving the mainland. Surrounded by palm trees, sun-dappled decks, and poolside wet bars, this retro-Polynesian retreat is the island's original resort hotel. The owners also run the adjacent **Humphrey's** restaurant (see below), as well as an outdoor amphitheater famous for its summertime Concerts by the Bay series. Many of the 182 rooms and suites have views of either the marina or bay, and though they're far from spectacular, they do have carpeting and ceiling fans, hair dryers, and coffeemakers. Room service from Humphrey's is available. The low-key ambiance and over-grown tropical isle landscaping make this a pleasant change from the more sterile high-rises. Special room rates are offered during slow times, but rooms are in big demand during the concert season. ◆ 2303 Shelter Island Dr. 224.3411, 800/542.7400; fax 224.3478. www.halfmooninn.com

Near Humphrey's Half Moon Inn & Suites:

HUMPHREY'S

★★$$$ The quintessential tropical décor is a bit dated, but the food—tasty mesquite-grilled fish, good lobster, excellent Cajun corn chowder—is consistently good. The adjoining **Casablanca** cocktail lounge has live music nightly. While away a Sunday at the lavish champagne brunch. ◆ Seafood ◆ M-Sa, breakfast, lunch, and dinner; Su, brunch and dinner. Reservations recommended for dinner. 2241 Shelter Island Dr. 224.3577

MISSION BAY AND BEACHES

First, a word about dress codes. Shoes are out; rubber thongs are in. Shades (preferably name brands like Ray Ban, Serengeti, or Vuarnet) are a must. Leave your cut-off jeans at home. Stock up on flimsy nylon runner's shorts and the briefest of tank tops in neon orange or pink. Cultivate a fondness for the aroma of coconut oil; tune your muscles until they're clearly defined. Practice catching a Frisbee and serving a volleyball. Assume a fun-comes-first attitude. Balance your beautiful bod atop skates or a bike and cruise like a pro.

Start at **Mission Bay Park**, a 4,600-acre panorama of Southern California at play. Spanish explorers called the area **False Bay** because the beautiful body of water they saw sometimes became swampy marshland with the fickle flow of the **San Diego River**. Channels were built to guide the river toward the open sea, but it wasn't until after World War II that San Diegans got serious about capitalizing on this area between the ocean and the **Clairemont Hills**. With public bonds and the Army Corps of Engineers, the river was successfully diverted to the sea by means of a channel that was deep enough for boats to travel in and out of the bay. The tidelands were dredged to create deep coves and sloping sandy beaches. The result was a park that was half land and half water, with two bridges linking 90 acres of developed public parks, 7,000 parking spaces, and slips for 2,500 boats. Seventy-five percent of Mission Bay is devoted to public parks and beaches; the remaining lands are leased to hotels, sportfishing companies, boatyards, and **Sea World**. To thousands of picnickers, joggers, water-skiers, and kite flyers, Mission Bay is where to go for company picnics and family reunions, marathon training and maximum relaxation, pre-dawn fishing expeditions and sunset bonfires. The bay is also home to the newest trend in water sports: kiteboarding, which combines elements of windsurfing and kite flying. As you bike the winding cement sidewalks curving along the water's edge, let your mind go, soak in the sun's warmth and the sea's salty smell, and imagine being able to come to the bay every day after work to unwind. Seems San Diego's developers had some good ideas after all.

To the south, **Ocean Beach**, or OB, as it's called, is a small town at the end of I-8, where all roads lead to the beach. OB developed gradually, with a main street, **Newport Avenue**, running toward the ocean, post-war tracts of California bungalows and Mission-style homes set in orderly straight lines up the hills toward Point Loma, and an abiding sense of neighborhood. Although fast-food chains and minimalls have been kept out, for the most part, antiques dealers have moved in, setting up shop after shop along Newport Avenue. OB is neither gentrified nor yuppified, with just enough drawbacks to keep it from being "discovered." Proximity to the airport is perhaps the biggest flaw—visitors are usually blasted from their beds at 7AM when the first jets take off overhead with reverberations that set off the neighbors' car alarms. Then there's the OB reputation, distorted and magnified by legend and lore. Outsiders hear that the place is seamy and unsafe, a magnet for drifters and derelicts, where community standards are entirely too tolerant. It's true that eccentricities are encouraged here, but so is responsibility and civic involvement. OB is just like any other small town—it just happens to be at the beach, with some of the best surfing waves in the county and the unparalleled vistas at **Sunset Cliffs**.

Just to the north, **Mission Beach** is a tourist attraction in search of a community. Its heart is a 2-mile-long peninsula, between the waters of Mission Bay and the Pacific Ocean, that's only a quarter-mile across at its widest point. The main drag, **Mission**

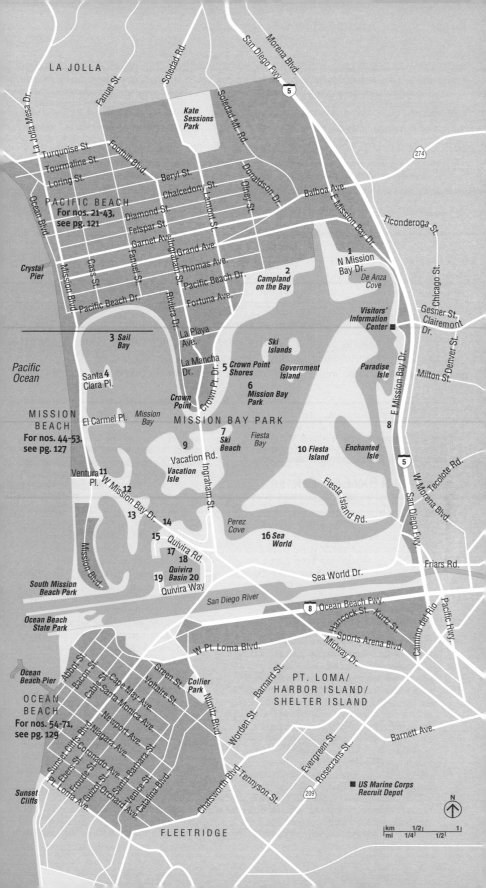

Boulevard, runs from the southern tip of the peninsula to **Pacific Beach.** It becomes so overcrowded on summer weekends that the police close it to incoming traffic by noon and get real serious about parking tickets. Forget side streets—the peninsula only has two narrow, one-way streets that run parallel to the boulevard, with alleys and walkways squeezed between beat-up bungalows that abut futuristic condos. Every inch of Mission Beach is covered by bodies, buildings, and sand. The noise level is intense: In addition to boom boxes and shouted conversations, there are the screams from the **Belmont Park** roller coaster, the whirring of police and Coast Guard choppers overhead, and, faintly, the constant pounding of the surf. The boardwalk is action central, the epitome of the SoCal beach scene, a Hieronymus Bosch–type confluence of humanity hanging it *all* out in the sun.

The madness calms down considerably when you head north to Pacific Beach and the **Crystal Pier.** The daredevils on wheels are more considerate of pedestrians, the boardwalk is bordered with jasmine shrubs and pretty parks, and the loiterers are likely to be families taking a break from hauling coolers and umbrellas to the beach. Trendy restaurants, bars, and shops line **Garnet Avenue,** attracting outsiders in search of the hippest hangouts. Pacific Beach still has the horrendous Mission Boulevard traffic, but the congested system of alleys and back-to-back housing is replaced by wide neighborhood streets shaded by towering palms. Side streets lead to the area's least congested beaches and lawns, along **Sail Bay** and **Crown Point Shores.**

MISSION BAY PARK

1 MISSION BAY GOLF CENTER

You can get in a sunset game on the night-lighted, 18-hole executive golf course; practice your form on the driving range; or take the kids to the miniature golf course. Watch for errant balls when you're playing 18 holes; this low-key course attracts more than its share of novice golfers. ♦ Admission. Daily. 2702 N Mission Bay Dr (between Clairemont Dr and Grand Ave). 858/490.3385

2 CAMPLAND ON THE BAY

Tucked away from the major thoroughfares of the bay is this 42-acre campground with 500 full-hookup spaces for RVs and 150 dirt spaces with fire rings. This is definitely the most scenic spot to park your motor home in the central San Diego area. Facilities include catamaran rentals, boat slips, pool, park areas, and a restaurant. Pets are allowed, and there's a 2-night minimum stay on summer weekends. The grounds are full much of the time; make reservations at least 6 months in advance for the spring and summer months. The spots by the marshlands (designated a wildlife reserve and a fabulous spot for bird-watching) are the most scenic; the view from the spots near the sandy bay beach and play-ground are also good, but you can count on

daytime noise. Spaces for RVs come in a variety of comfort levels, with some sites including a private Jacuzzi and washer-dryer. Tent camping is much more primitive and can be far from idyllic for those seeking to really get away from it all. ♦ 2211 Pacific Beach Dr (between E Mission Bay Dr and Olney St). 858/581.4224; reservations, 858/581.4260, 800/4BAYFUN

3 SAIL BAY

Private marinas, condos, and homes line the edges of this large inland bay formed by Santa Clara and Crown Points. When the bay was originally developed in 1926, homeowners were offered 50-year leases allowing them to create private beaches by extending their patios, fences, and retaining walls onto the sand. When the leases ran out in 1976, the city forced homeowners—after lengthy battles—to remove some 25 private docks from the beach, and by 1986 the private fences, walls, and patios were also outlawed. This bay is now like a park, with a walkway running along its edges and an ever-growing lineup of sailboats beached on the sand. ♦ Pacific Beach Dr (between Riviera Dr and Mission Blvd)

4 MISSION BAY SPORTCENTER

You can reach this isolated haven only via a boat through the bay or a drive through the congestion and madness of **Mission Beach.**

SURF LINGO

Bottom turn: turn back into the wave after riding atop it

Floater: riding off the tip of the wave into the air and landing back on the wave

Hang ten: hang your toes over the edge of the surfboard while riding a wave

The kind: the ultimate, as in *I bought the kind board today.*

Off the lip: a bottom turn on top of the wave

Tube: to surf inside a wave

For dedicated windsurfers, water-skiers, or sailors, the hassle of the journey is rewarded by the prime breezes along the cove forming **Sail Bay**. You say you don't know the difference between a keel and a kayak? You can learn as much as you want to know about sailing, water-skiing, or surfing here, then rent a boat and wet suit and practice until your burned skin and weary muscles demand relief. If you're feeling especially adventurous, check out the newest trend to hit the local waters: kiteboarding. The center offers lessons in this sport that combines a surfboard, a harness, the wind, and an enormous kite. Paddlers can rent kayaks, canoes, and rowboats; wave riders can try out surfboards and boogie boards at the nearby ocean beaches. Windsurfers, pro and amateur, rent their gear here, then stop in the sailing center next door for tips on the affairs of the wind and a browse through the gear and slick boards for sale. ◆ Daily. 1010 Santa Clara Pl (at Mission Blvd). 858/488.1004

Within Mission Bay SportCenter:

SAN DIEGO SAILING CENTER

Windsurfing has become one of the hottest sports in San Diego, and more than 23,000 beginners have learned about daggerboards, mast tracks, and tacking with this company, on Santa Clara Point. The point is one of the prime windsurfing spots in the county, and it's a good spot to become enthused enough to try balancing on a wet board while holding a sail aloft with the wind. ◆ Daily. 858/488.0651

YOUTH CAMPS

If you're bringing along a water-child who is addicted to the wind and sea, you might consider signing him or her up for a weeklong intensive summer camp by the bay. Children aged 6 to 16 learn sailing, kayaking, boogieboarding, water safety, water-skiing, windsurfing, and ocean surfing. ◆ 858/488.1004

5 CROWN POINT SHORES

One of the best spots for group gatherings, the shores face **Fiesta Island** and **Sea World**, with a spectacular view of the fireworks and the thunderboats that roar through the bay during the hydroplane races. This spot boasts fire rings, lifeguards, rest rooms, playgrounds, and best of all, a large parking lot. ◆ Crown Point Dr (between Lamont and Ingraham Sts)

6 MISSION BAY PARK

You've got to look at a map to grasp the immensity of this 4,600-acre park, an aquatic buffer zone between the beach towns and I-5. First-timers should pull into a parking lot by the **Visitors' Information Center** (see below) and consult their maps. Mission Bay's layout can be very overwhelming, and even locals get confused by the sheer number of channels, coves, islands, and bays along the curving 27-mile shoreline. I-5 runs along the park's eastern strip of lawns and rolling hills to Sea World Drive at the south. The Ingraham Street Bridge (aka the Glenn Rick Bridge, named for the park's builder) bisects the park about midway between the freeway and the ocean and leads to Pacific Beach. West Mission Bay Drive connects the park with Sea World Drive and Mission Beach. The entire area east of the Ingraham Street Bridge is open to water-skiing, except in the coves and channels marked with 5-mph buoys. The entire Northwest Bay is allocated for sailing. Fishing is permitted anyplace in the bay except official swimming areas: Bonita Cove, Ventura Cove, Crown Point Shores, De Anza Cove, Playa Pacifica, and Tecolote Shores. In recent years the swimming areas have been affected by pollution—heed the signs. Playa Pacifica and Tecolote Shores along the bay's eastern edge entice families with their calm waters, playground equipment, and wide expanses of lawns for picnicking and kite flying. By the way, kite flying is a performance art here—red, yellow, blue, and green boxes, tails, and triangles guided by professional

---

Restaurants/Clubs: Red | Hotels: Purple | Shops: Orange | Outdoors/Parks: Green | Sights/Culture: Blue

crews swirl against the blue sky. This is the land of joggers, boaters, swimmers, picnickers, loungers, and loafers. Don't try to figure it all out in one trip. ♦ Bounded by Mission Bay and Sea World Drs and by I-5

Within Mission Bay Park:

VISITORS' INFORMATION CENTER

Brochure collectors, get out your knapsacks to handle all the slick handouts from hotels, tour operators, restaurants, and other businesses. The desk clerks have good maps, advice on navigating your way about, and answers for most reasonable questions. Spread your finds out on a lawn by the water and soak in the bay's coconut-oil-scented ambiance. There's a big playground between the center and the water. ♦ Daily. 2688 E Mission Bay Dr (between Sea World and Clairemont Drs). 276.8200

7 SKI BEACH

It's amazing that all those bodies dangling from tow ropes don't end up in a huge tangle as amateur and pro water-skiers dodge, twist, and leap in the water, swooshing through one another's wakes. There's a continuous line of customized trucks and jeeps at the launch ramp, and an occasional incredible bottleneck in the parking lot. Thunderboats take over the course during the annual **Unlimited Hydroplane Races** each September; their roar can be heard clear to the Ocean Beach Pier. ♦ Ingraham St (between Sunset Cliffs Blvd and Crown Point Dr)

8 HILTON BEACH AND TENNIS RESORT

$$$ This resort came on the bay scene in 1963, when the hillsides framing the park were just starting to sprout homes. The property underwent a much-needed remodeling in 1994, with a complete obliteration of the outdated Polynesian theme. The improved hotel has a Mediterranean-style design with pale, sand-colored stucco walls, green shutters, and lots of balconies. The 357 rooms, spread over the property in several

two-story buildings and one seven-story tower, have a soothing beige-and-teal color scheme. Within steps of the guest rooms are plenty of attractions and distractions: a clean, half-mile-long beach; seven tennis courts and a health club; chartered yachts and deep-sea fishing boats; rental catamarans, Windsurfers, Aqua Cycles, bicycles, and other land and sea toys; a beyond-Olympic-size pool; several restaurants and bars; and easy access to the picnic areas, playgrounds, and miles of trails through the park. ♦ 1775 E Mission Bay Dr (between Sea World and Clairemont Drs). 276.4010, 800/HILTONS; fax 275.7991 &

9 PARADISE POINT RESORT AND SPA

$$$$ In the early 1960s, Hollywood producer Jack Skirball visited **Vacation Isle**, a 44-acre artificial island in the middle of Mission Bay, and decided to transform it into his own version of paradise. Skirball and architect **Eldridge Spencer** turned the barren island into the **Vacation Village South Seas Paradise**, with lagoons filled with water lilies, waterfalls, an abundance of palm trees and fragrant flowers, and a natural setting that can't be beat. Today, Noble House Hotels and Resorts owns the resort, with 462 rooms nestled among palm trees and tropical flowers and foliage. A true all-in-one resort, the facilities include three restaurants (including **Baleen**; see below); four swimming pools; eight tennis courts; shuffleboard, basketball, and volleyball courts; bike and boat rentals; an 18-hole putting green; jogging paths; and children's summer programs. One of the highlights of the property is the luxurious Balinese-style spa, which offers body treatments, massages, facials, and salon services. Accommodations are in single-story bungalows (a refreshing change from all the high-rise hotels around town), many overlooking the bay, with comfortable country-casual furnishings. Several suites are available with private patios. It's an ideal destination for families, and spacious enough for honeymoon couples to retain a sense of privacy. Rates are lowest between September and May; weekend rates are available all year. ♦ 1404 W Vacation Rd (between Ingraham St and W Mission Bay Dr). 858/274.4630, 800/344.2626; fax 858/581.5924. www.paradisepoint.com

9 BALEEN RESTAURANT AND BAR

★★$$$$ With its gorgeous bayside setting and whimsical tropical décor, **Baleen** is one of the prettiest restaurants in town, although the food can be inconsistent and the prices are in the luxury category. Still, the service is welcoming, and the place is popular with guests and locals for sunset cocktails and appetizers on the patio or a sunny Sunday

Legendary mountain man Jedediah Smith arrived in San Diego in the late 1880s, after establishing the overland trail that would become a wagon-train freeway for the westward bound.

A farmers' market is held in Pacific Beach every Saturday between 7 AM and noon. Located on the first floor of the Promenade, the event offers fresh produce and flowers as well as specialty products such as honey and preserves.

SAN DIEGO BY BIKE

San Diego, one of the most bicycle-friendly cities in the nation, offers over 300 miles of bike paths and ideal weather for cycling year round. Beach cruisers with thick tires are the latest fashion, although you'll see everything from sleek racing bikes to clunkers. Even police officers patrol the beach communities on two wheels. There are rows of bike racks (which fill quickly) in front of government buildings, shopping malls, tourist attractions, and park-and-ride trolley and bus stops; there are even bike racks on public buses. Drivers are far more considerate of bicyclists than you'd expect in a big city, and many of the scenic drives around the county have a separate right lane for bicycles.

Bicyclists seem to outnumber pedestrians on the **Mission Beach** boardwalk, where cyclists in bikinis and the briefest of bathing trunks cruise happily alongside in-line skaters. The boardwalk has become such a speedway that officials have instituted a speed limit of 8 mph—hard to enforce because few bikes sport speedometers. The pace is far calmer along the shores of **Mission Bay**, but if you ride along the sidewalks by the water, keep an eye out for stairs that seem to appear just when you've gained speed. Traffic is a bit of a problem along **San Diego Bay**, but you can follow a combination of bike paths and lanes from the **Embarcadero** to **Seaport Village** and the **San Diego Convention Center**, then take your bike on the ferry to **Coronado**, where the streets are flat and wide.

The most challenging and rewarding routes travel through **Ocean Beach** and **Point Loma** to **Cabrillo National Monument**, and along **Highway 101** from **La Jolla** to **Solana Beach**. Both involve hills and long stretches of spectacular scenery. Back-country cyclists with strong legs can make it up the 3,000-foot grade to the top of **Mount Palomar**; those with less energy can stick to the sea-level highways through the **Anza-Borrego Desert**. Off-road mountain bikes are restricted to certain trails in California state parks and are not allowed on the **Pacific Crest Trail**; for specific rules, contact the **California State Parks Department** (916/653.6995) and **San Diego County Parks Department** (858/565.3600). A free map of San Diego County bike routes is available by calling the **Caltrans Bicycle Information** line (231.BIKE). For more in-depth information and directions on specific biking routes, get a copy of *Cycling San Diego* by Jerry Schad (Centra Publications, P.O. Box 191029, San Diego, CA 92159).

Free bike racks are available on several public bus routes. Bikes are also allowed on the trolley. For information on bus and trolley bike services contact the **Transit Store** (449 Broadway, at Fifth Ave; 234.1060). Bikes are also allowed on the **San Diego Bay Ferry** (1050 N Harbor Dr, at Broadway; 234.4111). Organized bike tours are available through the **Sierra Club** (3820 Ray St, near 30th St in North Park; 299.1743). You can rent bikes, locks, and helmets (required by law for riders under 18 years of age) at **Bikes and Beyond** (1201 First St, at the Ferry Landing Marketplace, Coronado; 435.7180) and the **Beach Club** (704 Ventura Place, between Mission Blvd and the boardwalk, Mission Beach; 858/488.5050).

brunch. The cuisine runs the gamut from classic Americana—roast lamb and Maine lobster—to Asian-style bouillabaisse. ♦ Californian/seafood ♦ Daily, breakfast, lunch, and dinner. 1404 W Vacation Rd (between Ingraham St and W Mission Bay Dr). 858/274.4630

10 FIESTA ISLAND

Water-skiers and jet-skiers do their dervish whirls in the waters off this 465-acre man-made sandlot, and dogs of all breeds are allowed to cavort along the shore without leashes any time of day or night. The island's most infamous regulars are the players of Over-the-Line, an oddball (in more ways than one) game played by teams with indecent names and a general tendency toward rowdiness. The annual July **Over-the-Line Tournament** attracts groupies by the hordes.

Beer and bikinis are the norm. ♦ Fiesta Island Rd (between E Mission Bay and Sea World Drs)

11 BAYSIDE WALK

The best overall view of the Mission Bay neighborhoods is from a bike cruising this concrete pathway from **Mission Point**, the southwest tip of the bay, to **Santa Clara Point** at the north. Residents of the bay-front homes along the path somehow carry on normal lives in the midst of a 24-hour-a-day playground. Windsurfer boards are the most popular toys to the south; sailboats abound to the north. ♦ Bayside Walk (between Mission Pt and Santa Clara Pl)

12 BAHIA RESORT HOTEL

$$$ This 14-acre resort on a sandy peninsula curves into sheltering Mission Beach's inner

Restaurants/Clubs: Red | Hotels: Purple | Shops: Orange | Outdoors/Parks: Green | Sights/Culture: Blue

THE BEST

Jan Heying

Owner, Heying & Associates Public Relations and
Advertising

Is San Diego the country's best-kept secret? Not
anymore.

Food first:

Breakfast—**Kono's** at the entrance to **Crystal Pier** in
Pacific Beach, Where the real surfers hang out and
where you fit in with a pair of shorts and Pure Juice
flops. Be sure to get there before 10AM unless you
want to wait. People-watching is half the fun.

Lunch—has to be **Pt. Loma Seafood** on **Shelter
Island**—the freshest fish sandwiches in town. Sit
outside and watch the half-day boats bring in their
hauls.

Drinks—no better view of the city skyline than from
either the lounge at the top of the **Hyatt** downtown or
the outside deck atop **Bertrand's** at **Mr. A's**.

Dinner—favorite all-around—**George's** at the **Cove** in
La Jolla. Casual outside ocean-view patio. For an
elegant indoor dining experience, the best steakhouse
in town is **Donovan's**, located in the **University Towne
Centre** area. It's one of the few restaurants in town
with a sommelier.

While in **La Jolla**, take a walk around the cove and up
to **La Valencia Hotel** for a nightcap in the famous
Whaling Bar, frequented by many a Hollywood celeb.
Ask for their signature Whaler—this counts as dessert
as well with the magical ingredient of Häagen Dazs
vanilla ice cream. Yum!

Fun stuff to do:

Stroll along the **Boardwalk**, starting at the foot of
Pacific Beach Drive south along **Ocean Front Walk**
down to **Belmont Park** (home of the wooden roller
coaster). Cross over past the **Jack in the Box** for a
walk back; head north along **Bayside Walk**. Cut
through the **Catamaran Hotel**, cross over **Mission
Boulevard**, and head for the **Green Flash** on the
outside patio for a margarita and a chance of seeing
the green flash right at sunset. Rollerblades or a bike

rented at the **Mission Beach Club** near the roller
coaster are also acceptable modes of transportation.
Be sure to keep under 8 mph. Just a 1.5-hour drive
away, head to **Julian** for a Sunday-afternoon stroll
through this quaint mountain community famous for
its homemade apple pie, cider, and clean air. In
winter, it actually gets snow, so bring your sled. An
afternoon of walking and museum gazing in **Balboa
Park**—a picnic on the lawn and taking in the latest
original hit or soon-to-be hit Broadway show at the **Old
Globe Theatre**.

If you're lucky enough to be here in the summer during
Humphrey's Concerts by the Bay on Shelter Island,
don't miss a chance to see top-name jazz artists
performing live in this venue under the stars. For an
intimate indoor theater experience with the best
acoustics in town, check out the latest show at the
East County Performing Arts Center.

September affords an opportunity to experience **Street
Scene**, San Diego's version of the New Orleans Jazz
festival and Mardi Gras all wrapped up into 2 days in
the streets of downtown. Rest your feet, have a local
microbrew, and stop in at **Dick's Last Resort** for the
ultimate in fun-hearted harassment from crazy
waitstaff—the stuffed jalapeños are worth the price of
the abuse.

Pub crawling starts at the **Turf Club** in **Golden Hill**,
where you can start out with the best Long Island iced
tea in town while grilling your own $5 steak right in the
middle of the bar. Great neighborhood bar-grill. Head
into the **Gaslamp Quarter** for just about anything you
can think of, from **Martini Ranch** (you can guess their
specialty) to the **Field**, an authentic Irish pub, for
some Guinness on tap. Dance the night away at the
Belly Up in **Solana Beach**, or the hip new **On
Broadway** downtown.

Just 45 minutes south gets you to **Rosarito Beach** in
Mexico. For a relaxing weekend or even for the day,
make an appointment for a hot-rock massage or
hydro-bath at the spa at **Las Rocas**, a beautiful,
American-owned hotel overlooking the Pacific. While
you're there, stop by **Puerto Nuevo** for a traditional
lobster feast, complete with all the trimmings, rice,
beans, guacamole, tortillas, and of course,
margaritas—all for under $15. Olé!

bay, where sailboats nearly obliterate the sky
on sunny days. The location is ideal if you
want easy access to the frenetic party action
at Mission Beach; the roller coaster is just
across the street, and shrieks pierce the drone
of traffic and police helicopters. Despite its
proximity to the beach, the hotel is usually
peaceful. The one- and five-story buildings
with their 325 rooms are laid out in a loop
along the peninsula's outer edges, encircling
pools, tennis courts, and pansy-striped
gardens. There is also a casual restaurant
serving continental fare for breakfast, lunch,

and dinner. The general décor is pretty basic;
rooms on the west side have the best views.
It's a mainstream sort of place, good for
families. Special rates are available in winter;
weekend rates, throughout the year. ♦ 998 W
Mission Bay Dr (at Mission Blvd).
858/488.0551, 800/576.4229 in US,
800/233.8172 in Canada; fax
858/488.1387. www.bahiahotel.com

12 BAHIA BELLE

The sunset and night lights of **Mission** and
Pacific Beaches are more romantic when

viewed from the white curlicue railings of this Victorian-style sternwheeler, which has been cruising the bay between the **Bahia** and **Catamaran** resorts since the 1960s. The *Belle*, boasting warm mahogany paneling, red velvet curtains, brass railings, and a stained-glass skylight, is understandably popular as a wedding site. Her sister ship, the **William D. Evans**, is even more luxurious, with a 42-foot-long stained-glass skylight, formal dining rooms, and teak trimmings. Both ships are available for charters, and the *Bahia Belle* is used for drinking and dancing cruises open to the public. Admission. ♦ Cruises nightly, July–Labor Day; F-Sa, Sept–June. *Note:* At press time, the *Bahia Belle* was scheduled to be refurbished; call in advance to check the sailing schedule. The Bahia Resort, 998 W Mission Bay Dr (at Mission Blvd). 858/488.0551, 800/576.4229 in US, 800/233.8172 in Canada; fax 858/488.1387

13 BONITA COVE AND MARINERS POINT

Across the water and directly south of **Belmont Park**, this sandy peninsula is used for Over-the-Line and volleyball tournaments. The parking lots here fill up quickly because it's an easy walk through the lawns of the park to the boardwalk and ocean across Mission Boulevard. ♦ Mariner's Way (at W Mission Bay Dr)

14 DANA INN

$$ This is a good choice if you're more interested in playing outside than hanging around some fancy hotel room. Two-story gray-and-blue wooden barrackslike buildings sit by the foot of the Ventura Bridge, which leads to Mission Beach. The 196 rooms are equipped with coffeemakers, refrigerators, and hair dryers and are designed to be childproof; you need not worry about draping your wet towels about. Shuttles leave throughout the day for **Sea World**, and kids and adults can occupy themselves with shuffleboard, Ping-Pong, tennis (two courts), swimming, bike and skate rentals, and generally running amok on the lawns by the bay. The coffeeshop staffers are remarkably cordial, patient, and informative; the food, predictable. ♦ 1710 W Mission Bay Dr (entrance on Dana Landing Rd). 222.6440, 800/445.3339; fax 222.5916

15 HYATT REGENCY ISLANDIA

$$$$ The 18-story hotel tower seems out of place along the bay, but the tower rooms do have a top-notch view of the bay and ocean sides of Mission Beach. There's also a three-story addition, with rooms right next to the marina, whose 150 slips are often filled with enviable private yachts. The 422-room hotel boasts an ideal bayside location, great for those interested in boating and fishing. The hotel restaurant is best known for its lavish Sunday brunch, though the food has improved for dinners as well. ♦ 1441 Quivira Rd (between Sunset Cliffs Blvd and W Mission Bay Dr). 224.1234, 800/233.1234; fax 221.4887. www.hyatt.com

16 SEA WORLD

The bay's largest attraction is this 150-acre marine park. Four University of California, Los Angeles (UCLA) fraternity brothers opened the park in 1964 on just 22 acres. Now owned by Anheuser-Busch, **Sea World** has gradually expanded along the bay's southern shores and has seemingly endless parking lots and attractions to keep its guests amused. Once you've paid the steep entrance price, make sure you don't miss **Penguin Encounter**, where yellow-tufted emperor penguins preen and strut in an artificial Antarctic environment behind glass; the **Shark Encounter**'s fierce inhabitants; the **Forbidden Reef** display of moray eels and bat rays; and the playful bottlenose dolphins and sea otters at **Rocky Point Preserve**. Let the kids run wild in **Shamu's Happy Harbor**, with its water maze, funship, and sand play area. When the sun gets high, load the whole family onto the **Shipwreck Rapids** ride for cool sprays from waterfalls or board a simulated helicopter ride through the **Wild Arctic**. You can't get away without going to see the sleek black-and-white killer whales leap from their 6.7-million-gallon pool to splash the crowd. ♦ Admission. Daily. 1720 S Shores Rd (between Sea World Dr and Ingraham St). 226.3815; recorded information, 226.3901

17 SPORTSMEN'S SEAFOODS

★$ Fish and chips, fresh tuna burgers, and shrimp cocktails taste great when you're sitting at the small patio outside this self-service café by the rowboats and yachts moored in the bay. The adjacent fish market displays prize specimens from the daily catch. ♦ Seafood ♦ Daily, lunch and early dinner. 1617 Quivira Rd (between Sunset Cliffs Blvd and W Mission Bay Dr). 224.3551

17 SEAFORTH BOAT RENTALS

Sailboats, water-ski boats, and even low-tech rowboats are for rent here. ♦ Daily (closed Christmas Day). 1641 Quivira Rd (off W Mission Bay Dr). 223.1681

18 SEAFORTH SPORTFISHING

Bag an albacore, yellowtail, dorado, or snapper, depending on the season and your

---

Restaurants/Clubs: Red | Hotels: Purple | Shops: Orange | Outdoors/Parks: Green | Sights/Culture: Blue

OVER-THE-LINE

People in San Diego are addicted to sports trends. For example, in-line skating long ago replaced ordinary roller skating on the **Mission Beach Boardwalk**. Frisbee golf tournaments draw pros bearing a half-dozen different-sized discs for a variety of challenging shots at **Balboa Park**'s **Frisbee Golf Course** in **Morley Field**.

But the oddest sport of all has got to be **Over-the-Line**. The game itself is a simple version of sandlot softball with three-person teams. But the spectacle is another

story. Hedonism, debauchery, and decadence reign during the annual world championships held every July on **Fiesta Island**. Not only do the players compete with a ball and bat but they also put untoward energy into composing raunchy and ridiculous team names that would make Andrew Dice Clay blush. Their team T-shirts set the mood for the ultimate party, a dawn-to-dusk sunbake where naked flesh is at a premium and inhibitions are ignored. Not for the faint of heart.

---

expertise (or luck). Seaforth and its predecessor, **Mission Bay Sportfishing**, started fishing charters out of the bay in the early 1960s, when there actually were fish worth catching not far from shore. Most of today's anglers are headed for the banks off Point Loma or the Coronado Islands (in Mexican waters). Half- and full-day trips are offered, and scuba-diving charters are also available. ♦ Daily, from 4:30AM. 1717 Quivira Rd (between Sunset Cliffs Blvd and W Mission Bay Dr). 224.3383. www.seaforthlanding.com

18 THE LANDING

★★$ The crew members at this waterside coffee shop cheerfully begin their work day at 5 AM, serving coffee and eggs to hyped-up or half-asleep anglers. At the more humane hour of 9 or 10AM, they're still quick with a quip and coffeepot, and enough discarded newspapers have piled up that you don't have to purchase

your own. Settle into a heavy wooden captain's chair to devour your flaky golden hash browns with a melted-cheese-and-Ortega-chili omelette, raisin-bread French toast, or oatmeal with walnuts and brown sugar. Lunch at the counter, where you can watch the grill master flip your burger, fry your shrimp, and slice your fresh-baked turkey. The food all tastes expertly homemade. ♦ Coffee shop ♦ Daily, breakfast and lunch. 1729 Quivira Rd (between Sunset Cliffs Blvd and W Mission Bay Dr). 222.3317

19 MISSION BAY PARK HEADQUARTERS

A wood-shake-and-shingle South Seas–style bungalow serves as action central for park activities and development; maps, brochures, and permits for group functions are dispensed efficiently. ♦ M-F. 2581 Quivira Court (between Sunset Cliffs Blvd and W Mission Bay Dr). Offices, 221.8901

20 QUIVIRA BASIN

Sportfishers, boaters, and waterfront browsers roam these shores facing the Mission Bay Channel, which leads into the bay and open sea. The port office and park headquarters are located here, along with several boat sales and rental yards, marinas, a small shopping and dining center, sportfishing and whale-watching boats, and uncrowded picnic grounds. There's a fine view of Ocean and Mission Beaches from the rocky outcroppings along the channel mouth. ♦ Quivira Rd (between Sunset Cliffs Blvd and W Mission Bay Dr)

Pacific Beach is one of San Diego County's oldest suburbs, dating back to the late 1880s. In 1902, oceanfront lots could be purchased for as little as $350.

Books aren't the only attraction at the Earl & Birdie Taylor Library, a branch of the public library at 4275 Cass Street (858/581.9934). The striking building is also home to numerous special events, including jazz concerts, art exhibits, and reading discussion groups.

In 1850, San Diego became both a city and a county, and California became the 31st US state.

The Glenn Curtiss Flying School, established on North Island in 1911, was the first military aviation school in the US.

PACIFIC BEACH

21 KATE SESSIONS PARK

Here is another tribute to the indomitable **Kate Sessions**, who created much of San Diego's natural beauty with her early 1900s

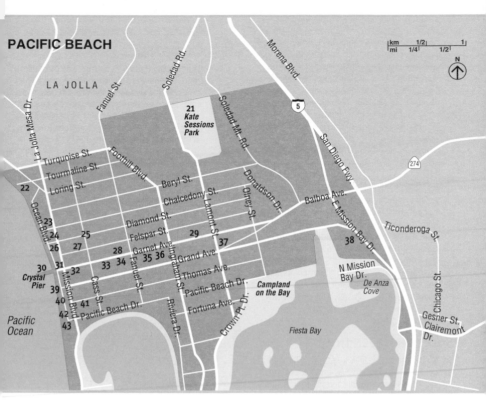

PACIFIC BEACH

LA JOLLA

21 Kate Sessions Park

22

23
24 25
26 27 28
29
30 31 32 33 34 35 36 37 38
Crystal 39
Pier 40 41
42 Pacific Beach Dr.
Pacific 43
Ocean

N Mission Bay Dr.
De Anza Cove
Campland on the Bay
Fiesta Bay

landscaping. Kate was a Pacific Beach resident and cherished the hillside of Soledad Mountain. In 1933, the city acquired 79 acres north of Lamont Street for this park, which wasn't landscaped and properly dedicated until 1957, on Sessions's 100th birthday. Don't miss the view from the flagpole atop the hill looking out south over the bay to Point Loma and beyond. ◆ Park Dr (between Soledad Mt and Soledad Rds)

22 TOURMALINE PARK

This small rocky beach isn't great for sunbathing, but the winds offshore are ideal for windsurfers, who balance on their narrow boards with brightly striped sails and capture the breeze seemingly effortlessly. The park has rest rooms and precious few parking spots. ◆ Tourmaline St (between Mission Blvd and Pacific View Dr)

23 PACIFIC SHORES INN

$$ Retirees and others looking for an escape from the sun and sounds of merriment find peace and shade at this small two-story inn. Many of the 55 plain rooms have refrigerators and kitchenettes. The quiet northern beaches are just a block west; restaurants and shops

are a few more blocks south. Facilities include a laundry room, a pool, and free continental breakfast; there is no restaurant. ◆ 4802 Mission Blvd (between Chalcedony and Law Sts). 858/483.6300,888/GR8.STAY; fax 858/483.9276. www.pacificshoresinn.com

24 PACIFIC TERRACE HOTEL

$$$ This pink condolike hotel is the best modern hotel on the boardwalk. It boasts two layers of balconies, encircled with cranberry-colored metal railings that jut past each other for the most advantageous views. The 73 totally up-to-date rooms have small refrigerators, TVs, and phones; half the units have kitchenettes. The complimentary cosmetics include a soothing aloe lotion (good for

---

Restaurants/Clubs: Red | Hotels: Purple | Shops: Orange | Outdoors/Parks: Green | Sights/Culture: Blue

sunburn); soft terry-cloth robes and hair dryers are standard in all rooms. Guests have access to a washer and dryer, underground parking, complimentary continental breakfast, and free lemonade and popcorn served all day; there's no restaurant on the premises, but there are plenty within walking distance. The pool and hot tub face a relatively quiet stretch of beach with fire rings. It's definitely a winner. ♦ 610 Diamond St (between Ocean and Mission Blvds). 858/581.3500, 800/344.3370; fax 858/274.3341. www.pacificterrace.com

25 Cream of the Crop

A prime destination for smart shoppers on a budget, this resale boutique specializes in high-quality, gently used women's clothing and shoes. You'll find a number of top designers represented, along with department-store brands and items from local boutiques. There's a particularly good selection of evening wear and accessories such as scarves, purses, and belts. Daily. 4683 Cass St (at Diamond St). 858/272.6601

26 Beach Haven Inn

$$$ Canadian families escaping the winter's cold and Arizona families racing from the summer's heat return annually to this small motel for clean, moderately priced accommodations near the beach yet away from the noisiest sections of Mission Boulevard. The heated pool and hot tub are enclosed with blue metal gates and wooden fences that block the traffic noise, and air conditioners are currently being installed in all the rooms (which helps blot out the noise). There is a washer and dryer on the premises, and several of the 23 units (18 with kitchenettes) have refrigerators. There is no restaurant. Rates drop significantly in winter. ♦ 4740 Mission Blvd (between Missouri and Diamond Sts). 858/272.3812, 800/831.6323; fax 858/272.3532. www.beachhaveninn.com

27 Cafe 976

Tables and chairs are set about in the brick patio, screened porch, and dining and living rooms of this Victorian-style beach house, which has been turned into a coffeehouse. It's far more peaceful than the coffeehouses along Garnet Avenue. ♦ Coffeehouse ♦ Daily. 976 Felspar St (at Cass St). 858/272.0976

27 Cass Street Bar & Grill

★$ Neighbors literally hang out from the street-side counters of this bar-café, shouting out greetings to friends parking their bikes and heading in for a cold one. Pictures of regulars with their favorite catches (marlin, tuna, and the like) decorate the walls, and the crowd has a sports-fan attitude. Several counters with bar stools line the walls and windows and surround two pool tables. You can't miss the wall-size mural of a tropical sunset. The burgers and chicken sandwiches are messy, flavorful, and guaranteed crowd pleasers. Also worth ordering: any of the fish specials of the day. ♦ American ♦ Daily, lunch and dinner (kitchen closes at 10PM). 4612 Cass St (between Felspar and Emerald Sts). 858/270.1320

28 Henry's Market Place

Expand your picnic spread with impeccably fresh avocados, breads, tortillas, oranges, brie, and goat cheese, and basics like environmentally correct paper towels. The market also offers freshly made sandwiches and has a nice selection of wines for sale. ♦ Daily. 1260 Garnet Ave (between Fanuel and Everts Sts). 858/270.8200

29 Cafe Athena

★★$ Step into this pretty blue-and-white Greek taverna, redolent with the aroma of olive oil, and feel your taste buds come alive. Dine with friends so you can split several dips—*tzatziki* (yogurt with cucumbers, garlic, and dill), *taramasalata* (caviar blended with olive oil and lemon juice), and *panaki salata* (spinach blended with feta cheese and water chestnuts)—served with warm pita bread. Move on to the great salads, *tyropites* (feta and mozzarella in phyllo pastry), and cream of roasted eggplant soup. If you still have room, try the tender chicken souvlaki, the lamb meatballs (called *keftedes*), or the swordfish brochettes, and force yourself to sample at least one bite of the baklava. Takeout is available. ♦ Greek ♦ Daily, lunch and dinner. 1846 Garnet Ave (at Lamont St). 858/274.1140 ♿

30 Crystal Pier

At first glance, the pier appears to be closed, but there is a chain-link gate that's open for

---

Glass bottles are not allowed on most beaches.

To tell whether the tide is coming in or going out, check the color of the sand near the water's edge. If there is a distinct dark band of sand, the tide is coming in and you'd better move your towels. If the sand is uniform in color, the tide is going out and it's a good time to look for sea critters in tide pools.

Ocean Beach's Wednesday evening Farmers' Market (4-7PM, until 8PM during the summer) draws crowds to Newport Avenue for fresh produce and flowers, along with baked goods, potted plants, jellies and salsas, and live music. Kids especially enjoy the enclosed trampoline and the rides on real llamas.

pedestrians daily from dawn until sunset. Blue-and-white hotel cottages line both sides of the 400-foot-long pier's entrance; the rest is operated by the city during daylight hours as a fishing pier, with a small bait-and-tackle shop and a cluster of craggy-faced anglers who dangle their lines for halibut, perch, mackerel, and the occasional lobster. Surfers line the break where the waves form on both sides of the pilings, and gulls swarm about, squawking and swooping after trashy tidbits. The hotel's operators keep a close eye on the goings-on along the pier and prohibit alcohol, profanity, and boom boxes on the premises. The present-day scenario is far more natural than its first incarnation as **Pickering's Pleasure Pier**, an aborted attempt to capitalize on the building boom brought to Mission Beach by the **Mission Beach Amusement Center** in 1925. The initial plan was designed by **Ernest Pickering**, who had built several amusement center piers in Los Angeles but failed to see the San Diego project through. The investors pushed on, with **Neil Nettleship** and **Ben Tye** as designers, and in 1927 opened their **Crystal Pier** and the **Crystal Ballroom**, with a cork dance floor that drove the flappers wild. Unfortunately, the pilings quickly became infested with marine borers and started swaying within 3 months, and the pier was condemned within a year. It was widened and reopened in 1935, then nearly destroyed by high tides and waves in 1982. After lengthy and costly renovations, including replacing the T-shaped fishing area at its far end, the pier reopened in time for the Pacific Beach Centennial in 1987. ♦ Daily, sunrise to sunset. Garnet Ave (at Ocean Blvd)

On Crystal Pier:

CRYSTAL PIER HOTEL & COTTAGES

$$$ You can't sleep any closer to the water than in these blue-and-white cottages, where the surf literally rocks you to sleep as it pounds the pier's pilings. Guests drive their cars right onto the pier and park in front of their doors. The wooden cottages, which were completely gutted and remodeled in 1994, are adorned with pink geraniums growing in window boxes under blue shutters. The 26 cottages and two second-story suites have full kitchens with large refrigerators, microwaves, and stovetops; separate bedrooms with queen beds covered in quilts; living rooms with TVs, futon couches, and wicker chairs; and patios looking almost straight down at the sea. The pier is closed to the public at sunset, giving the hotel's guests the privacy to quietly soak in the salty night air and dream above the pounding waves. The cottages are

available at very reasonable daily, weekly, and monthly rates (with a 2-night minimum stay) between 16 September and 14 June, although in the winter months the air can be damp and the sea rough. The daily rate doubles (with a 3-night minimum stay) between 15 June and 15 September, with no special rates for longer stays. ♦ Reservations essential in summer. 4500 Ocean Blvd (at the foot of Garnet Ave past Mission Blvd). 858/483.6983, 800/748.5894

31 KONO'S SURF CLUB

★★$ It's the food that packs the crowds into this tiny café, where the breakfast potatoes alone—laden with onions, green peppers, and cheese—warrant a visit. Surf movies play on TV, and gorgeous photos of great waves around the world line the walls. Be prepared to wait in line on weekend mornings. ♦ American ♦ Daily, breakfast and lunch. 704 Garnet Ave (at Ocean Blvd). 858/483.1669

32 KARINYA

★★$$ Owner Tajchai Navapanich was born in Bangkok and has a degree in engineering from the University of California, San Diego (UCSD). Obviously, his heritage held more promise than his degree. Navapanich and his two sisters prepare searingly spicy Thai dishes that bring tears to most eyes. To accommodate wimpy American palates, dishes are prepared mild, medium, or hot, but be forewarned that medium is about as hot as the seeds of a jalapeño. Try the *mee krob* (a crispy tangle of sweet noodles with shrimp, green onions, and bean sprouts), *nuah pad ped* (beef with sweet basil, garlic, chilies, and mint), and *gang ped* (chicken in red curry with coconut milk and bamboo shoots). ♦ Thai ♦ M-F, lunch and dinner; Sa-Su, dinner. 4475 Mission Blvd (between Hornblend St and Garnet Ave). 858/270.5050

33 SOCIETY BILLIARD CAFE

Players line up to pay major bucks to play at the 15 state-of-the-art pool tables in an industrial-chic setting with drainpipes as lighting columns and other heavy metal parts strewn about. Beer, wine, gourmet pizzas, and sandwiches are served. There are special day rates for die-hard players, and no minimum play time. ♦ Daily. 1051 Garnet Ave (between Fanuel and Cass Sts). 858/272.7665

34 TRADER JOE'S

Stock up your hotel room, condo, or cooler with discount wines (but remember, no glass bottles on the beach), imported beers, and exotic flavors of sparkling water, as well as reasonably priced gourmet treats such as

---

Restaurants/Clubs: Red | Hotels: Purple | Shops: Orange | Outdoors/Parks: Green | Sights/Culture: Blue

pretzels stuffed with peanut butter or chocolate-covered macadamia nuts. ◆ Daily. 1211 Garnet Ave (between Fanuel and Everts Sts). 858/272.7235. www.traderjoes.com

35 WORLD CURRY

★★$ With a selection of curries from Thailand, India, the Caribbean, and Japan, this informal eatery offers flavors to please just about everyone. The generous portions of curries range in strength from mild to fiery and can be ordered with either a choice of meats or strictly vegetarian. Side dishes include jasmine rice, fresh Indian breads, chicken skewers, and refreshing salads. Eat in the vibrantly painted dining room or order to go. ◆ International ◆ M-Sa, lunch; daily, dinner. 1433 Garnet Ave (between Haines and Gresham Sts). 858/270.4455

36 MR. SUSHI

★$$ As the name suggests, the menu consists mainly of sushi, prepared with deft showmanship in a wildly popular contemporary neon and black lacquer setting. The restaurant closes at midday, between 2 and 5PM. ◆ Sushi ◆ Tu-F, lunch and dinner; Sa-Su, dinner; closed M. 1535 Garnet Ave (at Ingraham St). 581.2664

37 LAMONT STREET GRILL

★★$$ Pacific Beach's best dining room is located in a converted beach bungalow in a partly residential neighborhood. Outside, tables surround a fireplace on the small patio; inside, there are several little dining rooms. Owners Steve and Kathy Bettles have a real sense of romance, and chef Robert Marnulis is so confident in his skills he's written a cookbook called *The Soups of Lamont Street Grill*. Naturally, you're well advised to start with his soup of the day, perhaps followed by shrimp sautéed with green-chili pesto, or the mélange of Italian sausage, chicken, and fresh fish over pasta with spicy beurre blanc. All meals are followed with fresh fruits dipped in chocolate. ◆ Californian ◆ Daily, dinner. Reservations recommended. 4445 Lamont St (at Hornblend St). 858/270.3060

38 RUBIO'S DELI-MEX

★★$ Owner Ralph Rubio relished the fish tacos he devoured at sidewalk stands in the Mexican fishing village of San Felipe year after year, finally securing a vendor's secret recipe in 1978. In 1983, he opened his first fish taco stand on this bustling boulevard, and gradually his beloved fish tacos caught on in a big way. Now Rubio has take-out stands scattered throughout San Diego County and even has the fans in the stands at **Qualcomm Stadium** spurning hot dogs for fried fish wrapped in corn tortillas. The original eatery isn't exactly conveniently located, but it's worth a visit if you're curious about this culinary creation that now appears on trendy menus all around town. The classic fish taco is made of a battered and deep-fried strip of fresh fish wrapped in a soft corn tortilla with shredded cabbage, a squeeze of lime juice, and a spicy secret sauce; for the seafood-shy, **Rubio's** also serves terrific *carnitas* (marinated pork) and tame chicken tacos. ◆ Mexican ◆ Daily, breakfast, lunch, and dinner. 4504 E Mission Bay Dr (at Bunker Hill St). 858/272.2801. Also at 901 Fourth Ave (at E St), downtown. 231.7731; 355 Rosecrans (between Midway Dr and Sports Arena Blvd), Point Loma. 223.2631. www.rubios.com

39 OCEAN PARK INN

$$ Sand-colored stucco helps this three-story hotel blend in with the surroundings; underground parking makes it convenient. The outdoor pool is heated (a plus in winter), and each of the rooms offers a patio or balcony with chairs and a small table. Other bonuses include kitchenettes in the suites, a coin-operated laundry, complimentary continental breakfast, and refrigerators in all of the 73 rooms and suites, which are well maintained and large. There's no restaurant in the hotel, but several are within easy walking distance. ◆ 710 Grand Ave (between Mission and Ocean Blvds). 858/483.5858, 800/231.7735; fax 858/274.0823. ♿ www.oceanparkinn.com

40 TERRIFIC PACIFIC BREWERY & GRILL

★★$$ The name fits—this restaurant offers some terrific suds and grub and a fine view of the Pacific. Beers, which are made on the premises, come in styles from pale ale to unfiltered wheat beer. Best bets, foodwise, are the fish and chips, fried calamari, fresh yellowtail sandwich, and any of the burgers. In addition to the first-floor dining room and patio, there's a second-floor deck that's a fine place for an alfresco lunch or dinner overlooking the sea. ◆ Brew pub/American ◆ Daily, lunch and dinner. 721 Grand Ave (at Mission Blvd). 858/270.3596

41 NICK'S AT THE BEACH

★★★$$ There's a lot to like about this two-story restaurant and bar, starting with the lengthy and eclectic menu served in the main-floor dining room. There's not a loser on the list, from the baked, broiled, or blackened fresh fish entrées to the seafood pasta with feta cheese, the meat loaf (with mushroom gravy), the grilled veggie salad, and the steamed mussels flavored with cilantro and lime. To wash it all down in style, Nick's offers a reasonably priced wine list, more than a dozen draft beers, and a full liquor selection. Upstairs, the lively bar area draws the 21-and-over crowd with pool tables, TVs, a CD jukebox, and plenty of ocean-view seating indoors and on the adjacent sun deck. Night owls will appreciate the fact that food is served until 1 AM nightly. ◆ Seafood/American ◆ Daily, lunch and dinner. 809 Thomas Ave (at Mission Blvd). 858/270.1730. www.nicksatthebeach.com

42 THE PROMENADE

This two-block-long shopping and dining complex hasn't been as successful as developers had hoped, so it may be transformed into a condo complex. But for now, take advantage of its wonderful underground parking lot—a real find in these crowded streets. Parking is free with validation from businesses in the complex, which include T-shirt and beachwear shops, take-out food stands, and mainstream restaurants. ◆ Daily. Mission Blvd (between Pacific Beach Dr and Thomas Ave)

Within the Promenade:

EGGERY ETC.

★$ Quantity is as important as quality among this crowd, who wolf down *chorizo* omelettes

smothered in hot salsa as a hangover cure, or piles of syrupy pancakes and French toast for that first sugar rush of the day. ◆ American ◆ Daily, breakfast and lunch. 4130 Mission Blvd (between Pacific Beach Dr and Reed Ave). 858/274.3122

Randy Strunk
Owner

PACIFIC BEACH SURF SHOP

If you need it to surf, they've got it here: wetsuits, bodyboards, surfboards and wax, along with skateboards, skimboards, clothing, and sunscreen. The shop also offers rentals on bikes, swim fins, beach chairs, and in-line or roller skates. Surfing lessons are offered by appointment year-round. ◆ Daily. 4150 Mission Blvd (between Pacific Beach Dr and Reed Ave). 858/373.1138

42 GREEN FLASH

★$ The glassed-in patio is the perfect spot for a sunset dinner (salads, fish, pastas), whereas the dining room and bar inside are great

THE BEST

Abigail Padgett
Award-Winning Mystery Author

Crawl the used-book stores on **Adams Avenue**, then have coffee at **Lestat's**.

Watch the sunset from the cave beneath the parking lot across from the **Spaulding Mansion** on **Sunset Cliffs Boulevard**. Quite dramatic at high tide!

Walk north up **Torrey Pines Beach** from the I-5 overpass to the big drainage pipe; scuttle through it and up the hill a bit. Great view from a magically isolated spot.

Picnic in **Balboa Park** before a play. A blanket, wine, and candles in silver holders are essential.

Walk at least 10 blocks of **Garnet** from the beach and back, checking out all the shops.

Do the same in the **Gaslamp** on a Saturday afternoon.

Take the dachshund to **Dog Beach** for a waddle and then to the **Dog Beach Dog Wash** for something fabulous from the boutique.

Hike the **Oak Canyon Trail** from the **Old Mission Dam** in **Mission Trails Park** while listening to Mozart on the Walkman, or Mahler if it's cloudy.

Take out-of-town guests to the **Gulf Coast Grill** and order all the appetizers.

Walk the boardwalk from **Pacific Beach** to **Mission Beach** on a winter night.

Restaurants/Clubs: Red | Hotels: Purple | Shops: Orange | Outdoors/Parks: Green | Sights/Culture: Blue

places to meet locals. This is one of the nicest eateries on the boardwalk. ◆ Continental ◆ Daily, lunch and dinner. 701 Thomas Ave (at Ocean Blvd). 858/270.7715 &

World Famous

california coastal cuisine

43 WORLD FAMOUS

★★$$$ Set right on the boardwalk, this beachy restaurant features "California coastal cuisine," which can be anything from lobster bisque and grilled fresh fish to seafood salads, fish and chips, or prime rib. The food is generally quite good, not to mention filling, and service is informal but pleasant. Both the bar and dining room offer ocean views, but the best seating (if you want to view the nonstop boardwalk action) is out on the patio. ◆ American/continental ◆ Daily, breakfast, lunch, and dinner. 711 Pacific Beach Dr (at Ocean Blvd). 858/272.3100

MISSION BEACH

44 CATAMARAN

$$$ The South Seas theme is taken to the max at this tropical resort hidden behind Polynesian pagoda-style green copper roofs facing the pandemonium on Mission Boulevard. The two-story atrium lobby is a misty green oasis of ferns and waterfalls, and streams run through the grounds between the tower and two-story buildings facing Sail Bay. The hotel was renovated in 1987; the 312 rooms and suites are decorated in cool corals and greens; some have refrigerators and balconies. Facilities include a restaurant that is well-regarded for its Sunday brunch, the **Cannibal Bar** (with frequent live music performances), a fitness room, pool (not as lavish as you would expect), and bike and watersports equipment rental. The hotel is owned by the William Evans family, who also own the **Bahia** in Mission Bay and the *Bahia Belle* sternwheeler (see page 118), which offers nighttime cruises between the two hotels. The service isn't always the best, and the rates are

high for what you get. Check on weekend rates, family packages, and other discounts. ◆ 3999 Mission Blvd (between Zanzibar Ct and Pacific Beach Dr). 858/488.1081, 800/422.8386 in US, 800/233.8172 in Canada; fax 858/488.1387. www.catamaranresort.com

45 MISSION CAFÉ AND COFFEE SHOP

★★$ Breakfast is the featured meal of the day at this funky neighborhood hangout. Waffles, breakfast burritos, eggs (in various incarnations), and French toast are standouts on the wide-ranging menu, and the pancakes are simply some of the best in town (check out the strawberry-granola and the banana-blackberry versions). Lunch offers plenty of satisfaction too, with spicy "Chino-Latino" fare such as Baja shrimp burritos and Asian chicken pasta, along with imaginative sandwiches and salads. No need to dress up. Because reservations aren't accepted, expect to wait for a table on the weekends. ◆ American/international ◆ Daily, breakfast and lunch. 3795 Mission Blvd (between Santa Clara Pl and San Jose Pl). 858/488.9060

46 SASKA'S

★★$$ This place started out as a decent, reasonably priced steak and seafood restaurant with dependable grilled fresh catches, uninspired but fresh salads, and gigantic baked potatoes. The restaurant is a godsend at 1AM when everywhere else is closed. **Saska's** updated its image with the help of architect **Tom Grondona**, known for his wacky, playful designs. Grondona added an arch, a fish market, and an upstairs open-air café, with neon stripes and cut-out palm trees. ◆ Steak/seafood ◆ Daily, lunch and dinner until 1 AM. 3768 Mission Blvd (between Pismo and Redondo Cts). 858/488.7311. www.saskas.com

47 PILAR'S BEACH WEAR

Every female body must someday encounter the bathing suit. At this shop, the choice is wide enough to camouflage most flaws and help make the best of what you've got. The shop is mostly devoted to women's swimwear, but there are also a few pairs of swim trunks in stock. ◆ Daily. 3745 Mission Blvd (between Portsmouth and Queenstown Cts). 858/488.3056

48 MISSION BEACH CLUB

Brothers Dan and Ray Hamel opened their bike shop, formerly known as **Hamel's**, back in 1966. Things have changed a lot since then—the façade has been rebuilt to resemble a Gothic castle, the bike shop has expanded to include lots of other sporting equipment, and the brothers sold the place a few years ago. But bathing beauties in string bikinis and briefs still wait in line to rent bikes, boogie boards, roller skates, and in-line skates. Tourists and locals drop by to peruse the selection of clothing, accessories, and beach gear on sale. Daring skateboarders perform nearby, entertaining the crowd. A cautionary note: first-time skaters should practice their skills south of **Belmont Park** before attempting to blend with the boardwalk crowd. ◆ Daily. 704 Ventura Pl (between Mission Blvd and Boardwalk). 858/488.5050; fax 858/488.9811

49 HOMIE'S CINNAMON ROLLS

★★$ The intoxicating scent of freshly baked cinnamon rolls marks the spot of this cool little neighborhood bakery. Owner Harold Rose, alias Butch the Baker, turns out several varieties of his signature treats, including Pecan Pleasure, Awesome Apple, and the cinnamon-packed Homie's Original. (They've gotten so popular, they're now served at **Qualcomm Stadium**.) There's seating inside the shop (which serves coffees and juices) and on the small patio out front. ◆ Daily, 7 AM–noon. 735 Santa Clara Pl (between Mission Blvd and Boardwalk). 858/488.2354. www.homies.com

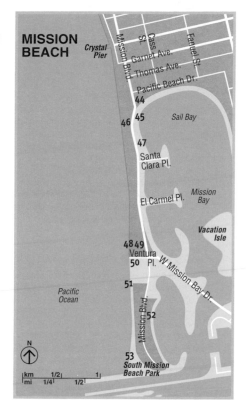

Ocean Beach is home to the "Ocean Beach Geriatric Surf Club and Precision Marching Surfboard Drill Team and Gidget Patrol," a group of over-30 surfers known for their annual appearances (complete with longboards, Beach Boys music, and tongue-in-cheek synchronized routines) at the OB Christmas Parade and other civic events.

Two magnificent specimens of the Torrey pine can be seen on Saratoga Street (between Froude and Ebers Streets) in Ocean Beach.

The Mission Beach wildlife isn't all of the two-legged variety. According to the official City of San Diego Web site (www.sannet.gov/), in December 1998 a Mission Beach resident called 911 to report a seal running loose in the alley off of Kennebeck Court. Lifeguards responded and learned that the disoriented seal been wandering through some yards facing Mission Bay. They walked it across Mission Boulevard to the Mission Beach boardwalk, where the seal made its way over the seawall, down the beach, and into the ocean.

50 BELMONT PARK

Belmont Park is the closest San Diego comes to the Jersey shore approach, replete with screams from the roller coaster, the aroma of hot dogs and cotton candy, and a toned-down, carnival-like ambiance. The Mission Beach scene received a much-needed commercial boost when this 18-acre shopping-dining-amusement complex opened in 1990, ending nearly a decade of acrimonious discourse about the future of the priceless chunk of real estate between Mission Boulevard and the beach. The park had been Mission Beach's centerpiece since 1925, through prosperous highs and seedy lows. When first developed by John D. Spreckels as a distraction from the raging success of his Coronado Tent City, it was a fanciful, elaborate amusement park with a **Natorium** (now called **The Plunge**), a dance hall, and a roller rink. The midway rides and arcades were contained in **Luna Park**, which was fenced in by the wooden trestles of the **Giant Dipper**. The park survived the ravages of the Depression and peaked in popularity during World War II, when sailors and their dates escaped reality and partied hearty before being parted by the war. By 1976, the park had deteriorated to the point where the city was forced to close it. Gradually the roller coaster's frame became home to a growing huddle of drifters, and the neighbors grew more anxious. In the end, the interests of commerce and nature were integrated into this controversial complex that still hasn't quite caught on. Restaurants and shops have a tendency to disappear after a few months of high rents and low returns. Still, its impact can hardly be ignored, as the **Giant Dipper**'s passengers echo the screams of all roller coaster riders through history. Other attractions here include a merry-go-round and a games arcade. ♦ Daily. 3126 Mission Blvd (between San Fernando and Ventura Pls). 858/488.0668. www.giantdipper.com

Within Belmont Park:

GIANT DIPPER ROLLER COASTER

The retro mint green and cotton-candy pink color scheme of this 1925 coaster seems out of place against the blue summer sky and takes away a bit of the charm of the half-mile of wooden tracks swooping and dipping on the horizon. But at night the 1,600 twinkling white lights outlining its curves are downright romantic. Thanks to the volunteer efforts of the Save the Coaster Foundation, the **Giant Dipper** became a National Historic Landmark on its 65th birthday (4 July 1990). Nearly one third of the wooden framework and all the tracks were replaced, along with all the nuts and bolts, as restorers faithfully followed the 1925 Frank Prior and Frederick Church design. Granted, there are far more exciting roller coasters around today, but nothing beats this one for nostalgia. ♦ Admission. M-Th, 11AM-8PM; F-Sa, 11AM-10PM. 488.1549

THE PLUNGE

If you like swimming pools, don't miss this one, billed as the largest indoor saltwater swimming pool in the world when built in 1925. Architect **Lincoln Rogers** housed the 175-foot-long pool in a grand Spanish-Renaissance palace reminiscent of the **Balboa Park** buildings from the 1915 exposition. The pool was inlaid with painted tiles brought by horse and buggy from Ensenada, Mexico, and both the building and tiles were at the heart of all controversies over changes in the park for the next 65 years. Unlike other **Belmont Park** landmarks, this one has remained open to the public since 1925, and its preservation became a condition of later development. Lap swimmers who were addicted to 60-foot lanes were bereft when the building was closed for renovations in 1987 and had a hard time coping with its transformation from a slightly seedy, mildewy hideaway into a gorgeous showplace at the

heart of an upscale fitness club that opened in 1988. The second-story mezzanine that once overlooked the pool was replaced with a two-story-high mural of orca whales. The pool is still open to the public (the hours change with the seasons) for a fee and is also used for swimming classes and occasional **Dive-In Movies**, where viewers recline in inner tubes while watching *The Abyss* or *Jaws* from the pool. ♦ Admission. Daily; call ahead for hours. 3115 Ocean Front Walk (between San Fernando and Ventura Pls). 858/488.3110

51 BOARDWALK

To attempt a peaceful Sunday-afternoon stroll down the 3-mile boardwalk from **Belmont Park** to **Pacific Beach** is to definitely risk life and limb. Bicyclists with beer-can holders on their handlebars whip through clusters of pedestrians as if determined to win an obstacle-course race. At the same time, roller skaters in string bikinis charge oncoming traffic with fearless abandon, passing the males loitering on the wall between the boardwalk and sand, who respond with whistles and catcalls. In 1994, the city instituted an 8-mph speed limit on the boardwalk; because bikes and skates don't typically have speedometers, the law is difficult to enforce, but it does give the cops a chance to nab the worst offenders. It's difficult to imagine how anyone over the age of 25 could bear to spend the night in any of the rental houses along this stretch, which is patrolled frequently by police officers wearing tan shorts, riding herd on the crowd from their beach-cruiser bicycles. Fortunately, weekdays are much calmer, except at summer's height. Unless you're determined to witness beach life at its rowdiest, stick with the boardwalk's northern stretches near the **Crystal Pier** (see page 122). ♦ South Mission Beach Park to Palisades Park

52 THE PENNANT

This classic beach bar is popular with the members of OMBAC (the Old Mission Beach Athletic Club)—including police officers, postal workers, and teachers—who thrive on sports and beer. Spend an hour or two on the second-story open-air deck quaffing pitchers of beer and take in yet another view of the beach scene. ♦ Daily, 8AM-2AM. 2893 Mission Blvd (between San Gabriel La and Deal Ct). 488.1671

53 SOUTH MISSION BEACH PARK

This spit of land at the south end of the park has beaches facing both the bay and the open sea. The neighborhood's streets are far less crowded than in central Mission Beach, and the homes far more luxurious. There are several sand volleyball courts and fire rings on the ocean side of South Mission Beach and bicycle paths on the bay side. ♦ Ocean Front Walk (between Belmont Park and San Luis Rey Pl)

OCEAN BEACH

54 DOG BEACH

Rover and Spot can frolic in the waves without leashes here, where the San Diego River flows (or rather trickles) into the sea. It's obviously paradise for dogs, who race in and out of the waves with glee. Dog owners are required to clean up after their pets; compliance, however, can be very spotty. Their territory is separated from the rest of OB by the rock jetty that forms the flood channel; another jetty to the north blocks the river's natural course into the bay. The river floodway is a fertile feeding ground for mussels, clams, egrets, herons, and countless other creatures who appear and disappear with the tides, and the jetty is a popular courseway for bicyclists and joggers heading from the beach to **Robb Field** (see below). ♦ W Point Loma Blvd (at Abbott St)

55 THEE BUNGALOW

★★★$$ Owner-chef Ed Moore is an alumnus of many fine local establishments, including the now defunct but fondly remembered **Gustaf Anders**, which reigned as the hottest restaurant in La Jolla for many years. Moore chose this small, venerable restaurant as his solo venture, banking on the establishment's long-standing reputation as one of the most romantic hideaways in town. The small converted bungalow at the edge of **Robb Field** has two intimate dining rooms that glow with candlelight and warmth from the fireplaces, as well as a sheltered patio. Guests dine on pâté; lobster bisque topped with puff pastry; roast duck (the house specialty) with black cherry, orange, or peppercorn sauce; or game specials such as venison, pheasant, and goose. The wine list features more than 1,000 selections and is revered by connoisseurs for its fair pricing and depth. For bargain hunters, Moore offers an early-bird special, including soup or salad and entrée, nightly. ♦ French/continental ♦ Daily, dinner. Reservations recommended. 4996 W Point Loma Blvd (near Bacon St). 224.2884. www.theebungalow.com

55 THE 3RD CORNER

★★★$$ Just across the street from **Thee Bungalow**, the **3rd Corner** restaurant was formerly the site of the **Belgian Lion**. When the Coulon family (longtime owners of the much-missed Belgian Lion) decided to sell, Ed Moore purchased the space, extensively remodeled it, and created an eye-pleasing new dining room, patio, and bar devoted mostly to fresh fish and seafood. Guests are welcome to dine at the bar counter or simply savor a glass or two of imported beer or fine wine. The menu, a fetching blend of Southern French and Mediterranean influences, features sampler-size "small plates" of classic dishes, such as steamed or stuffed mussels, country pâté, ahi tartare and scallops niçoise, as well as full-size entrées, such as cassoulet, bouillabaisse, roasted monkfish, and lamb loin. An offbeat wine list eschews familiar Chardonnays and Merlots in favor of an international lineup of whites and reds from Italy, Spain, Argentina, France, and Chile. The interior is chic yet inviting, with faux-finished walls, flattering lighting (with lots of candles), and a small fireplace in the bar. ♦ French/Mediterranean ♦ Daily, dinner. Reservations recommended. 2265 Bacon St (at W Point Loma Blvd). 223.2700. ᕗ www.thethirdcorner.com

55 ROBB FIELD

Rugby players collide over leather balls on the playing fields beside the flood channel, in full

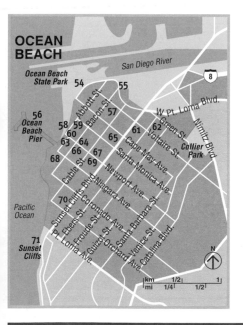

OCEAN BEACH

Ocean Beach State Park 54

San Diego River

8

56
Ocean Beach Pier

Pacific Ocean

71 Sunset Cliffs

58 59 57
60
63 64 65
66 67
68 69
55
61 62
W Pt. Loma Blvd.
Green St
Nimitz Blvd
Voltaire St.
Cape May Ave.
Collier Park
Santa Monica Ave.
Newport Ave.
70
Abbott St.
Bacon St.
Cable St.
Sunset Cliffs Blvd.
Coronado Ave.
Niagara Ave.
Pt. Ebers St.
Froude St.
Guizot St.
Orchard Ave.
Venice St.
Santa Barbara St.
Catalina Blvd
Pt. Loma Ave.

N

km 1/2 1
mi 1/4 1/2

view of the cars streaming into OB off I-8. On spring and fall weekends, the field is packed with players and fans, and there's a steady stream of joggers passing by. The vast grass fields are also home to soccer leagues, softball teams, model-plane enthusiasts, dog walkers, bird watchers, and picnickers and sunbathers. Bicyclists favor the asphalt path that runs east from **Dog Beach** along the floodway and over Sunset Cliffs Boulevard Bridge to Mission Bay. ◆ W Point Loma Blvd (between Sunset Cliffs Blvd and Bacon St)

Within Robb Field:

ROBB FIELD SKATE PARK

With the addition of this spacious, well-designed skate park in 2000, **Robb Field**'s cool quotient soared. Young boarders flock here from throughout the county, attracted by bowls, rails, quarter pipes, and other features of this all-concrete facility. Guests must be 6 or older, and pads are required. The fenced park is at the north end of Robb Field, near the bridge over the San Diego River. ◆ Admission (both daily and annual passes are sold). Daily (closes at sunset). 525.8486

PENINSULA TENNIS CLUB

This club has well-maintained courts and is open to both members and the general public. Members play for free; there's a daily fee for nonmembers. ◆ Daily. 2525 Bacon St (in Robb Field). 226.3407

56 OCEAN BEACH PIER

The half-mile-long walk to the T at the end of the pier relaxes both body and mind, blowing away tensions in salty breezes. The air seems 10 degrees cooler no matter what time of day, and the waves seem ever more powerful as they pound against the concrete pilings. At the peak of summer's heat, the sun's glare leaves wrinkles around your eyes and sand leaves a fine white crust on your broiled skin.

John D. Spreckels developed much of early San Diego by building spectacular gardens, amusement parks, and other tourist attractions such as Coronado's Tent City, the Mission Beach Amusement Park, and the Mission Cliff Gardens above Mission Valley at the end of his rail lines, where investors were needed to establish new communities.

San Diego's first health club was established downtown in 1924. It was an elaborate affair, with 96 sleeping rooms, 2 solariums, 4 handball courts, a gymnasium, and pool. There was also a separate dining room, lounge, and entrance for women.

And when the fog of winter rolls in, your body disappears into a cool gray cocoon. The pier has its ardent admirers who barely pass a day without strolling its length. Fishing is part of the daily routine for a few, who dangle their lines from carefully calculated perches for their dinner of mackerel, halibut, or bass. You won't need a fishing license to join the pier anglers, but you will need squid, hooks, and advice from the crusty characters at the small bait-and-tackle shop near the far end of the pier. Be prepared to dodge dive-bombing seagulls that brazenly swarm along the rails, snatching any even remotely edible snacks. Beneath the pier's boardwalk daredevil surfers dodge past the pilings atop curling waves, performing for wanderers who loiter mindlessly, soaking in the scene. The view is even more spectacular on summer nights, when the fireworks from **Sea World** explode on the midnight-blue horizon. ◆ Daily, 8AM-8PM. Park in the lot at the foot of Newport and Abbott Sts. Niagara Ave (at Bacon St)

On Ocean Beach Pier:

OCEAN BEACH PIER CAFE

$ Welcome to the latest of several restaurants/cafés whose only distinction is an enviable setting. Think of it as a resting spot, a place to write postcards with the sea pounding at your feet. Don't count on the food. ◆ American ◆ Daily, breakfast, lunch, and early dinner. Almost one-half mile beyond the foot of Niagara (at the end of the pier). 226.3474

57 DOG BEACH DOG WASH

Dogs of all shapes and sizes (and their owners) abound at this bright, friendly establishment devoted to the do-it-yourself washing, grooming, and general pampering of canines. The large elevated tubs (with warm water, towels, and shampoo included in the price) are the centerpiece of the operation, but you can also rent training videos; sign up for various classes; and purchase a variety of shampoos, toys, collars, bandannas, and treats for your best friend. The helpful and enthusiastic staff keeps the place clean and running smoothly. ◆ Daily. 4933 Voltaire St (between Cable and Bacon Sts). 523.1700. www.dogwash.com

THE BEST

Georgeanne Irvine

Development Communications Manager, San Diego Zoo

I'm one of those rare San Diego natives, and although I've traveled all over the world, I've discovered that there's no place I'd rather live than here. And even if I didn't live in San Diego, I would most certainly vacation here . . . often . . . because our wonderful city has an amazing array of things to do and see.

One of my all-time favorite places to visit is the **San Diego Zoo**, which is saying a lot, because I've worked at the zoo the past 24 years but never tire of it and still enjoy a busman's holiday. Every day is a new adventure. Some small hidden zoo pleasures for me include the walk through the **Hummingbird Aviary**, which is filled with colorful flowers and jewels of the bird world, and the adjacent bromeliad garden. Both areas are off the beaten track at the zoo but easy to find. I also love **Hippo Habitat** in **Ituri Forest**. It's my favorite major exhibit because it brings back memories of my canoe trip down the Zambezi River in Africa, where hippos seemed to congregate around every bend of the river. What's really exciting about the zoo's hippo exhibit is that visitors can view the underwater world of hippos through thick glass! It truly looks as if the 2-ton creatures are performing hippo ballet as they glide through the water and delicately bounce off the bottom of the pool.

Our sister facility, the **San Diego Wild Animal Park**, is another fantastic animal adventure that reminds me of Africa. An excellent way to see the park is via a **Photo Caravan**, an open flatbed truck that takes you right into the enormous field areas where you can feed giraffes and pet rhinoceroses.

In **Balboa Park**, adjacent to the zoo, rides on the miniature railroad and the colorful carousel (where you can reach for a real brass ring) are great fun. Also, **Spanish Village**, a local artists' colony, is a great shopping spot for a variety of art from paintings and pottery to jewelry and gems.

A down-home way to spend a Sunday afternoon is a walk or drive through northwestern **Mission Hills** to check out the **Open Houses**. The homes, especially the Craftsman-style houses and the yards, are gorgeous. **Coronado** neighborhoods are wonderful for browsing too.

I've recently discovered the beauty and serenity of the **Rancho Penasquitos Nature Reserve**, located about 20 minutes north of downtown, just to the west of Interstate 15. You can hike, bike, jog, or ride horseback through this native terrain, and the trails lead almost all the way to the coast. In the restaurant arena, **Athens Market Taverna** in downtown is my absolute favorite. The Greek food, especially the lemon chicken, is delectable, and owner Mary Pappas is San Diego's most gracious, gregarious host.

Alfonso's in **La Jolla** has the best nachos and salsa anywhere in San Diego plus magical margaritas. After my meals at **Alfonso's**, I always stroll down to the **Children's Pool** at **La Jolla Cove** to watch the harbor seals come in for the night. I've counted as many as 100 seals inching their way up from the surf for a good night's sleep on the sand.

Other neighborhoods that are fun to explore and have many good restaurants are **Hillcrest**, **University Heights**, and **Kensington**. My favorite restaurants in those areas include **Montana's**, the **Parkhouse Eatery**, the **Adams Avenue Grille**, and the **Antique Row Cafe**. There are many, many antique shops along **Adams Avenue** between **University Heights** and **Kensington**, so a meal and antique shopping are another great way to spend part of a San Diego day.

58 OCEAN BEACH

These sands are known for their volleyball courts, playgrounds, fire rings, and crowds; the waves are legendary among board and body surfers. North of the pier, oceanfront cliffs crumble into rocky shores, creating tide pools for starfish and hermit crabs. As the rock piles give way to sand south of the pier, the beach widens and surfers congregate at the foot of Newport Avenue, territory also popular with clientele familiar to the police officers on the beach beat. The main lifeguard tower is at the foot of Santa Monica Avenue, and five outposts are scattered north to the end of Voltaire Street and the beginning of **Dog Beach** (see page 130). The lifeguards post flags noting safe swimming areas. Pay attention to them: OB is known for its rip currents that can sweep an unsuspecting swimmer out to sea. Large groups of revelers tend to congregate early around the fire rings, where they bake their bodies in the sun, roast hot dogs over the coals, and burn wooden pallets in an orange blaze against the darkening sky. Lifeguards are on duty at the beach 24 hours a day, 365 days a year; they can see you on the beach, even if you can't see them. Parking lots at Abbott St and Newport Ave and Abbott St and West Point Loma Boulevard. ♦ Abbott St (between Newport Ave and W Point Loma Blvd)

59 CECIL'S CAFE AND FISH MARKET

★★$$ This popular spot offers a dynamite location across from the beach and consistently top-notch food. The small dining room is framed with full-length windows, and the tables and booths are judiciously placed for optimum views. Breakfast fare includes the traditional bacon and eggs as well as some unusual creations, such as macadamia nut pancakes or calamari and eggs. At dinner, light eaters can get by with the excellent house salad and fish tacos; hearty appetites should be sated with the hamburger and grilled fish selections. Groups divvy up portions of gourmet pizzas, and few can resist the macadamia ice-cream pie. ◆ Californian ◆ Daily, breakfast and dinner. 5083 Santa Monica Ave (between Bacon and Abbott Sts). 222.0501 ♿

59 QWIIG'S BAR & GRILL

★★$$ Some folk were not all that happy about this upscale yuppie-looking restaurant when it opened in 1985 in a new two-story wooden plaza across the street from the beach. But the first-rate food served with a welcome lack of pretense won over the resisters before long, and now it's easily the most popular restaurant in a 5-mile radius of OB. The consistent quality of the food is a major attraction. The hamburgers topped with melted cheese and grilled bacon could quite possibly be the best in all of San Diego; the calamari sandwich runs a close second. The Cobb salad with chunks of white chicken breast, bleu cheese, avocado, and eggs in artful rows atop a platter of crisp lettuce makes an unparalleled lunch, supplemented by fragrant hunks of sourdough bread and foccaccia. At dusk the elevated bar area looking out toward the ocean is packed with the after-work crowd nibbling on fried calamari, artichokes, and oysters, and the adjacent sushi bar is usually busy as well. Diners have an even better view of the sunset from the cushy, crescent-shaped booths facing the ceiling-to-floor windows (covered with tinted shades when the sun's glare is too bright). For an awesome repast, have the creamy clam chowder with peppered sherry, the house salad topped with crumbled walnuts, and any fresh fish—ahi in wasabi butter, yellowtail with red pepper, or salmon tossed with pasta. By the way, the restaurant was named after a group of surfers the owners hung out with at a secret beach along Sunset Cliffs. ◆ Seafood ◆ M-F, lunch and dinner; Sa, dinner; Su, brunch and

In 1927 San Diegans passed a $650,000 bond issue to deepen San Diego Bay, which built up the tidelands near downtown, making them suitable for airport runways. San Diegans have vehemently debated the wisdom of having an ever-growing international airport in one of the most congested areas of the county for decades. But the airport has been expanded, and it seems destined to remain at the edge of downtown.

dinner. 5083 Santa Monica Ave (between Bacon and Abbott Sts). 222.1101

60 HODAD'S

★★$ Lunch at this burger joint is a true OB experience. Surfing and cartoon memorabilia cover every wall; you can even dine inside a VW bus. The menu is simple: big greasy burgers, steak fries, and thick shakes and malts. ◆ American ◆ Daily, lunch and dinner. 5010 Newport Ave (between Bacon and Abbott Sts). 224.4623

61 OB PEOPLE'S NATURAL FOODS

Flash into the past as you select your kefir of choice to the sounds of Joni Mitchell or the Grateful Dead. This 1960s food co-op entered the 1990s with computerized cash registers but still remains one of the precious few markets with organic veggies and fruits; bins of granola and brown rice; coolers with carrot juice and rennetless cheese; and shelves filled with herbal and nonchemical lotions, shampoos, and soaps. Members get a 10-percent discount on purchases. ◆ Daily. 4765 Voltaire St (between Ebers St and Sunset Cliffs Blvd). 224.1387. www.obpeoplesfood.com

62 KAISERHOF

★★$$ San Diego's best German restaurant, **Kaiserhof** is a favored destination for anyone who loves a good beef *rouladen* or wiener schnitzel. Entrée portions are enormous, and just to make sure no one leaves hungry, dinners include soup or salad, two side dishes, and lots of hearty breads. As befits a *biergarten*, there's a sizable collection of German beers on tap. In addition to the covered patio (the best place to sit on sunny days and balmy evenings), there's seating in the cozy bar area and the dining room with a fireplace. Come here with a big appetite and don't be afraid to request a doggie bag. ◆ German ◆ Daily, lunch and dinner. 2253 Sunset Cliffs Blvd (between Voltaire St and W Point Loma Blvd). 224.0606

63 SOUTH BEACH BAR & GRILLE

★$ The windows by the bar look out across the parking lot to the ocean and right onto the sidewalk, allowing patrons to visit with friends passing by without even leaving their stools. The fish tacos and oyster shooters are good and popular with the beach crowd. ◆ American ◆ Daily, lunch and dinner. 5059 Newport Ave (between Bacon and Abbott Sts). 226.4577 ♿

63 SAPPORO JAPANESE RESTAURANT

★★$ Drop by this tiny dining room for tasty, very reasonable Japanese fare—sushi, teriyaki chicken, tempura, and assorted noodle dishes are all specialties of the house. Combo meals generally include miso soup and a salad,

NATURE'S CALENDAR

San Diego's seasonal changes are subtle and even invisible to the untrained eye until a few years have gone by. Then, it slowly sinks in. Winter means whales; spring brings flowers and showers; summer belongs to the beach. Check out these signs when you visit.

January

Over 10,000 gray whales migrate past San Diego on their way from the Bering Strait to **Baja California**. Whales' spouts can be spotted from **Point Loma**, **Sunset Cliffs**, and whale-watching boats.

February

More whales, rough seas, and cold nights—sometimes as low as 50 degrees! There's the possibility of snow in the mountains, which causes bumper-to-bumper traffic on mountain roads as San Diego natives race to get a peek at winter.

March

If it's going to rain, this is the most likely time. In March 1991, the city got 7 inches of precipitation all at once—that's almost the normal annual rainfall.

April

Ocotillo and other cacti bloom in the **Anza-Borrego Desert**.

May

Wild lilacs bloom along mountain roads; tulip and daffodil bulbs are coaxed into production; orange blossoms fill the air with their heady perfume.

June

Jacaranda trees cast a feathery purple haze over neighborhood streets; June Gloom descends, covering the skies with gray clouds through most of the day; June bugs attack windows, lamp shades, and walls with their brittle shells; grunion season begins.

July

Skies clear for the fireworks; the ocean temperature reaches the high 60s; brush and forest fires fill the skies with smoke and soot.

August

The Perseid meteor showers fill the back-country skies with streaks of shooting stars; drive to **Sunrise Highway** near **Mount Laguna** and set out your beach chair in an empty field for the show.

September

Ocean temperatures hit the mid-70s; the kids are back in school, and the beaches are nearly empty; hot, dry Santa Ana winds blow at 40–50 mph, challenging drivers to stay in their lanes; apples ripen in **Julian**.

October

Golden leaves and bushels of acorns fall from the oak trees in the **Cuyamaca**, **Palomar**, and **Laguna Mountains**; coastal fogs are so thick you can hear the foghorns for miles.

November

Expect the Taurid meteor showers (see August); red and white poinsettias bloom in front yards all over town.

December

Ocean waves are whipped by the winds into whitecaps, and wool sweaters actually get some wear.

making them an especially good buy for foodies on a budget. ♦ Japanese/sushi ♦ M-F, lunch; daily, dinner. 5049 Newport Ave (between Bacon and Abbott Sts). 222.6686

63 SOUTHCOAST SURF SHOP

This is possibly the best shop in San Diego for surfboards, boogie boards, wet suits, and all the appropriate gear for the hang-ten set; there's also a great selection of beach wear and T-shirts. ♦ Daily. 5023 Newport Ave (between Bacon and Abbott Sts). 223.7017

63 THE BLACK

The 1960s are alive and well in this head shop reeking of incense and patchouli oil. Drug paraphernalia is *verboten* in San Diego these days, but this shop still has an impressive collection of bongs, pipes, roach clips, and rolling papers—presumably for use by tobacco smokers. There's lots of other merchandise as well, ranging from clothing and jewelry to posters, magazines, and a huge selection of beads (for creating your own jewelry). ♦ Daily. 5017 Newport Ave (between Bacon and Abbott Sts). 222.5498

64 GOLDEN SEASHELL

The selection of silver and gold charms at this small jewelry shop is worth perusing, especially if you're looking for a sea-motif gift, like a sterling silver manta ray or a marlin in 14-karat gold. ♦ M-Sa. 4920 Newport Ave (between Cable and Bacon Sts). 225.0481

Restaurants/Clubs: Red | Hotels: Purple | Shops: Orange | Outdoors/Parks: Green | Sights/Culture: Blue

64 LITTLE CHEF

★$ An OB institution for cheap breakfasts, this eatery now also offers pretty good American, Greek, and Chinese dishes. Try the omelette with feta cheese and tomatoes, or the dependable burgers, but skip the Greek salad. The Chinese take-out counter offers good *kung pao* chicken and other standards. ◆ International ◆ Daily, breakfast, lunch, and early dinner. 4902 Newport Ave (between Cable and Bacon Sts). 222.3255

65 IN HARMONY HERBS AND SPICES

Stop in this unusual little shop for an incredible selection of spices, seeds, herbs (for cooking or medicinal purposes), aromatherapy products, herbal extracts, and books. Live herb plants, some of them rare or hard to find, are also available for gardeners. Definitely an OB treasure, with savvy staffers and some fun and unusual gift items. ◆ M-Sa. 4808 Santa Monica Ave (between Sunset Cliffs Blvd and Cable St). 223.8051. www.inharmonyherbs.com

66 OCEAN BEACH INTERNATIONAL HOSTEL

$ Also called the OBI Hostel, this is the latest incarnation of the old **Newport Hotel**. The hostel (not affiliated with American Youth Hostels) has 60 beds, a kitchen and lounge for guests' use, and a great front porch for watching the street action. Passports or other ID are required, to keep out the riffraff tired of sleeping on the beach. Also, only international travelers are accepted; you'll need to have proof of travel, such as current visas, international travel tickets, or foreign ID cards. ◆ 4961 Newport Ave (between Cable and Bacon Sts). 223.SURF, 800/339.SAND; fax 223.7881. obihostel@aol.com

66 PACIFIC SHORES BAR

Aficionados of dive beach bars need look no farther than the kidney-shaped table embedded with seashells and kelp near the front door. Order a round of Schlitz and shots of Rock & Rye, punch up a Frankie Laine tune on the jukebox, and pretend you're a beach bum circa 1950. For a change of flavor, arrive late at night on a weekend and mingle with a young crowd more into martinis, multiple piercings, and modern music. ◆ Daily. 4927 Newport Ave (between Cable and Bacon Sts). 223.7549

66 OB ATTIC

Among the proliferation of antiques shops along Newport Avenue, this shop stands out for its low prices on items such as garish lamps and used furniture. ◆ Daily. 4921

Newport Ave (between Cable and Bacon Sts). 223.5048

67 NEWPORT AVENUE ANTIQUE CENTER

Locals mourn the demise of **Coronet**, the classic five-and-dime store that closed on this spot in 1993. Its place was soon taken by yet another antiques emporium, this one divided into sections for dozens of different vendors, some selling treasures and some selling junk. ◆ Daily. 4864 Newport Ave (between Sunset Cliffs Blvd and Cable St). 222.8686

67 NEWPORT AVENUE ANTIQUES

Just across the parking lot from **Newport Avenue Antique Center** (see above), this shop offers a nice diversity of items, from Victoriana to Asian furniture. ◆ Daily. 4836 Newport Ave (between Sunset Cliffs Blvd and Cable St). 224.1994

67 ORTEGA'S

★★$$ One of the best Mexican restaurants in all San Diego, this family-run place is usually packed. With only a handful of tables and a small counter, expect a wait during peak hours—then dig into excellent dishes such as tamales, enchiladas, *huevos rancheros*, *tortas* (sandwiches), and daily fresh fish specials. Don't miss the fresh lemonade. ◆ Mexican ◆ Daily, breakfast, lunch, and dinner. 4888 Newport Ave (between Sunset Cliffs Blvd and Cable St). 222.4205

68 POMA'S

★★$ Leonard Poma tried to give up his sub shop and retire to Hawaii, but he couldn't stay away from OB. When he returned, the word spread quickly—aided by enormous signs hanging from the small shop proclaiming "Leonard's Back!" Soon the hungry hordes clamored for Leonard's subs: the Newport packed with cold cuts and cheese, the hot roast beef, the salami, the pastrami, and the mortadella. Thick-crusted pizzas are piled high with toppings, and the antipasto has plenty of marinated vegetables, oil-cured olives, and lip-puckering peppers. There are tables and a TV inside, but you're much better off taking your lunch to the pier or beach. ◆ Subs/Pizza ◆ Daily, lunch and dinner. 1846 Bacon St (at Niagara Ave). 223.3027

68 NATI'S MEXICAN RESTAURANT

$$ A couple of generations of OB residents have grown up on **Nati's** Americanized Mexican fare. No, the cheese crisps and ground-beef tacos aren't particularly authentic, but prices are reasonable and the atmosphere is ultra casual, making it a popular spot for families with kids. Indoor and patio seating. ◆ Mexican ◆ Daily, lunch and

dinner. 1852 Bacon St (at Niagara Ave). 224.3369

69 GARY GILMORE GOLDSMITH

Gorgeous emeralds and pearls grace the display windows outside this elegant jewelry shop. The perfect souvenir might just be the OB charms with the peace symbol in the O (these need to be ordered in advance, as they're cast on-site). The jewelers will willingly indulge your fantasies with their trays of minerals and gems—everything from turquoise to fine diamonds—and their inspirations in jewelry design. ♦ Tu-Sa. 4857 Newport Ave (between Sunset Cliffs Blvd and Cable St). 225.1137

69 DAZE OF FUTURE PAST

Looking for that perfect satin bowling jacket or plaid shirtwaist dress to complete your 1950s look? This is the place to check out stacks of tacky shoes and accessories and rows of bizarre getups. The window displays are always completely garish. ♦ Daily, except M. 4879 Newport Ave (between Sunset Cliffs Blvd and Cable St). 222.0220

69 OCEAN BEACH ANTIQUES MALL

The displays alone are worth a visit, making you long for items you couldn't possibly adapt to your décor: gorgeous furniture, holiday ornaments, and plenty of objets d'art and vintage jewelry. ♦ Daily. 4847 Newport Ave (between Sunset Cliffs Blvd and Cable St). 223.6170

70 O.B. DONUTS

Local food critics always include this shop in their lists of San Diego's best doughnut makers, and with good cause. From the basic cake to the airy twists and rich buttermilk bars, these are some darn good doughnuts. The cheerful, hard-working family who runs the place also makes croissants, scones, and other pastries. ♦ Doughnuts/coffeehouse ♦ Daily. 1830 Sunset Cliffs Blvd (between Narragansett and Coronado Aves). 222.0298

71 SUNSET CLIFFS

Guess what you're supposed to do here? Focus your lens, brace your sandal-clad feet a few steps away from the crumbly edge of the cliffs, and press the shutter studiously as the orange ball sinks into the golden sea. Most town residents have a hefty portfolio of sunset shots. And it's pretty hard to resist. The setting is pure drama—the ragged edge of the continent battered by the spray of the wild sea. Since the turn of the 19th century, speculators and developers have coveted the cliffs. Albert Goodwell Spaulding, the sporting-goods magnate, attempted to tame them with studied civility in 1910 when he bought a dramatic chunk of hillside facing the cliffs and the sea. When the **1915–1916 Panama California Exposition** opened, so did Spaulding's Japanese gardens, with arched bridges across canyons dug by the surf, palm-thatch umbrellas shading benches on rocky points above the water's foam, and pebbled paths curving through gardens of serenity. Nature scoffed at the $2 million investment and blew the plantings away like shredded dollar bills. Be careful here: Don't become so entranced by the beauty that you forget your personal safety. The cliffs' edges are as unpredictable as the surge of water below and can crumble all too easily. Cliff rescues, complete with screaming sirens, whirring helicopters, and tragic consequences, are common—and largely unnecessary. Pay attention to signs warning you to stay away from the edges, and stick to populated paths. ♦ Sunset Cliffs Blvd (between Hill St and Point Loma Ave)

71 MILLS MANOR

You would expect the homes closest to **Sunset Cliffs** to be particularly elegant and grand, given the breathtaking view. John P. Mills, real estate salesman extraordinaire, certainly thought so in the early 1920s, when he hustled a lot for his imaginary residential community of winding paved streets and red-roofed, white-stucco homes staggering up the hillside above the Japanese gardens. Mills and his partners bought the land from Spaulding's widow, gave their new streets Italian and Spanish names, and hosted lavish gatherings to entice potential buyers. The centerpiece of Mills's development scheme is still an attention grabber, dwarfing its neighbors in both style and size. The 1926 pink-stucco, red-tile-roofed, 12-bedroom mansion was meant to rival any similar estate along the California coast. A wall partially hides the Corinthian columns and arched stained-glass windows of the main house; the adjoining 19-horse stable has been converted to a four-car garage with apartments on the second floor. Mills didn't have a lot of time to enjoy his palace (equipped with a $40,000 chinchilla rug, polished rosewood paneling, and hand-carved Italian furnishings): His development company ran smack up against the Great Depression. By 1929, Mills was destitute, and his development was never revived. The manor has had several owners since then; when last sold, it went for several million. It remains a private residence. ♦ Sunset Cliffs Blvd (at Osprey St)

Restaurants/Clubs: Red | Hotels: Purple | Shops: Orange | Outdoors/Parks: Green | Sights/Culture: Blue

LA JOLLA

L a Jolla can be thought of as a series of snapshots: a panorama of green palms and pines, turquoise sky and amethyst sea, white domes and red-tile roofs adorned with bougainvillea; an underwater closeup of an orange garibaldi surrounded by iridescent neon fish; a formal wedding portrait on the lawn of a seaside park; an action shot of a Frisbee in flight; a wide-angle view of surfers gliding on white foam toward a wall of sun-baked bodies on hazy brown sand.

It's an understatement to say that La Jolla is a wealthy community. It's hard to keep the dollar signs out of your mind as you stroll through the tony, eucalyptus-lined streets. La Jollans motor in Mercedes, Range Rovers, and BMWs. Their sweats are by Polo, their suits by Armani, their dresses by Yves Saint Laurent. Homes nestled in foliage line the coast and punctuate the palm-studded hills, boasting columned terraces and tiled swimming pools in glistening shades of blue. Much of La Jolla's character can be attributed to its founders, who understood the potential of the rugged coastline and chaparral-covered hills. Frank Bosford and George Heald of the 1887 Pacific Coast Land Bureau had the sense to lay out the streets of their new town along its natural lines, following the curve of the coastline with boulevards 80 feet wide. They planted 2,000 eucalyptus, cedar, and palm trees from the waterfront into the hills.

Ellen Browning Scripps gave La Jolla its soul. Scripps, who amassed a small fortune in the newspaper business, started buying land here in 1896, moved into her La Jolla cottage a year later, and immediately assumed the role of benefactor. Over the next 50 years, she gave the village a bounty of lasting gifts. With her brother and half sister, she funded the **Scripps Institution of Oceanography (SIO)**. She created the **Children's Pool** south of **La Jolla Bay** and donated much of **Torrey Pines Park** to the city. Employing architect **Irving Gill**, she started **Bishop's School** and **La Jolla Recreation Center**, the **Wisteria Cottage**, and the **Woman's Club House**. With **Louis Gill** (Irving's nephew), she added a bell tower to **St. James-by-the-Sea Episcopalian Church**. This cluster of Gill buildings and vast, undisturbed lawns is a treasured cultural zone, protected by Scripps's wise investments and good taste. In 1927 La Jollans gratefully dedicated their most picturesque park to Ellen Scripps on her 91st birthday. The Monterey cypress that twists and bends around the simple brick marker bearing her name was planted in 1936 in a posthumous celebration of her 100th birthday.

La Jolla's heart is the **Village**, roughly delineated by **Pearl Street** to the south, **Prospect Street** to the north, **Torrey Pines Road** to the east, and the rugged coast to the west. Within these boundaries are **La Jolla Cove** and **Scripps Park**, and the restaurants, shops, galleries, and glamour that entrance visitors and make this such a perfect neighborhood for simply strolling about. North of the cove is **La Jolla Shores**, a long stretch of waves on sand. Early La Jollans dreamed of establishing a yacht club here, but F.W. Kellogg realized the folly of the scheme (boats couldn't moor along the open coast) and established **La Jolla Beach & Tennis Club** in 1935, a members-only establishment now run by his descendants. In 1951 Florence Scripps Kellogg donated a large park north of the club to the city; **Kellogg Park** now borders a long beach unequaled by any other in San Diego. **Scripps Pier** is the shore's northern boundary, where the sandstone cliffs prevent further coastline development.

To the east lies the La Jolla of the future—the **University of California, San Diego (UCSD)** and the **Golden Triangle**. Largely undeveloped until the late 1970s, the Golden

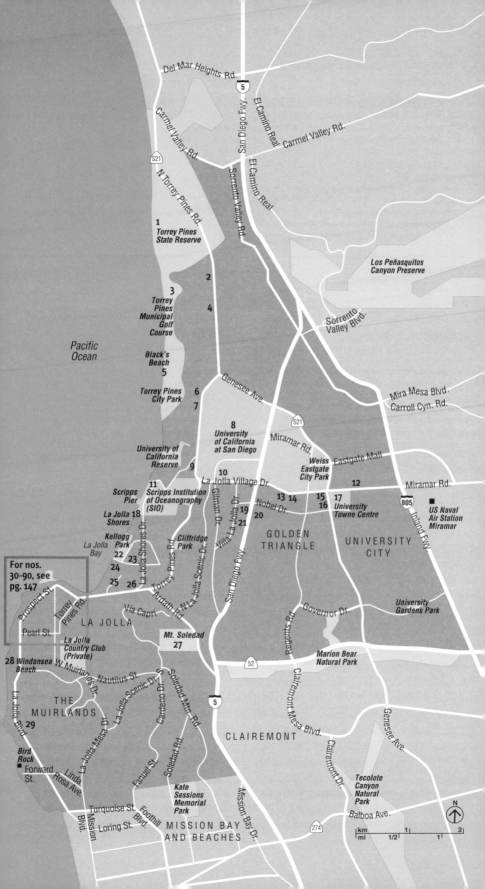

Del Mar Heights Rd.

5

San Diego Fwy.

El Camino Real

Carmel Valley Rd.

Carmel Valley Rd.

S21

N Torrey Pines Rd.

El Camino Real

Sorrento Valley Rd.

Los Peñasquitos
Canyon Preserve

1
Torrey Pines
State Reserve

2

Sorrento
Valley Blvd.

3
Torrey
Pines
Municipal
Golf
Course

4

*Pacific
Ocean*

Black's
Beach
5

Genesee Ave.

Mira Mesa Blvd.
Carroll Cyn. Rd.

Torrey Pines
City Park

6

7

S21

Miramar Rd.

8
University
of California
at San Diego

Weiss
Eastgate
City Park

Eastgate Mall

Miramar Rd.

University of
California
Reserve

9

La Jolla Village Dr.

10

Gilman Dr.

12

805

US Naval
Air Station
Miramar

11
Scripps
Pier

Scripps Institution
of Oceanography
(SIO)

13 14

15

16

17 University
Towne Centre

Nobel Dr.

La Jolla Dr.

19

20

*La Jolla
Shores*

18

Cliffridge
Park

21

GOLDEN
TRIANGLE

UNIVERSITY
CITY

Villa La Jolla Dr.

*La Jolla
Bay*

Kellogg
Park

22

23

24

25

26

La Jolla Shores Dr.

Torrey Pines Rd.

N La Jolla Scenic Dr.

For nos.
30-90, see
pg. 147

Ardath Rd.

San Diego Fwy.

University
Gardens Park

Via Capri

Governor Dr.

Prospect St.

Torrey
Pines Rd.

LA JOLLA

Regents Rd.

Pearl St.

La Jolla
Country Club
(Private)

Mt. Soledad
27

52

Marion Bear
Natural Park

28 Windansea
Beach

W. Muirlands Dr.

Nautilus St.

5

Clairemont Mesa Blvd.

THE
MUIRLANDS

La Jolla Scenic Dr.

Soledad Mtn. Rd.

Cardeno Dr.

La Jolla Blvd.

29

La Jolla Mesa Dr.

Soledad Rd.

CLAIREMONT

Clairemont Dr.

Genesee Ave.

Bird
Rock

Forward
St.

Linda
Rosa Ave.

Fanuel St.

Kate
Sessions
Memorial
Park

Mission Bay Dr.

Tecolote
Canyon
Natural
Park

Turquoise St.

Foothill
Blvd.

Mission
Blvd.

Loring St.

MISSION BAY
AND BEACHES

274

Balboa Ave.

N

km   1   2
mi   1/2   1

Triangle has been a challenge for urban planners, developers, and architects who have made the most of an area bisected by the eight lanes of traffic on **Interstate 5**. Whole new communities of red-roofed condos, towering apartment buildings, and family homes fill canyons where coyotes roamed not long ago, adding to the general sense of urban sprawl.

Visible from the freeway are architectural statements galore: Try to spot the **Aventine**, a complex of buildings that looks like a gigantic piece of burned toast. You can't miss the alabaster spires of the **San Diego, California Temple for the Church of Jesus Christ of Latter-Day Saints**. With the mishmash of building styles and burgeoning population in this area, there's no chance of mimicking the sedate cohesiveness of the original La Jolla by the cove.

All phone numbers carry the 858 prefix.

1 TORREY PINES STATE RESERVE

The twisted and gnarled limbs of rare Torrey pines stand like sentries atop the 300-foot-high sandstone cliffs at this 1,700-acre reserve between La Jolla and Del Mar. From the beaches below, the cliffs appear washed in shades of red, orange, and gold by the sun; from above, amid the centuries-old twisted trees, the coast appears untouched. Spanish explorers of the 1500s used the trees as a navigational landmark and called the hilltop, which stood out against the barren landscape, Punta de los Arboles (Point of Trees). In 1850, the *Pinus torreyana* was named by Dr. C.C. Parry, who discovered the tree to be indigenous to only two small areas in San Diego and on Santa Rosa Island, part of the Channel Islands southwest of Santa Barbara. From that time on, San Diegans have fought to preserve the trees and their rugged habitat. This reserve was established in 1921, under the protection of Guy L. Fleming, who lived here and tended to the pines until his death in 1960. The **Guy Fleming Trail**, winding through the pine groves overlooking the sea, is his tribute. The adobe lodge used as the park headquarters was built in 1922 as a gift from Ellen Browning Scripps. Combine a day at **Torrey Pines Beach**—one of the prettiest in the county—with a late-afternoon hike up the park road to the top of the cliffs, where sunsets are always spectacular. ◆ Admission and parking fee. Torrey Pines Park Rd (between Callan and N Torrey Pines Rds). 755.2063

2 THE LODGE AT TORREY PINES

$$$ One of the most impressive redevelopment projects in the county has transformed the old **Lodge at Torrey Pines** into a stunning new world-class resort. Once a comfortable but unexceptional place to stay, the new Lodge is a fabulous sight to behold. Designed to pay homage to the early California Craftsman style of architecture, the buildings feature shingled exteriors, rich woodwork, and soaring ceilings. In addition to 175 elegant rooms and suites, the new hotel (built on 6.5 acres adjacent to the **Torrey Pines Golf Course**) features a full-service spa, two restaurants (including one that will specialize in seasonal and local products as well as California wines), a fitness center, and swimming pool. Guests can also take advantage of guaranteed tee times and special golf packages. ◆ 11480 N Torrey Pines Rd (between Science Park and Callan Rds). 453.4420, 800/656.0087, fax 453.7464. ᏻ www.thelodgeattorreypines.com

3 TORREY PINES MUNICIPAL GOLF COURSE

Golfers have good reason to drag out their games at these two 18-hole courses above the sea. The view is outstanding, and the winds create quite a challenge even for the pros who compete in the Buick Invitational held here in late January each year. ◆ Admission. 11480 N Torrey Pines Rd (between Science Park and Callan Rds). 453.8148

4 HILTON LA JOLLA TORREY PINES

$$$ The hotel's low profile is nearly invisible from Torrey Pines Road; all you can see is a driveway leading to the pay garage (there is no free parking, by the way). Walk through to the back of the hotel, however, and you get a panoramic, wide-screen view of a wild, windswept bluff above the open sea. To the north is **Torrey Pines Municipal Golf Course**,

THE BEST

Jack O'Brien
Artistic Director, Old Globe Theatre

San Diego is dependent only on the imagination and the desire of the person surrounded by it. Sports enthusiast? Try for tickets to a **Chargers** game and tailgate with the rest of the crazies, or if you are a golfer, golf courses are to San Diego what restaurants are to New York—a different one for every day of the year!

Sightseer? Try Sunday morning on the **Boardwalk** at **Mission Beach**, and watch for the rollerbladers; or drive out to the end of **Point Loma** to the **Cabrillo Monument** and let the harbor take your breath away. Drive across the **Coronado Bridge** and either have a sunset drink at **Peohe's** or go Sunday morning for brunch at the famed **Hotel del Coronado**.

How about cuisine? Play "Italian roulette" either with the downtown swirl at **Fio's** in the **Gaslamp**—and cross the street to **Croce's** for great music afterwards!—or twilight above **Del Mar** at **Il Fornaio**. And still the best fish in the area, for my money, is **Cafe Pacifica** in **Old Town**.

See? I haven't even *mentioned* **Sea World** or the **zoo** yet!

which provides a backdrop of immaculate lawns and wind-twisted trees for the angular white lines of the hotel, designed by **Welton Becket** in 1989. Jutting balconies afford private views of formal gardens, rugged bluffs, and open ocean. Interiors rich in cherry wood, granite, and marble emphasize the hotel's elegance—this 400-room hotel has butlers on every floor, 24-hour concierge and room service, and limousine transportation. The restaurant here does an admirable job and is particularly popular for its upscale Sunday brunch. ♦ 10950 North Torrey Pines Rd (between Science Park and Callan Rds). 558.1500, 800/445.8667; fax 450.4584

5 BLACK'S BEACH

Prior to 1978, this was San Diego's only legal nude beach, and hordes of sun worshipers braved the arduous climb down steep cliffs to reach the sands where they could strip and sunbathe, body surf, and leap after volleyballs in the buff. It's no longer a *legal* nude beach, but that doesn't stop devotees from dropping their drawers, and regulars have established a system of warning signals when the law arrives. Access to the beach is difficult and should be attempted only by those accustomed to steep climbs. Stick to the well-traveled paths that lead down the cliffs just north of the gliderport, or walk south about 1.5 miles along the sand from **Torrey Pines State Beach**. Don't try to make your way down the cliffs alone; lifeguards and paramedics have performed enough cliff rescues here. ♦ Torrey Pines Scenic Dr (at Torrey Pines Rd)

6 TORREY PINES GLIDERPORT

Hang gliders seem to leap effortlessly from atop the cliffs into the winds that carry them over the sea. Actually, it takes a considerable amount of strength and skill to guide the gliders into the updrafts and back to the top of the cliffs; landings on **Black's Beach** some 360 feet below the starting point are not uncommon. Pity the poor athlete lugging his or her gear back up those rocky precipices, and envy those who fly so grandly and land on their feet with aplomb. ♦ 10020 N Torrey Pines Rd (at Torrey Pines Scenic Dr). No phone

7 SALK INSTITUTE FOR BIOLOGICAL STUDIES

Engineer August Komendant called this an "Acropolis of Science." Jonas Salk said the building is "a living organism of artistic expression." Twin three-story concrete buildings face each other across a smooth travertine marble plaza broken only by a silver channel of water that flows toward the framed expanse of blue sky and sea. Architect **Louis I. Kahn** and scientist Jonas Salk combined forces to design an ideal environment for scientists to pursue their research. Architects **Anshen+Allen** designed a much-discussed expansion to Kahn's original buildings. ♦ 10010 N Torrey Pines Rd (between Torrey Pines Scenic Dr and Genesee Ave). 453.4100

8 UNIVERSITY OF CALIFORNIA, SAN DIEGO (UCSD)

Established in 1960, **UCSD** is one of the top 10 research universities in the nation, with a prestigious faculty that includes several Nobel laureates and 18,000 students. A large number of undergraduates go on to medical school, and UCSD ranks first in the nation in the percentage of undergrads who pursue doctoral degrees. It all takes place on a 1,200-acre spread of eucalyptus forests, canyons, and mesas that sprawls from the Pacific to the rim of the Golden Triangle. The university includes five undergraduate colleges, the **Scripps Institution of Oceanography**, the **School of Medicine**, and the

---

Restaurants/Clubs: Red | Hotels: Purple | Shops: Orange | Outdoors/Parks: Green | Sights/Culture: Blue

IN THE SWING

San Diego County and northern **Baja** combined have an extraordinary number of golf courses—at least 90 at last count—with more on the way. Duffers say it's the spectacular weather that makes them haul those cumbersome golf bags through airports en route to their favorite courses.

Golf also keeps San Diego citizens at work—Callaway, the second-largest golf equipment manufacturer in the country, is the leading employer in **Carlsbad**, with over 2,000 employees. A number of national golf tournaments are held in San Diego annually, including the February **Buick Invitational** PGA tournament at **Torrey Pines**.

San Diego Magazine readers voted the **Torrey Pines Municipal Golf Course** their favorite public course, which makes sense because it has spectacular views of the ocean and is regularly shown during frequent televised tournaments. Both the north and south courses offer several holes that border the ocean and include challenges such as deep canyons and heavy vegetation. The south course has been completely remodeled, with greens enlarged, 60 bunkers added, and tee boxes lengthened for championship play. For a list of all the golf courses in the San Diego area, log on to the web site of the **San Diego Convention and Visitors Bureau**, www.sandiego.org, and order the free golf guide.

School of Architecture. Despite the emphasis on the sciences, the university has historically attracted a brilliant roster in the humanities as well, including the late philosopher Herbert Marcuse; radical Angela Davis; writers Alice McDermott and William Murray; artists Faith Ringold, the late Italo Scanga, and Russell Forester; and musician John Cage. *Note*: When visiting the university by car, be sure to park in metered spaces or obtain a parking permit from one of the university's visitor information centers. ◆ N Torrey Pines Rd (between La Jolla Village Dr and Genesee Ave). 534.8273

Within UCSD:

SOCIAL SCIENCES AND HUMANITIES LIBRARY

The tiered, steep pyramid of glass cubes rising from a two-story concrete pedestal has become both a beloved and abhorred landmark on the campus since it was first designed in the late 1960s by **William Peirera** and opened in 1977. But it is so much a part of the campus that architect **Gunner Birkerts** was required to set a 1992 expansion around and under the pedestal, making it, in effect, a nonbuilding. The addition is nearly hidden by landscaping, leaving the library's image as a hovering spaceship intact. ◆ M-Th, 8AM-midnight; F, 8AM-6PM; Sa, 10AM-6PM; Su, 10AM-midnight. 534.3339

UNIVERSITY BOOKSTORE

Book lovers from throughout San Diego visit this enormous bookstore for its excellent selection, housed in the **Price Center**, designed by **Kaplan McLaughlin Diaz**.

Opened in 1988, the center also has study lounges, a ballroom, a recreation room with wide-screen TV, video games, pool tables, fast-food outlets, and offices for student organizations. ◆ M-Sa. 534.READ

STUART COLLECTION

Thanks to arts patron James DeSilva, commissioned works of art are spread throughout the 1,200-acre campus—in eucalyptus groves and lawns and even atop buildings. The 11 pieces of sculpture include Terry Allen's *Talking Trees*, three lead-covered eucalyptus trees that stand initially unnoticeable near the library. Passersby are more likely to hear the trees before they see them, and the sound of a tree "reciting" Aztec poetry or country-western songs startles the unsuspecting. Sculptor Robert Irwin wrapped sections of another eucalyptus grove with blue-violet, plastic-coated, small-gauge chain-link fencing atop 25-foot-high stainless steel poles; French artist Niki de Saint Phalle built a 14-foot fiberglass *Sun God* that stands on top of a 15-foot ivy-laced arch in a grassy park near the **Mandeville Auditorium**. The Scottish avant-garde gardener Hamilton Finlay created a park with chiseled stone benches and bird-baths shaped like aircraft carriers, and Jenny Holzer engraved a massive green granite table with thought-provoking quotes. ◆ For a map of the collection, write to the Stuart Collection, UCSD B-027, La Jolla, CA 92093, or call 534.2117

9 STEPHEN BIRCH AQUARIUM-MUSEUM

Opened in 1992, this 49,000-square-foot, $14 million facility replaced the beloved, ramshackle **Scripps Aquarium** that had entertained and educated hundreds of thousands of visitors since 1950. The current museum, designed by San Diego architects **Wheeler, Wimer, Blackman & Associates**, sits on a bluff above La Jolla Shores and has 33 tanks filled with lobsters, octopus, eels, sharks, and all the colorful creatures that keep us fascinated with underwater realms. An outdoor tide pool displays the starfish, urchins, anemones, and crabs like those found on San Diego's beaches during low tide, and the museum includes interactive displays explaining tides, waves, and earthquakes. The museum runs educational programs and great field trips, including visits to tide pools, snorkeling excursions, and specimen collecting in Mission Bay. The bookshop has an imaginative collection of sea-life–oriented gifts. ◆ Admission. Daily. 2300 Expedition Way (at N Torrey Pines Rd). 534.3474 ᴖ

10 LA JOLLA PLAYHOUSE

San Diego's reputation as a center for theater has been bolstered by this playhouse, formally called the **Mandell Weiss Center for the Performing Arts**. The summer season has become nationally known for its elaborate and innovative sets and its eclectic selection of plays. It was established in 1947 by the **Actors Company**, a repertory company founded by San Diegan Gregory Peck and Hollywood friends Dorothy McGuire and Mel Ferrer, using a high school auditorium on Nautilus Street. Peck and company staged a series of acclaimed plays for 17 years; then, in 1964, the theater closed down. It wasn't until 1983 that it reopened under the aegis of **UCSD**. Since then, several of its productions have moved east, to Broadway, including the rock musical *Tommy* and the more sedate *A Walk in the Woods*. The season generally runs from May through October; call ahead for exact schedule. ◆ Admission. 2910 La Jolla Village Dr N (between Gilman Dr and Torrey Pines Rd). 550.1070

11 SCRIPPS INSTITUTION OF OCEANOGRAPHY (SIO)

The **Scripps Pier**, where biologists have run all sorts of unusual experiments, has been a local landmark since 1916, when Ellen Browning Scripps established an endowment fund for the institution. The pier was replaced by a new one in 1987–1988 and renamed the **Ellen Browning Scripps Memorial Pier**—yet another testament to a beloved benefactor. Currently the largest and oldest oceanographic institution in the world, **SIO** began as the Marine Biological Association of San Diego in 1903, when scientists led by Berkeley professor William E. Ritter worked

out of a boathouse and a wooden shack that they called the "little green laboratory." By 1910, the scientists had a permanent laboratory overlooking the Pacific. In 1912, the institute became part of the **University of California** system and was the first college to award doctorates in oceanography. It now has a staff of more than 1,200 biologists, oceanographers, geologists, and other scientists and support personnel researching the greenhouse effect, global warming, earthquake prediction, the marine food chain, pharmaceuticals derived from sea life, and other subjects. The campus on both sides of La Jolla Shores Drive includes one of the original 1910 **Irving Gill** buildings, a library by **Liebhard & Weston**, and a library by **Lloyd Ruocco**. ◆ 8602 La Jolla Shores Dr (off El Paseo Grande, a mile north of Torrey Pines Rd). 534.3624

12 EMBASSY SUITES

$$$ The Golden Triangle's most reasonably priced rooms are to be found at this chain hotel. All 335 suites have separate living rooms and kitchenettes and are as popular with business travelers as with families. Complimentary full breakfast and afternoon cocktails are served in the atrium lounge, and the **Coast Cafe** restaurant is one of the few places in the area open for breakfast as well as lunch and dinner. Facilities include a fitness center and indoor pool. Ask about special weekend and family rates. ◆ 4550 La Jolla Village Dr (between I-805 and Genesee Ave). 453.0400, 800/EMBASSY; fax 453.4226 ᴖ

13 THE AVENTINE

People either love or hate architect **Michael Graves**'s monumental attention-grabber on a hillside, rising above I-5 (and anything else in its way). Named after one of Rome's seven hills, it has been criticized for lack of harmony with its neighbors. The complex, which includes a 400-room **Hyatt Regency** hotel, an office building, an upscale health club, and a restaurant court, is an architectural landmark—one often compared to an Art Deco radio, a monstrous piece of whole-wheat toast, or a modernistic tombstone. Parking can be confusing: There is one enclosed lot on La Jolla Village Drive and another on Executive Way, and the hike from either lot to the restaurants can be lengthy. ◆ 3777 La Jolla Village Dr (between Regents Rd and I-5)

Within The Aventine:

HYATT REGENCY LA JOLLA

$$$ You can't miss the golden-ochre, crescent-shaped roof of this 16-story hotel

---

looming on the horizon, surrounded by rust-colored pillars and imposing lawns. **Michael Graves** went far beyond designing the façade, also acting as interior design and art consultant and even including his own paintings and sketches on the walls. Graves responded to developer Jack Naiman's challenge for a romantic designer hotel by blending neoclassical, Mediterranean, and Postmodern elements, using towers, campaniles, colonnades, and a collection of classical sculptures. The earth-toned stucco walls and rose, gray, and red Italian marble floors add warmth to the massive public spaces; white harem tents and terra-cotta pillars shade sunbathers by the pool; and palms are used inside and out. The 400 guest rooms have cherry wood furnishings with black lacquered designs that repeat the pattern of square glass panes on the hotel's exterior. The adjacent 32,000-square-foot health club has basketball, squash, tennis, and racquetball courts (there is an extra charge for guests to use the facility). **Camp Hyatt for Kids** offers activities to distract children from the opulence, though business travelers are far more prevalent than families. ♦ 3777 La Jolla Village Dr (between Lebon Dr and University Center La). 552.1234, 800/233.1234; fax 552.6066

CAFÉ JAPENGO

★★$$ This sleek and sophisticated dining room attracts office workers from the Golden

---

Theodor Seuss Geisel—better known as Dr. Seuss, author of *The Cat in the Hat* and *The Grinch Who Stole Christmas*, among other books—lived in La Jolla from the late 1940s until his death in 1991. He won a Pulitzer Prize in 1984 for his contributions to children's literature.

Author Raymond Chandler lived in La Jolla between 1949-1959. His novel *Playback* is set in La Jolla (called Esmeralda in the book).

My first impulse was to get out in the street at high noon and shout four-letter words.

—Raymond Chandler, on arriving in the genteel village of La Jolla

---

Scuba divers used to pry green and red abalone from under algae-encrusted rocks off La Jolla's shores. The meat itself is wonderful, but more beautiful are the insides of the shells, with opalescent bands of turquoise, rose, and green. Unfortunately, the abalone are now endangered and divers are forbidden to collect them.

Triangle, lots of good-looking singles from all over town, and the theater crowd headed for the **La Jolla Playhouse**. The most popular seats in the house are at the sushi bar, where everything is prepared to order. Other entrées include a succulent slow-roasted duckling, several different grilled fish dishes, and a filling 10-ingredient fried rice. The sushi bar is open until 11PM on Fridays and Saturdays. ♦ Asian ♦ M-F, lunch and dinner; Sa-Su, dinner. 8960 University Center La (between Nobel and La Jolla Village Drs). 450.3355

14 PALOMINO

★★$$ Just a few steps away from **Café Japengo**, this Mediterranean-Californian bistro attracts a lively, generally young crowd at lunch and dinner. Specialties of the house include hardwood-roasted salmon, crab cakes, assorted pastas, and a delicious bread pudding. Be sure to check the chef's daily menu, which stars imaginative preparations of local seafood and other products. The **Palomino** is a good spot for people watching, with seating at the bar and a front patio as well as the artfully decorated dining room. Californian. ♦ M-F, lunch; daily, dinner. 8990 University Center La (between Nobel and La Jolla Village Drs). 452.9000

15 COSTA VERDE CENTER

Another in the series of shopping malls that serve as the Golden Triangle's neighborhood centers, this one is significant for its wide range of great restaurants. The multilevel complex can be confusing, as it is completely oriented to the automobile and various parking lots. Shop and restaurant hours vary. ♦ Daily. Genesee Ave (at La Jolla Village Dr)

Within Costa Verde Center:

AESOP'S TABLES

★★★$$ Whether you dine in or order your dinner to go, you'll be delighted with the results. The Greek salads are legendary, and anchovy lovers will want to order the *horiatiki* salad, with chunks of tomato, cucumber, red onions, artichoke hearts, feta, olives, and salty anchovies. The gyros, souvlaki, *spanakopita* (spinach pie), and moussaka are all first rate, and the chef also prepares specials such as lamb shanks, fish stews, and an unusual Greek *pitza* made with pita bread and lamb sausage. Don't miss the baklava for dessert. Several small dining rooms opening toward a deli area and the open kitchen give a sense of privacy. ♦ Greek ♦ M-Sa, lunch and dinner; Su, dinner. Lower level. 455.1535 &

16 ROY'S

★★★$$$$ Part of an ultra-upscale chain founded by top Hawaiian chef Roy Yamaguchi, this restaurant specializes in a winning blend of

AVIATION IN SAN DIEGO

1883   The first controlled-wing flight is performed on 9 August by John and James Montgomery, who carry their soaring machine on a hay wagon to its first test flight in what is now known as **Otay Mesa**. John sits in the bicycle saddle between two 20-foot muslin-covered wings while James stands on the crest of a hill with the 40-foot towrope. At the signal, he runs downhill, pulling the 40-foot glider behind him. John glides to a graceful landing 600 feet away.

1922   The first airplane manufacturing plant is started by Claude Ryan on **Dutch Flats**.

1925   The first daily scheduled year-round passenger

airline is inaugurated when **Ryan Airlines** starts operating the **San Diego–Los Angeles Air Line**.

1926   San Diego becomes the first city to establish a municipal board of air control and issue a complete set of air ordinances.

1927   Colonel Charles A. Lindbergh starts his historic flight on 10 May in the ***Spirit of Saint Louis*** from a small private landing strip adjacent to the **Ryan Aircraft Company**. Lindbergh flies over **San Diego Bay** to **North Island** to refuel, then flies to New York and eventually across the Atlantic to Paris.

Asian, European, and Pacific Rim cuisine. Fresh fish in a variety of guises is always a good bet, but other top contenders include potstickers, grilled teriyaki scallops, roast lamb, and a delicious Mongolian pot roast. The vast, modish dining room, complete with exhibition kitchen, can be noisy, and the wine list is pricey indeed. Still, **Roy's** offers some terrific food (as well as a fun sake-tasting menu and cool atmosphere) for whenever you're feeling flush. If you'd like to watch the chefs in action, ask for a seat at the counter; otherwise, quietest tables are at the far edges of the room. ♦ Asian-fusion. ♦ Daily, dinner. 8670 Genesee Ave (near Esplanade Ct). 455.1616

17 WESTFIELD SHOPPINGTOWN UTC

Developer Ernest Hahn turned the shopping center of the 1960s into a faux center city when he built UTC on 90 acres of barren hillsides in the late 1970s. His mall begat the Golden Triangle, and ultimately became the commercial district for the sprawling, red-roofed condo communities and spiraling office towers that now fill the rolling hills between Interstates 5 and 805. But UTC is far more than a shopping mall. Its tenants include an indoor ice-skating rink surrounded by a video-game arcade and a food court with take-out delicacies from egg rolls to *spanako-pita*; a child-care center; the **Well Being Center**, with health education and exercise classes; a full-scale fitness center; a bank; four major department stores (**Macy's**, **Nordstrom**, **Robinson's-May**, and **Sears**); and enough clothing and specialty shops to keep those plastic cards shuffled. It's a great spot

for mall browsers, and those who know the layout well enough to park near their destination get in and out quickly. Developer Hahn went on to build downtown's fantastical **Horton Plaza** and the blessedly cool, indoor **North County Fair** in Escondido. ♦ Daily. 4545 La Jolla Village Dr (between Towne Centre Dr and Genesee Ave). 546.8858

18 LA JOLLA SHORES

The mile-long beach from the **La Jolla Beach & Tennis Club** to the 1,000-foot-long **Scripps Pier** is one of the most popular playgrounds in San Diego, offering plenty of room for scuba divers, surfers, boogie boarders, body surfers, swimmers, and toddlers running from the surf. **Kellogg Park**, the grassy lawn at the south end of the shores, was donated to the city by Florence Scripps Kellogg, niece of Ellen Browning Scripps and wife of William Kellogg, creator of the **Beach and Tennis Club**. Scuba divers enter the water here, headed for the underwater canyons offshore, and kids are quite happy at the playground by the sand. Lifeguards patrol the beach during the summer months, performing hundreds of rescues of unwary swimmers caught in riptides, unruly surfers in over their heads, and lost children wandering the shoreline. There are rest rooms, showers, and parking lots, all of which are full from dawn until dusk in the summertime. The best areas for solitude and tide pools are at the far north end of the beach, toward the **Scripps Pier** (see page 141). Keep an eye on the tides; you can easily lose your strip of sand and watch your towels get washed away when the tide comes in. ♦ La Jolla Shores Dr (between Camino del Sol and Scripps Pier)

Restaurants/Clubs: Red | **Hotels: Purple** | Shops: Orange | **Outdoors/Parks: Green** | Sights/Culture: Blue

19 SamSons Deli Restaurant

$$ Given the scarcity of Jewish delis in San Diego, this is a blessing, albeit an overpriced one. A Hollywood theme prevails, with the walls covered in celebrity photos and movie stills. The menu is traditionally lengthy—a dozen omelettes; lox and whitefish platters; eight soups including matzo ball and borscht; and mammoth pastrami, chopped liver, knockwurst, and kosher bologna sandwiches. A trip to the adjoining bakery for chocolate-chip *rugelach*, pumpernickel bagels, and lox should clean your wallet out. ◆ Deli ◆ Daily, breakfast, lunch, and dinner. 8861 Villa La Jolla Dr (between Via Mallorca and Nobel Dr). 455.1462

20 San Diego, California, Temple for the Church of Jesus Christ of Latter-Day Saints

Motorists on I-5 can be expected to gawk when they first see the 10 alabaster spires of this Gothic temple. A 10-foot gold-leaf statue of Moroni (the angel who spoke with the church's founder, Joseph Smith) tops the temple, designed by **Deems Lewis McKinley Architects**. When it opened in 1993, outsiders were allowed to tour its interior; now the temple is used only for special religious occasions and is closed to the public. ◆ 7474 Charmant Ave (off Nobel Dr)

21 La Jolla Village Square

When it opened in 1979, the mall was the only enclosed shopping center in San Diego—an idea that never took off. New owners took over the mall in 1991 and literally turned it inside out, updating the exterior façades and placing all shop entrances outside, close to the parking lots. High-priced tenants moved out and were replaced by low-priced mega-stores: a **Cost Plus**, **Trader Joe's** liquor and specialty food market, several discount shops, and numerous take-out food stands and restaurants. The mall has become a popular destination for neighborhood residents running errands and picking up dinner. Store and restaurant hours vary. ◆ Daily. 8657 Villa La Jolla Dr (between Via Mallorca and Nobel Dr). 455.7550 &

Within La Jolla Village Square:

California Pizza Kitchen

★$ This is a family favorite because of its hefty portions, inexpensive prices, and eclectic menu sure to please everyone. Finicky eaters can have pasta with plain tomato sauce; more adventurous types might like the Thai chicken pasta with ginger peanut sauce. Thin-crust pizzas for two have toppings ranging from pepperoni to pineapple, and the desserts get rave reviews from all ages. ◆ Californian/Italian ◆ Daily, lunch and dinner. 457.4222. Also at 437 S Hwy 101 (near Lomas Santa Fe), Solana Beach. 793.0999

22 Sea Lodge

$$$ Smack up against the sidewalk at the southern end of La Jolla Shores beach is an ocean lover's delight. The hotel, designed by **Liebhardt, Weston and Goldman**, opened in 1967; renovations have repaired any aging caused by the sun and salt air. The hotel retains a peaceful, colonial Mexican ambiance, with three-story, tile-roofed buildings encircling courtyards and fountains and open-air walkways offering sudden glimpses of the waves. The 128 rooms come in a variety of shapes and sizes. All have refrigerators, irons and ironing boards, hair dryers, and coffeemakers; some have full kitchens. Oceanfront rooms have wooden balconies as big as porches. Families check in for weeks at a time in the summer; the children's pool, beach, and nearby playground are big draws. But there's also a large contingent of business travelers combining work with time on the two tennis courts, in the fitness center, or on the beach. Book summer reservations early. ◆ 8110 Camino del Oro (between Camino del Sol and Ave De Vallecitos). 459.8271, 800/237.5211; fax 456.9346 &

Within Sea Lodge:

The Shores Restaurant

★★$$ Even if you're not staying at the hotel, stop in the oceanfront restaurant for inexpensive happy hour munchies, the daily breakfast buffet, Friday- and Saturday-night seafood buffets, Sunday brunch, or the early-bird dinner specials. The setting can't be beat, with a series of arched windows facing the surf, and the service is friendly, cheerful, and rapid. ◆ American ◆ Daily, breakfast, lunch, and dinner. 459.8271

23 Ristorante Piatti

★★$$$ You should definitely make reservations for dinner at this little Italian café, where trompe l'oeil murals enliven the Mexican-style rough-wood and tile décor of the dining rooms. It's so popular with the locals, there's rarely an open table. In addition to the attractive dining rooms, there's a plant-filled patio shaded by an enormous tree; it's a choice spot among La Jollans for an alfresco lunch or dinner. The open kitchen stimulates the appetite for pizza margherita, assorted panini (sandwiches), herbed bruschetta (grilled bread), and perfect rotisserie chicken. ◆ Italian/Californian ◆ Daily, lunch and dinner. Reservations highly recommended. 2182 Avenida de la Playa (between El Paseo Grande and Calle de la Plata). 454.1589

24 LA JOLLA BEACH & TENNIS CLUB

$$$ Stately palm trees gracefully outline the 22-acre oceanfront spread where the elite hobnob on 12 championship tennis courts and an immaculate quarter-mile beach. The club's facilities (including a heated 25-yard-long tiled pool and a pitch-and-putt course around a tropical lagoon) are closed to the public. The only way for nonmembers to use them is to rent one of the club's 90 hotel rooms. Back when cattle roamed free on this beach, some enterprising La Jollans decided to establish a yacht club and laid its cornerstone in 1927. The yacht harbor never materialized. In 1935, Frederick William (F.W.) Kellogg, a retired newspaper publisher from Pasadena who often summered in La Jolla, bought the property, envisioning a beach and tennis club. His son, W.S. Kellogg, took over in 1940, planted the palms along the club's entrance, donated 800 more palms to the La Jolla Shores community, and commenced to create a picturesque private enclave that remains the pride of La Jolla. ♦ 2000 Spindrift Dr (between Paseo Dorado and Ave de la Playa). 454.7126; fax 456.3805. www.ljbtc.com.

25 THE MARINE ROOM

★★★$$$ If you happen to be in town during high tide (the highest are in December and January), by all means stop here at least for a drink and the literally smashing view of the waves crashing against the restaurant's windows. This spot opened in 1941, and in 1944 guests were treated to a startling show of windows shattering against the force of the waves. In 1948 tempered glass was installed and withstood every storm for 35 years, until the window frames caved in during a 1982 storm. Thus far, the latest windows are holding strong. It's part of the **La Jolla Beach & Tennis Club** (see above) but is open to the public. The view even on calm days can't be beat, and the food—an artful mix of Pacific Rim, French, Mediterranean, and California influences—is consistently pleasing. Best bets include fresh fish and seafood, steaks, and the occasional wild-game specials. The service is courtly and gracious. All in all, a good spot for a romantic dinner or a special occasion. In addition to the main dining rooms, where just about every table has an ocean view, there's a cozy bar just right for sipping martinis at sunset. ♦ Californian/continental ♦ M-Sa, lunch and dinner; Su, brunch and dinner. Reservations recommended. 2000 Spindrift Dr (between Paseo Dorado and Ave de la Playa). 459.7222

26 CASA DE LAS JOYAS

Three white domes topped with what looks like a dollop of whipped cream rise above a red-tile roof on the west side of Torrey Pines Road, to your left as you leave the Village heading toward **La Jolla Shores**. The house is nicknamed Little Taj Mahal for its startling resemblance to the Indian palace, much admired by architect **Herbert Palmer**. Palmer intended to form a school of architecture on this hillside, with classsrooms by the beach. The school did not materialize. Instead, his 1927 house has gone through incarnations as a harem, casino, and smuggler's den; it's presently an enviable private home. ♦ 2040 Torrey Pines Rd (between Camino de la Plata and Lowery Terrace)

27 MOUNT SOLEDAD

For a close-up look at a real earthquake fault (**Rose Canyon**) topped by a 43-foot-high cross, navigate the winding roads to the top of the 800-foot-high hill, which is grandly called **Mount Soledad** (Spanish for "solitude"). Several crosses (including a flaming one, courtesy of the Ku Klux Klan) have stood atop the hill since 1913; the latest was designed by architect **Don Campbell** in 1954, as a memorial to servicepeople in the world wars and the Korean conflict. The cross itself is an ongoing subject of conflict and controversy over the separation of church and state. ♦ Soledad Mountain Rd (between Via Casa Alta and Via Capri)

28 WINDANSEA BEACH

If you're not accustomed to shooting the tube or riding the curl, you're best off staying on the sand at this serious surfer hangout. Strangers are barely tolerated on the waves but certainly welcome as admiring fans. Tom Wolfe memorialized the **Windansea** surfers of the 1960s in *The Pump House Gang*, graphically describing the shocking lifestyle of the Max Meda Destruction Company (MMDC), a group of surfers who hung out at a pink water-pump house facing the waves. Members were known to harass outsiders who attempted to set up their beach umbrellas on MMDC turf and were given to holding "conventions," or rowdy beer parties, and driving the neighbors mad. MMDC alumni and admirers still sport T-shirts and decals bearing the group's logo (though at the height of the group's notoriety, police were known to stop anyone who would so brazenly support the renegade tribe). The beach is much calmer now, but the waves are still wild. Parking is scarce, so be prepared for a hike to and from your car. ♦ Neptune Pl (between Rosemont and Fern Sts)

Restaurants/Clubs: Red | Hotels: Purple | Shops: Orange | Outdoors/Parks: Green | Sights/Culture: Blue

29 UNITED METHODIST CHURCH

These striking, cream-colored church buildings were once home to the San Carlos trolley depot (designed by **Eugene Hoffman**) and the **La Plaza** Mexican restaurant and **El Toro Bar**, favorite haunts of Raymond Chandler, Billy Wilder, and other La Jolla celebs. In 1959, church members remodeled the buildings into a sanctuary, library, and chapel (using the appropriate blessings to drive away any questionable spirits) and have since added on several buildings in faithful adherence to the original Mission-style lines and arches. ♦ 6063 La Jolla Blvd (between La Cañada and Mira Monte Drs). 454.7108

30 LA JOLLA COVE

Craggy sandstone cliffs edge this pocket of aquamarine water where bright orange garibaldi, iridescent pink and blue neons, and silvery swarms of smelt swim in an underwater preserve. On sunny afternoons when the underwater visibility reaches 10 to 15 feet, the sea's surface seems to be composed of human bodies, snorkels, and fins. The tiny beach fills quickly, and nearby parking spots are claimed by 10AM. Scuba divers hang out at the patch of grass above the stairs to the beach, near the showers and rest rooms. The flat-topped rocky ledges framing the south side of the cove are popular spots for photographers, sunset worshipers, and explorers examining pools of water for a glimpse of a sea anemone or hermit crab. Youngsters are often tempted to dive from the top of the cliffs to the water below—a very dangerous prospect which usually leads to serious injury. ♦ Coast Blvd (between Prospect St and Girard Ave)

31 THE CAVE STORE

Claustrophobes, beware! To visit **Sunny Jim Cave**, you must creep down 133 dark, narrow stairs—or you could swim a quarter-mile or so north from the cove. La Jolla has seven natural caves along the coastline, the largest of which is Sunny Jim. The land entrance to the cave is through this funky little store, which has assorted knickknacks and paintings for sale but no longer the extensive shell collection of years past. If you're wearing walking shoes, be sure to wander along the **Coast Walk Trail**, a dirt path which starts just past the entrance to the shop (it's marked with a Historical Landmark sign). Along the way, you'll get spectacular views of the ocean (and the multi-million-dollar homes nestled on the cliffs), as well as the shores north past La Jolla to Del Mar, Encinitas, and beyond. ♦ Admission to cave. Daily. 1325 Coast Blvd (off Prospect St). 454.6080

32 LA JOLLA COVE SUITES

$$ It's a miracle this 1950s-style motel hasn't been replaced by a $500-a-night penthouse palace. It's literally across the street from the cove, and it would be worth staying here just for the free parking. There are 117 suites spread throughout several squat cement buildings, furnished in a mishmash of colors and styles. There's a wide range of prices and amenities, from wood-shingled terrace condos with full kitchens and living rooms on a hill at the back of the complex to small studios toward the back of the complex. The ocean-front rooms on the top floors are the most expensive and desirable. All suites have kitchen facilities. The long, narrow pool, sundeck, and putting green sit on a strip of cement between the condos and hotel. A good-size, clean-looking launderette is available for guests. There's no restaurant, but a continental breakfast is served on the rooftop terrace every morning. This is one of the best places to stay if you're into sleeping to the sound of pounding surf and don't mind the less-than-palatial atmosphere. Book early for summer stays. ♦ 1155 Coast Blvd (between Prospect St and Girard Ave). 459.2621, 800/248.2683; fax 454.3522 &

33 PANNIKIN BROCKTON VILLA

★★$$ The tables on the front porch face the sea and are almost never empty. Breakfast selections include steamed eggs with feta or Jarlsberg cheese and the bagel-and-lox plate; lunch items range from light salads to stacked-high sandwiches filled with turkey, meat loaf, or other fresh choices. If the café is full, order a coffee and muffin to go and take them to the cove. ♦ Coffeehouse ♦ Tu-Su, breakfast, lunch, and dinner; M, breakfast and lunch. 1235 Coast Blvd (off Prospect St). 454.7393

34 RED ROOST AND RED REST

These two rundown brown-and-red cottages are smack across the street from the cove. Less romantic types might exclaim, "What a prime piece of turf!" Ongoing legal struggles over the cottages' historic status (they were built in 1894) have prevented the owner from replacing them, so instead they accumulate "No Trespassing" signs and continue to disintegrate. ♦ 1179 and 1187 Coast Blvd (off Prospect St)

35 ELLEN BROWNING SCRIPPS PARK

Washington palms nearly 100 years old stretch from **La Jolla Cove** to the **Children's Pool** (see page 151), curving in harmony with the bay's natural outline and framing lush lawns that cool bare feet. Walter Lieber, who first visited La Jolla in 1904, is credited with convincing his neighbors to clean up the area around the cove (which was littered with tents, bottles, and cans) and plant the palms.

LA JOLLA

But the park that eventually developed within the palms was named for Ellen Browning Scripps in 1927, on her 91st birthday. A Monterey cypress that has been twisted into dramatic contortions by the force of the sea winds was planted at the corner of Girard and Coast in 1936, again in honor of Scripps. A walk through this park is an essential part of any visit to San Diego. ♦ Coast Blvd (between Prospect St and Girard Ave)

36 939 Coast

This 17-story cliff of closed drapes and tiny balconies rose up across from La Jolla Cove in 1965, prompting outrage and a 50-foot height limit on any new construction in La Jolla. The apartment building is a private residence. ♦ 939 Coast Blvd (between Prospect St and Girard Ave)

36 Shell Beach Apartment Motel

$ Regulars settle in for weeks and months at the 45 apartment-like units with kitchen facilities and comfortably worn furnishings. Studios are available as well as one-, two- and three-bedroom suites. Families and retirees are

Restaurants/Clubs: **Red** | Hotels: **Purple** | Shops: **Orange** | Outdoors/Parks: **Green** | Sights/Culture: **Blue**

more common here than surfers or college kids. There's nothing pretty or elegant about the place, but the low price and proximity to the water more than make up for any shortcomings. Senior citizens and AAA members usually get a discount. ◆ 981 Coast Blvd (off S Coast Blvd). 459.4306, 800/248.2683; fax 454.3523

37 PROSPECT PLACE

The understated white arches and subdued signage at this shopping-dining-office complex designed by **William Lumpkins** in 1963 are far easier on the eye than the neon hype of the newer minimalls a few blocks away on Girard Avenue. Wander past the second-story galleries to the back balconies that overlook the coastline to La Jolla Shores. ◆ 1250 Prospect St (off Torrey Pines Rd)

Within Prospect Place:

GEORGE'S AT THE COVE

★★★★$$$ Gregarious host George Hauer greets old friends and initiates with the confidence of one who knows his guests will be more than satisfied with their dining experience. His restaurant is a consistent award winner for its cordial service, gorgeous view of the cove, and classic California cuisine—not to mention an impressive and eclectic selection of modern art displayed throughout the dining rooms. Try fresh saffron linguine with peekytoe crab, or Pacific swordfish garnished with grilled portobello mushrooms. Upstairs at the bar (always a lively place on weekend nights) and on the informal **Ocean Terrace** on the top floor, a more casual crowd watches the sun set while dining on pasta and fish. ◆ Californian ◆ Daily, lunch and dinner. Reservations recommended. 454.4244. www.georgesatthecove.com

AFRICA & BEYOND

This tiny shop is filled with wood carvings, bead work, garish masks, woven baskets, tapestries, conga drums, and xylophones. ◆ Daily. 454.9983

AZUL LA JOLLA

★★$$ One of La Jolla's prettiest restaurants, indoors and out, **Azul** offers ocean-view dining and capable California cuisine. In addition to the main dining room overlooking the sea, there's a sleek, inviting bar area and an outdoor patio complete with fireplace and additional views. Best bets on the menu are the herb-roasted sea bass, double pork chops, and any of the innovative appetizers. ◆ California/Mediterranean. ◆ Tu-Sa, lunch; daily, dinner. Su, brunch. 454.9616; fax 454.0934. www.azul-lajolla.com

38 TRATTORIA ACQUA

★★$$ Several restaurants have opened and closed in this location, down several flights of stairs in the **Coast Walk** building. This delightful trattoria opened in 1994 and deserves its many rave reviews. White-clothed tables are set in several dining rooms, along the patio, and in a separate gazebo overlooking the cove (views from here are the best in the restaurant). Highlights of the Mediterranean-based menu include osso buco, lobster ravioli, spicy seafood pasta, and lasagna with four cheeses. Panini sandwiches are both filling and inexpensive—try the grilled number with roasted peppers and mozzarella cheese or the excellent Portobello mushroom version. The tiramisù is not to be missed, and the wine list is excellent. By the way, if you're not up to taking the stairs, there's an elevator that connects the street-level entrance to the subterranean restaurant and parking lot. ◆ Italian/Mediterranean ◆ M-F, lunch and dinner; Sa-Su, brunch and dinner. Reservations recommended. 1298 Prospect St (off Coast Walk). 454.0709 &

39 TOP O' THE COVE

★★★$$$$ Table 6 should have a brass plaque bearing the names of couples who have become engaged while watching the sunset over the cove from this most romantic of settings. This wooden cliffside bungalow, originally built as a private home by **Thorpe and Kennedy** in 1893, has resisted the fate of its neighbors and remained intact. It became the **Top O' the Cove** in 1955 and immediately earned the title of "San Diego's most romantic restaurant." It's equally worthy for its cuisine. The menu is continental with California overtones, and the wine list has more than 1,000 selections. Everything is superb, and executive chef Alain Redelsperger has lightened and brightened the menu with influences from Asia, France, and the Mediterranean. If you're into a walk on the wild side, order the northern elk with Pinot Noir shallot sauce; tamer tastes might go for baked Chilean sea bass or seared salmon. Don't miss the chef's signature French toast with vanilla bean–custard filling for dessert. The second-story **Bar at the Top O' the Cove** was constructed against formidable odds in 1990. A crane with a 200-foot reach had to be used to hoist steel beams and posts above the Morton fig trees planted before the turn of the 19th century. A ramp leads from the street up to the bar, which, of course, offers a knockout

UP, UP, AND AWAY

Every evening near dusk (conditions permitting), the cloudless blue sky east of **Del Mar** is dotted with glowing hot-air balloons drifting toward the hills. One of the best views of this sky show is from **Interstate 5**, near the **Del Mar Fairgrounds** exit. Fortunately, traffic moves so slowly during rush hour that you'll have plenty of time to gawk and to dial the following companies on your cellular phone: **Skysurfer Balloon Company** (481.6800, 800/660.6809) and **Panorama Balloon Tours** (481.9561, 888/455.3592; www.gohotair.com). Vintage biplanes, including an open-cockpit biplane, are the specialty of **Aviation Adventures** (760/438.7680, 800/759.5667).

For an even greater rush, head to the **Torrey Pines Gliderpark** in **La Jolla**, where hang gliders step ever so gracefully from atop a 300-foot cliff and fly above the ocean, suspended from multicolored wings.

The ultimate in soaring sans machinery is in a silent sailplane swooping over back country valleys and hills, under the expert guidance of a pilot from **Sky Sailing** (760/782.0404) in **Warner Springs**. And should you care to do it totally alone, visit the parachute-jump range at **Skydive San Diego** (619/661.6671, 800/FREEFALL; www.airadventures.com) on **Otay Lakes Road**.

view of **Scripps Park** and the cove and a much more laid-back atmosphere than downstairs. ◆ Continental/Californian ◆ Daily, lunch and dinner. Jacket requested. Reservations required. 1216 Prospect St (at Ivanhoe Ave). 454.7779. rrz@topofthecove.com; www.topofthecove.com

40 ALFONSO'S

★★★$$ After you've window-shopped until you're ready to drop, plop your weary body down at one of the patio tables here and indulge in some of San Diego's best margaritas, corn chips, salsa, and marinated carrots. Still hungry? Try the *nachos con chorizo* (with sausage) lathered with sour cream, or the *carne asada* (grilled beef) burrito, a La Jolla tradition. The inside cantina and restaurant are dark and noisy, but the food is hearty and crowd-pleasing. And nothing beats a sidewalk table on a warm summer night for a real treat. ◆ Mexican ◆ Daily, lunch and dinner. 1251 Prospect St (between Cave St and Ivanhoe Ave). 454.2232

41 WINE BAR AND GRILLE OF LA JOLLA

★★$$$ Wines from around the world are sold here by the taste, glass, or bottle, along with gourmet fare such as Hudson Valley foie gras, potato-wrapped sea bass, and nori-crusted ahi. In addition to the chic, spare bar area, there's seating on the front sidewalk. ◆ Californian. ◆ Daily, lunch and dinner. 1271 Prospect St (between Cave St and Ivanhoe Ave). 456.0536

42 GENTLEMEN'S QUARTER

Drop by this upscale clothing store for the latest fashions from European designers such as Ermenegildo Zegna, Dolce and Gabbana, and Armani. Despite the name, both men's and women's clothing and accessories are sold here. ◆ 1200 Prospect St (at Ivanhoe Ave). 459.3351; fax 459.8581. sales@gentlemens-quarter.com

43 POMEGRANATE

Women delight in the one-of-a-kind hats, purses, jewelry, and dresses that make up the selection here. ◆ Daily. 1152 Prospect St (between Ivanhoe and Herschel Aves). 459.0629

44 CHOCOLATE FACTORY

Sugarholics can indulge their cravings here with frozen chocolate-covered bananas and caramel apples dipped in nuts or M&M's. There's also a great selection of sugar-free chocolates. ◆ Daily. 1145 Prospect St (between Ivanhoe and Herschel Aves). 454.0077

45 LA VALENCIA

$$$$ Beauty, elegance, and charm live inside the pink stucco walls of this property, known colloquially as La V. It has been the centerpiece of Prospect Street since 1926, when **William Templeton Johnson** designed the building. La Jolla brides and grooms pose in front of the many windows overlooking La Jolla Cove; neighborhood nabobs quaff martinis with their cronies in the woodsy **Whaling Bar**; stylish women lunch in the rosy glow on the patio. Summon your most refined attitude and walk through the wrought-iron gates, under the trellis, and into the lobby. Stunning views are everywhere: from the picture window in the richly appointed **La**

Restaurants/Clubs: Red | Hotels: Purple | Shops: Orange | Outdoors/Parks: Green | Sights/Culture: Blue

Sala room (where there's piano music just about every night) to the vistas from the main dining room overlooking the pool. Even the balcony in the women's rest room overlooks the sea. The hotel has undergone a complete remodel, refurbishing the 100-plus original guest rooms and adding a stunning collection of luxury villas just beyond the pool area. The 15 new villas each boast an ocean view, whirlpool tub, and king-size bed, and range from 400 to 1,200 square feet. Several have fireplaces as well, and personalized butler service is included for the duration of your stay. Rooms at the back of the main building are built into the hillside and overlook the hotel's terraced gardens and pool and on to the sea. Don't try to find floors numbered 1 through 3, however; owing to the way the hotel was originally constructed, they simply don't exist. ◆ 1132 Prospect St (between Ivanhoe and Herschel Aves). 454.0771, 800/451.0772; fax 456.3921. ໄ www.lavalencia.com

Within La Valencia:

THE SKY ROOM

★★★★$$$$ Situated on the top floor of the hotel, this 12-table dining room is one of the best restaurants in town. The 300-degree ocean view doesn't hurt, but it's the creative, consistently well-prepared fare that really makes the **Sky Room** worth a visit. Preparations range from updated French classics to imaginative variations on Pacific Rim and Mediterranean, with specialties including foie gras, Kobe beef, Dover sole, and freshwater prawns. Truly a special-occasion place, with a topnotch wine list and service that matches the elegant décor. ◆ French-Californian. ◆ Dinner, nightly. Reservations required. 454.0771 ໄ

46 16 ANCIENT MARINER

The window display of shells, fossils, and geodes stimulates the curious at this shop. Inside are fascinating finds like cauliflower coral, pencil urchins, fossils from Morocco, Indonesia, and Florida, and amethyst and quartz jewelry. ◆ Daily. 1137 Prospect St (between Ivanhoe and Herschel Aves). 459.6858

47 LA JOLLA INN

$$ This European-style inn, next door to the posh **La Valencia** (see above), has comfy sitting areas scattered throughout and a cozy lounge where guests can browse through magazines and books. It was formerly known as the **Prospect Park Inn**. Smoking is not allowed in the inn but is tolerated on the sundeck. The 22 small rooms have narrow balconies looking out to Girard Street and **Scripps Park**. Kitchenettes and weekly and monthly rates are available. Many of the guests are Europeans who return for their

annual La Jolla vacations. Continental breakfast, afternoon beverages, and parking are included in the rate. ◆ 1110 Prospect St (between Herschel and Girard Aves). 454.0133, 800/345.8577 in CA, 800/433.1609; fax 454.2056

hotelparisi

48 HOTEL PARISI

$$$ Sleek and contemporary without being cold, the **Hotel Parisi** is a hip alternative to La Jolla's older hotels. Situated just across from **La Valencia** (see above), the **Hotel Parisi** has 20 spacious rooms with soaring ceilings, restful neutral colors, and spare, sophisticated décor. Several of the rooms have balconies, and many offer delicious ocean views. Be aware that live music is often played on weekend evenings on the streetside courtyard under several of the rooms. The hotel is located over retail shops and galleries; climb the winding staircase to reach the inviting lobby centered by a fountain. Feng shui principles were used throughout the hotel; maybe that's why it feels so cool and comfortable. Complimentary parking and breakfast. No restaurant, but the hotel offers priority reservations at two of proprietor Sami Ladeki's nearby restaurants, **Roppongi** and **Sammy's California Woodfired Pizza**. ◆ 1111 Prospect St (at Herschel Ave). 454.1511, 888/4PARISI; fax 454.1531. www.hotelparisi.com

49 DANSK OUTLET STORE

Like the clean, stylish dinnerware and other items created by Dansk? Here, you can stock up on everything for your kitchen and dining table, from napkin rings and place-card holders to place settings, ceramic platters and jugs, wineglasses, acrylic ware, and holiday décor. The store specializes in selected seconds, overstocks, discontinued, and irregular (but good-looking) merchandise, so your savings can be considerable. Note: Although the official address is on Wall Street, the entrance to the store is on Herschel between Wall and Prospect streets. Chalk it up to a bit of quirky area character. ◆ Daily. 1044 Wall St, Ste. G (enter between Herschel Ave and Prospect St). 459.2655. www.dansk.com

50 MODERN DOG AND CAT

Stop by this fun, friendly little shop to find the latest gear for the well-outfitted pet, from intricate beaded collars to hand-painted food bowls and water bowls to scented shampoos and other potions. For owners, there are pet-print flannel pajamas and other whimsical gifts. Pet grooming available by appointment. ♦ Daily. 7932 Ivanhoe Ave (at Cave St). 551.9696; fax 551.2828

51 CHILDREN'S POOL

Up until 1997, when it was closed to the public, this calm and sheltered cove was home to snorkelers, swimmers, and of course, lots of children. Now, however, it's home to scores of harbor seals, who have effectively taken over the beach and waters as their own. Although the beach is closed to humans, you can still get a close-up view of the seals (which spend much of their time sleeping and sunning on the sand) from the breakwater wall and the sidewalks above the beach. ♦ Coast Blvd (between Jenner St and Eads Ave)

52 THE GRANDE COLONIAL

$$$ The dark polished mahogany and brass fittings of this delightful 1913 hotel make it seem as if it should be in Georgetown or London rather than La Jolla. The 55 rooms, 17 junior suites, and 3 one-bedroom suites have been completely remodeled in country florals and plaids, and have all the modern amenities. The designers incorporated many vintage touches, including antique furnishings, steam radiators, bathrooms with 1920s tile, and the original elevator. The best views are from the fourth-floor rooms at the back of the main building; the best setting is the 1913 wooden cottage surrounded by flowers and vines that's home to eight of the suites. All of the rooms have been designated as nonsmoking. Situated on a quiet block of Prospect Street, the yellow-and-white inn has a peaceful pool area in back, a genteel lobby and adjacent bar, and a bright, cheerful sunroom that can be reserved for meetings and banquets. ♦ 910 Prospect St (between Girard Ave and Jenner St). 454.2181, 800/826.1278; fax 454.5679. & info@the grandecolonial.com; www.thegrandecolonial.com

Within the Grande Colonial:

NINE-TEN

★★★$$$ Executive chef Michael Stebner has turned the former **Putnam's** restaurant into a stylish new dining destination frequented by the Who's Who of La Jolla. The menu, based on the freshest seasonal items the chef can obtain each day, ranges from soups and salads to lobster risotto, sautéed scallops, soft-shell crabs done tempura style, and duck confit. Both full and half portions are available, so you can choose to make a meal of several different entrees if you wish. For dessert, it's hard to beat a molten-centered warm chocolate cake. In addition to the dramatic-looking dining room and bar, seating is available on the sidewalk patio and garden-view terrace. ♦ California/French ♦ Daily, breakfast, lunch, and dinner. Reservations recommended. 454.2181

52 LIVING ROOM COFFEEHOUSE

★★$ Appropriately named, the coffeehouse is furnished with an assortment of couches, tables, and chairs set about a large, sunny room facing the sea (though you can only glimpse it between the rooftops). The décor is a bit funky by La Jolla standards but utterly comfortable for students and writers as well as families with young children. Bonus: the sidewalk patio is a dog-friendly place to sit with your canine companions. Choose from steamed eggs or bagels for breakfast, quiche or croissant sandwiches for lunch or dinner, or any of the tempting sweets displayed throughout the day. ♦ Coffeehouse ♦ Daily, breakfast, lunch, and dinner (closes at midnight). 1010 Prospect St (between Girard Ave and Drury La). 459.1187

53 JOSE'S COURT ROOM

★$ Casual, fun, and occasionally a bit rowdy, this place is a tradition among La Jolla's younger set, who gather for beers and great chicken burritos and *pollo asado* (grilled, marinated chicken breast) plates. ♦ Mexican ♦ Daily, lunch and dinner. 1037 Prospect St (between Girard Ave and Drury La). 454.1891

53 CARA

Women who travel frequently will be tempted to fill their suitcases with the easy-care, wrinkle-free clothing from this boutique. Many of the outfits come from India and Indonesia in colors and patterns guaranteed to hide spills and stains. ♦ Daily. 7938 Girard Ave (at Prospect St). 459.6618

54 THE ATHENAEUM

The original **La Jolla Library**, designed by **William Templeton Johnson** in 1921, and this building, designed by **William Lumpkins** in 1957, were linked together in 1991 with an unobtrusive design by **David Raphael Singer**. The complex makes an incomparable setting

---

for chamber concerts, lectures, and an impressive collection of rare books and manuscripts on music, architecture, design, and the arts. ♦ Tu-Sa; W, until 8:30PM. 1008 Wall St (between Herschel and Girard Aves). 454.5872

54 THE SILVER STORE

The name says it all: This inviting little shop carries everything silver, from imaginative jewelry designs and a variety of gifts for under $10 (napkin rings, candle holders, holiday ornaments) to elegant silverware collections in innumerable patterns. You can also stock up on basic flatware in stainless steel. ♦ Daily. 7909 Girard Ave (between Wall and Prospect Sts). 459.3241; fax 459.6773

55 LA JOLLA POST OFFICE

Outlying areas may claim to be within La Jolla, but the postal service knows better, and only those living and doing business within the village can have the prestigious 92037 ZIP code. They pick up their packages at this simple stucco, red-tile-roofed office (built in 1935) fronted by eucalyptus trees. ♦ M-F; Sa, 8:30AM-1:30PM. 1140 Wall St (between Ivanhoe and Herschel Aves). 454.7139

56 CASA DE MAÑANA

If you have to retire, you'd couldn't do better than in the utterly magnificent style at this Spanish-Colonial spread designed by **Edgar Ullrich** in 1924. Originally a coastal resort, the building was taken over by the Methodist church in 1953 and remodeled as a retirement home. It's a private facility. ♦ 849 Coast Blvd (between Jenner St and Eads Ave). 454.2151

57 GALLERY ALEXANDER

Browse among a colorful collection of works from contemporary American crafts artists. Over 600 different artists are represented by the gallery, and the exhibits change every 6 weeks. Of particular note: the classy-looking colored glass wind chimes, and the beautiful menorahs fashioned from such materials as glass, steel, and wood. ♦ Daily. 7925 Girard Ave (between Prospect and Wall Sts). 459.9433

58 TASENDE GALLERY

Since the 1990s, Jose Tasende has made a bold imprint on the La Jolla art scene, staging dramatic exhibitions of sculpture and drawings by Henry Moore, Jose Luis Cuevas, Eduardo Chillida, Isamu Noguchi, and others in his visually understated gallery, designed by **Robert Mosher** in 1979. When Tasende first came to town in 1979, he attempted to influence local culture by installing a Henry Moore sculpture at La Jolla Cove, but the public reaction was virulent. Ten years later he got the community's approval and support for an anniversary exhibition with nine large sculptures installed on the grounds of some of Prospect Street's most beloved buildings. The gallery's exhibitions focus on art of the post–World War II era, with group shows by such artists as Jiacomo Manzu, Andres Nagel, and Lynn Chadwick. ♦ Tu-Sa. 820 Prospect St (between Eads Ave and Jenner St). 454.3691

59 ROPPONGI RESTAURANT, BAR AND CAFE

★★$$$ Owned by Sami Ladeki, the successful restaurateur who also founded **Sammy's California Woodfired Pizza** (see page 156), Roppongi offers upmarket atmosphere and a trendy menu. The high-style dining room features booth and table seating (as well as a private room that can be reserved in advance) and is anchored by an eye-popping oversize aquarium. The fare is best described as Asian fusion meets tapas bar, with signature dishes such as kung pao calamari, a savory crab napoleon, and scallop satay. Out front, the patio centered by a fire pit is a favorite spot from which to watch the world go by. ♦ Asian/Pacific Rim ♦ Daily lunch and dinner. 875 Prospect St (at Fay Ave). 551.5252 ⑤

60 SANTE

★★★$$$ Two small California bungalows and a patio surrounding an old oak tree have been transformed into a romantic Italian eatery. Tony Buonsante operated Manhattan's posh La Fenice for 10 years before escaping to La Jolla with his recipe file. The homemade gnocchi are the house favorite, and the calf's liver is a pungent treat hard to find anywhere else. The host is very protective of his guests, and the dining room feels more like a private club than a public restaurant. ♦ Italian ♦ M-F, lunch and dinner; Sa-Su, dinner. Jacket requested. Reservations recommended. 7811 Herschel Ave (between Silverado and Wall Sts). 454.1315

61 WARWICK'S

Faithful patrons mill around the display tables and shelves for lectures and signings by local writers Judith and Neil Morgan, and out-of-town best-selling authors like Thomas Keneally, Amy Tan, and George Will. The intelligentsia of La Jolla orders its more obscure tomes here, and mainstream readers get valuable advice and suggestions from a knowledgeable staff. The bookstore has been in the Warwick family since 1902. ◆ Daily. 7812 Girard Ave (between Silverado and Wall Sts). 454.0347

62 GIRARD GOURMET

★★$ The crowds at the sidewalk tables and at the deli counter are a tipoff. In the morning, office workers stop by to pick up egg sandwiches and almond croissants, and the place really gets packed at lunchtime as regulars place their orders for gargantuan ham-and-cheese sandwiches, smoked salmon sandwiches, or BLTs; salad plates accompanied by homemade bread; or such hot specialties of the day as lamb stew, turkey stuffed with broccoli, eggplant stuffed with spinach and cheese, or tortellini marinara. The crowds pick up again in early evening as neighborhood folks stop by for gourmet dinners to take home. It's a great place to stock up on picnic supplies before a day at the cove. ◆ Deli ◆ Daily, breakfast, lunch, and takeout. 7837 Girard Ave (between Silverado and Wall Sts). 454.3321

63 GIRARD AVENUE SHOPS

La Jolla is one of San Diego's greatest shopping centers, and much of the action takes place on this stretch of Girard Avenue. One-of-a-kind galleries and boutiques are interspersed among upscale chain stores, including the **Gap**, **Gap Kids**, **Banana Republic**, **Polo Ralph Lauren**, and **A/X Armani Exchange**. ◆ Daily. Girard Ave (between Torrey Pines Rd and Prospect St)

64 MUSEUM OF CONTEMPORARY ART SAN DIEGO

It seems fitting that the former estate of Ellen Browning Scripps, designed by **Irving Gill** in 1916, is now La Jolla's cultural centerpiece. Since its founding in 1941, the museum has become San Diego's resource for innovative exhibitions of post-1950s art, and for its music and film programs, including the annual Animation Film Festival. The museum has undergone several changes in name and appearance and was closed betweem 1992 and 1996 for a radical renovation and expansion. Architect **Robert Venturi**'s design restores and complements the original Gill arches and cubes while expanding the museum to incorporate new exhibition space on the western side of the existing building, a large sculpture garden, more space for the excellent bookstore, and a café on Prospect Street. The museum's permanent collection includes works by Andy Warhol, Robert Rauschenberg, Frank Stella,

Edward Ruscha, Edward Kienholz, John Baldessari, Kiki Smith, and Agnes Martin. A second location in downtown San Diego presents temporary exhibitions and film screenings and has a branch of the museum shop. ◆ Admission. Th-Tu; closed W. 700 Prospect St (between Eads and Draper Aves). 454.3541. & Also at 1001 Kettner Blvd (at Broadway). 454.3541

65 JOHN COLE'S BOOK SHOP

Purple wisteria cascades over the yellow trellis above the path to the leaf-green **Wisteria Cottage** and an imaginative, captivating collection of books, cards, trinkets, and treasures. The cottage was built in 1903 or 1904, then purchased in 1905 by Ellen Browning Scripps and remodeled by **Irving Gill**. Scripps's sister Virginia had a passion for the color purple; she was responsible for the 60-foot-long wisteria trellis. The cottage hosted many famous guests, served as the temporary quarters for **St. James Episcopalian Church**, and was headquarters for the exclusive **Balmer School**, predecessor of the **La Jolla Country Day School**. The Cole family, who has owned the building since 1966, created a literary haven. Zachary Cole transformed a side room of the house into **Zach's Music Corner**, with an excellent selection of tapes and CDs. ◆ Tu-Sa. 780 Prospect St (between Eads and Draper Aves). 454.4766

66 ST. JAMES-BY-THE-SEA EPISCOPALIAN CHURCH

Several angular tiers of red-tile roofs cast shadows across the pale pink stucco walls of this imposing structure, where Deagan chimes toll the hour from a brick bell tower. The original church on this site was designed by **Irving Gill** in 1907. In 1928, **Louis Gill** added the tower (modeled after one destroyed by Porfirio Díaz's forces in Campo Florida, Mexico) at the request and bequest of Elizabeth Scripps for her sister Virginia. Six months later, the first building was moved and an entire new compound designed. Although the original church was soft and rounded with white arches, the new one was far more elaborate, with a peaked roof and inset cloverleaf windows. The chapel was donated by relatives of Scripps, who followed her commitment to sharing their wealth with La Jolla. A gift shop, which is open daily, offers a surprisingly eclectic selection of objets d'art and children's toys along with books and devotional materials. The church building is open each day; hours vary. ◆ 743 Prospect St (between Eads and Draper Aves). 459.3421

Restaurants/Clubs: Red | Hotels: Purple | Shops: Orange | Outdoors/Parks: Green | Sights/Culture: Blue

67 LA JOLLA VILLAGE LODGE

$$ This motor hotel, just a 10-minute walk from the cove, isn't fancy, but the rooms are worth checking out, especially if you're seeking reasonable rates. Good news for folks who travel with their dogs (or cats or parrots, etc.): It's a pet-friendly establishment. There's an extra fee of $20 (per stay, not per night), and owners are asked not to leave pets in the rooms alone. All 30 rooms have been remodeled in a cool gray-blue color scheme, many have refrigerators, and free parking is available right outside each room. Some of the accommodations are designated nonsmoking. There's no restaurant on the premises, but several are within easy walking distance. ♦ 1141 Silverado St (at Herschel Ave). 551.2001; fax 551.3277. www.lajollavillagelodge.com

68 LA TAVERNA

★★$$ This tiny Italian restaurant seats only about two dozen people indoors, but it's big on heart and style. The very reasonably priced lunches and dinners include excellent risottos (which change daily), superb salmon fettuccine with Parmesan cream, and hearty potato gnocchi served with Gorgonzola sauce. Don't miss the bittersweet chocolate layer cake for dessert. Additional seating is available on the sidewalk patio. Beer and wine are served. ♦ Italian. ♦ Tu-Sa, lunch and dinner. 927 Silverado St (between Girard and Fay Aves). 454.0100

69 LA JOLLA WOMAN'S CLUB

This elegant white building is one of architect **Irving Gill**'s purest designs, featuring simple arches and cubes framed by green lawns and modest shrubs. It was first called the **Reading Club**, then the **Literary Club**, and in 1902 joined the state and national federations of Woman's Clubs. Ellen Browning Scripps donated the money for the building, joining with Gill in 1914 to create yet another lasting landmark in her neighborhood. The building is open during club events and is a popular site for weddings and receptions. ♦ 715 Silverado St (between Eads and Draper Aves). 454.2354

70 COVE THEATRE

Dating from 1952, this is one of the few remaining neighborhood theaters in San Diego. The bill often includes new releases of foreign films. ♦ Admission. 7730 Girard Ave (between Kline and Silverado Sts). 459.5404

71 J&S BEAUTY SUPPLY

Locals and tourists alike love browsing the product-packed aisles here. There's an incredible array of beauty supplies, including hair and skin-care products, aromatherapy potions, makeup and hair accessories, and discounted designer perfumes in both regular and miniature sizes. This is a great place to stock up on fun and unusual gift items or special treats for yourself. ♦ Daily. 7734 Girard Ave (between Kline and Silverado Sts). 551.4056

71 SUSHI ON THE ROCK

★★$$ This trendy sushi bar is *the* place to go for California rolls, smoked eel, and red tuna sashimi, as well as less-traditional concoctions such as Monkey Balls (mushrooms stuffed with spicy seafood) and a variety of cooked Asian dishes. It's lively, generally packed, and noisy, especially on the weekends, so don't come expecting a quiet dinner for two. ♦ Sushi ♦ M-F, lunch and dinner; Sa-Su, dinner. 7734 Girard Ave (between Kline and Silverado Sts). 456.1138. sushiontherock@aol.com

72 WHITE RABBIT

A 4-foot-high, two-dimensional wooden *Alice in Wonderland* rabbit holds his trumpet aloft at the front door, beckoning diminutive book lovers into a fantasyland inhabited by Curious George, Babar, and the Little Engine That Could. The shop's newsletter has a nationwide circulation and includes reviews of current children's titles and an order form for easy shopping. Special events include frequent author readings and signings, and a children's storytime every Wednesday at 10:30AM (for kids over 3 years old). ♦ Daily. 7755 Girard Ave (between Kline and Silverado Sts). 454.3518, 800/920.9000; fax 454.5705

73 SCRIPPS INN

$$$ It's easy to miss this quiet, dark brown, 13-room bed-and-breakfast tucked in a corner of Coast Boulevard. Many guests check in for a month or more each year, taking advantage of the reasonable rates, parklike setting, and kitchen facilities. The best rooms are **No. 6** and **No. 12**, each with a fireplace and ocean view. Croissants from the **French Gourmet**, a nearby bakery, are served every morning in the lobby. Reserve far in advance. ♦ 555 S Coast Blvd (at Cuvier St). 454.3391; fax 459.6758

74 ADELAIDE'S FLOWERS AND GIFTS

White tulips, violet freesias, buttercup daffodils, and branches of lilacs, forsythia, and pussy willows herald the coming of spring from the fragrant sidewalk display. Inside, gorgeous orchids and bromeliads are tucked into crystal vases, bronze pots, and other attractive receptacles. Take a fragrant tuberose or two back to your hotel room. Or, for a souvenir that will last years instead of days, buy some of the gorgeous artificial flowers made with a variety of materials. Hint: A gift from this shop is always appreciated by San Diego hosts and hostesses. ♦ M-Sa; closed Su. 7766 Girard Ave (between Kline and Silverado Sts). 454.0146, 800/322.2771; fax 454.1474

75 MARY STAR OF THE SEA

For ecclesiastical beauty, few local buildings are as impressive as this Catholic church. It reigns over the shops on Girard Avenue like a California version of St. Patrick's Cathedral. The church was designed in 1937 by **Carleton Winslow** as a tribute to the early missions, and it manages to be austere and elegant at the same time. A mural above the church's front door was painted by Alfredo Ramos Martinez in 1937; by 1960, it had faded and aged irreparably in the salt air. The image of the Virgin standing atop rippled blue waves was reproduced in a tile mosaic installed in 1967. ♦ 7727 Girard Ave (between Kline and Silverado Sts). 454.2631

76 LA JOLLA RECREATION CENTER

The junction of La Jolla Boulevard and Prospect Street is one of the prettiest stretches of land left in the city, thanks largely to the beneficence of Ellen Browning Scripps, who donated the land for a community center. Amateur painters, potters, and poets practice their skills in the center's classrooms, looking out through classic 1915 **Irving** and **Louis Gill** arches toward vast lawns and shaggy palms. Children climb aboard dragons and butterflies in the playground, and the constant plop of tennis balls keeps a rhythmic sound in the air. In 1926, the schoolchildren of La Jolla supposedly donated one penny apiece for a monument to Scripps on the southwest corner of Draper Street. Sculptor James Porter created a bronze child kneeling on the ground, cupping water from a silken pond. ♦ 615 Prospect St (between Draper Ave and Cuvier St). 552.1658

77 BED & BREAKFAST INN AT LA JOLLA

$$ There is no better introduction to the **Irving Gill** era than this charming hideaway at the end of a flower-lined path. Gill designed the house in 1913 for George Kautz, and **Kate Sessions**, who designed much of early San Diego's landscaping, planted the original gardens. Gill's signature nooks and crannies and arched passageways have been incorporated into each of the 15 enchanting guest rooms, each with private bath. The **Pacific View Room** has a fireplace beside an antique

desk and wood-framed window that looks out to sea; the **Gill Penthouse** has an upstairs deck. Fresh fruit, a decanter of sherry, cut flowers, and terry robes are standard amenities; some rooms also have wonderful bathtubs perfect for a leisurely soak. Call for midweek specials. ♦ 7753 Draper Ave (between Kline and Silverado Sts). 456.2066, 800/582.2466

78 K. NATHAN GALLERY

California's own Impressionist period flourished in the early 1900s, giving rise to the gorgeous landscapes and ocean scenes featured at this small but fascinating gallery. Along with this selection of California plein air paintings, the proprietor has a number of other pre-1950s American works. Daily. 7723 Fay Ave (between Kline and Silverado Sts). 459-3490. www.knathangallery.com

OF LA JOLLA

79 ENCORE OF LA JOLLA

Treasured by fashion-conscious bargain hunters, **Encore** is one of the best consignment clothing stores in the county. This is the place to find gently used (or occasionally, never-worn) clothing and accessories from top designers. Although there's a small men's section, the two-story store (with discounted merchandise upstairs) is basically for women. The selection is incredible, as well as ever changing, as local socialites tend to drop off their party finery here after wearing it only once. Just about every designer imaginable is represented here, from Armani to Zegna. ♦ Daily. 7655 Girard Ave (between Torrey Pines Rd and Kline St). 454.7540.

80 THE CHOPRA CENTER FOR WELL BEING

Founded by Deepak Chopra, the well-known specialist in alternative medicine, this stately building houses a variety of mind- and body-oriented services. Classes include seminars in yoga, meditation, healing, wellness, and spiritual development and range from 1-day workshops to weeklong (or longer) programs. The peaceful and inviting day spa offers facials, massages, and body treatments using various oils, herbal wraps, and aromas. And the on-site **Store of Infinite Possibilities** sells books, CDs, candles, herbal supplements, jewelry, and a variety of other unusual products. All in all, the center is an oasis of

---

Restaurants/Clubs: Red | Hotels: Purple | Shops: Orange | Outdoors/Parks: Green | Sights/Culture: Blue

calm and thoughtfulness in an otherwise bustling community. Call or visit the web site for a schedule of classes and services. ♦ Daily. ♦ 7630 Fay Ave (between Pearl and Kline Sts). 551.7788, 888/424.6772. www.chopra.com

81 PORKYLAND

★★$ Yes, the name is strange, but the take-out Mexican food is *delicioso*. All you need is one taste of the *carnitas* or a tamale to forget such mundane concerns as fat and cholesterol. The fresh tortillas have replaced sliced bread in many a gringo household, and the *tacos al pastor* (pork with spices) will make you swear off burgers forever. Outdoor seating available in a tree-shaded courtyard adjacent to the parking lot. ♦ Mexican ♦ Daily, lunch and dinner. 1030 Torrey Pines Rd (between Herschel and Girard Aves). 459.1708

82 BISHOP'S SCHOOL

Ellen and Virginia Scripps donated much of the land and funds for this venerable private school, and successive benefactors, parents, and alumni have preserved the school's heritage. **Irving Gill** designed the first building in graceful Minimalist style. Then San Diegans became entranced with the more formal and decorative style used to create **Balboa Park**'s **El Prado** and hired **Carleton Winslow** to design a more ornate church and bell tower topped with a yellow-and-blue dome. The tower wasn't actually built until 1930, after **Louis Gill** had designed an addition to the original building, complete with a simple white dome, tying the two styles together and creating a picturesque landmark enhanced by blue skies and emerald green lawns. ♦ 7607 La Jolla Blvd (between Pearl and Prospect Sts). 459.4021

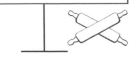

83 MICHELE COULON DESSERTIER

★★$ A gifted pastry chef, Michele Coulon makes some of the finest desserts in

Southern California. One bite of her Belgian chocolate torte, white chocolate mousse cake, or pleasantly boozy rum walnut torte and you'll be hooked. Her cozy café, furnished with antiques, makes a lovely place to linger over breakfast pastries or a light salad or soup for lunch. There's also a tree-sheltered patio for dining alfresco. And of course, you'll want to bring something home for dessert. Beer and wine are served. ♦ M-Sa, breakfast and lunch. 7556 Fay Ave in the Sycamore Court square (between Pearl and Kline Sts). 456.5098. www.dessertier.com

84 LA JOLLA LIBRARY

The village's original library has been mated with the **Athenaeum** (see page 151), and this new facility, designed by **Robert Mosher** and **Roy Drew** in 1989, reflects some of the style of the old with its red-tile roof and stucco walls. The inside, though, is purely modern, with 10,000 square feet of space devoted to efficiency and curiosity. ♦ Daily; hours vary. 7555 Draper Ave (between Pearl and Silver Sts). 552.1657

85 HARRY'S

★★$ This spot has been a popular breakfast institution since the early 1960s, and the banter behind the counter is heavily sprinkled with familiarity. The works of local artists are displayed and occasionally purchased. Your breakfast—banana pancakes, a bacon-and-cheese omelette, hot oatmeal with raisins—comes with an individual fresh-brewed pot of coffee. Lunch is served too, but people come for the breakfast dishes, which are served until closing. ♦ American ♦ Daily, breakfast and lunch. 7545 Girard Ave (between Pearl St and Torrey Pines Rd). 454.7381

86 COMEDY STORE

Up-and-coming and famous comedians perfect their shticks here before easily amused audiences. ♦ Admission. Shows: nightly; call for specific acts. 916 Pearl St (between Drury La and Fay Ave). 454.9176

87 SAMMY'S CALIFORNIA WOODFIRED PIZZA

★★★$ Try any of the 20 variations of gourmet pizza, including garlic chicken, duck sausage, and Jamaican shrimp with fire-hot jerk seasoning. Pasta lovers can opt for chicken tequila fettuccine flavored with cilantro or angel hair with sun-dried tomatoes. Salads are enormous and excel-lent; choose a half-order if you're sharing a pizza. For dessert, the signature "messy sundae" with chocolate and caramel sauce is big enough for two or more. La Jollans of all social persuasions come here for casual, inexpensive meals. ◆ Californian/pizza ◆ Daily, lunch and dinner. 702 Pearl St (between Eads and Draper Aves). 619/456.5222. ♿ Also at 770 Fourth Ave (between F and G Sts). 230.8888; 12925 El Camino Real (at Del Mar Heights Rd), Del Mar. 259.6600

87 PSYCHIC EYE BOOK SHOP

The sign offering daily psychic readings is enough to draw the curious inside to browse through aisle after aisle of crystal balls, candles, beads, New Age tapes, and books on every possible psychic, astrological theme. ◆ Daily. 702 Pearl St (between Eads and Draper Aves). 551.8877

88 MARRAKESH

★★$$$ Dining here is a night-long event. Guests sit on the floor or on low padded banquettes around enormous inlaid wooden tables. Multicourse Moroccan feasts are presented stylishly, augmented by belly dancers on weekends. Try the excellent lamb with prunes and honey, grilled prawns over rice, or pastry stuffed with chicken, raisins, and eggs. ◆ Moroccan ◆ Daily, dinner. Reservations recommended. Pearl St (between Draper Ave and Cuvier St). 454.2500

89 D.G. WILLS BOOKS

Indulge your urge to browse among the new and used scholarly books in this appropriately musty setting. Book signings and poetry readings are held frequently. ◆ Daily. 7461 Girard Ave (between Genter and Pearl Sts). 456.1800

90 PANNIKIN STORE

Loyal shoppers make regular visits here for fresh roasted coffee beans from all over the world, herb teas, and unusual coffee accoutrements. The coffees are available by mail order; ask for a catalog. ◆ Daily. 7458 Girard Ave (between Genter and Pearl Sts). 454.6365. Also at 675 G St (between Sixth and Seventh Aves). 619/239.7891; 3145 Rosecrans St (between Lytton St and Sellers Dr), Point Loma. 619/224.2891. Mail order, 800/232.6482

90 GALLERY EIGHT

Prices here range from $10 to thousands of dollars for gorgeous contemporary crafts, including silver jewelry by Steven Brixner, ceramics by Patrick Crabb, and unique baskets woven with needles from the endangered Torrey pines by Neil and Fran Prince. ◆ M-Sa. 7464 Girard Ave (between Genter and Pearl Sts). 454.9781

Restaurants/Clubs: Red | Hotels: Purple | Shops: Orange | Outdoors/Parks: Green | Sights/Culture: Blue

DAY TRIPS

COASTAL NORTH COUNTY

The drive along **Coast Highway (S21)** from **Torrey Pines State Reserve** to **Oceanside** is a must for anyone who wants a real glimpse of life along the Pacific Coast.

The trend-setting town of **Del Mar** marks the entry into North County, the fastest-growing segment of San Diego County. As famous for its thoroughbreds as it is for its nitpicky city ordinances—no skateboarding, no washing your car on the street, no noisy leaf blowers, Del Mar is a small town trying desperately to stay tranquil and exclusive despite bumper-to-bumper popularity.

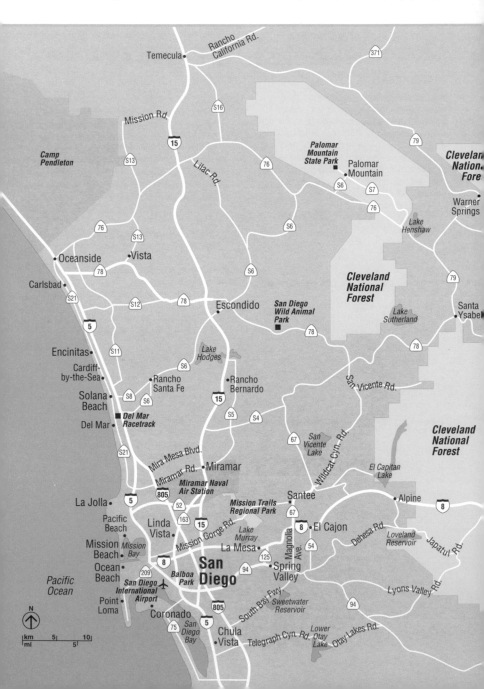

Architect **Jon Jerde**'s Mediterranean-inspired **Del Mar Plaza** (1555 Camino del Mar, at 15th St; 858/792.1555) proved that a new commercial center in the heart of Del Mar's villagelike downtown need not be intrusive or garish. Modeled on an Italian hillside village, this ritzy, multilayered, sun-splashed piazza with panoramic views of the Pacific is filled with chic clothing boutiques, galleries, and gourmet restaurants. Great for both shopping and people watching, this is where the beautiful people come to pose. Favorite spots include a wonderful bookstore-coffeehouse called **Esmerelda** (858/755.2707), whose whimsically tiled alfresco patio invites hours of leisurely reading and sipping. **Il Fornaio Cucina Italiana** (858/755.8876), has the best ocean view in the county from its top-deck patio and seems like a place where paparazzi would hang out waiting for celebs. The Northern Italian, Tuscany-style breads, pizzas, and roasted chicken, duck, and rabbit are baked in an enormous oak-fired oven. Architects **Backen, Arrigoni & Ross** designed the restaurant using vaulted ceilings, arched windows, Carrara marble, terra-cotta floor coverings, and mahogany furnishings; a 165-foot hand-painted trompe l'oeil Pompeiian frieze wraps around the indoor dining area. Also in **Del Mar Plaza**, the award-winning **Pacifica Del Mar** (858/792.0476) serves highly imaginative and delicious Pacific Rim cuisine. For the greatest margaritas in town, grab a bar stool at **Epazote** (858/259.9966). Immediately south of the plaza is a strip of **Camino del Mar** well worth a leisurely stroll. **Earth Song Bookstore** (1440 Camino del Mar, between 13th and 15th Sts; 858/755.4254) is part bookstore, part New Age boutique selling books and beautifully handcrafted jewelry and clothing amidst crystals, inspirational tapes, and folk arts. **Americana Restaurant** (1454 Camino del Mar, between 13th and 15th Sts; 858/794.6838) serves innovative fusion cuisine at a breezy sidewalk café and is a great spot for soaking up Del Mar's unique beachy-chic charm. The inn **L'Auberge Del Mar** (1540 Camino del Mar, between 15th and 18th Sts; 858/259.1515) is an elegant hotel on a slight hill looking toward the sea, with posh rooms and suites, an indulgent, upscale restaurant, and a sybaritic spa. On the downscale side, the blue-and-white **Del Mar Motel** (1702 Coast Blvd, between 15th and 18th Sts; 858/755.1534, 800/223.8449) sits right on the beach (guests are asked to shower the sand off their feet before entering) and offers simple rooms with the background sounds of surf pounding on sand. For more unusual digs, check out **Les Artistes** (1540 Camino del Mar; 858/755.4646), where each room has a theme to match a different artist's works.

And of course, there's the famed **Del Mar Racetrack and Fairgrounds** (2260 Jimmy Durante Blvd, at Via de la Valle; 858/755.1141). It was popular with the Hollywood crowd during the 1940s and 1950s; at one time many a star could be seen lunching and betting inside the track's exclusive **Turf Club**. It won't take you long to figure out that summer, specifically the weeks of the Del Mar Fair between mid-June and the first week in July, is high season in Del Mar.

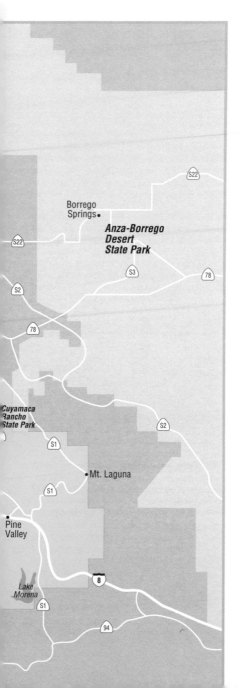

159

THE BEST

Ann Jarmusch

Architecture Critic, *San Diego Union-Tribune*

Ditch the car and ramble through **Little Italy**, a downtown neighborhood undergoing a housing boom without (we hope) losing its Italian accent. India Street is *La Strada* if you're looking for cappuccino and cannoli, hand-painted Italian pottery, or art supplies.

The gemlike **Pacific Rim Park**, at the western tip of **Shelter Island**, is a work of art and place of peace. An exuberant expression of friendship for San Diego's sister cities on the Pacific Rim, the park unites brilliant mosaics, fluid ironwork, and a pearl-shaped fountain with cultural symbolism. It's one in an ongoing series of international parks designed and built by artist-designer James Hubbell and students from Mexico, China, Russia, and San Diego.

Natural canyons, which run like crooked green fingers through San Diego neighborhoods, are among the area's natural treasures. Experience a bit of urban wilderness by traversing the **Spruce Street footbridge**, a suspension bridge that dates to 1912.

Get a glimpse of how modest yet challenging life could be 150 years ago by visiting the **Point Loma Lighthouse**, now a museum, at **Cabrillo National Monument**. This park also offers panoramic views of the San Diego–Tijuana region, from the mountains to San Diego Bay and the ocean.

South Chula Vista Library is a colorful, inviting complex of indoor-outdoor rooms, fountains, and gardens. Designed by Ricardo Legorreta, this building features splendid views onto courtyard gardens, a reading area for young children, and a literacy program.

Housed in a charmingly restored historic beach cottage, **Pannikin Brockton Villa** serves reasonably priced meals with million-dollar views of **La Jolla Cove**. Sit in front of the fireplace, on the breezy veranda, or outside on a terrace shaded by old pepper trees.

The **Salk Institute for Biological Studies** (1965) and the **Neurosciences Institute** (1995) are neighboring architectural masterpieces, the former overlooking the Pacific, the latter facing east on **Torrey Pines Mesa**. In designing the **Neurosciences Institute**, architects **Tod Williams, Billie Tsien & Associates** of New York City paid homage to the Salk, a world-acclaimed, influential design by **Louis I. Kahn** with Jonas Salk's input. In addition, Williams and Tsien created an extraordinary place infused with a spare, serene beauty and the spirit of nature.

The **Self-Realization Fellowship Meditation Gardens** in Encinitas offer a series of small, lush garden experiences and surprises. Quiet reflection is encouraged, as you'll see from the numerous benches placed in lovely spots.

The **Santa Fe Depot** (1914–1915) is a restored downtown landmark still humming with passenger train traffic. A great example of Mission Revival style, this faux adobe building is ablaze with colorful tile, from its twin domes to the waiting room.

Stroll along the arcades of **Balboa Park**'s **El Prado**, which is lined with reconstructed 1915 exposition buildings and punctuated with grand fountains. Among the pearls of fine architecture on this strand: the painstakingly reconstructed **House of Hospitality**, the **San Diego Museum of Art**, and the **Museum of Man**'s **California Tower**.

Your first clue is the perpetually backed-up traffic on **I-5** for several miles preceding the **Via de la Valle** exit. This gridlock keeps residents grumbling throughout the season. But it's worth the frustration to go to the fair, if only to ride the mammoth Ferris wheel—one of the few existing wheels with an ocean view. After the fair ends, the thoroughbreds take over; racing season lasts from mid-July through September. Restaurants near the track include the ever-popular **Fish Market** (640 Via de la Valle, between Del Mar Downs Rd and S21; 858/755.2277), a busy, noisy dining room where the fresh fish can't be beat. **Prime 10 Steakhouse** (3702 Via de la Valle, at El Camino Real; 858/523.0007, 259.8777) is the place to go for steaks and prime rib.

Just north of Del Mar is sleepy **Solana Beach**. Within this residential beachside burb is the Mexican enclave of **Eden Gardens**, also called Little Mexico. Home to Mexican-American families for generations, the area has several good, unpretentious family-run restaurants along **Valley Avenue**, including **Fidel's** (607 Valley Ave, between Genevieve and Hernandez Sts; 858/755.5292) and **Tony's Jacal** (621 Valley Ave, between Genevieve and Hernandez Sts; 858/755.2274), which has been serving home-style Mexican favorites since 1946. Solana Beach is perhaps most famous for the **Cedros Design District** (Cedros Ave at Lomas Santa Fe Dr), where shops selling imported furnishings, fine arts and jewelry, chic housewares, and antiques have replaced a strip of old underused buildings. The anchor of the neighborhood is the **Belly Up Tavern** (143 S Cedros Ave, at Lomas Santa Fe; 858/481.9022). It's a whale of a nightclub and one of the few venues in North County that books national and international musical acts, from big bands to reggae. The club's interior, with its rounded ceiling and wood-paneled walls, resembles the hull of an overturned ship. Stop for lunch at the District's **Café Zinc** (132 S Cedros Ave; 858/793.5436), where stylish shoppers sip coffee drinks on the patio. Or visit the trendy **Pacific Coast Grill** (437 S Highway 101; 858/794.4632).

A short jaunt east along **S6** will take you to **Rancho Santa Fe**. Easily the wealthiest community in San Diego County, "the Ranch" exudes old money and taste. The tony, secretive enclave lost its privacy when the Heaven's Gate cult chose it for a mass suicide in 1997, but that was merely a blip on the otherwise serene scene. During the early part of the 20th century, Douglas Fairbanks Jr. bought a sprawling ranch just across the river valley from Rancho Santa Fe. This land, aptly named **Fairbanks Ranch**, now consists of ultraluxurious private estates. Horse stables and equestrian events abound within the area. If Rancho Santa Fe has a hub, it's the quiet cluster of shops and restaurants known as the **Village**, near the peaceful **Inn at Rancho Santa Fe** (5951 Linea Del Cielo, between El Guego and Ave de Acacias; 858/756.1131; fax 858/759.1604). The inn has 100 units spread over 20 acres in small cottages. As for dining, the elegant French country **Mille Fleurs** (6009 Paseo Delicias, at La Granada; 858/756.3085) is housed within a restored 1926 adobe, with whitewashed walls, wood-beamed ceilings, fresh flowers, and a crackling fireplace. Gregarious owner Bertrand Hug is forever circulating around the room chatting with guests, and chef Martin Woesle is revered by diners for his roasted rabbit, herb-crusted lamb, and silken foie gras. Every morning, home gourmets and professional chefs line up to buy exotic produce from the **Vegetable Shop**, aka **Chino's** (6123 Calzada del Bosque, at Via de Santa Fe, 858/756.3184). An unpretentious little stand with lots of clout, it's been called the Rolls Royce of roadsiders for its homegrown perfect arugula, radicchio, baby vegetables, and culinary herbs. If it's love you're after, you'll find it in serves and volleys at the **Rancho Valencia Resort** (5921 Valencia Cir, at Rancho Valencia Dr; 756.1123, 800/548.3664; fax 756.0165). One of the country's premier tennis clubs, this high-end resort helps amateurs and pros hone their backhand on its 18 courts. Guests stay in 43 casita suites complete with wet bars, fireplaces, and private patios, and dine on French cuisine with a California twist at **Rancho Valencia Restaurant**.

Back on **S21** (also called **Highway 101**), continue north and you'll hit **Cardiff-by-the-Sea**, the ultimate California beach town. Totally without pretension, Cardiff is cherished by locals and visitors alike. A handful of

dining favorites includes **Las Olas** (2655 N Hwy 101, at Dublin Rd; 760/942.1860), a beachy Mexican eatery famous for fish tacos and *carne asada* (grilled beef). For good prime rib and seafood and a dazzling view of the Pacific, try the **Beach House** (2530 S Hwy 101, at Dublin Rd; 760/753.1321). Finally, let the crashing waves lull you to sleep at **San Elijo State Beach** (S21, between Manchester Rd and Schubert Dr; 760/753.5091, 800/444.7275), one of the few beachside campgrounds in the county.

Next up is **Encinitas**. On entering this picturesque beach community, you'll immediately spot the immaculate white walls and gleaming gold spires of the **Self-Realization Fellowship Retreat and Hermitage** (939 Second St; 760/436.7220), founded by disciples of Yogi Paramahansa Yogananda. The lush tropical cliffside meditation gardens are open to the public; cameras, smoking, and loud talking are prohibited. The view of the Pacific, especially at dusk, is absolutely awe-inspiring.

The beach adjacent to the Fellowship, fittingly called **Swami's**, is one of California's prime surfing spots. Highway 101 runs into **First Street** through the center of town, past funky shops and cafés that dot the strip. **Lou's Records** (434 N Hwy 101; 760/753.1382) is famous for its extensive collection of rare and used vinyl and is proof that the CD revolution has not entirely conquered the music retail industry. One of the last old movie theaters in the county, **La Paloma** (471 S Hwy 101; 760/436.9466) hosts film festivals throughout the year. On the coastal side, **Moonlight Beach**, as its name suggests, is best suited to a romantic evening stroll, whereas inland, the **Quail Botanical Gardens** (230 Quail Gardens Dr, between Encinitas Blvd and Leucadia Blvd; 760/436.3036) is perfect on a sunny day when you can tour the 30 acres of bamboo groves, California native plants, and exotic tropicals. Encinitas is also the poinsettia capital of the world, thanks to the efforts of the Paul Ecke family and its prodigious flower farms. **Leucadia**, the next town up the line, is a throwback to pre-yuppie times.

Carlsbad, due north on Highway 101, is home to **La Costa Resort & Spa** (2100 Costa del Mar Rd; 760/438.9111, 800/854.5000). This world-renowned 478-unit resort, opened in 1965, is a mecca of civilized sporting pleasures. Two luxuriously landscaped courses attract golfers from around the world and host various tournaments. Tennis tournaments are held at the resort's 21-court tennis complex. The rich and famous relax and rejuvenate at the ultra-

---

Restaurants/Clubs: Red | Hotels: Purple | Shops: Orange | Outdoors/Parks: Green | Sights/Culture: Blue

FOUR SEASONS RESORT
Aviara, North San Diego

sybaritic spa and health center. Seven restaurants on the premises cater to a variety of tastes and diets. Even more luxurious is the **Four Seasons Resort Aviara** (7100 Four Seasons Point; 760/6800, 800/819.5053; fax 760/603.6801), where San Diegans escape when they want seclusion, fine dining, and the most comfortable beds in the world. The resort has a full spa with every exotic treatment you might desire, plus an 18-hole golf course. Summer jazz concerts on the lawn fill the hotel with guests, so make reservations early. Carlsbad's other big attraction is the spring bloom of ranunculus flowers on the hillsides east of I-5. The flower fields are open to the public in April and May. For the kiddies, **Legoland** (One Lego Dr at Cannon Rd; 760/916.5346, 877/534.6526) is a fantasy of rides and attractions built out of Legos. It's best for the toddler set. Unless they're totally devoted to Legos, kids over 8 or so tend to grow bored quickly.

Oceanside, on San Diego County's northwest borderline, is home to **Camp Pendleton**, the Marine Corps' largest amphibious training base. The 125,000 acres of government land, bisected by I-5, was originally the **San Margarita Valley**, named by Spanish explorer Don Gaspar de Portola in 1769. In the mid-1800s, during the reign of Don Pio Pico, the last governor of Alta California from Spain, the land became home to a military unit—Los Galgos (the Greyhounds), a small cavalry squadron formed to combat *los Americanos* coming into California. In 1942, shortly after

---

One of the more unusual annual events held in the desert is the Pegleg Smith Liar's Contest, named after a gold miner who supposedly found gold nuggets near Borrego Springs but could never find his gold mine again.

Long before Oceanside was a city it consisted of two Native American villages—Hepuwwoo and Enekelkawa—inhabited by Luiseño Indians.

The last sighting of a California condor in the wilds of San Diego County was in 1933 at Mount Palomar. The nearly extinct condor is now being bred at the Wild Animal Park, where Molloko, the first California condor conceived in captivity, was born in 1988.

---

the bombing of Pearl Harbor, Camp Pendleton was established. Dedicated to the corps by FDR and named for Major General Joseph H. Pendleton, who later became the mayor of Coronado, the base trained the Marine infantrymen who fought in World War II, Korea, Vietnam, and the Persian Gulf. When not under high-security measures, Camp Pendleton is open to civilian visitors 7 days a week. A self-guided driving tour offers a glimpse into the military life, with barracks, training ranges, and a helicopter air station among the sights. An amphibious-vehicle museum features prototype vehicles used during World War II and in the Korean War. Visitors must have a valid driver's license, vehicle registration, and proof of insurance before they are admitted. Call 725.5566 for further information.

The **Mission San Luis Rey** (4050 Mission Ave, between I-5 and I-15; 760/757.3651), a National Historic Landmark and the largest of California's missions, is open to the public. The mission includes a retreat center and a museum devoted to the history of California's missions. It's open daily, and charges admission.

INLAND NORTH COUNTY

Heading north from San Diego on **Highway 163** to Interstate 15 will take you past the **Miramar Naval Air Station**, where fighter jets and bombers streak through the air, and on to **Rancho Bernardo**, San Diego's first planned community, established in 1961. When it comes to mass-produced Southern California architecture, Rancho Bernardo is the undisputed queen of the California-Mediterranean look, with hillsides covered with endless rows of white stucco houses with red Spanish tile roofs. Strict guidelines for architecture, landscaping, and home alterations give RB, as it's known to locals, a pristine, rural, communal look. Expect lots of golf courses, parks, and hiking and riding trails. The **Rancho Bernardo Inn** (17550 Bernardo Oaks Dr, at Rancho Bernardo Rd; 858/675.8500, 877/517.9342; fax 858/675.8501) boasts 12 tennis courts, 108 holes of golf, 287 rooms and suites, great children's programs, and a health and fitness center. The resort's award-winning gourmet restaurant, **El Bizcocho**, is revered among discerning diners throughout the county. For a totally indulgent weekend, spend a night in a private villa by the golf course—with a private fireplace and hot tub, of course. Play golf or tennis if you must, and reward yourself with a multicourse dinner or seemingly endless Sunday brunch (or both) at **El Bizcocho**.

Continue north along I-15 to **Escondido**, rural North County's minimetropolis. Though its name is Spanish for "hidden valley," Escondido is hardly hidden. In fact, several celebrated attractions call it home. The **San Diego Wild Animal Park** (the WAP; 15500 San Pasqual Valley Rd, at Old Pasqual Rd; 760/747.8702) occupies 1,800 acres of natural preserve in the foothills of the **San Pasqual Valley**. Established in 1972 by the San Diego Zoological Society, the WAP (sister to the **San Diego Zoo** in **Balboa Park**) is sanctuary to about 3,500 critters that roam in herds along the plains and hillsides, making it a truly unique zoo experience. A monorail carries visitors past gazelles, zebras, and giraffes who seem to roam free in the distance. Animal shows have a definite educational bent, and the gift shops are stocked with safari-oriented souvenirs. Early morning and evening are the best animal-watching times. The WAP is open daily; there's an admission charge.

Vigorous exercise is combined with elegant pampering at Escondido's world-known superspa of the rich and famous, the **Golden Door** (777 Deer Springs Rd, 1 mile off I-15; 760/744.5777, 800/424.5777; fax 760/471.2393). Established in 1958 by health and fitness guru Deborah Szekely, the facility caters almost exclusively to women. (Nine weeks of the year are dedicated to men.) A minimum 7-day stay promises a decadently luxurious experience for the body and mind. Flanked by mountains and shaded by oaks is the **Lawrence Welk Resort** (8860 Lawrence Welk Dr, at Champagne Blvd; 760/749.3000, 800/932.9355; fax 749.9537). Established in 1964 by the famed bandleader, the sprawling stucco and Spanish-tile resort encompasses 1,000 acres of verdant foothills, 132 rooms and suites, a dinner theater, and a shopping plaza. Golf is the sport of choice here—the resort boasts three courses—and there's a **Lawrence Welk Museum** (749.3448) with memorabilia from the *Lawrence Welk Show*'s history. The museum is open daily; hours are erratic, so call ahead. Admission is free.

Although Escondido's wineries are overshadowed by the popularity of those in **Temecula** (see below), there are still a few small wineries here worth visiting. **Deer Park Winery** (29013 Champagne Blvd, between Castle Rd and Welk View Dr; 760/749.1666) is both a winery and a vintage car museum. Take a self-guided tour of both the winery and museum and finish up with tastings. One admission charge applies to both. **Orfila Vineyards/Thomas Jaeger Winery** (13455 San Pasqual Rd, at Zermant La; 760/738.6500) offers daily tours and wine tastings. The **Ferrara Winery** (1120 W 15th Ave, between Juniper and Maple Sts;

760/745.7632) began producing wines in 1932; the facilities are a designated California State Historical Point of Interest. And finally, the city's **California Center for the Arts** (340 N Escondido Blvd, between Espanas Green and Lincoln Ave; 760/839.4100) showcases dance, music, and theater performances. For dining before the theater—or any time—try **150 Grand Café** (150 W Grand Ave; 760/738.6868), known for its inspired California-French cuisine.

WINE COUNTRY

If you've got wine on your mind, head for **Temecula Valley**'s wine country. Though not part of San Diego County (it's part of **Riverside County**), Temecula is only an hour's drive north of downtown San Diego on I-15. To reach Temecula's wineries and main business district, take the **Rancho California Road** exit and head east. Don't let the surrounding scenery throw you off—eventually the mammoth peach-and-gray stucco housing projects will give way to sprawling, vine-covered hills. Because it takes about 2 days to visit all of the wineries, you might want to check into the cozy, six-room **Loma Vista Bed & Breakfast** (33350 La Serena Way, at Rancho California Rd; 909/676.7047). This rustic inn near the famed **Callaway Winery** (see below) makes a perfect stopover. Rooms and suites are named after vintages, and the room price includes a wine-and-cheese evening repast and a champagne continental breakfast. **Embassy Suites** (29345 Rancho California Rd, at I-15; 909/676.5656, 800/EMBASSY; fax 909/699-3928) has 136 suites perfect for those who like to spread out a bit.

If you only have a day to spend here, be sure to visit the beautiful, castlelike **Thornton Winery** (32575 Rancho California Rd, between Margarita Rd and Calle Contento; 909/699.0099; fax 909/699.5536). Famous for its Culbertson sparkling wines made in the classic French *méthode champenoise*, Thornton offers tours and tasting on weekends only. The tour, which is free, is one of the best in the Valley. The winery's on-site restaurant (and the only one in the vicinity), **Cafe Champagne** (909/699.0088), serves tasty renditions of Californian cuisine classics like mesquite-grilled fish and chicken. Have

---

THE BEST

Rob Wellington Quigley and Everyone Else in the Office

Architects

Fidel's, **Solana Beach**—great Mexican food in a building with courtyards that ramble on forever.

Point Loma Seafoods—this bustling waterfront take-out seafood restaurant has the best fresh seafood for sale and a wonderfully crispy, fried fish sandwich served on sourdough bread. Ask for it sloppy so you get lots of tartar sauce.

Chicano Park, under the San Diego side of the **Coronado Bridge**—after the freeway bisected their community, local Chicano artists reclaimed their turf and created a park by painting the supports under the bridge in colorful murals.

Salk Institute—every architect that visits the San Diego area has to see **Louis Kahn**'s best building.

Baltic Inn (521 6th Ave), **J Street Inn** (222 J Street),

and **La Pensione** (India and Date)—San Diego has set an example for the country in providing housing for the lower economic levels in single-room-occupancy hotels.

La Jolla Women's Club—Irving Gill innovated the use of tilt-slab construction on this wonderfully regional building located across the street from the **Museum of Contemporary Art, San Diego** on Prospect in **La Jolla**.

Crystal Pier (Garnet Avenue, Pacific Beach)—the little cottages on this pier are a great place to stay and be lulled to sleep by the waves. Not recommended during big storms!

163 through Balboa Park—the best inner-city freeway experience in California; a true gateway to the city. Hopefully they'll never widen this and destroy the special feeling of driving through the canyon and trees under the **Cabrillo Bridge**.

Stuart Collection, UCSD—an inspired series of site-specific sculptures scattered throughout the **UCSD** campus in an ongoing program.

---

an alfresco lunch on the breezy patio. A 1-day trip should also include a stop at the **Callaway Winery** (32720 Rancho California Rd, between Margarita Rd and Calle Contento; 909/676.4001, 800/472.2377), which is best known for its exceptional Chardonnay. The winery is open for tours daily. **Santa Margarita Winery** (33490 Madera de la Playa, between Margarita Rd and Calle Contento; 909/676.4431) specializes in aged Cabernet Sauvignons and offers tours on weekends or weekdays by appointment. **Hart Winery** (41300 Avenida Biona, at Rancho California Rd; 909/676.6300) has daily tastings of their handcrafted red wines. Most of the wineries (13 at last count) offer a tour of the facilities and a wine tasting, some for a fee. Contact the **Temecula Valley Wine-growers Association** (P.O. Box 1601; Temecula, CA 92593-1601; 909/699.6586, 800/801.9463) for a brochure on the wineries and other area services.

EAST TO THE MOUNTAINS AND DESERT

San Diegans longing for a change of scenery and season head east on **I-8** to the **Cleveland National Forest** or **Anza-Borrego Desert State Park**, both of which are within a couple of hours' drive of downtown. Heading east on

I-8, you'll bypass the communities of **La Mesa**, **El Cajon**, and **Alpine**, and see the mountain peaks looming ever closer as you climb the gradual grades from sea level to the junction of I-8 and **Highway 79**, at 3,370 feet.

If you head north on Highway 79, you'll come to **Cleveland National Forest**. The 26,000-acre **Cuyamaca Rancho State Park** (760/765.0755, 800/777.0369) is the most accessible and popular area of the forest. Several campgrounds are available by mountain streams and hiking paths. The road then passes through the mountain town of **Julian**, best known for its Annual Apple Days Festival held in October, when San Diegans drive through town by the hundreds in search of homemade apple pies. **Santa Ysabel**, a few miles north, is famous because of **Dudley's** restaurant and bakery (30218 Hwy 78, at Hwy 79; 760/765.0488, 800/225.3348), and its selection of dozens of varieties of home-baked breads. The next town, **Warner Springs**, has an airfield where glider planes land soundlessly. Back west off **Highway 76** is **Palomar Mountain State Park** (760/742.3462) and the **Palomar Observatory** (742.2119), with the 200-inch Hale Telescope, one of the largest reflecting telescopes in the world. The white-domed observatory building is open to the public daily; admission is free.

For an alternate mountain experience, take I-8 east from San Diego to **Pine Valley** and the turnoff for **Highway S1**, also called **Sunrise Highway**, through the **Laguna Mountains**. From the lookouts near the 5,975-foot-high **Mount Laguna** you can see east across the desert to the vast unknown beyond. The **San Diego State University Observatory** (SDSU) on Mount Laguna is open *most* Friday and Saturday summer nights at sunset for stargazing; call the SDSU Astronomy Department (619/594.1415) to check the schedule. There's no charge for admission, but you must obtain your free tickets the afternoon of the evening you want to attend. The tickets are available at the United States Forest Service Visitor's Center (in Mount Laguna, Highway S1 near mileage marker 23.5, at Los Huecos Rd; 619/473.8547).

The **Anza-Borrego Desert State Park** comprises some 600,000 acres of parched, undeveloped land where cactus bloom in the spring and snowbirds in motor homes migrate in winter months. The park's **Visitor Information Center** (760/767.4205) is the best place to begin your desert explorations with a hike through the cactus gardens and museums. The town of **Borrego Springs** has several campgrounds and hotels; call the **Chamber of Commerce** (760/767.5555, 800/559.5524) for information. **La Casa del Zorro Resort** (3845 Yaqui Pass Rd, at Borrego Springs Rd; 760/767.5323, 800/824.1884; fax 760/767.5963) offers 77 rooms and suites in several two-story buildings and private casitas beside pools, gardens, and putting greens. Jazz concerts are held in the summer; book early during the spring wildflower season.

South to Chula Vista

Chula Vista, the second-largest city in San Diego County, is just 7 miles south of downtown and easily accessible by freeway or the **San Diego Trolley**. Its greatest attraction, at least for nature lovers, is the **Sweetwater Marsh National Wildlife Refuge** and the **Chula Vista Nature Center** (1000 Gunpowder Point Dr, at E Street; 409.5900). One of the few remaining salt marsh bird habitats on California's coast, the 316-acre plot of priceless waterfront property stretches along the southern end of **San Diego Bay**. Graceful blue and white herons glide above the glassy ponds and burrowing owls nest in simple cages; bird watchers have spotted more than 130 species of birds from the center's wooden lookout tower. Bat rays, sand sharks, and guitarfish populate an outdoor petting tank, and several indoor exhibits highlight the natural inhabitants of the coast. The park, which charges admission, is open Tuesday through Sunday.

Coors Amphitheatre (2050 Entertainment Circle; 671.3600) is an open-air concert venue with 20,000 seats. Its excellent acoustics make it a favorite of top musical acts, including the Dixie Chicks, Dave Matthews Band, Sting, and Aerosmith.

The US Olympic Committee's **ARCO Training Center** (2800 Olympic Pkwy; 656.1500) is a state-of-the-art facility for athletes, many of whom live on-site and train in such sports as soccer, field hockey, and archery. Tours are offered Monday through Saturday (call ahead to make sure it's open), and sports memorabilia is available in the Spirit Store. Let the kids test their bravura on the water slides and rides at **Knott's Soak City USA** (2052 Entertainment Cir; 661.7373), a water park open during summer months.

One of the most traditional eateries in the area is **Anthony's Fish Grotto** (215 West Bay Blvd, at E St; 425.4200), one in a small chain of family restaurants. Crab, lobster, shrimp, and swordfish are all expertly prepared.

Nearby are the **Chula Vista Harbor** and **California Yacht Marina**, pleasant places for boat connoisseurs to stroll waterside pathways and admire the yachts. Chula Vista has managed to surpass San Diego City when it comes to public libraries, with its spectacular **South Chula Vista Library**, which opened in April 1994. Mexican architect **Ricardo Legoretta** designed the sunflower-yellow building with bright purple trim, which has received rave reviews from architectural organizations and a few pans from its neighbors.

Restaurants/Clubs: Red | Hotels: Purple | Shops: Orange | Outdoors/Parks: Green | Sights/Culture: Blue

To really appreciate Tijuana, you've got to leave your timidity at the border. You'll have to see the blatant poverty and cope with the crush of the crowd. You'll have to consider the culture, customs, and laws of a foreign land, despite its proximity to your home. Then you'll see Tijuana for what it is: a young city, only about 100 years old; the fourth largest city in Mexico; entryway to the 1,000-mile-long Baja California peninsula. Many of its inhabitants have come from throughout Latin America looking for opportunity along the border. City leaders boast that Tijuana's unemployment is among the lowest in the nation, owing to the large number of factory jobs at *maquiladoras*. These manufacturing plants, many foreign owned, are strung along the border in a region that casual travelers rarely see.

Avenida Revolución is the traditional tourist destination—a strip of restaurants, bars, and shopping arcades where gringos run wild, chasing bargains, cheap drinks and eats, and good times. It's been that way since the 1920s. Today's Avenida Revolución is largely the province of bands of college-aged kids and wide-eyed tourists looking timidly back at their buses. All that said, you absolutely must cruise Revolución for an hour or so. Check out the *pasajes* (shopping arcades), the restaurants, and the **Palacio Frontón**. Buy a paper flower, woven bracelet, or pack of gum from the children on the street. Then retreat to the **Centro Cultural** to see exhibits, films, and performances about Mexico's cultures and history.

Day-trippers have traditionally made up the bulk of Tijuana's guests, but there are more and more reasons to spend the night. You can easily fill a weekend with shopping, restaurant hopping, and visiting cultural sights. The Centro Cultural features dance troupes, symphonies, and performers from throughout Latin America and Cuba, hosting those who never make it to the US—as well as those who do. The discos and clubs are as extravagant and exciting as those in Acapulco or L.A., and they don't even begin to rock until after midnight. Rock bands play at trendy nightclubs. When it comes to nightlife, Tijuana is pure Mexican—vibrant, jazzy, dazzling, and inexhaustible.

The country code is 52. Phone numbers and area codes changed in 2001. The new area code is 664; phone numbers should be seven digits.

Getting to Tijuana

By Air

Travelers visiting from mainland Mexico arrive at the **Abelardo Rodríguez International Airport** in the **Otay Mesa** area, a 15-minute cab ride from downtown Tijuana. Airlines serving Tijuana include **Mexicana** (800/531.7921), **Aeroméxico** (800/237.6639), and **AeroCalifornia** (800/428.2163).

By Bus

Greyhound (619/239.3266, 800/231.2222) offers frequent bus service from downtown San Diego to downtown Tijuana. The Greyhound terminal (686.0695) in Tijuana is at **Avenida México**, at Madero. **Five-Star Tours** (619/232.5049), at the **Santa Fe Depot** on

Broadway at Kettner, offers bus service to the **San Ysidro** border crossing, and across the border to the company's terminal on Avenida Revolución by the **Palacio Frontón**.

By Car

Many drivers prefer to leave their cars in the large parking lots in San Ysidro on the US side of the border and walk across rather than hassle with driving in Tijuana. If you must leave valuables in the car, at least stash them in the trunk, as car break-ins are common. It's worth the extra money to leave your car in a guarded lot. And if you do take your car, it's essential to buy auto insurance, because most US policies do not

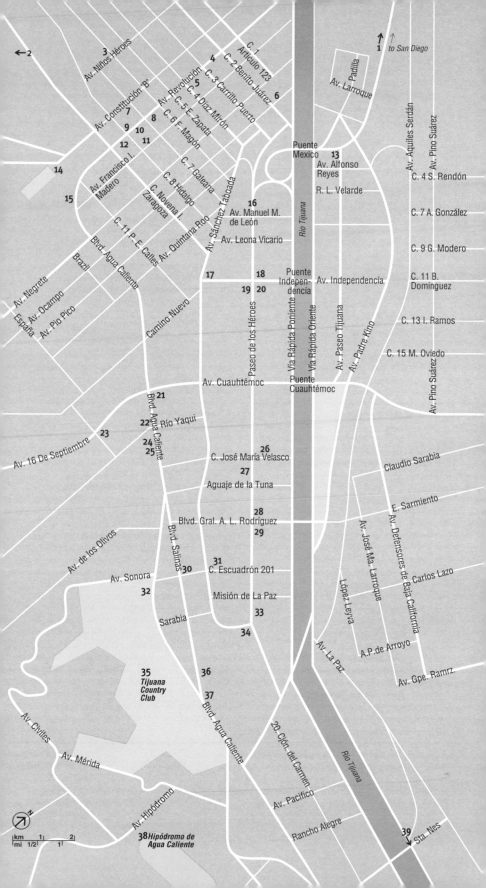

cover driving in Mexico. Stop at one of the Mexican auto insurance stands at the San Ysidro exit off **I-5** just north of the border; some are open 24 hours daily. You'll need to show your driver's license and the car's current registration.

Also, most car-rental companies do not allow their cars into Mexico; if you're renting in San Diego, be sure to check this out. **Avis** (800/331.1212) and **Courtesy** (619/424.8606) do let their cars across the border, with certain restrictions.

By Trolley

The **San Diego Trolley** (619/233.3004; www. sdcommute.com) travels from downtown San Diego to the border every 15 minutes between 5AM and midnight.

FYI

Health Precautions

Despite its proximity to the United States, Tijuana is a foreign land, so you should observe the same health and safety precautions you would elsewhere in Mexico. Don't drink the tap water, and except in better hotels and restaurants, avoid uncooked vegetables and ice cubes. Trust your instincts. If you tend toward queasiness, take a spoonful of Pepto-Bismol before you eat.

Language

Mexican (as opposed to Castilian) Spanish is the native tongue of Tijuana, but English in various degrees of clarity is nearly as common. The language along the border can best be called "Spanglish," a great, often amusing mix that locals and guests manage to communicate with quite well. Tijuana is pronounced "Tee-WHA-na," not "Tee-a-WHA-na." *Gracias* ("thank you") goes a long, long way, as does *por favor* ("please"). The border is called *la frontera* or, more often, *la línea*; a bathroom is a *baño*; the check (which most waiters will not bring unless you ask for it) is *la cuenta*. *¿Dónde?* means "Where?"; *¿Cuánto es?* means "How much?"; *¿Mande?* or *¿Cómo?* means "What did you say?" When trying to pass someone or get through a crowd, say, "*Con permiso*." When introduced to someone, say, "*Mucho gusto*" ("Pleased to meet you"). And when you blow it, say, "*Desculpe*" ("Forgive me").

Money

As compared to the US dollar, the peso has inched steadily upward since its devastating 1995 devaluation, but it recently stabilized. Prices in dollars are readily quoted, and US currency is accepted nearly everywhere. Money-exchange stands, called *casas de cambio*, are

clustered on the US side of the border and along Avenida Revolución. Some say that as the peso devalues, the bargains get better, but it seems most shopkeepers and restaurateurs have grown adept at adjusting their prices quickly.

Shopping

Bargaining—it's an art and a sport for some travelers, and a way of life in Tijuana. When shopping at a market or street stand, offer at least a third less than the asking price and work from there. Prices in department stores and nicer shops are normally not negotiable.

Street Plan

Street signs can be hard to find in Tijuana, and directions are normally given relating to landmarks. When searching for a street's name, look at the outer walls of buildings at the intersections; often there's a tiny plaque with the name there. The streets crossing Avenida Revolución in downtown Tijuana have both names and numbers; for example, Calle 2 is also called Calle Segunda (Second Street) or Calle Benito Juárez. Check the street signs; the numbers, however, are minuscule and hard to read.

Telephones

To call Tijuana from the US, dial 011-52-664 before the seven-digit number. To call the US from Tijuana, dial 001 before the area code and number. Unless otherwise indicated, phone numbers in this chapter are in the (664) area code.

Visitors' Information Offices

The **Tijuana Tourism & Convention Bureau** (683.1405) has an information office just inside the San Ysidro border crossing; it's open Monday through Saturday between 9AM and 7PM and Sunday between 9AM and 2PM. The **Tourism Bureau** also operates an information booth on Avenida Revolución between **Calles 3** and **4**, which is open daily. An information office at the intersection of **Calle 1** and Avenida Revolución is open daily between 9AM and 7PM. The **State Secretary of Tourism** office (Calle Primera 711, at Av Revolución; 688.0555) can help visitors with complaints or legal woes. **Fondo Mixto/Tijuana Tourism Board** (Av Paseo de los Héroes 9365-201; 684.2854, 888/775.2417; info@venatijuana.com; www.venatijuana.com) has information regarding accommodations, restaurants, and local events. In the US, **Baja Information** (6855 Friars Rd, suite 26, San Diego, CA 92108; 619/298.4105, 800/522.1516 in Arizona, California, and Nevada; 800/225.2786 elsewhere in the US; impamexicoinfo@juno.com) is a valuable resource for hotel reservations and advice before you go.

1 TIJUANA/SAN YSIDRO BORDER CROSSING

Welcome to the busiest border crossing in the world. Most tourists enter Tijuana here, either by car, bus, or on foot. No matter the mode,

the experience is often overwhelming. If you're driving, a Mexican guard will wave you past the booth. Take a deep breath, steady your nerves, and get ready to bump and grind (your gears, that is). Lanes take on only a semblance of order a few yards inside the border, and signs point in incredibly confusing directions. After bypassing an immediate right-hand exit, you must stay right, center, or left, depending on your destination. The first right-hand exit leads to **Pueblo Amigo Center** and the **Zona del Río**. Head straight and you may make it onto the toll road to Playas de Tijuana, Rosarito Beach, and Ensenada (misleadingly labeled "Rosarito Ensenada Scenic Road"). Veer to the left and enter the puzzling maze of downtown (follow signs for El Centro and Avenida Revolución). If you're in the midst of auto-body shops, you're on the right track. Don't be alarmed by the men racing toward you, waving their arms and yelling. They're only trying to give you an on-the-spot estimate for painting your car. And don't count on getting any of it right the first time around; driving in a befuddled daze is part of the total experience.

Pedestrians have a much easier time. Walkways lead to all the main sights, and cabs fill a nearby parking lot. The aroma of sizzling pork soon fills the air from a lineup of taco stands; salesmen flash their cases of silver jewelry with practiced persistence; children selling Chiclets and woven bracelets tug on your arm. The walkways are busy most of the day and night; guard your possessions as you would on a rush-hour Manhattan subway.

The border is open 24 hours a day, and there's usually only a short wait to enter Mexico. Coming back to the US is a different story. If you're driving, the line for the border can be 17 lanes wide and 3 miles long, and the wait may last well over an hour. Avoid weekday rush hours (the same as in the US) and weekend mornings and evenings. Sunday nights are a nightmare, because all those vacationing below must eventually pass through here. There is another crossing east of downtown, in the Otay Mesa area, but it's hard for a beginner to find. (To attempt this, take Calle 2a to Vía Rápida Oriente and follow signs to Otay.) If you're walking through the border, the wait is considerably less, but the line (or mass) of bodies sometimes packs the enclosed tunnel-like pathway leading toward the customs agents. Either way, an officer will ask your nationality; US residents don't need passports, but travelers from other countries should carry theirs, as well as visas if appropriate. You'll also be required to state what you're bringing back. ♦ Signs clearly mark entrances to the border from Paseo Tijuana and Calle 2.

2 PLAYAS DE TIJUANA

The coast seems secondary in the overall scheme of Tijuana, and there are no great beaches. The *playas* area has become a neighborhood of condominiums and private homes with a large shopping center and a campus of the private **Mexico City Universidad Iberoamericana**, with a school of architecture. There was talk about placing another border entry here, so travelers headed south could completely bypass the city. But the combination of influential residents on the Mexican side and environmental concerns along the US coast seems to have nixed the idea. ♦ Take the Ensenada Toll (Cuota) Rd from the border and exit at the Playas de Tijuana sign.

At Playas de Tijuana:

PLAZA DE TOROS MONUMENTAL

Bullfights are held in this spectacular seaside setting on summer Sundays, alternating with the bullring downtown. ♦ Admission. Su, about 4:30PM, July-Aug. At the Ensenada Hwy. 685.2210, 619/232.5049 in San Diego

3 EL TAURINO

★★★$ A courtly maître d' greets American tourists, presents them with an English-language menu, and escorts them to cozy booths in an ambiance far more soothing than any place on Revolución. The menu includes huge portions of roasted quail, baked chicken, shrimp in several styles, and a grilled fillet of New York steak. The prices are shockingly low (when compared to those in San Diego) and the quality of the food and service pleasingly high. ♦ Grilled meats/Mexican ♦ Daily, lunch and dinner. Calle 6 7531 (at Av Niños Héroes). 685.7075

4 AVENIDA REVOLUCIÓN

The historic soul of tourist Tijuana rests uneasily on this boulevard of bawdy bars and tawdry trinkets. During the two world wars (and every other US military buildup), Revolución was the place sailors went before they shipped out. The girlie shows are long gone, and city leaders have tried mightily to class up the strip. But its character remains questionable. Youngsters (primarily from the US) knock back beers and tequila with an intensity that's almost frightening. They literally dangle from the banisters of second- and third-story rooftop restaurants, each building more outrageously decked out in neon than the next.

The avenue's other consistent attraction is shopping. All the basic curios flow from cluttered storefronts onto the sidewalks, and sellers maintain a running spiel that would exhaust a circus barker. The most expansive souvenir shopping is in the *pasajes*, or arcades filled with individual sellers, but indi-

---

Restaurants/Clubs: Red | **Hotels: Purple** | Shops: Orange | **Outdoors/Parks: Green** | Sights/Culture: Blue

vidual stores are well worth browsing as well, and some have better-quality merchandise. Department stores fill out the shopping options, and restaurants abound.

Most of the interesting businesses are in a seven-block walk between Calles 2 and 9. Cross streets lead to the locals' downtown Tijuana. Especially busy are Avenida Constitución, one block west, and Avenida Madero to the east. ♦ Between Calles 9 and 2

5 LA ESPECIAL

★★★$ For down-home Mexican cooking, descend the stairway midblock on the south side of the street and enter the bustling din of the most popular restaurant on Revolución. Locals and visitors who appreciate *real* Mexican food have been coming here for nearly 50 years. The corn chips are fried on the premises, the salsa even looks hot, and the marinated carrots and jalapeños will spark a craving for a frosty beer. The most popular item on the menu is *carne asada*, a thin, plate-size filet of marinated grilled beef served with tortillas, beans, and rice. Tacos, enchiladas, and burritos have an earthy, savory flavor that can't be duplicated. The waiters, dressed in black slacks and vests, move with unruffled efficiency and speak enough English to answer your questions. The dark dining rooms are never empty, no matter the time of day. If you're into people watching, try for a table in the middle of the first room; for privacy, hold out for a booth. The same stairs that lead to the restaurant also enter a cool, dark *pasaje* where vendors display an above-average collection of silver and turquoise jewelry. ♦ Mexican ♦ Daily, breakfast, lunch, and dinner. Av Revolución 718 (between Calles 4 and 3). 685.6654

5 H. ARNOLD

This newish store where both prices and quality are relatively high is typically packed with gawkers and shoppers on the weekends. Eyes glazed from ogling the sixteenth velveteen sombrero or striped Saltillo-style blanket in previous stores, shoppers can't help but fondle the beautiful gifts and home decorations from mainland Mexico. These are nearly the same things you'll find elsewhere, but they're of the best selection and highest quality—for example, exquisite decorative tiles from Tonalá, Jalisco, and unusual blown glass vases from Guanajuato. ♦ Av Revolución 1968. 685.5660

6 MERCADO DE ARTESANÍAS

Bargains abound at this collection of stands that spreads over a full block along the walkway to downtown. Browse through baskets, serapes, piñatas, sombreros, and pottery; then make your purchases on the way back. You are likely to be deluged with offers from the sellers. Just keep your cool and don't get rattled by the pressure tactics. Though at first glance it all looks alike, you'll soon learn to judge quality and originality. ♦ Daily. Calle 2 and Av Ocampo

7 LA COSTA

★★★$$ Consistently fresh and abundant seafood keeps this restaurant full while newer ventures come and go. Try any fish prepared with garlic and butter or *veracruzano* style with tomatoes and onions. The abalone, when in season, is tender and delicious, and if you're in the mood for lobster, splurge here. Entrée prices include soup or salad, rice, and dessert. ♦ Seafood ♦ Daily, lunch and dinner. Calle 7 8131 (between Avs Revolución and Constitución). 685.8494

8 CHIKI JAI

★★$ The Spanish jai alai players from the nearby **Palacio Frontón** made this tiny café their headquarters during the years the game was played. For decades, this was the only place in town where you could get *pulpo en su tinto* (octopus in its own ink) and Basque-style chicken. Despite the arrival of newer, trendier restaurants, this cheerful and clean eatery maintains a faithful lunch clientele of locals and visitors. Congenial owners-hosts Manuel and Paquita Monje still keep a watchful eye on their business and are proud to show off the recently renovated kitchen and bathrooms. ♦ Spanish ♦ Daily, lunch and dinner. Av Revolución 1388 (between Calles 7 and 6). 685.4955

9 TOLÁN

When you've grown weary of seeing a million copies of the same onyx chess sets, visit this shop, one of the original purveyors of Mexican folk art in Tijuana. Señor Jesús Pérez Sánchez consistently impresses regulars with an ever-expanding selection of traditional glassware, woodcarvings, tin and papier-mâché sculptures, place settings and tablecloths, Christmas ornaments, and lacquerware chests. You won't leave empty-handed. ♦ Daily. Av Revolución 1471 (between Calles 8 and 7). 688.3637

10 PALACIO FRONTÓN

Bizarre as it may seem, the most significant edifice on Revolución is a mock Moorish palace fronted by a fountain and a statue of a jai alai player in midleap. The *frontón* (or ball court) opened at the end of World War II after 2 decades of false starts and enjoyed instantaneous success as Hollywood stars and post-war partiers jammed into the viewing stands. The glamour eventually faded, and the games were abandoned in the late 1990s. Today the venue is rented out for boxing matches and exhibitions. Horse races are broadcast via satellite at the adjacent **Caliente Race and Sports Book**, and tour buses meet passengers in front of the building. ♦ Av Revolución (between Calles 8 and 7)

11 LA VILLA DE ZARAGOZA HOTEL

$ Your best bet for comfort, safety, and cleanliness right near Avenida Revolución is this 42-room motel-like complex near the **Palacio Frontón**. You won't escape the traffic noise from the busy city center, but the management does try to keep the clientele subdued enough to let their neighbors sleep. After trudging through Tijuana all day, it's nice to be able to take a break in an air-conditioned room and down free bottles of purified water; there's also free parking (a plus in downtown) plus a funky restaurant and bar upstairs. ♦ Av Madero 1120 (between Calles 8 and 7). 685.1832

12 SANBORN'S

The original blue-tiled **Sanborn's** in Mexico City has been a haven for American travelers for nearly a century, and offshoots of the chain have gradually cropped up throughout the country. The Tijuana branch lacks the Old World charm of the Casa de Azulejos (House of Tiles) but looks exactly like its sister outlets inside, displaying a little bit of everything the consumer needs. The selection of folk art is impressive, with lacquered boxes from Guerrero, papier-mâché sculptures from Guanajuato, and silver filigree earrings from Taxco displayed tastefully. The chocolates counter and bakery are legendary: Be sure to pick up a sweet treat. The book and periodicals section has many classic books about Mexico in Spanish and English and a good selection of postcards. The restaurant is best at breakfast, when you can sit by the French doors in the sunlit room and feast on a bountiful buffet or order French toast, *huevos rancheros*, or fresh Danishes from the menu. Another bonus: an underground parking lot on Calle 9. ♦ Daily, 8AM-10PM. Av Revolución (between Calles 9 and 8). 688.1462

13 PUEBLO AMIGO

Architect **Federico Lara** designed this fanciful re-creation of a Mexican village in 1989 as a one-stop pseudo-Mexican experience just 300 yards from the border. Shops and restaurants are painted blue, peach, and green; pathways are named after picturesque Mexican towns; a brick kiosk built by hand by a family from Querétaro stands nobly in the middle. Over the years, the complex has become more a nightlife center than a tourist attraction. Families gather to shop at the grocery store and eat at the take-out stands. Visitors come for the clubs and restaurants. A pedestrian walkway runs between the border and the complex; pedestrians who want to move on to Avenida Revolución will need to take a cab. ♦ Paseo Tijuana (between Av Alfonso Reyes and Puente Mexico) &

Within Pueblo Amigo:

LEY

Don't miss the experience of shopping in a full-scale Mexican grocery-department store. The *tortillería* makes fresh corn tortillas all day long, the *panadería* pumps out fresh rolls and baked goods, and the deli section offers a fascinating selection of cheeses, salads, sauces, and vats of tamales and casseroles for a serve-yourself take-out meal. ♦ Daily. No phone

SEÑOR FROGS

★★★$ Most major Mexican cities have at least one restaurant from the Carlos Anderson chain, but the mood differs considerably between beach resorts and business cities. The 22,000-square-foot Tijuana venue has a hugely popular restaurant on the first floor and a raucous bar on the second. Red neon lights cast a pink glow over the Warhol-like paintings and escaped carousel horses that decorate the restaurant. Spectators usually head here after a bullfight to sample the delicious *antojitos* (tamales, chalupas, tostadas, and other traditional Mexican snacks) or barbecued chicken and ribs. The waiters are more than attentive, the food is always good, and the ambiance is consistently festive. ♦ Mexican/American ♦ Daily, lunch and dinner. 682.4962. www.senorfrogs.com

HOTEL
PUEBLO AMIGO

13 HOTEL PUEBLO AMIGO

$$$ This modern seven-story inn is the best place to stay in downtown Tijuana. The 108 rooms have either one king-size or two queen-size beds, direct-dial international phone service, minibars, and purified tap water; facilities include a restaurant and bar and an indoor pool. The clientele is a mix of tourists and business travelers using the business center, secretarial services, and convention and meeting rooms. The hotel is ideally located if you're touring Tijuana's major attractions. ♦ Vía Rápida Oriente 9211 (at

---

Restaurants/Clubs: **Red** | Hotels: **Purple** | Shops: **Orange** | Outdoors/Parks: **Green** | Sights/Culture: **Blue**

171

WINERIES

Northern Baja is Mexico's leading source of domestic wine. Most wineries, launched by Russian immigrants in the early 1900s, are located in the fertile valleys around **Ensenada**, primarily in the **Guadalupe Valley** east of the city and at **Santo Tomás** south of the city. In late August, the wineries join together for a weeklong wine festival that includes the blessing of the grapes and all sorts of culinary and cultural events. **Baja California Tours** (see Guided Tours, page 179) offers a special tour for the wine festival, and winery tours are also available through the **Hotel San Nicolás** (646/176.1901) in Ensenada.

Wineries that are open to the public include **L.A. Cetto** in Tijuana (664/685.3031), **L.A. Cetto** in the Guadalupe Valley (646/155.2264), **Casa Domecq** in the Guadalupe Valley (646/165.2249); and **Santo Tomás** in Ensenada (646/178.3333).

Pueblo Amigo). 683.5030, 800/386.6985; fax 683.5032. htlpueblo@telnor.net; www.hotelpuebloamigo.com

Within Hotel Pueblo Amigo:

CALIENTE RACE AND SPORTS BOOK

Satellite betting is a big attraction in Tijuana, especially because the horses have ceased racing at the **Agua Caliente** track. The **Caliente Sports Book** clubs are spread throughout the city; at last count there were 11, with 3 located in **Pueblo Amigo**. The clubs feature satellite broadcasts of sporting events, horse races, and even beauty pageants from the US and Mexico. Bettors settle in comfy chairs in cocktail lounges and watch the action on wide-screen TVs. ♦ 647.4730, 619/231.1919 in San Diego, 800/PIKBAJA in the US. www.caliente.com.mx

14 L.A. CETTO WINERY

Mexico's best wines come from Baja California, and **Cetto** is one of Baja's premier wineries. Tours of the Tijuana facilities include visits to the aging room and bottling plant, a generous wine tasting ($2), and plenty of time in the gift and wine shop. The winery is a short walk from Revolución, one block west on Calle 9 and two blocks south on Constitución. ♦ M-Sa; Cañón Johnson 2108 (at Av Constitución). 685.3031; fax 638.7121

15 TOWER OF AGUA CALIENTE

A replica of the tiled tower at the entrance to the old Agua Caliente casino was built by the Lions Clubs of Tijuana in 1988. It marks the point where Avenida Revolución becomes Boulevard Agua Caliente, leading toward the bullring, racetrack, country club, and exclusive neighborhoods. ♦ Av Revolución (between Blvd Agua Caliente and Calle 11)

16 ZONA RÍO

The river zone is Tijuana's cultural and commercial zone, with sophisticated restaurants, discos, office buildings, and shopping centers lining broad boulevards. The main thoroughfares here are a thrill a minute for brave and brazen drivers, because they all lead to *glorietas*—maddeningly confusing traffic circles that leave novices cringing. The secret to driving around these circles is to maneuver your car between two other vehicles (preferably already dented), then go with the flow. There is a perceptible pattern of stops and starts that you'll eventually understand. The *glorietas* also boast fine monuments to world leaders and noble ideas, from Abraham Lincoln and the Aztec emperor Cuauhtémoc to the concept of independence. It's nearly impossible to get a look at the statues, however, unless you walk along the boulevard instead of driving. ♦ Paseo de los Héroes (between Avs Rodríguez and León)

17 MERCADO HIDALGO

For a touch of authentic Mexico, stop by this busy marketplace with stands displaying fresh flowers, produce, dried and fresh chilies, herbs, and beans. The large selection of piñatas, along with the candy to fill them, makes, if nothing else, an excellent photo opportunity. You'll find a few souvenirs ensconced among the household necessities, and they're sure to cost less than in the tourist shops. ♦ Daily. Av Independencia (at Av Sánchez Taboada). No phone

18 TIJUANA CENTRO CULTURAL

The cultural center, designed in 1974 by **Pedro Ramírez Vázquez** and **Manuel Rosen**, is the centerpiece of Tijuana's art community and a must-see for those interested in exploring Mexico beyond Tijuana. An Omnimax theater rises above the low-profile museum buildings, looking like a sand-colored UFO. Films on space, travel, and science are shown in the theater throughout the day. Inaugurated in 1999, the **California Museum** (admission) houses a permanent display explaining life throughout the peninsula, from pre-Hispanic times to the modern era. Kids and adults will enjoy the variety of exhibits, from a gray whale skull to a series of old ships built to scale, models of early missions, and a Kumayaay Indian willow hut, as well as oil paintings and icons. The museum space itself is a pleasure to explore, with exposed metal beams and tract lighting illuminating items in Lucite display cases. The museum's café is a nice place to rejuvenate. Music, theater, and dance performances are held in the concert hall and courtyard; a schedule of upcoming performances is available at the museum's information desk. The bookstore has a great collection of art books in Spanish, and a few postcards and souvenirs. ♦ Paseo de los Héroes (between Avs Independencia and Mina). 687.9600

19 PLAZA FIESTA

This pretty shopping complex has worn poorly with time; a murder here in 1989 did nothing to improve public relations. It once hosted popular restaurants; the current tenants are bars that attract packs of serious-looking youths draped in black on weekend nights. There is little to distinguish one bar from another except the favored flavor of music: techno, pop, rock, and Latin tunes compete like a battle of the bands, bursting forth from dark rooms with video screens and small dance floors onto screened-in patios. ♦ Paseo de los Héroes (between Avs E. Castellanos and Independencia)

20 PLAZA RÍO TIJUANA

Comparable in size and selection to many US malls, this complex has several department stores, including **Sara's** and **Dorian's**, dozens of specialty shops, a **Sanborn's** restaurant and shop, and a multiplex movie theater (showing first-run US films in many of its 17 salons). ♦ Paseo de los Héroes (between Avs Cuauhtémoc and Independencia). 684.0402

21 TOREO DE TIJUANA

Here top matadors from Mexico and Spain perform their rituals with polished flair before approving crowds; as a rule, the bulls don't stand a chance. The crowd is a mix of cultures and classes, with the elite seated in the shade near the ring and masses packed together on bleachers in the sun. Bullfights are held on Sunday afternoons between May and September, with no fights in June. The venue alternates between this ring and the **Plaza de Toros Monumental** in Playas de Tijuana (see page 169). ♦ Admission. Blvd Agua Caliente (at Av Cuauhtémoc). No phone in Mexico; 619/232.5049 in San Diego

22 CORONA PLAZA

$ Don't be fooled by the understated office-like edifice of this hotel—the décor inside is quite sophisticated. It mimics the newer hotels in other parts of Mexico, where the landscaping and public spaces are arranged atriumlike in the center of the building, with its 100 rooms overlooking the open restaurant. For less noise and more light and fresh air, take a room on the second or third floor at the back near the swimming pool. The color scheme is a subdued gray, peach, and blue combo with bleached wood furnishings. The hotel is just south of the bullring, on the same side of the street; the entrance to the underground parking garage is just beyond the hotel's entrance. The only attraction within reasonable walking distance is the bullring, but all the rest are within a short cab ride. ♦ Blvd Agua Caliente 1426 (between Río Yaqui and Av Cuauhtémoc). 681.8183; fax 681.8185

23 LA FONDA DE ROBERTO

★★★$$ Though it's hard to find (take a cab), this stalwart restaurant serves authentic regional Mexican cuisine that is worth the search. Transplants from the mainland stop by when they're homesick for Yucatán's *cochinita pibil* (marinated pork baked in banana leaves), Puebla's *mole* (a sauce of chocolate and spices), or *chiles en nogada* (chilies stuffed with ground meat, raisins, and nuts, topped with cream and pomegranate seeds). The daily specials are always worth trying, though the flavors may be unusual. Try to dine here with a group so you can sample several dishes. The restaurant is located off Boulevard Agua Caliente on the old road to Ensenada. ♦ Mexican ♦ Tu-Su, lunch and dinner. Cuauhtémoc Sureste 2800, Col. América (at the Motel La Sierra). 686.4687

24 PARROQUIA ESPÍRITU SANTO

The parish church for the wealthy residents of Colonia Chapultepec rises behind the racetrack in a series of seven white arches inlaid with stained glass. Legend has it that the pastor's mother dreamed of a church that appeared like a rainbow, with arcs of color changing in hue with the sun. The designer Jaime Sandoval Hernández (an engineer from Michoacán) relied on stained glass to cast a rainbow on the stark white arches, the colors changing in intensity with the movement of the sun. The effect is best seen from inside the building. As you look toward the altar, the arches appear to be softly washed in gold, green, lavender, and blue; as you look from the altar toward the pews, the series of stained-glass arcs come into sight, framing

---

Restaurants/Clubs: Red | Hotels: Purple | Shops: Orange | Outdoors/Parks: Green | Sights/Culture: Blue

the stained-glass wall at the rear of the church. Additional ornamentation has been kept to a bare minimum. The altar is backed by a sky blue wall and simple crucifix. A framed painting of the Virgin of Guadalupe hangs nearby. The church is overwhelmingly beautiful, particularly during a midday wedding. ♦ Avs Rosales and Cumpas (at Blvd Agua Caliente). 621.8355

25 GRAND HOTEL

$$ The twin mirrored towers of the **Plaza Agua Caliente** and this hotel rise 18 stories above the clutter and congestion of the city, acting as landmarks for confused travelers and hallmarks of a prosperous Tijuana at its height in the early 1980s. Architect **Alfredo Lauren** designed the hotel, which opened in 1982 as a **Fiesta Americana** and is still referred to by that name by many locals. Although the spare look of the hotel's lobby and public spaces is no longer in vogue, this is still a gathering spot for Tijuana society hosting charity balls, beauty contests, and fashion shows. The 422 rooms—all with minibars and direct-dial phones—are popular with business travelers, visiting celebrities, and tourists alike. Facilities include a pool, two tennis courts, a health club, shops, three restaurants, a lively bar, and a branch of the **Caliente Race and Sports Book**. ♦ Blvd Agua Caliente 4558 (between Blvd Rodríguez and Av Cuauhtémoc). 681.7000, 800/472.6385 in the US; fax 686.7016. ghotelt2@telnor.net; www.grandhoteltijuana.com

26 CIEN AÑOS

★★$$ Dine with well-off Mexicans and tourists who've bolted from the beer-slinging bars of Avenida Revolución in this simple yet elegant, upscale eatery. Waiters are helpful and attentive yet unobtrusive and happy to explain some of the unusual nouvelle Mexican specialties. Pre-Hispanic favorites include items made with nopal cactus, *huitlacoche* corn fungus, a wide range of chilies, and of course, the humble corn tortilla. These are artfully combined with such Spanish contributions to Mexican *comida* as beef, pork, and cheese as well as just the right seasonings and spices. ♦ Mexican ♦ Daily. Calle José María Velazco 1407, between Paseo de los

In 2000, there were 28 million border crossings into Baja California. Tourism professionals estimate that on average, 25 million people visit Tijuana annually.

The Kingston Trio's hit *"The Tijuana Jail"* is based on a 1958 raid of illegal gambling halls in Baja that left many Americans behind bars below the border.

Héroes and Vía Rápida Poniente, Zona Río. 634.3039

27 MUNDO DIVERTIDO

A roller coaster rises high above the **Zona Río**, providing a welcome focal point for those trying to drive to this amusement park. As with most local attractions, the park is more fun at night, when lights streak the sky with garish colors and the noises seem intensified. Attractions include a miniature golf course, batting cage, rides for the little ones, and a video-game parlor guaranteed to keep the teens occupied. ♦ Admission is free; tickets for the rides are on sale at several stands inside the park. Calle José M. Velasco 2578 (at Paseo de los Héroes). 634.3213

28 BABY ROCK

Ask architecture buffs to name the most striking building in town and they'll inevitably mention this one, designed by **Jaime Bejar**. The disco to beat all discos, it is shaped like— you guessed it—a big brown outcropping of boulders half buried in rocks. The line winds far down the boulevard on Friday and Saturday nights as a chic crowd of young adults waits to be judged cool enough to be admitted to the cavelike dance hall filled with tropical plants, soaring lights, and the throbbing beat of the latest tunes. ♦ Th-Su, 9PM-5AM. Av Diego Rivera 30 (at Blvd Paseo de los Héroes). 634.1313

29 HOTEL LUCERNA

$$$ When President Miguel de la Madrid inaugurated this hotel in 1980, it was the only four-star facility in town. Today the hotel has an Old World ambiance in the lobby and restaurants, and a somewhat worn appearance in the 179 rooms and suites. The style seems more from the 1960s than 1990s, with brocade wallpaper, gilded chandeliers, wrought-iron balconies, and ornate bedside lamps that turn down low enough to be nightlights. The color scheme is mostly gold, brown, and green. The location is probably the quietest of any hotel in town, and the heavy drapes, air conditioning, and lack of outside noise make for a superb night's sleep. Of its two restaurants, **El Acueducto** is often recommended by locals; the travel agency is a great help if you're planning on traveling into mainland Mexico. ♦ Paseo de los Héroes 10902 (at Blvd Rodríguez). 633.3900, 800/LUCERNA; fax 634.2400. lucerna@telnor.net; www.hotel-lucerna.com.mx

30 LOS ARCOS

★★★$$ No matter how much this restaurant expands, the business crowd still packs it full between 2 and 4PM on weekday afternoons for the traditional midday feast. It's hard to imagine how they ever manage to get back to work. The typical meal might include smoked marlin tacos, fresh seviche, and *caldo de lobina* (chunks of sea bass in lime broth) served with crisp corn tortillas. And those are just the appetizers. Should you still be hungry, order the specialty: a whole grilled snapper served on a giant platter. Ask for *cebollitas* and get a plate of grilled green onions and chilies to wrap in tortillas with your fish. The room gets noisier and livelier as the afternoon wears on, and everyone seems reluctant to get on with the day. Being on vacation, you can linger as long as you like. ♦ Mexican/seafood ♦ Daily, lunch, and dinner. Blvd Salinas 201 (at Calle Escuadrón). 686.3171

31 VILLA SAVERIOS

★★★$$$ This chic, modern restaurant is the place to try Tijuana's version of haute Italian cuisine. The antipasto alone is a delight, and the homemade pastas melt in your mouth. The scene is quite hip—dress up a bit. ♦ Italian ♦ Daily, lunch and dinner. Calle Escuadrón 201 at Blvd Sánchez Taboada, Zona Río. 686.6502

32 LA LEÑA

★★★$$ The golf course green seen through a huge plate-glass window is just about the only decoration or distraction in this restaurant's single spare, square dining

room. Soft, romantic music encourages conversation, whereas ceiling fans lazily distribute the delicious smell of meat grilling in the open kitchen. **La Leña** (which means "the firewood") is famous for its grilled meats; the *gaonera*, a tender fillet of beef stuffed with cheese and guacamole, is a must. The waiters are friendly and helpful and teasingly encourage first-timers to sample the tripe. ♦ Mexican ♦ Daily, lunch and dinner. Blvd Agua Caliente 11191 (between Avs Mérida and Sonora). 686.2920

33 FIESTA INN

$$$ The original Vita Spa Agua Caliente has metamorphosed as several hotel chains to reopen in 1995, restored and rejuvenated, as a **Fiesta Inn**. The restaurant is wedged between the lobby and the pool area, where under a Moorish-style cement canopy you can relax in the slightly sulfurous waters of the original thermal spring. Rooms are slightly more elegant than other Tijuana accommodations of this price range—with dark pink carpets, cream walls, forest green upholstery, and floral accents in the same palate. Each room has a writing desk and reading lamps above the beds. The mineral springs are diverted to individual tubs at the second-floor spa (reservations, 888/848.2928), where you can also get massage, facials, pedicures, and other treatment, at US prices. ♦ Paseo de los Héroes 18818, Zona Río (at Av Sánchez Taboada). 634.6901, 800/343.7821; fax 634.6912. www.fiestamexico.com

34 RUINAS DE AGUA CALIENTE

In the 1920s Hollywood's wildest leading men and ladies converged on this out-of-the-way pleasure palace to gamble and drink—Prohibition and prudishness be damned. The few film clips from the era show a sultry Rita Hayworth singing Spanish love songs and long-legged sybarites sunning by the pool. The entire **Agua Caliente** resort complex included a racetrack, golf course, hotel, spa, riding stables, and even an airstrip. Today, several elementary and secondary schools have a campus on the hotel and casino's grounds. The tiled point of the sky-high minaret that marked the entrance pokes above a cluster of basketball courts and hoops. The beyond—Olympic-size pool, edged in gorgeous blue-and-yellow hand-painted tile, is empty; a rusted diving board stands to one side; a chipped green fountain sits stolidly above the adjoining wading pool. A larger-than-life-size statue of President Lázaro Cárdenas stands at the corner of the property, his back toward the minaret. Cárdenas banned gambling in Mexico in 1935; the rest is history. You can get a good glimpse of the minaret from Paseo de los Héroes and Avenida Sánchez Taboada. To see the pool, drive up the small hill to your right just after the intersection, and into the large parking lot. ♦ Av Sánchez Taboada (at Paseo de los Héroes)

35 TIJUANA COUNTRY CLUB

🅟 The 18-hole golf course and country club were first established in the 1920s, when Tijuana was a popular escape for Hollywood's elite. Among the course's current clients are foreign business travelers involved with the city's *maquiladoras*. Guests at some hotels have privileges at the club; others can golf for a fee. The least expensive green fees for nonmembers are Monday, Tuesday, Thursday, and Friday. Caddies and carts available at extra charge. ♦ Admission. Blvd Agua Caliente (between Avs Hipódromo and de los Olivos). 681.7855

36 CASA MEXICANA

A wonderful selection of home accessories can be found at this shop a few blocks up from the **Grand Hotel**. There are stone bird-baths, large mirrors in tin frames, decorative tiles (sold individually or by the box), and innovative housewares and home accessories of ceramic, wrought iron, and glass. It's a wonderful shop for browsing and getting inspiration for home redecoration. ♦ Blvd Salinas 11111 (at Calle G. de León). 686.5491

37 EL POTRERO

★★$$$ What a funny place! Because it's shaped like a gigantic Mexican hat, you'd think this family-owned restaurant would be full of gringos eating pseudo-Mexi-food. Instead, local lawyers and other professionals chat amiably over business lunches and personal dinners. Pastoral scenes—a cornfield, a burro, a young country girl—decorate seven stained-glass windows at the front of the round restaurant. The food is Mexican, but instead of *antojitos* (tacos, enchiladas, and other fare most familiar to foreigners), you'll enjoy delicious traditional dishes with an international touch. For an appetizer, try the grilled Portobello mushrooms stuffed with crunchy garlic sautéed in olive oil. Move on to lentil soup ("like Grandma used to make") or a green salad before attacking a main course: perhaps meatball stew, rabbit in rich dark *mole* sauce, or the super tender *carne ahumado* (beef grilled over charcoal and then deliciously seasoned). The descriptive English-language menu makes choosing easier. ♦ Mexican ♦ Daily, breakfast, lunch, and dinner. Blvd Salinas 4700 at Blvd Agua Caliente. 681.8082

38 HIPÓDROMO DE AGUA CALIENTE

Greyhounds, rather than horses, race at this track. But those who are devoted to the ponies can head for the **Caliente Race and Sports Book** franchise here and watch satellite-TV broadcasts of US horse races. Gamblers can place their bets on either quadruped. ♦ Greyhounds race daily except W; Sports Book open daily. Blvd Agua Caliente (at Av Salinas). 633.7300; 619/231.1919 in San Diego

39 CAFÉ RITZ

★★$$$ If you sit for long in this café-pub-restaurant, something will go up in flames. It may be the house specialty—spinach flambé, ignited to unite olive oil, brown sugar, and Cointreau and then topped with mandarin orange slices and pine nuts. Or the delicious sweet banana flambé, blackened with liqueur and cinnamon and served with a huge chunk of vanilla ice cream. Vases here and there hold bird of paradise and calla lilies, mimicking the design in the delicate stained-glass windows. Situated near the Otay area factories and border crossing, this intimate restaurant's lunch clientele includes foreign and national businesspeople talking shop. At night, candlelight and a piano man crooning *epoca de oro* ballads invite romantic tête-à-têtes. ♦ Continental ♦ Daily, breakfast, lunch, and dinner. Blvd Lázaro Cárdenas L-6, Zona Otay Constituyentes. 624.3608

SOUTH OF TIJUANA

Tijuana is foreign and familiar at the same time, simultaneously confusing and reassuring her American guests. Probably 75% of first-time visitors to TJ (as the city is nicknamed) speak absolutely no Spanish, wouldn't know a peso from a yen, and have only a vague sense that there must be laws and customs to be followed. It usually works out okay, but to make the most of the experience, try to pick up at least a sprinkling of the language and also bring some common sense.

The country code is 52; the area codes for phone numbers in this chapter are listed with each number.

Transpeninsular Highway 1, which stretches the 1,000-mile length of the **Baja California** peninsula, begins just south of the border in Tijuana. The more heavily traveled northern Baja cities of Tijuana and **Ensenada** are connected by Carretera 1D: Look for signs for the **Ensenada Cuota** or **Rosarito Ensenada Scenic Highway**, which leads up into the hills west of the city past **Playas de Tijuana**. The Ensenada Toll Road (about $6.60 from TJ to Ensenada) then heads south to the weekend coastal getaways between Tijuana and Ensenada, 68 miles down a picturesque shoreline. Keep a close watch on the road signs just south of Playas de Tijuana and *don't* head east to Tecate.

The first tourism-oriented complex you come upon is **Real Del Mar Golf Club** (Ensenada Toll Rd Km 19.5; 664/613.3401, 800/662.6180; www.realdelmar.com.mx), an 18-hole course that covers the hills and valleys east of the highway. The course is open to the public. Within the complex is the **Marriott Real Del Mar Residence Inn** ($$$; 664/631.3670; 800/331.3131 in the US), a peaceful, secluded golfer's hotel with fully equipped suites, including kitchens; some have fireplaces, and there's a pool on the premises.

Rosarito Beach, where investors are determined to create a full-scale resort city, has grown into a major community of more than 100,000 residents and a prime weekend getaway for thousands of Southern Californians. Traffic grinds slowly through town along **Boulevard Benito Juárez** on Saturday and Sunday afternoons. The north-ernmost exit for Rosarito puts you at the outskirts of town; cruise Boulevard Juárez slowly, keeping an eye out for pedestrians and easily missed stop (*alto*) signs. The biggest complex at this end of town is the **Quinta del Mar Resort** ($$-$$$; 25500 Blvd Juárez, a block from the beach;

661/612.1648; 800/678.7244 in the US) consisting of condos, time-shares, and hotel rooms. Within the complex, the **Hotel Quinta Terranova** has luxury condominiums and beachfront town homes, tennis courts, restaurants, and a shopping arcade. Rosarito has become a center for carved furnishings, and several shops have cropped up along Boulevard Juárez. Newer shops farther south have diverted business from the moribund **Quinta Plaza**, next to the hotel, but still worthwhile is a **Caliente Race & Sports Book** gambler's hall and **Comercial Mexicana** supermarket. The most compelling reason to visit, however, is to have lunch or dinner at **La Leña de Rosarito** ($$; 661/612.0826). Every afternoon, owner Jaime Ramirez beats a path from his government job in Tecate to whip up his signature flan (custard) and greet longtime customers. After a free appetizer, order the steak-and-lobster dinner or one of the grilled steak-house specials. A few blocks south, savvy locals stream throughout the day to **Ortega's** ($; 661/612.0022, Blvd Juárez 200), which serves inexpensive yet endless buffet meals. Roughly across the street, **Arte Mexicano** (Blvd Juárez 2400; 661/612.0125) is *the* place to visit if you're about to furnish a castle or other monumental building. The 15,000-square-foot building is crammed with massive iron architectural elements (door frames, gates, and giant chandeliers), heavy dark-wood furniture, and other fascinating pieces, in addition to a smattering of smaller keepsakes. Less than a mile south on the ocean side of the street, you'll find **Vince's Seafood Restaurant** ($$; Blvd Juárez 97-A; 661/612.1253), an unassuming place with Formica tables and battered wood chairs. Atmosphere notwithstanding, Vince's is the people's choice for a seafood lunch, where you can get a small lobster for $10 or a large lobster meal for about twice that much. The breaded halibut, another favorite, includes soup, salad, tortillas, and rice or potatoes. A dozen oysters or fresh shrimp or tuna salad make a wonderful meal—despite being served on plastic plates. At the back of the 28-year-old restaurant is a fish market that sells to homemakers and other area restaurants. One block farther, the **Rosarito Tourist & Visitors Bureau** (Blvd Juárez 907, suite 14; 66/612.0396; 800/962-BAJA, toll-free in the US; www.rosaritobch.com) folks hand out brochures in the Oceana Plaza, which houses mainly government agencies, not retail stores.

Continuing south, **El Nido** ($$; Blvd Juárez 67;

San Diego — Ensenada:
68 miles / 1.5 hours

661/612.1430) is simultaneously lively and intimate, with at least five dining rooms decorated in rustic but upbeat style, with lamp shades and wood trim of the curious trunk of the cirio cactus, brick walls, and lots of wrought iron. Signature dishes of this longtime Rosarito restaurant are quail and venison, but you can choose from a range of more conventional meats. Tortillas are handmade over an open fire, and near the back of the restaurant, a round bar adds another unique touch to the pretty premises. Across the street and a block or two south, **Le Cousteau** ($$; Blvd Juárez 184; 661/612.2655) is moderately priced and French-country comfortable. A fireplace warms the single cottage-style restaurant with knotty pine ceiling and exposed beams, white café curtains, brick walls, and rustic cement floor. On the menu are vegetarian crepes and grape leaves as well as filet mignon, lasagne, four-cheese fettuccine, and daily specials (no credit cards accepted).

It's impossible to overlook the garish façade of the **Festival Plaza** ($-$$; Calle Nogal 1207-1 at Boulevard Benito Juárez; phone and fax 661/612-2950, 800/453.8606; www.festivalbaja.com), a 145-room hotel and entertainment complex. Rooms run from simple studios to two-story casitas with kitchenettes and hot tubs. Noise is a definite factor throughout the property; the sound system blares rock and pop and is silent only between 2AM and 9AM, if then. Concerts are frequently held in the hotel's outdoor arena by the large playground; other fun facilities include a pool, a concert stage, several restaurants, and the dusky **Museo Cantina Tequila**, a bar masquerading as a museum serving 130 varieties of tequila. Just behind

Festival Plaza, **Papas & Beer** (661/612.0444) is a strange and somewhat wonderful bar that seems well suited for a rave: *Swiss Family Robinson* meets modern funk and techno. Young people party in small enclaves at different levels surrounding a central sandy area or run up the cement stairs to perform to no one in particular from a large, raised stage. Small groups shout to each other above the music under palapa shelters or the palm trees and the stars. The bar is adorned with tangas and microbikini bottoms.

But for most people the reason to visit Rosarito on your drive down the coast is to see the **Rosarito Beach Hotel** ($$; Blvd Juárez 31; 661/612.1106; 800/343.8582 in the US; fax 661/612.1125; reserv@telnor.net; www. rosaritobeachhotel.com). There is an exit from the highway right by the hotel—you'll see the arched entryway to the west. The red-tile-roofed, white-stucco hotel was built in the

GUIDED TOURS

First-timers are likely to get more from their Baja experience by joining a guided tour that handles transportation through the border and within Mexico in addition to offering information on what you're seeing along the way. Check with the following companies for information:

Baja California Tours (858/454.7166 or 800/336.5454, both in the US; www.bajatours. signonsandiego.com) offers guided day and overnight tours to **Tijuana**, **Rosarito**, and **Ensenada**. They also offer specialized tours, including tours of art galleries and wineries; customized tours are available.

San Diego Contactours (619/477.8687, 800/235.5393; fax 619/477.0705; www.contactours.com) has guided day and overnight tours from San Diego to **Tijuana**, **Rosarito**, and **Ensenada**. For example, their midweek Ensenada Tour, under $100 per person, includes lunch the first day, a tour, and room at a three- or four-star hotel.

San Diego Scenic Tours (858/273.8687) offers a 4-hour narrated tour of the major sights in **Tijuana**, with free time for shopping and dining.

same era as Agua Caliente in Tijuana and has been open continuously since the 1920s. Luckily, it survived the end of gambling and the arrival of Prohibition that destroyed Agua Caliente. One of the prettiest original buildings now houses the spa, offering first-class massage, facials, wraps, and other treatments. Further vestiges of its former glamour are evident in **Chabert's**, a glamorous restaurant with heavy brocade drapes, handmade rugs, and luscious chandeliers. In the French restaurant's large anteroom, patrons sip wine or spirits and admire the tiles depicting scenes from Don Quijote de la Mancha as they wait for a table in the luxurious dining room. In the hotel itself, 275 rooms vary in comfort and amenities: The most charming are in the original building on the two floors above the pool; the most comfortable are in the newer tower facing the sea. Stop by for a margarita in the **Azteca** bar restaurant, another of the town's recommended eateries. The hotel hosts a buffet dinner and folkloric dance show every Friday and Saturday night, and a popular Sunday brunch.

South of Rosarito, the **Old Ensenada Highway** (Carretera 1) runs parallel to 1D past several resort communities and hotels. Less than 10 miles beyond Rosarito is **Foxploration** (Carretera Libre a Ensenada Km 32.8, Popotla; 661/614.9499; admission; closed Tu, W in summer, and closed in off season), a theme park built on the set of *Titanic* after its 1997 wrap. See costumes from *Titanic*, tour a film set, and learn how movies are made. On weekends, local artists perform on the oceanfront stage. There's also a shopping arcade,

children's play area, and food court with the usual fast-food suspects. Just beyond, **Calafia** ($; Km 35.5 Old Ensenada Hwy; 661/612.1580, 877/700.2093; fax 661/612.0296; calafia1@telnor.net; www.calafia.com.mx) is the most dramatic of the enclaves that have for years drawn repeat visitors from the US. The long-standing trailer park has closed, and the inn's 50 rooms are but an adjunct to the property's popular restaurant, decorated with old photos of Baja and historical artifacts and overlooking steep cliffs to the sea. Many opt to eat at tables on individual landings staggering down the cliffs to a sea-level stage and dance floor. For wonderful modern art, visit **Galería Giorgio Santini** (closed W; Carretera 1 Km 40; 661/614.1459; www.giorgiosantini.com), which shows contemporary Mexican, European, and US artists' work and fine jewelry from Mexico.

A trip down the coast isn't complete without a visit to **Puerto Nuevo** (Km 44 Old Ensenada Hwy). The attraction is a simple but bountiful feast of lobster, beans, rice, and homemade tortillas. Puerto Nuevo (also called Newport) began as a tiny village of fishermen's shacks where families served lobster dinners from small dining rooms often built onto the front of their houses. Now Puerto Nuevo has more than 25 restaurants, all serving the same basic lobster dinner, though the local waters have long been fished out and the lobsters are shipped here from elsewhere. The Pacific spiny lobster is not sweet like those from Maine but has a distinctive salty flavor. Most of the restaurants are open between noon and 10PM, but some do close earlier when the crowd is light. Crafts vendors have set up

---

Restaurants/Clubs: Red | Hotels: Purple | Shops: Orange | Outdoors/Parks: Green | Sights/Culture: Blue

A MEXICAN SAMPLER

A visit to San Diego is the perfect opportunity to get a taste of Mexican dishes. Far more varied and interesting than the stereotypical tacos and burritos would lead you to think, Mexico's cuisine is a blend of several different influences, including Maya, Aztec, Spanish, French, and American. Whether you're actually heading south of the border to **Tijuana** or **Ensenada** or staying in the San Diego area, you're bound to encounter at least one Mexican restaurant worthy of a stop. The following glossary of terms will help you find your way around a typical menu:

Buñuelo A deep-fried flour tortilla sprinkled with sugar and cinnamon.

Burrito An oversize flour tortilla wrapped just so to encase beans, various styles of meat, or even fish or seafood.

Carne asada Thin strips of beef marinated to a spicy perfection, then grilled and served with tortillas.

Carnitas Marinated chunks of pork, often served with a basket of tortillas and a tray of condiments (salsa, onions, cilantro, guacamole) for a do-it-yourself feast.

Chiles rellenos Mild or hot green peppers stuffed with cheese or meat, coated with egg batter, and fried.

Chimichanga A deep-fried burrito, Texas-style.

Chorizo Spicy sausage. It's often mixed with scrambled eggs and salsa, then wrapped in a flour tortilla.

Churro A deep-fried twisted strip of sweet dough rolled in cinnamon and sugar.

Cilantro That taste you can't quite figure out. Cilantro (aka Chinese parsley, coriander leaves) grows like a weed in local gardens and appears as a garnish on *carnitas*, fajitas, *carne asada*, and other dishes; usually included in salsa and other sauces.

Enchilada A bit of cheese or meat wrapped in a corn tortilla, covered with red or green sauce, and baked. Great with melted cheese, sour cream, or guacamole on top.

Fajitas The Californization of Mexican food at its best—sautéed chicken, beef, or shrimp with strips of onions, green peppers, and other veggies served on a sizzling griddle with a basket of fresh tortillas.

Fish taco Grilled or batter-fried fish with shredded cabbage, lime, and secret sauce in a soft corn tortilla.

Flan Caramel custard.

Guacamole Mashed avocado mixed with lemon juice, cilantro, onion, tomatoes, and chilies. Because avocados are priced like gold these days, guacamole is often stretched with sour cream or mayonnaise.

Huevos rancheros Fried eggs on a corn tortilla topped with mild tomato sauce.

Nachos The ultimate snack feast, based on a layer of corn chips topped with melted cheese, as common as popcorn at baseball games, movies, and bars. The toppings make the meal—beans, sour cream, guacamole, chopped jalapeños, *chorizo*, and more.

Quesadilla A Mexican grilled-cheese sandwich on a flour (or corn) tortilla, good topped with Ortega chili strips, guacamole, or sour cream.

Salsa A generic term for the ubiquitous dip/sauce/condiment made of any combination of red or green tomatoes, onions, chilies, and cilantro. It can be cool as ketchup or hot as hell.

Tamale A rectangle of finely ground cornmeal with a portion of meats in chili sauce, also made with a sweet inside filling, or plain. Wrapped in corn husks and steamed.

Tortilla Flour or cornmeal dough patted into a thin, round pancake, then griddle-cooked—few foods are as simply superb as a fresh tortilla.

---

stands on the road leading to Puerto Nuevo and along the parking lot; the best bets are the terra-cotta planters and statues.

Return to the toll road for the rest of the trip to Ensenada. You'll soon see sand dunes near **Cantamar**, where hang gliders practice their landings and takeoffs and off-road enthusiasts spin their tires in the sand.

Bajamar (661/155.0151, 800/342.2644), about 7.5 miles south of La Fonda, is the granddaddy of resort communities along the coast, with one 18-hole golf course on the cliffs above the sea and another 9 holes (Scottish-links style) right by the rocky beach. Several private home and condo developments are scattered along the course. At the heart of the development is the charming **Hacienda Las Glorias** ($$$; 661/155.0151, 800/342.2644; fax 661/155.0150), with 80 rooms in a two-story hacienda-style building around a central courtyard. The hotel is one of the loveliest along the coast, with handcrafted wood furnishings and French doors opening to flower gardens and the golf course. The toll road from here curves dramatically along steep cliffs with breathtaking views of the ocean below, out to the **Todos Santos** islands. **El Mirador**, a roadside rest stop, is about 5 miles south of Bajamar.

The road drops down a steep hillside and flattens out outside Ensenada by two of the

---

Between 1825 and 1831, California was a part of Mexico, with San Diego as its capital.

area's prettiest hotels. **Las Rosas** ($$$;
Ensenada Hwy Km 105, Tijuana;
646/174.4320; fax 646/174.4595;
www.lasrosas.com) sits on a slight rise above
the ocean. Its swimming pool, level with the
horizon, seems to flow right into the surf.
Locals and tourists mingle in the hotel's
atrium lobby and dining room; many of the 31
rooms have fireplaces, and all have sea
views. Take tennis lessons, swim, bake in the
sauna, or soak in the spa overlooking the sea.
Punta Morro ($$; 646/178.3507,
800/526.6676; fax 646/174.4490;
pmorro@telnor.net; www.punta-morro.com) is
located on a small point off the highway north
of Ensenada. All 30 rooms and suites have
kitchenettes and terraces facing the ocean;
some have fireplaces. The pool and hot tub sit
right above the sea, and the restaurant is set
on pilings above the waves.

Ensenada is the largest port in northern Baja,
and a busy, somewhat picturesque city struggling to attract tourists. There's little to admire
along the **malecón**, or waterfront promenade,
home to nearly empty shopping plazas that
block the water view. However, the **Fish
Market**, near the entrance to town, is a must-
see, with fish and crustaceans artfully
arranged on ice. Fresh seafood from all over
Baja is displayed in the covered market,
where vendors beckon shoppers with claims
of the freshest shrimp, crab, tuna, squid, and
whatever else they hooked that morning. Fish-
taco stands face the market to the north,
offering Ensenada's greatest culinary treat—
hunks of batter-fried fish wrapped in fresh
corn tortillas and topped with shredded
cabbage, cilantro, salsa, a dollop of mayo,
and a generous squeeze of lime. At the end of
the lane, head one street inland to **Boulevard
Costero**, the town's main north–south artery,
whose name soon changes to **Boulevard
Lázaro Cárdenas**. At the intersection of
Cárdenas and Riviera is **Riviera del Pacífico**,
Ensenada's version of the 1920s-style casino
and resort. The sparkling white Prohibition-era
building has been well maintained and is
used for civic and social functions; guests can
tour the ballrooms or small regional museum
daily.

Another block east of the waterfront is
Avenida López Mateos. Ensenada's primary
shopping, restaurant, and hotel strip has been
renamed **Calle Primera** along its eight mostly
tourist-oriented blocks between Calles Castillo
and Obregón, although locals pay this little
mind. There's more *there* there than in
Rosarito, and the town has several good
restaurants and plenty of bars ranging from
rowdy to nearly genteel. Far and away the
most famous watering hole is **Hussong's**

Cantina (Av Ruíz 113, at Av López Mateos;
646/178.3210). Juan Hussong, a German
immigrant, opened the bar in 1892, and it's
been packed with revelers ever since. The
building hasn't changed too much over the
years, although today there's just a hint of
sawdust on the wood floors, and a TV in each
of two corners. Still, the cavernous room—
sometimes dusky and smoky and other times
respectably smoke-free—is just what you'd
expect in a traditional Mexican cantina. It's
even more fun and romantic when celebrating
locals or gringos spring for a round of heart-
breaking songs from the resident mariachis.
Far more upscale (but also an Ensenada insti-
tution) is **El Rey Sol** ($$; Av López Mateos
1000; 646/178.1733), a French restaurant
with chandeliers, heavy wooden furnishings,
stained-glass windows, and great food. There
are Mexican dishes as well. For instance, you
can have chicken in *mole* or *chipotle* sauces
(two classic dishes from the interior) or
Cordon Bleu; or try a seafood puff pastry
stuffed with chopped scallops, shrimp, clams,
and fish in white sauce.

East of this zone but within walking distance (or
a short cab ride), **Hotel San Nicolás** ($$; Av
López Mateos, at Av Guadalupe; 646/
176.1901, toll-free 877/287.6906; fax
646/176.4930; nico@sannicolas.com.mx;
www.sannicolas.com.mx) is one of Ensenada's
most venerable hostelries. The 150 rooms and
suites are decorated with heavy wooden
Colonial-style furnishings, and the enormous
rectangular outdoor pool is the centerpiece of
an attractive garden patio. Facilities include a
restaurant, discotheque, travel agency, shops,
and a branch of the **Caliente Race and Sports
Book**. The hotel also offers guided tours to the
wineries in the **Guadalupe Valley** outside
Ensenada.

To gain a better look at the locals' Ensenada,
head inland to **Parque Obrero** (between
Calles 8 and 7 and Avs Iturbide and Hidalgo)
and, a few blocks away, the **Catedral Nuestra
Señora de Guadalupe** (Av Floresta at Av
Juárez), a church with lovely stained-glass
windows. Munch some of Ensenada's finest
seafood tacos (pay in advance for the shrimp
tacos, but not for the fish) at **Tacos el Fénix**,
a humble but extremely popular sidewalk
eatery in front of a hardware store at Avenidas
Juárez (aka Calle 5a) and Espinosa.

On Avenida Miramar between Calles 6a and
7a, both sides of the block are dedicated to
the grape at the wine seller **Bodegas de
Santo Tomás** (Av Miramar 666;
646/178.3333). The south side is the winery
itself, where you can taste and purchase their
vintages; across the street are an art gallery
and small café.

Restaurants/Clubs: Red | Hotels: Purple | Shops: Orange | Outdoors/Parks: Green | Sights/Culture: Blue

GAY SAN DIEGO

In 1972, San Diego responded to a perceived snub (the Republican Party rejected the city as the site of its 1972 convention) by adopting the nickname America's Finest. Pure boosterism? Perhaps. But to be fair, the local folks (including gay and lesbian groups) who chose the moniker really do have good cause to boast—their city offers one of the finest blends of climate, culture, and lifestyle in the US.

The country's seventh largest metropolis, with a population of about 1.2 million, San Diego is blessed with more than 300 sunny days per year, and its heart lies in its beaches, jock culture (it has hosted many high-profile sporting events such as the **America's Cup** sailing races and the **Super Bowl**), and the great outdoors. But the city also has top-notch art galleries, museums, performing-arts venues, and restaurants, making it not only an attractive spot to live but also a great place to visit—as almost 14 million people do each year.

For the gay or lesbian visitor, San Diego offers a slew of gay-oriented retailers, clubs, dining spots, and lodging, along with a rich panoply of queer political, social, sports, religious, and cultural organizations. The gay community here, though somewhat low key, is as friendly, accessible, and varied as that of any urban spot in America.

To be sure, the city's heritage as a military outpost has left a certain starchiness to the place, and a semicloseted mentality remains in certain areas. But paradoxically, the military was also instrumental in building San Diego's queer community in the first place—an estimated one third of the gay population is made up of ex-sailors and ex-marines.

Situated right on the **Pacific Ocean,** just a half hour from the Mexican border, San Diego is California's birthplace—the Spaniards founded the territory's first fort and mission here in 1769, and it eventually grew into an important port and agricultural center. Whaling thrived here until about 1870, and seafood processing and distribution is still economically viable. With its proximity to key agricultural areas, San Diego also remains a vital regional center for produce shipping. World War II changed the tone and substance of the place, as San Diego grew into a huge center for military bases. Along with the military came the aeronautics industry, which drew related institutions, until the city became headquarters for many important scientific and technological enterprises, public and private.

In keeping with its military bearing, San Diego has traditionally maintained a right-leaning political stance, but there have been a few shifts toward the center here since the early 1990s. In 1990, the city council adopted the Human Dignity Ordinance, banning discrimination in housing and hiring on the basis of sexual orientation. In 1993, Christine Kehoe, the city council's first openly lesbian member, was elected. She was reelected in 1996, the same year that the GOP rectified its 1972 "snub" and held its national convention here.

Hillcrest, San Diego's main gay neighborhood, started out as the city's first suburb in the 1920s and eventually evolved in the 1960s and 1970s into a bohemian stronghold with a plethora of alternative venues, from beatniky coffeehouses to gay bars. As it began gentrifying in the late 1970s and 1980s, Hillcrest became the guppie (gay urban professional) neighborhood of choice and turned increasingly upscale. Located north of downtown, the area is an amalgam of housing styles, with apartment buildings

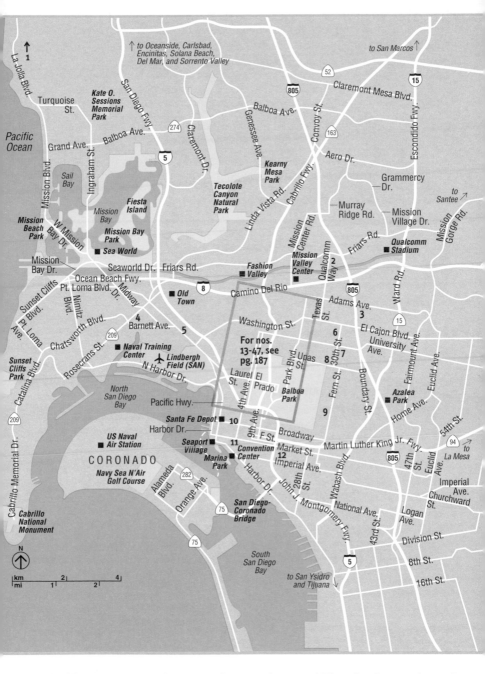

↑
1

↑ to Oceanside, Carlsbad,
Encinitas, Solana Beach,
Del Mar, and Sorrento Valley

to San Marcos ↑

52

805

Claremont Mesa Blvd.

15

La Jolla Blvd.

Turquoise St.

Kate O. Sessions Memorial Park

San Diego Fwy.

Balboa Ave.

Genesee Ave.

Convoy St.

163

Escondido Fwy.

Grand Ave.

274

Balboa Ave.

Claremont Dr.

Aero Dr.

Grammercy Dr.

to Santee ↗

Pacific Ocean

Mission Blvd.

Ingraham St.

5

Kearny Mesa Park

Linda Vista Rd.

Murray Ridge Rd.

Mission Village Dr.

Mission Gorge Rd.

Sail Bay

Mission Bay

Fiesta Island

Tecolote Canyon Natural Park

Cabrillo Fwy.

Mission Center Rd.

Qualcomm Way

Friars Rd.

Qualcomm Stadium

Mission Beach Park

W. Mission Bay Dr.

Mission Bay Park

Mission Bay Park

Sea World

Mission Valley Center

2

Mission Bay Dr.

Seaworld Dr.

Friars Rd.

Fashion Valley

Camino Del Rio

Adams Ave.

805

Ward Rd.

Ocean Beach Fwy.
Pt. Loma Blvd.

Sunset Cliffs Blvd.

Nimitz Blvd.

Midway Dr.

8

Old Town

Texas St.

3

15

Pt. Loma

Chatsworth Blvd.

Barnett Ave.

4

5

Washington St.

For nos. 13–47, see pg. 187

6

El Cajon Blvd.

University Ave.

Sunset Cliffs Park

Catalina Blvd.

Rosecrans St.

209

Naval Training Center

Lindbergh Field (SAN)

N. Harbor Dr.

Laurel St.

El Prado

4th Ave.

Park Blvd.

Upas St.

30th St.

Fern St.

7

Boundary St.

Fairmount Ave.

Euclid Ave.

209

North San Diego Bay

Pacific Hwy.

9th Ave.

Balboa Park

9

Azalea Park

Home Ave.

54th St.

Cabrillo Memorial Dr.

Santa Fe Depot

10

F St.

Broadway

Martin Luther King Jr. Fwy.

94

to La Mesa

US Naval Air Station

Harbor Dr.

Seaport Village

11

Convention Center

Market St.

12

47th St.

Euclid St.

CORONADO

Marina Park

Imperial Ave.

Wabash Blvd.

805

Imperial Ave.
Churchward St.

Navy Sea N'Air Golf Course

Alameda Blvd.

Orange Ave.

282

Harbor Dr.

John J. Montgomery Fwy.

28th St.

National Ave.

43rd St.

Logan Ave.

Cabrillo National Monument

75

San Diego–Coronado Bridge

Division St.

75

South San Diego Bay

5

8th St.

N

↑

to San Ysidro and Tijuana ↓

16th St.

km
mi

2
1

4
2

sandwiched between pricey older bungalows, and restored Victorian houses down the street from quaint groupings of cottages. The **Uptown District** here is a European-style complex of town houses and shops.

Although Hillcrest remains the heart of the homo community, since the 1990s the rainbow tide also has washed eastward to less pricey areas, such as **University Heights**,

Restaurants/Clubs: Red | Hotels: Purple | Shops: Orange | Outdoors/Parks: Green | Sights/Culture: Blue

North Park, Kensington, and **Talmadge**. More recently, a small gay outpost has been established in a low-rent but up-and-coming district called **Azalea Park**.

Both gay men and lesbians live and hang out in these neighborhoods—unlike in New York and other cities, there isn't a big division between the sexes in San Diego's queer community. Local lesbians have long worked closely with their male counterparts to effect change, and that sense of purpose is still quite evident today. In fact, San Diego is considered to have one of the strongest lesbian communities in California, and proof of that is in the number of women who hold fairly visible positions in political and social community groups.

For the gay visitor, San Diego offers a most appealing balance: It's a laid-back beach city that nonetheless offers a host of cosmopolitan pleasures. America's Finest? Maybe the name is not such an exaggeration after all.

SYMBOLS

♂ predominantly/exclusively gay-male-oriented

♀ predominantly/exclusively lesbian-oriented

♂ predominantly/exclusively gay-oriented, with a male and
♀ female clientele

1 MUSEUM OF CONTEMPORARY ART SAN DIEGO

La Jolla's cultural centerpiece, built in 1941 and refashioned by architects **Venturi, Scott Brown and Associates** for a 1996 reopening, is known for its special exhibits, as well as a permanent collection that includes works by Frank Stella, Robert Rauschenberg, Edward Kienholz, and that ubiquitous artistic queen Andy Warhol. The complex also includes an excellent bookstore, a large sculpture garden, and a café. **MCA Downtown** (1001 Kettner Blvd, at W Broadway; 234.1001), an intimate branch museum, usually hosts special exhibits by California artists. ♦ Admission. Tu-Sa, 10AM-5PM; Su, noon-5PM. 700 Prospect St (a quarter-mile north of La Jolla Blvd). 454.3541 &

1 BLACK'S BEACH

🅟 Possibly the best-known nude beach in America, here is where you'll still find sun worshipers in the altogether, even though
♂ going au naturel hasn't been legal here since
♀ 1978. The gay section is north of the **Torrey Pines Gliderport**. Head for the farthest parking area (which can be rather cruisy), then very cautiously descend the steep, treacherous cliffs to the sand on paths more suited to goats than humans. To the left, the straights play volleyball and picnic with their kids; to the right, up about three quarters of a

mile, is the rainbow-colored buoy and plenty of butt-naked guys (and some women too). A saner, safer approach is to take the paths just north of the gliderport and walk past the straight beach, which adds about a quarter-mile to the journey. *Note:* This is a popular cruising spot, but it may be monitored by the police. ♦ Torrey Pines Scenic Dr (off N Torrey Pines Rd)

2 SAN DIEGO MARRIOTT MISSION VALLEY

$$$ A former host hotel for the annual gay rodeo, this reliable chain property has lots of marble and granite, as well as 350 rooms and 6 suites with some great views of the valley (especially as you ascend its 12 stories). Just down the road from **Qualcomm Stadium** (where the **Chargers** and the **Padres** play), it attracts lots of pro jocks, who like to hang out in the Modernist pool area, with its sleek waterfalls and ample lounging space. About a mile away is the University Heights–Park Boulevard district, with its coffeehouses, antiques shops, and gay bars. The **Mission Valley Center** mall is another area attraction (the **AMC 20-Plex** theater there is a homo magnet). On-premises amenities include a tennis court, a health club with whirlpool and sauna, and an Italian restaurant. ♦ 8757 Rio San Diego Dr (at Qualcomm Way). 692.3800, 800/842.5329; fax 692.0769 &

3 LESTAT'S COFFEE HOUSE

Yep, the name's a nod to one of the bisexy bloodsuckers in Anne Rice's *Interview with the Vampire*, as well as a tie-in to the neighboring stores on Adams Avenue's informal "Book Row." Don't expect dark, Gothic premises and bitter brew, though—it's all lavish Victorian-style sconces, chandeliers, and stuffed chairs, creating a plush setting for sipping a darn good cup of coffee, nibbling on pastry, and

FESTIVALS

In April, the weekend-long **LeatherFest** (685.5149) presents workshops and exhibitions in various venues. The **Del Mar Fair** (692.2077 ext 500) in early July has a **Gay Day**, and drag queens crown their emperor and empress during mid-July's **Coronation Weekend**, sponsored by the **Imperial Court de San Diego** (629.1967). The last weekend of July, **Pride Weekend** (297.7683) sweeps through Hillcrest and **Balboa Park** with a rally, a parade, a 2-day festival, and the ever-popular **Zoo Party** at the **San Diego Zoo**. Around the same time, the **Gay and Lesbian Film Series** takes place at the **Ken Cinema** (4061 Adams Ave, between Kensington and Terrace Drs, Kensington; 283.5909). Hillcrest's **CityFest** (299.3330), one of the city's largest

street fairs, is typically held the first weekend in August. It isn't a gay event per se but is heavily queer nonetheless, drawing those who couldn't come out for **Pride Weekend**.

In September, the **Del Mar Thoroughbred Club** (692.2077) hosts a **Gay Day** at the races. Later that month, the **Golden State Gay Rodeo Association, San Diego Chapter** (298.4708), sponsors the country's best-attended annual **Gay and Lesbian Rodeo** (see "Yee-Haw, Mary—The Homo Rodeo Comes to Town" on page 191). San Diego County's largest HIV/AIDS fund-raiser, **AIDS Walk San Diego** (291.9255), winds through **Balboa Park** in early October.

listening to nightly entertainment, from Dixieland jazz to folk. The crowd is mixed— men and women, queer and not. ♦ M-Th, 6:30AM-11PM; F-Sa, 6:30AM-midnight; Su, 7AM-10PM. 3343 Adams Ave (at Felton St). 282.0437 &

4 THE HOLE

♂ You'll know how this Levi's bar close to the **Naval Training Center** got its name when you descend into a courtyard filled with men out to have a good time, especially during the Monday-evening wet-underwear contest— dubbed "Wet 'N' Wilder"—that starts at 9PM. On Sunday afternoons the barbecue is lit on the patio, and later in the evenings, the guys get a lot chummier with each other. ♦ M-F, 2PM-2AM; Sa-Su, noon-2AM. 2820 Lytton St (between St. Charles and Rosecrans Sts). 226.9019

5 CLUB MONTAGE

♂
♀
The city's largest gay dance club is a veritable homo Habitrail, with five rooms on three levels, plus three massive bars, a dance floor, a video bar with a wall of 12 boob tubes, and, when a breather is called for, a spacious rooftop patio. Wednesday nights are devoted to the collegiate set and thirty-somethings who want to relive their glory days with tunes from the 70s and 80s. Hip straights wiggle their tushes with the queers on Thursday nights when the venue becomes "Recess." Recess, Club Montage Thursday draws the most women (lesbian and straight), too; gay men predominate on Wednesdays and weekends. ♦ Cover. W-Th, 9PM-2AM; F-Sa, 9PM-4AM. 2028 Hancock St (between

Estudillo and Witherby Sts). 294.9590. & www.clubmontage.com

6 NORTH PARK ADULT VIDEO

♂ A subsidiary of **The Crypt** (see page 189), this shop also stocks an elegant sufficiency of erotic playthings and movies to rent. There's also a video arcade in back (once cruisy, now heavily monitored). ♦ Daily, 24 hours. 4094 30th St (at Polk Ave). 284.4724

7 EAGLE SAN DIEGO

♂ Big mustachioed daddies, men in black, bears of all ages, and hot beefcake (in chaps, if you're lucky) cram into this dark hole-in-the-wall with a testosterone-heavy atmosphere. A serious leathermen's bar, it also hosts theme nights for community groups. ♦ Daily, 4PM-2AM. 3040 North Park Way (between Grim Ave and Ray St). 295.8072 &

7 SHOOTERZ/CLUB ODYSSEY

♂ Billiards are serious business at **Shooterz**, a pool-and-darts bar that attracts the jeans-and-rolled-up-T-shirt crowd, and attitude is minimal. If it gets too low key, duck through the door to the recently opened **Club Odyssey**. One of the area's newest dance clubs is a dramatic, upbeat venue—complete with Roman columns, marble-top bar in the back, and seamlessly mixed house music. The dance floor is filled with cute young guys and the occasional well-dressed (and probably straight) woman. ♦ Cover for dance club. Bar: daily, noon-2AM. Dance club: Sa-Su, 9PM-2AM. 3815 30th St (between North Park Way and University Ave). 574.0744 &

Restaurants/Clubs: Red | Hotels: Purple | Shops: Orange | Outdoors/Parks: Green | Sights/Culture: Blue

8 WOLFS

♂ You'll stumble into bears, uniform aficionados, and bare-chested leathermen at this industrial-looking Levi's-leather joint serving wine and beer (only) in North Park. Surprisingly good dance music sets the mood for some heavy cruising. In back is a small leather accessories store enclosed in a chain-link cage. ♦ Bar: daily, 6PM-4AM. Store: Th-Sa, 9PM-3AM. 3404 30th St (at Upas St). 291.3730 &

9 BIG KITCHEN CAFE

★$ Breakfast at this earthy, gay- and lesbian-friendly eatery is not just tradition, it's de rigueur for anyone who wants to experience the essence of San Diego. The close tables and the almost-like-home ambiance promote camaraderie—chat up your neighbor (who's likely to be family) or just gaze at the artwork and photos of customers past and present that cover the walls (including several of Whoopi Goldberg, who worked here in her early days). The food isn't fancy, just homey and tasty—try the specialty egg dishes or Bunyanesque pancakes, for example—and if you're waited on by the owner, Judy ("the Beauty on Duty") she'll make you feel like her only customer. ♦ American ♦ Daily, breakfast and lunch. 3003 Grape St (between Fern and 30th Sts). 234.5789 &

10 WYNDHAM U.S. GRANT HOTEL

$$$ Downtown's grande dame was built in 1910 and restored in 1985. The 280-room property serves as San Diego Pride Weekend's host hotel and also as a venue for the Imperial Court's coronation activities. Its location especially appeals to convention-goers and shoppers—across the street is the urban consumers' playground **Horton Plaza**, and a few blocks southwest, the high-end **Paladion**. Elegant but a tad stuffy, the rooms are furnished with Queen Anne winged-back chairs and armoires and come with travertine-marble baths. Jacuzzis and comfy robes are standard in all of the 60 suites—serious pleasures after a day on the town. ♦ 326 Broadway (between Fourth and Third Aves). 232.3121, 800/334.6957; fax 232.3626

11 BAYOU BAR & GRILL

★★$$ One of the more popular **Gaslamp Quarter** restaurants, catering to both straight and gay diners, this eatery serves up some mighty tasty soft-shell crabs, jambalaya, and other Cajun/Creole specialties that are distinctive without being too heavily spiced. The New Orleans–style coffee and traditional beignets evoke that city's **Café du Monde**. The tables are a bit too close together for romantic tête-à-têtes, but the dining room is bright and comfortable. There are sidewalk tables as well.

♦ Cajun/Creole ♦ M-Sa, lunch and dinner; Su, brunch and dinner. 329 Market St (between Fourth and Third Aves). 696.9747 &

12 VILLA MONTEZUMA

♂ This elaborate, eccentric house museum is a nonpareil Queen Anne Victorian, complete with tower and turrets, that lingers in a neighborhood whose fortunes have long since declined. Operated by the **San Diego Historical Society** and located near downtown, the house was built in 1887 for Jesse Shepard, a spiritualist, pianist, mystic, and "professional guest" of royalty who would later change his name to Francis Grierson and pen several notable books of the era, including *The Valley of Shadows*. Shepard, a charismatic, handsome dandy, lived here only 2 years with his "man Friday" (and lifelong companion) Lauritz Waldemar Tonner, but his influence on the house remains. Inside it's a showplace with polished redwood and walnut walls, fireplaces, silvery Lincrusta Walton ceilings, and art-glass windows, among them a representation of the face of the Orient (thought to be Shepard's likeness) and a depiction of Sappho attended by two cupids. ♦ Admission. Sa-Su, noon-4:30PM.1925 K St (between 20th and 19th Sts). 239.2211

13 BOURBON STREET

♂ The French Quarter has been lovingly re-created at this casual bar—if it weren't for the lack of humidity, you'd swear you were in N'awlins. The neighborhood fave attracts a crowd of all ages who come for a drink or to listen to nightly performances by talented pianists and contemporary or jazz singers. There's also a gameroom with dart boards, a pool table, and a jukebox. On Sunday afternoons and evenings, the guys congregate in front of the barbecue grill on the intimate back patio and feast on $2 burgers. ♦ M-Sa, noon-2AM; Su, 9AM-2AM. 4612 Park Blvd (between Madison and Adams Aves). 291.0173 &

14 TWIGGS TEA & COFFEE

You might find a budding homo novelist curled up in a big comfortable chair in this spacious coffeehouse, or card players, gay and straight, lounging on the sofa. Neighborhood couples bring their dogs, order double cappuccinos and pastries, and have *Kaffeeklatsches* at the sidewalk tables. The adjacent **Green Room**, with a 75-person capacity, hosts jazz and other music, one-act plays, poetry readings, and acting workshops. ♦ M-F, 6:30AM-11PM; Sa, 7AM-11PM; Su, 7:30AM-11PM. 4590 Park Blvd (at Madison Ave). 296.0616 &

14 PARKHOUSE EATERY

★★$$ An attractive, gay-popular café decorated like a page out of a Pottery Barn

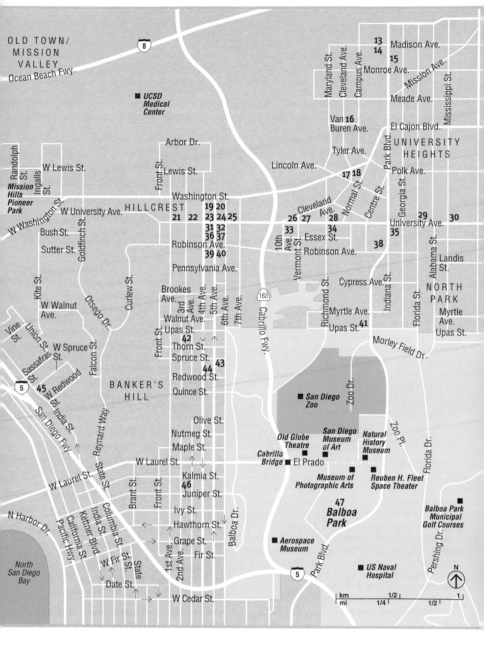

catalogue and located in what was once a thrift store, this casual place is a sleeper that took off on word of mouth. The cuisine, which the owners call "American ethnic grub," is kicky—where else would you find a smoked-sirloin burrito with black beans and cabbage, an ahi tuna and grilled-pear salad sandwich, or gingersnap-banana tiramisù? ◆ American ◆ Daily, breakfast, lunch, and dinner. 4574

Park Blvd (between Monroe and Madison Aves). 295.7275 ら

15 DIVERSIONARY THEATRE

♂
♀
San Diego's homegrown gay and lesbian playhouse stages both original works by talented local playwrights (like the holiday favorite *Our Gay Apparel*) and nationally known workhorses including *Love! Valour! Compassion!*

Restaurants/Clubs: Red | Hotels: Purple | Shops: Orange | Outdoors/Parks: Green | Sights/Culture: Blue

TIJUANA NIGHTS

The teeming city of **Tijuana**, in Mexico's 400-mile-long state of **Baja California**, is only a half hour away from downtown San Diego (though it seems almost worlds away once you cross the border). The fourth largest population center in Mexico, with about 1.8 million inhabitants, it's noisy, poor in some areas, and a bit overwhelming to first-time visitors. Yet it's also a gloriously diverse metropolis with its share of notable restaurants, major tourist attractions, and shopping action (see the "Tijuana" chapter)—not to mention an active *ambiente gay* that catches fire at night.

Park your car at any of the numerous parking lots at the border and take their shuttles across (much simpler and safer than driving across, and easier than walking). Most provide maps of the town as well, or you can get one at the **Tijuana Tourism & Convention Bureau** (83.1405) just inside the border crossing. You'll probably want to head to the bustling business and tourist strip called **Avenida Revolución**, the center of Tijuana (or TJ, as it's known in Southern California). Revolución is a hurly-burly of vendors hawking their wares and restaurant and bar owners beckoning gringos to stop in for a bite and a drink (often in English, nearly as common as Spanish here; note also that US dollars are pretty much as fungible as pesos). Note that street signs are in short supply and some of the major numbered streets also have names—for example, **Calle 2** is also known as **Calle 2a Benito Juárez**.

The gay community in Tijuana has been slowly growing. The mid-June Orgullo Sin Fronteras (Pride Without Borders) march attracted 85 participants in 1995, its first year; by 1999, the fifth, it was up to 400 (half of them marching on the sidewalk, out of range of press cameras, though).

Gay nightlife is literally as close as the border. Once you've crossed into Mexico, walk over to the **Viva Tijuana Shopping Center**, to **Club Extasis**, a state-of-the-art disco with go-go boys and tea dances that attract a significant American following (don't go before 10PM). Other popular clubs include **Mike's Disco** (Av Revolución, south of Calle 6) and **Los Equipales** (Calle 7, east of Av Revolución). Drag shows are especially big here, and in addition to those at Mike's and Equipales, good ones can be seen at **Noa Noa Disco** (Av D, near Calle 1) in the red-light district and at the **Terraza 9 Club** (Calle 6, between Avs Revolución and Constitución). **Plaza Santa Cecilia**, a pedestrian shopping mall between Calles 1 and 2 and slanting southwest from Revolución to **Constitución**, is home to the neighborhood taverns **El Ranchero** (open 24 hours) and **Villa García**. Villa García is predominantly locals only. However, the folks at El Ranchero are incredibly approachable and can answer most of your questions about local places to eat and/or stay. One of the most traditional gay bars in TJ is **El Taurino** (Av C, north of Calle 1).

A note about personal safety: The stories of Americanos being hauled into Tijuana jails are legion, but Tijuana is no more dangerous than parts of San Diego. Just don't draw attention to yourself with valuables or showy jewelry, and watch out for pickpockets. And don't forget that this is a religiously conservative country, so you might encounter the occasional unwillingness to allow couples to rent rooms with a single bed.

There are almost no specifically gay eateries, though the popular chain store–restaurant **Sanborn's** (Av Revolución, between Calles 9 and 8; 88.1462) does have a books and periodicals section with a considerable gay following. For seafood, try **La Costa** (★★★$$; Calle 7 8131, between Avs Revolución and Constitución; 85.8494). For authentic regional Mexican cuisine, take a cab to the hard-to-find **La Fonda Roberto** at the **La Siesta Motel** (★★★$$; Cuauhtemoc Sur Oeste; 86.4687).

For those who want to stay a night or more, there's **Villa Playas** ($; 80.1052), a gay bed-and-breakfast establishment in the **Playas de Tijuana** (the beach area). The two-story, eight-bedroom, five-bathroom house in an upper-middle-class neighborhood is usually rented out, but with advance notice the rooms can be made available to travelers. For additional information, write to P.O. Box 620219, San Diego, CA 92162. Another lodging option is the 100-room **Corona Plaza** ($; Blvd Agua Caliente 1426, between Rio Yaqui and Av Cuauhtémoc; 81.8183; fax 81.8185); it's not specifically gay-oriented, but it is pleasant. If you're going to stay in town, the hotels on Avenida Revolución are usually cheap and clean, though not in the greatest of shape maintenance-wise.

The **San Diego Trolley** (about $1.75 one way) runs from downtown San Diego to the Mexican border every 15 minutes between 5AM and midnight. **Greyhound** also offers frequent service from downtown to downtown. By car, take **I-5** to the border and park in one of the guarded lots (for about $7 per day), then walk across. If you're driving across the border, make sure to stop at one of the Mexican auto insurance dealers off I-5 in **San Ysidro** and purchase auto insurance, as most US policies do not cover driving in Mexico. Also check to see if your rental company allows its cars to be taken across the border.

For further information, check out Don Pato's Gay Tijuana Website at www.donpato.simplenet.com/tijuana.html. Also contact the **Tijuana Tourism and Convention Bureau** (see above), the **Tijuana Chamber of Commerce** (88.1685), the **State Secretary of Tourism** (81.9492; fax 81.9579), or **Baja Information** in San Diego (619/298.4105, 800/522.1516 in Arizona, California, and Nevada; 800/225.2786 elsewhere in the US). The **Attorney General for the Protection of Tourists Hotline** (88.0555) assists visitors with legal problems.

and Phyllis Nagy's *Girl Bar*. Even straight theater critics rave about productions in this intimate venue. ♦ 4545 Park Blvd (between Monroe and Madison Aves). 220.0097 &

16 KASA KORBETT

♂ $ Gay-owned and with a primarily queer clien-
♀ tele, one of the smallest bed-and-breakfasts in the area more often than not lives up to its motto: "Where a guest is at home." It's a convivial Craftsman house, more than 7 decades old, spruced up with Easter egg colors. Each of the three bedrooms is decorated in a different style—country cottage, Key West, and Southwest. All are charming, although none has a telephone and only one has a private bath. The outdoor hot tub is a nice plus. This is a good choice if you don't mind becoming a bit chummy with the other guests in a close, communal setting. ♦ 1526 Van Buren Ave (at Campus Ave). 291.3962, 800/757.5272. www.gsdba.org/members/kasakorbett

17 TOPSY'S

★$ In a world where change prevails, this gay-friendly round-the-clock diner has been standing guard on the same prime triangle-shaped patch of ground for what seems like an eternity. Despite several changes of own-ership, the grub has remained true to the classic diner formula (meat loaf, fried chicken, and the like). The interior likewise has been spruced up over the years but still retains that homey, coffee-shop feel. Its proximity to Hill-crest draws an *après*-club crowd for the bargain egg-and-meat combo breakfasts. ♦ American ♦ Daily, 24 hours. 1451 Washington St (at Lincoln Ave). 296.8268 &

18 THE CRYPT ON PARK

Restrain yourself—with clamps, handcuffs, slings, and other erotic accoutrements, of course. This is a boutique for the leather crowd both homo and hetero, stocked with plenty of playwear of rubber and hide, as well as various lubes and lotions. ♦ M-Sa, 11AM-10PM; Su, 11AM-7PM. 3841 Park Blvd. 692.9499

19 INTERNATIONAL MALE

The mail-order catalogue rivals Victoria's Secret in lasciviousness. The trendy clothing is generally superbly crafted, and women are as fond of the styles as men are. ♦ M-Sa, 10AM-9PM; Su, 11AM-7PM. 3964 Fifth Ave (between University Ave and Washington St). 294.8600. Also at 741 F Street. 544.9900 &

19 CLUB SAN DIEGO

♂ The largest gay bathhouse in Hillcrest, situated in a nondescript, unmarked building,

houses a maze of 53 private rooms, 300 lockers, a Jacuzzi, a sauna, a steam room, a tanning room, and Universal gym equipment. The clientele leans toward the 19-to-35 bar crowd. Day memberships are available. ♦ Daily, 24 hours. 3955 Fourth Ave (between University Ave and Washington St). 295.0850

20 HILLCREST CINEMAS

With the sudden demise of the Park and Guild movie theaters in 1996, this six-screen miniplex took on the responsibility of bringing art films, foreign flicks, and gay cinema to the community. Enjoy the latest "alternative" movies in plushy, comfortable seats. ♦ Daily. Village Hillcrest, 3965 Fifth Ave (between University Ave and Washington St), second level. 299.2100 &

21 HILLCREST GYM AND FITNESS CENTER

Members of the most convenient and gay-popular gym in Hillcrest are serious about fitness. They don't come merely to cruise but to use the free weights, Circuit Line machines, and Lifecycles or join in the aerobics, yoga, or tai chi classes. The intimate rooms give one the feeling of working out in a well-equipped home gym. Day memberships are available. ♦ M-F, 6AM-10PM; Sa, 8AM-8PM; Su, 8AM-6PM. 142 University Ave (between Third and First Aves). 299.7867

22 KICKERS

♂ San Diego's only gay and lesbian country-
♀ western dance venue packs cowboys and cowgirls onto the medium-size dance floor after 9PM. Patrons also crowd the mirror-lined viewing area along the sides of the dance floor; the oval bar allows customers in full Western regalia to keep an eye on the cowpoke of their choice. Complimentary two-step and line-dance lessons are offered throughout the week. On Sunday, the club becomes "Detour," a big tea dance with high-energy music (and men). ♦ Cover for Detour. M-Sa, 7PM-2AM; Su, 5PM-2AM. 308 Univer-sity Ave (between Fourth and Third Aves). 491.0400. & Calendar at www.hamburgermarys.com

22 HAMBURGER MARY'S

★$ Adjacent to and under the same own-ership as **Kickers**, this local branch of the West Coast chain of casual, fun eateries is the neighborhood's premier see-and-be-seen spot. Well-scrubbed boys and girls mingle on the outdoor patio (with heat lamps for when the weather turns a little cool) or sidle up to the covered bar. The burgers, salads, and café cuisine are nicely prepared. Especially

---

Restaurants/Clubs: Red | Hotels: Purple | Shops: Orange | Outdoors/Parks: Green | Sights/Culture: Blue

popular is the Sunday buffet brunch, a spread that will send you flying to the **Hillcrest Gym and Fitness Center** (see above). ♦ American ♦ M-Sa, breakfast, lunch, and dinner; Su, brunch and dinner. 308 University Ave (between Fourth and Third Aves). 491.0400. www.hamburgermarys.com

23 California Man

When in San Diego, get yourself outfitted like a local—for the beach or boys' night out—with an impressive selection of ties and dressier shirts, trendy T-shirts, and bod-flaunting shorts and jeans. It's also a ticket outlet for some of the larger community events. ♦ M-Sa, 10AM-9PM; Su, 10AM-6PM. 3930 Fifth Ave (between University Ave and Washington St). 294.9108 ♿

24 Gay Mart

♂ ♀ When it first opened in Hillcrest in 1996, vandals broke this store's windows several times, and it was the object of frequent verbal attacks from people on the street. But today it's business as usual, with non-Hillcresters accustomed to the bold public display of the word *gay*. The store brings in gays and some lesbians browsing through the stock of tan-line shorts, tank tops, swimsuits, videos, "Billy" dolls, lube, and condoms. ♦ M-Sa, 10AM-midnight; Su, 10AM-10PM. 550 University Ave (at Sixth Ave). 543.1221 ♿

25 Taste of Szechuan

★★$ Consistently good Szechuan and Mandarin fare is the lure here. Offerings include can't-miss lo mein dishes and tantalizing Szechuan orange beef. The peach-colored dining room is appointed with comfortable banquettes (and a lithograph of Marilyn Monroe accented by neon). Come early—at night it fills quickly with regulars, among them same-sex couples and large parties of gay diners. ♦ Chinese ♦ Daily, lunch and dinner. Hillcrest Center, 670 University Ave (between Seventh and Sixth Aves). 291.1668 ♿

26 Laguna Trends

Looking for a little something for your main squeeze? This attractive card and gift emporium caters to just about every taste. The stock includes more than 10,000 cards—including a handsome selection with gay themes (both male and female)—along with forget-me-not postcards, stationery, gift wrap, and jewelry. ♦ M-Sa, 9AM-9PM; Su, 9AM-7PM. 1092 University Ave. 298.2555 ♿

27 Condoms Plus

A gifty condom emporium affiliated with **F Street**, this brightly lit, flashy place stocks a complete range of rubbers, in addition to novelty items, sex toys, videos, and cards for men and women, gay and straight. ♦ M-F, 11AM-midnight; Sa-Su, 11AM-2AM. 1220 University Ave (between Richmond and Vermont Sts). 291.7400

28 Cafe Eleven

♂ ★★★$$ A cherished Hillcrest venue favored by business types who want to wind down or people looking for an elegant and intimate spot for their anniversary fetes, this charming and low-key place calls to mind the private dining room of a French country villa. The kitchen does a masterful job with continental offerings like pork chops with black-cherry sauce, green-peppercorn duck, and beef Wellington. ♦ Continental/country French ♦ Tu-Su, dinner. Reservations recommended. 1440 University Ave (at Normal St). 260.8023 ♿

29 Pecs

♂ Heads crane when new faces enter this subdued neighborhood leather bar, which is not as hard-core as the **Eagle** (see page 185). Reflecting the diversity of the area, Anglo, Hispanic, and African-American guys of all ages (late twenties to fifties) chat it up, cruise, and watch each other play pool or darts. ♦ M-Th, Su, noon-2AM; F-Sa, noon-4AM. 2046 University Ave (at Alabama St). 296.0889 ♿

29 F Street

One of a chain of 10 adult book/video stores throughout the county, the North Park branch is the gay-friendliest of the bunch. Your typical

The first lesbian palimony suit was settled in San Diego in June 1978. Denease Conley was ordered to pay $100 per month in support to Sherry D. Richardson, whom she had wed in February 1978 in a holy union ceremony performed by the Metropolitan Community Church.

Hillcrest by the numbers: median age, 39; approximately 37% have college degrees; almost 10 times as many residents rent as own homes. What the census figures don't indicate is that of the estimated 36,000 folks who reside here, about half are gay.

Bruce Springsteen wrote the song "Balboa Park," on his 1995 album *The Ghost of Tom Joad*, based on reports of undocumented Mexican minors engaging in "survival sex" in the park.

Dignity, the organization for Catholic gays and lesbians, originally started out as a discussion group in San Diego in 1969.

YEE-HAW, MARY—THE HOMO RODEO COMES TO TOWN

On America's gay rodeo circuit, San Diego's 4-day barn-raiser, held the last weekend in September, is considered one of the most visible and best organized. Certainly it's the best attended, with some 15,000 gay, lesbian, and straight spectators attending (and overrunning local hotels) in 1997. It is San Diego's second-largest convergence of gays and lesbians, after Pride Weekend.

What lures so many cowpokes to the dusty corrals and sawdust-strewn dance floors here? It's the enormous variety of rodeo- and Western-related activities, say the officers of the **Greater San Diego Chapter** of the **Golden State Gay Rodeo Association** (**GSGRA**), who've been organizing the city's **Gay and Lesbian Rodeo** since its 1989 inception. Indeed, the guy or gal intent on catching every single event would be hard-pressed to squeeze in a shower and some shut-eye during the whole of **Rodeo Weekend**. The kickoff on Thursday is the annual **Boots & Briefs Contest**, a signature charity fund-raiser pioneered by the **GSGRA/SD**, in which 10 to 15 men and women appear on stage in Western costume, then strip down to their skivvies, which are later auctioned off to the highest bidders. Colt model Steve Kelso put in an appearance at the 1995 and 1996 contests. After a Friday-afternoon party around the pool of the host hotel, the first of three big country-western dance parties takes place.

The real meat of the matter, though, lies in the impressive lineup of events in four categories: horse speed (pole bending, flag racing, barrel racing), rough stock (bull riding, steer riding, bareback bronc riding, and chute dogging), roping (breakaway calf roping, calf roping on foot, and team roping), and the camp events. It's this last set of three events that give the rodeo its distinctively queer flavor. They include "wild drag," with a team made up of a man, a woman, and another person (man or woman) in drag who try to control and mount a wild steer; "steer decorating," in which two-person teams try to tie a ribbon around the tail of a wild steer; and "goat dressing," created especially for gay rodeo, in which a two-person team catches a goat and outfits it with a pair of jockey shorts. Overall winners in each of the individual events receive coveted belt buckles; prize money also is awarded to first- through fourth-place winners in specific categories.

After considerable dillydallying, the date of the rodeo (traditionally—and inconveniently—held the same weekend as San Francisco's Folsom Street Fair) has finally been moved to mid-September. For more information, call 298.4708; fax 298.4709; write to **GSGRA/SD**, 3768 30th Street, San Diego, CA 92103; or visit their web site at www.gaywired.com/gayrodeo.

---

porn outlet, it's chockablock with videos, magazines, and adult toys geared to all orientations. It's worth a trip in at 3AM to check out the wide-eyed dudes congregated on the left-hand, man-to-man side of the store. ♦ Daily 24 hours. 2004 University Ave (at Florida St). 298.2644

30 MUSTANG SPA

♂ A health club and fitness center in a former lifetime, this bathhouse has all the amenities of a true-blue European spa: Olympic indoor swimming pool, 20-man Jacuzzi, and sauna. It also has the requisite video lounges and cruisy rooms—all on one floor. The place is very popular with travelers, and the Spanish, German, and Australian accents lend an international touch. A one-day membership lasts 12 hours. ♦ Daily 24 hours. 2200 University Ave (at Mississippi St). 297.1661

31 BABETTE SCHWARTZ, THE STORE

♂
♀
Doll, you haven't lived until you've bopped by Babette's Babulous boutique, known for its astounding selection of campy cards, loungewear, Indonesian folk art, and *Día de*

los Muertos (Mexican Day of the Dead) paraphernalia. Before she turned entrepreneur, Babette, one of San Diego's most celebrated drag queens, did her thing here when this space was a bar. ♦ M-Sa, 11AM-9PM; Su, 11AM-5PM. 421 University Ave (between Fifth and Fourth Aves). 220.7048 ⑤

31 SRO

★$$ This gay and lesbian neighborhood tavern is a kitschy, cool hangout for theater buffs. It's doubly favored for its twice-daily happy hour—that's right—once between 2PM and 7PM and then again for those later roamers between 11PM and 1AM. Pool table and video screens furnish additional amusement. ♦ Daily, 10AM-2AM. 1807 Fifth Ave. 232.1886 ⑤

32 CITY DELICATESSEN

★★$ Nosh until you drop on loads of New York-style deli fare and all-day breakfast goodies at this gay-owned spot. Bringing in the mixed gay and straight crowds are the homemade knishes, latkes, hearty stuffed cabbage rolls, and bevy of specialty sandwiches. It's all pretty darn good for California—and oy, the German chocolate cake

---

Restaurants/Clubs: Red | **Hotels: Purple** | **Shops: Orange** | **Outdoors/Parks: Green** | **Sights/Culture: Blue**

is like none you've ever tasted. ♦ Deli ♦ M-Th, breakfast, lunch, and dinner; F-Sa, breakfast, lunch, and dinner until 2AM. 535 University Ave (between Sixth and Fifth Aves). 295.2747 ♿

33 RICH'S

♂ All the hot young studs (and their admirers) preside here. As close as San Diego is going to get to New York or Los Angeles queer nightlife, this trendy club features a groove house and tribal rhythm night on Thursdays called "Club Hedonism," which has attracted the likes of former **Chicago Bulls** player Dennis Rodman. The dance floor at the back of the club remains just as crowded on the weekends. ♦ Cover. Th-Sa, 9PM-2AM; Su, 7PM-2AM. 1051 University Ave (between Vermont St and 10th Ave). 497.4588. www.richs-sandiego.com

33 EUPHORIA

★$ A hip and homo-owned European-style coffeehouse sandwiched between **Rich's** and **Flicks**, it's a top gathering spot for pre- and post-nightclubbing, attracting a diverse crowd of gays and straights. The menu offers coffee, desserts, and other light fare, and the comfortable leather chairs invite patrons to lounge and gab for hours. The seats fill up quickly after 8PM on weekends, and the predominantly young crowd spills out past the sidewalk café area. The interior walls serve as gallery space for work by gay artists; the exhibit changes monthly. ♦ Coffeehouse ♦ M-Th, 6:15AM-1:30AM; F-Su, 6:30AM-2:30AM. 1045 University Ave (between Vermont St and 10th Ave). 295.1769 ♿

33 OBELISK—THE BOOKSTORE

♂ San Diego's only all-lesbigay bookseller
♀ stocks much of the latest homosexual fiction and nonfiction titles, the community papers, and a huge selection of gay magazines (mainstream and "adult"). Equally ample is the collection of music, videos, Pride gear, and stickers. The shop also sells tickets to most of the lesbian and gay events held throughout the year. ♦ M-F, 10AM-10PM; Sa-Su, 10AM-11PM. 1029 University Ave (between Vermont St and 10th Ave). 297.4171 ♿

33 CALIFORNIA CUISINE

★★★$$$ One of Hillcrest's most popular restaurants, this intimate spot is an art-fancier's dream, from the stunning works that grace the walls to the beautifully arranged entrées. Chef Chris Walsh's black-and-white sesame seed ahi appetizer with hot-and-sour raspberry sauce is a must. Any of the fish, lamb, or veal entrées excel; favorites include mahimahi with fruit salsa, and lamb loin with dijon-sherry cream sauce. The garden patio in back is so intimate, you might forget you're in the midst of bustling Hillcrest. ♦ Continental

♦ Tu-F, lunch and dinner; Sa-Su, dinner. Reservations recommended. Valet parking F-Sa. 1027 University Ave (between Vermont St and 10th Ave). 543.0790 ♿

33 FLICKS

♂ The two darkened rooms in this S&M (stand-and-model) video bar are packed most nights with a fresh-faced, sun-worshiping crowd cruising for Mr. Right—or, perhaps more accurately, "Mr. Right-Now." Music videos fluctuate between the current hits and the daring. The last Thursday of every month features live comedy. ♦ Daily, 2PM-2AM. 1017 University Ave (between Vermont St and 10th Ave). 297.2056 ♿

34 MONTANA'S AMERICAN GRILL

★★★$$ Bring an appetite to the grill of your dreams. The Western-style menu includes T-bone steaks, pork chops, and fresh fish with bold, smoky flavors, all exquisitely prepared and served in an engagingly lighted room adorned with marble, granite, and mahogany. This is a favorite dinner spot for groups of gay men and lesbians. ♦ American ♦ M-F, lunch and dinner; Sa-Su, dinner. Dinner reservations required. 1421 University Ave (between Herbert and Richmond Sts). 297.0722 ♿

35 CAFE ON PARK

♂ ★★★$ On weekends, the crowds line up early for the signature breakfasts at this gay-friendly, San Francisco–style neighborhood café; if you arrive after 9:30AM, you'd better have a book or at least a chatty companion to pass the time with. The breakfast menu tempts with inventive specialties, from the Hangtown Fry (marinated and breaded oysters sautéed with three eggs) to the cornmeal and honey batter waffles; there's even a Cap'n Crunch and blackberry pancake that is—believe it or not—quite yummy. Lunch and dinner don't get huge throngs of customers, but the prodigious helpings make them true bargains. ♦ American ♦ M, Su, breakfast and lunch; Tu-Sa, breakfast, lunch, and dinner. 3831 Park Blvd (between Robinson and University Aves). 293.7275 ♿

35 NUMBERS

♂ A must-see on the bar circuit, this place has—or tries to have—something for almost everyone. Hang out and watch videos at one of three bars, shoot pool or throw darts, soak up some rays on the sloping outdoor patio during the afternoon, or enjoy the daily entertainment/activities (like a takeoff on *Wheel of Fortune*) in the lounge. The darkened surroundings are ideal for video watching or clandestinely scoping out that man in the athletic gear or trendy clubwear. Whatever you fancy, you're bound to find something (or someone) to amuse you here. ♦ Daily, noon-

2AM. 3811 Park Blvd (between Robinson and University Aves). 294.9005. & www.numbers-mansbar.com

36 CAFÉ LULU

♂
♀ A very young, late-night crowd keeps this coffeehouse hoppin' until the wee hours. Not far from the waterfront or most of the action, this eclectic hangout is a great place to go if you're still looking for more fun after hours, or a bite to eat, ranging from bagels to lasagna. ♦ M-Th, Su, 9AM-2AM; F-Sa, 9AM-4AM. 419 F St (at Fourth Ave). 238.0114 &

37 NO. 1 FIFTH AVENUE

♂
♀ Regulars chat up new friends in this dimly lighted bar festooned with fake tropical garlands hanging from the ceiling. Couples (most male) perch on the seats on the platform above the bar and watch the crowd. The back patio is a delight after work on Friday or during the summer. ♦ Daily, noon-2AM. 3845 Fifth Ave (between Robinson and University Aves). 299.1911 &

38 THE FLAME

♀ The city's premier lesbian bar, housed in an Egyptian Revival building, has a large dance floor, pool tables, and a long bar area called the **Ultra Suede Lounge**, as well as the area's most prominent neon sign. Lively throughout the week, it's especially hot on Wednesday when disco and dance standards—past and present—bounce off the walls. Friday evening draws a young crowd that ranges from lipstick to biker chick, all packed in for martinis and cigars. Sunday afternoons attract a more mature group of women, who stop by to socialize. Even the boys get their own night on Tuesdays. ♦ Cover some nights. M-Th, Sa-Su, 5PM-2AM; F, 4PM-2AM. 3780 Park Blvd (between Robinson and University Aves). 295.4163 &

39 CREST CAFE

★★$ An Art Deco delight packed for brunch on weekends with lesbians, gays, and straights alike, this café tempts diners with niçoise and Cobb salads, specialty burgers, and wonderful homemade desserts such as peach cobbler and crème brûlée. Don't even think about leaving without munching on the french-fried onion loaf. Try to grab a window table to check out the "scenery." ♦ American ♦ Daily, breakfast, lunch, and dinner. 425 Robinson Ave (between Fifth and Fourth Aves). 295.2510 &

39 THE BRASS RAIL

♂ No, it's not a time warp, just San Diego's oldest fag bar—and one of its most racially diverse as well. Drop in on Thursday nights for hot Hispanic men and *música latina*, or Wednesday and Friday nights when a predominantly black crowd gathers. The campy and comedic *Dreamgirls Revue*, showcasing celebrity look-alikes, takes the stage Monday, Tuesday, and Saturday. On the patio, an inexpensive café serves appetizers and pub snacks. ♦ Daily, 10AM-2AM. 3796 Fifth Ave (at Robinson Ave). 298.2233 &

39 DAVID'S PLACE

♂ The gathering spot for "positive people and their friends," this not-for-profit coffeehouse and oasis for the HIV community has a covered patio out front that always seems to be crowded with friendly Joes who nurse their cups of joe and nibble on their desserts late into the night. Inside, a diverse group of singers and bands entertains throughout the week. Artwork by local gay artists is occasionally exhibited. ♦ M-Th, Su, 7AM-midnight; F-Sa, 7AM-3AM. 3766 Fifth Ave (between Pennsylvania and Robinson Aves). 294.8908 &

39 HILLCREST INN

$ Rooms are extremely basic at this gay-popular property, but the rates are rock-bottom and the location is convenient to the central Hillcrest bars and all the restaurants and coffeehouses. Each of the 45 rooms comes with a kitchenette equipped with microwave and refrigerator, and a telephone and TV set. The sundeck and hot tub offer great views of the park and downtown, but there's no restaurant on the premises. If you want to know where to go for the hottest happy hour or the best after-hours action, just quiz the extremely knowledgeable front-desk personnel. ♦ 3754 Fifth Ave (between Pennsylvania and Robinson Aves). 293.7078, 800/258.2280; fax 298.3861

40 MIXX

★★★$$ The cozy dining room of this stunning restaurant has the feel of a plush Italian villa. It draws a crowd of well-dressed lesbian and gay couples and groups on weekends; couples of all orientations drop by the rest of the week. Chef Deborah Helm offers innovative preparations with Pacific Rim, Italian, and Indonesian influences; it's called "cuisine without boundaries," and it's consistently exciting. Among the stars are crab-cake sandwiches, tequila-lime rock shrimp linguine, and Szechuan chicken with mango-chile glaze. ♦ Eclectic ♦ Daily, dinner. Reservations recommended. 3671 Fifth Ave (between Pennsylvania and Robinson Aves). 299.6499 &

Restaurants/Clubs: Red | Hotels: Purple | Shops: Orange | Outdoors/Parks: Green | Sights/Culture: Blue

41 BALBOA PARK INN

$$ Pretty and pink, this Spanish Colonial–style bed-and-breakfast is spotless and home-away-from-homey inside. Bordering **Balboa Park**, the cluster of four buildings also lures a mixed gay and straight clientele with its proximity to the zoo and park attractions, as well as to some of the nightspots on Park Boulevard. Each of the 19 suites and seven bedrooms with baths is individually decorated and quaintly appointed; some have Jacuzzis, fireplaces, kitchens, and private decks. Guests can unwind in the private courtyard or out on the terrace. ♦ 3402 Park Blvd (at Upas St). 298.0823, 800/938.8181; fax 294.8070

42 BANKER'S HILL BED AND BREAKFAST

♂ ♀ $$ An unexpected find in the upscale Banker's Hill area west of **Balboa Park**, this gay-owned bed-and-breakfast in a fully restored 1912 Craftsman home serves a mixed lesbian and gay clientele. The five rooms feature Victorian-style furnishings and faux-finish walls, and the shared bathroom isn't a terrible inconvenience. Visitors can also take advantage of the attractive heated pool and spa in the backyard. ♦ 3315 Second Ave (between Thorn and Upas Sts). 260.0673, 800/338.3748; fax 260.0674

43 PARK MANOR SUITES

$$ Built around 1926, this attractive seven-story brick building was designed by **Frank P. Allen Jr.**, the chief architect for the 1915 Panama-California Exposition in **Balboa Park** across the street. Refurbished in 1991, the hotel exudes European charm. The 80 comfortable suites are furnished with Louis XIV chairs, Chippendale chests, and other Old World trappings. The **Top of the Park**, with some of the best views of Hillcrest, downtown, and the bay, most definitely is *the* spot for gay men to wind down Friday evenings. The street-level **Inn at the Park Restaurant and Bar** (296.0057) serves moderately priced continental specialties, including steaks, seafood, and pastas. ♦ 525 Spruce St (between Sixth and Fifth Aves). 291.0999, 800/874.2649; fax 291.8844 &

44 THE CALIPH

♂ A mostly older cadre stops by this intimate neighborhood piano bar to be entertained or to "Let Us Entertain You!" in the manner of show-tune queens everywhere. The décor alone is worth a look-see; it's a kitschy and truly surrealistic take on a Middle Eastern fantasia that's a little like being trapped in Disney's *Aladdin*. ♦ Daily 11AM-2AM. 3100 Fifth Ave (at Redwood St). 298.9495 &

45 CLUB BOM BAY

♀ Lesbians from femme to butch and from all walks of life surround the central bar pit at this casual hangout that is as extremely friendly as it is extremely busy. They gather to hear karaoke and live music, dance to popular tunes, or head out to the back patio for barbecue and the weekend kegger. There's a martini and cigar night too. ♦ M-F, 2PM-2AM; Sa-Su, 11AM-2AM. 3175 India St (at W Spruce St). 296.6789 &

46 KEATING HOUSE

$ The closest guest house to the downtown area, this 1888 Victorian is a step back in time and an ideal place if you're looking for a weekend away from the telephone, TV set, and all other high-tech gadgetry. The six rooms, filled with antiques and collectibles and adorned with friezes, complete the turn-of-the-19th-century atmosphere. Guests can also stay in the two-room cottage in back, near the lush garden. ♦ 2331 Second Ave (between Juniper and Kalmia Sts). 239.8585, 800/995.8644; fax 239.5774

47 BALBOA PARK

⬤ ♂ Considering that Spanish conquistador Vasco Núñez de Balboa used to set wild dogs on Native American men who dressed as women, he would be spinning in his grave if he knew how gay-popular his verdant, 1,200-acre namesake near downtown has become. It percolates with activity throughout the week, and weekends can be a real mob scene. Home to several of the city's major museums (including the **San Diego Museum of Art**, the **Natural History Museum**, and the **Museum of Man**), the world-famous **San Diego Zoo**, an 18-hole public golf course, and the acclaimed **Old Globe Theatre**, it's also been the site of two international expositions (one in 1915, when many of the Spanish Colonial–style buildings were constructed, and the other in 1935).

The park fairly swarms with homos. At its southwestern tip, **Marston Point** (on Balboa Dr south of El Prado) is better known as "the Fruit Loop," because of the men who cruise on foot or in autos. Near the corner of Balboa and Quince Drives is a broad sweep of lawn sometimes known as "the gay beach," where sun-worshiping boys in tiny bikinis lie out and gossip. Gay volleyball players set up their courts on the lawns on Sunday afternoons; gay runners and walkers congregate at the tree at Sixth Avenue and Laurel Street. An extension of the park, east of Florida Drive, is **Morley Field**, a sports complex that's notoriously cruisy after dark. ♦ Bounded by 28th St and Sixth Ave and by Russ Blvd, I-5, and Upas St. 239.0512

HISTORY

1542   On 28 September, the Spanish ships *San Salvador* and *La Victoria* arrive in **San Diego Bay**, which the Spanish call **San Miguel**. Explorer Juan Rodríguez Cabrillo leads his men ashore, where they rest for a few days among the local Kumeyaay people and then sail north.

1602   On 10 November, Spanish explorer Sebastián Vizcaíno sails into San Miguel and officially renames the bay San Diego after the saint San Diego de Alcalá.

1769   On 11 April, the Spanish ship *San Antonio* anchors in San Diego Bay; days later, the *San Carlos* arrives. In the following months, Spanish troops arrive by land from Baja California. Led by Gaspar de Portola, the troops move north toward San Francisco, leaving behind a small group of settlers. On 16 July, Padre Junípero Serra celebrates Mass at the new settlement atop **Presidio Hill**, beginning the first of a chain of missions in Alta California. The Spaniards place the Kumeyaay and other local Native Americans under the jurisdiction of the mission and rename them the Digueños. On 15 August, the Kumeyaay attack the settlement, killing one Spaniard. The settlers stay.

1770   Portola and his troops return from the north to the garrison on Presidio Hill.

1774   Serra and other priests move their mission up the **San Diego River** to get away from the soldiers' cruel treatment of the local Indians and to take advantage of the river valley's water supply and fertile land.

1775   On 4 November, the Kumeyaay attack and destroy the mission, which is rebuilt a few months later. Father Luis Jayme is killed in the attack.

1778   The Franciscans found the **Mission San Luis Rey** in northern San Diego near what is now **Oceanside**. The mission becomes the largest and most prosperous in California.

1800   The Presidio is enlarged and fortified, and a second fortress is built at **Point Loma**.

1807   The San Diego River is dammed to create grazing lands for cattle and sheep. About 1,600 Kumeyaay are listed as having been baptized by the priests in the previous decade. Records also show that about 9,000 of those Native Americans subsequently die from diseases brought by the Spaniards.

1821   Mexico gains independence from Spain, and the Mexican government claims Spain's territory in California. The Spanish flag continues to fly above the Presidio until 1823 or 1824, when it is replaced by the Mexican flag. The settlers begin moving from the guarded Presidio to the area now called **Old Town**.

1833   Mexico's Secularization Act places church property into private ownership and dissolves the mission system, creating vast ranches from mission lands. Mexican settlers begin arriving and creating prosperous cattle ranches.

1835   On 1 January, San Diego becomes an official civil pueblo with some 400 Mexican residents. Juan Osuna is elected the first mayor and judge.

1840   Sailor Richard Henry Dana, who arrived in San Diego 5 years earlier on the trading ship *Pilgrim* from New England, publishes his book *Two Years Before the Mast*, describing the people of California, called the Californios.

1846   The Mexican-American War begins. On 12 December, after fierce battles between the Californios and the Americans, the US Army enters and claims San Diego.

1847   On 17 January, the Californios surrender to US Colonel John Fremont.

1848   On 2 February, the Mexican-American War ends with the signing of the Treaty of Guadalupe Hidalgo; the US pays Mexico $15 million for much of what is now the southwestern US, including California.

1850   On 18 February, the San Diego region becomes a US county. On 27 March, San Diego becomes a city. On 9 September, California becomes the 31st state in the union. William Heath Davis and several partners purchase 160 acres of land facing San Diego Bay for $2,304 and begin building a new community where downtown San Diego now stands. Streets are laid, prefabricated houses are put up, and a wharf is built. But the citizens of Old Town prefer to stay where they are, and call the new settlement Davis's Folly. Davis's rising debt halts construction, and his fledgling metropolis becomes a ghost town.

1851 The city of San Diego declares bankruptcy.

1855 The **Old Point Loma Lighthouse** is lit.

1862 President Abraham Lincoln gives the mission back to the Catholic church.

1867 Alonzo Horton arrives in San Diego, intent on building a new city. A month later, he buys 960 acres in the downtown area at a land auction. Picking up where William Heath Davis left off 17 years earlier, he establishes **New Town**.

1868 William Gatewood and Edward Bushyhead found the *San Diego Union*. It begins as a weekly but becomes a daily in 1871.

1869 The population of San Diego hits 3,000 as newcomers are drawn to Horton's new city, which now includes **Horton's Wharf**, the **Horton House Hotel**, and **Horton Plaza**. Rancher Fred Coleman discovers gold in the mountains outside San Diego, and the Northern California gold rush moves south. Gold mining attracts thousands of settlers, but by 1874 the gold is gone and the rush is over.

1870 Whalers from New England begin hunting the gray whales that migrate every winter from the Bering Strait to San Diego and Baja California. The whales soon learn to bypass San Diego Bay. Chinese immigrants begin settling in the **Stingaree** district of downtown in what's now called the **Gaslamp Quarter**.

1871 The cornerstone is laid for San Diego's **courthouse**.

1872 Fire destroys much of the business district of Old Town. Merchants abandon the neighborhood and move into Horton's New Town.

1885 Train tracks are laid and the first transcontinental train arrives in San Diego.

1886 The first electric lights shine over downtown's streets.

1888 Trolley tracks and telephone lines are installed in the city. The **Hotel del Coronado** opens in **Coronado**.

1890 San Diego's population reaches 16,000.

1891 The train tracks are washed away in a storm and San Diego is once again isolated, except for a small supply line to Los Angeles.

The city of Coronado secedes from San Diego. The new lighthouse on the tip of Point Loma is lit, and the old one becomes a tourist attraction.

1895 The same company behind the *San Diego Union* begins publishing the **San Diego Evening Tribune**, a daily afternoon paper.

1897 Madame Katherine Tingley and the Universal Brotherhood and Theosophical Society purchase 130 acres on Point Loma and begin building **Lomaland**'s outdoor Greek theater and school buildings.

1898 The iron gunboat the *USS Pinta* enters San Diego Harbor, beginning the navy's ongoing presence in San Diego Bay.

1905 The *USS Bennington*'s boiler explodes in San Diego Harbor, killing 60 and injuring 47.

1908 The navy's battleship fleet visits San Diego while on a world tour to demonstrate US naval power. The ships are greeted with great fanfare, and the War Department starts planning to dredge San Diego Bay to accommodate larger ships.

1911 Aviator Glenn Curtiss lands his floating biplane beside the navy cruiser *USS Pennsylvania* in San Diego Bay, inspiring the navy to allot $25,000 to the development of naval aviation. Curtiss establishes the first military aviation school in the country at **North Island**. The first tuna cannery opens in San Diego, and commercial fishing becomes a leading industry. By 1950, there are six large canneries in San Diego, making it the leading commercial fishing port in the country. Competition from Japanese and South American boats and canneries cuts into the San Diego market, and by 1960 only one cannery will remain.

1915 The **Panama-California Exposition** opens in **Balboa Park**.

1916 The Zoological Society of San Diego is formed under the direction of Dr. Harry Wegeforth.

1919 The US Marine Corps recruiting depot opens.

1922 The San Diego Naval Training Station opens, and ground is broken for a naval hospital at **Balboa Park**.

1923 San Diego is named the headquarters of the Eleventh Naval District and the Pacific Fleet. The first known photographs of a solar eclipse are taken in San Diego.

1925 Pioneer aviator T. Claude Ryan starts Ryan Airlines, offering the first scheduled commuter flights from San Diego to Los Angeles. Ryan's company eventually becomes Teledyne Ryan Aeronautical, a leading manufacturer of military and civilian aircraft and equipment.

1927 Charles Lindbergh hires T. Claude Ryan to build a plane that can handle a solo flight across the Atlantic Ocean. Two months later, the *Spirit of St. Louis* is ready for flight. On 28 April, Lindbergh pilots the *Spirit of St. Louis* on a test flight at **Dutch Flats,** where San Diego's Midway Drive Post Office now stands. On 20 May, Lindbergh flies his new plane from New York to Paris.

1928 San Diego's airport, **Lindbergh Field**, is dedicated as 222 military planes roar in the sky. Colonel Ira C. Copley purchases the *San Diego Union* and the *San Diego Evening Tribune* as part of his Copley chain of newspapers.

1929 Archaeologists from the **Museum of Man** discover the prehistoric bones of the Del Mar Man.

1931 San Diego weathers the Great Depression with assistance from President Franklin Roosevelt's relief programs. Workers in the Works Progress Administration build animal cages at the zoo, a fairgrounds and race track in **Del Mar**, and the first buildings for **San Diego State University**. The CCC (California Conservation Corps) is put to work in the mountains of East County, clearing trails and planting trees.

1933 Reuben H. Fleet moves his Consolidated Aircraft factory to San Diego. It later merges with other companies as Convair, and then General Dynamics, becoming one of the region's largest employers, along with the Ryan, Solar, and Rohr aircraft companies. San Diego's first migrant workers' camps begin to appear. Most of the workers are homeless Dust Bowl families looking for work. Though the faces and nationalities change, migrant camps will continue to appear in the decades to come.

1935 Banking on a rise in prosperity and the imminent end of the Depression, San Diegans decide to host a second exposition in Balboa Park, using many of the buildings from the 1915-1916 Panama-California Exposition. On 29 May, the **California-Pacific Exposition** opens and runs for 2 years.

1941 On 7 December, loudspeakers at the San Diego Zoo broadcast a command for all military personnel to report for duty as news of the Japanese attack on Pearl Harbor, Hawaii, spreads. San Diego becomes mobilized as the US enters World War II. Balboa Park is declared off-limits to civilians, renamed **Camp Kidd**, and used as a training center and military hospital. Only the zoo and golf course remain open to the public. Local aircraft factories operate around the clock, and San Diego's population swells with an influx of workers. Military units patrol the beaches; large nets are strung into the bay to prevent submarines from entering the harbor.

1942 The War Department begins detaining Japanese-Americans in inland camps; by the end of the war, approximately 2,000 San Diegans of Japanese ancestry are interred in the camps.

1945 As the war ends, San Diego switches its focus from military defense to tourism. Voters pass a bond to create an aquatic center and tourist attraction at **Mission Bay**. The postwar housing boom creates new neighborhoods throughout the county, and real estate prices soar. By the 1980s, tourism will be San Diego's third largest industry, after manufacturing and military interests.

1948 *San Diego Magazine*, the first city magazine in the nation, begins publication.

1963 Ground is broken for the city's first convention center at the downtown **Community Concourse**.

1964 **Sea World** opens on 22 acres at the edge of Mission Bay; the **University of California** opens a 1,000-acre campus in **La Jolla**.

1965 The **Salk Institute for Biological Studies**, headed by Dr. Jonas Salk, opens in an architectural masterpiece designed by **Louis I. Kahn**.

1968 Old Town becomes a state historic park.

1969 The **San Diego–Coronado Bay Bridge**, which spans San Diego Bay, is completed and the ferries between downtown and Coronado cease operation.

1971 Pete Wilson becomes the mayor of San Diego; 24 years later, while governor of California, he will declare his intention to run for president as a Republican. (After only a few months, he withdraws his candidacy.)

1972 The **San Diego Wild Animal Park** opens in **Escondido**.

1974 The **Gaslamp Quarter Association** (now the Gaslamp Quarter Council) is founded to oversee preservation and development in the historic area of downtown.

1975 Nearly 20,000 Vietnamese immigrants are housed at **Camp Pendleton** in north San Diego county as the Vietnam War ends.

1978 On 25 September, **PSA Flight 182** from Sacramento collides with a private plane over the **North Park** neighborhood, taking 144 lives.

1983 The navy begins construction on a new hospital in **Florida Canyon** near its original hospital.

1984 The one remaining house from William Heath Davis's original community is moved to the Gaslamp Quarter to serve as the offices for the Gaslamp Quarter Council.

1985 The worst brush fire in San Diego's history destroys 116 homes in the neighborhood of **Normal Heights**.

1989 The **San Diego Convention Center** opens.

1991 On 29 January, radio station **B100** puts out a call to San Diegans to go to **Jack Murphy Stadium** to show their support for the US troops fighting in the Persian Gulf War. More than 30,000 people show up; 3,000 of them form a human American flag, which is photographed and sent to the troops.

1994 On 8 November, Californians pass Proposition 187, making illegal immigrants ineligible for public services, including education and nonemergency health care, and denying some benefits to legal immigrants as well. Opponents stage demonstrations at the border and vow to boycott San Diego businesses. Lawsuits immediately follow the proposition's passage, and enforcement is stalled.

1995 In January, the **San Diego Chargers** win the AFC (American Football Conference) championship and go to the **Super Bowl**, where they are soundly defeated by the **San Francisco 49ers**.

1996 The **Republican National Convention** is held in August at the San Diego Convention Center.

1997 While the Naval Training Center at Point Loma is closed to all active military duty, the reconstructed **House of Hospitality** reopens in Balboa Park.

1998 The **Padres** win the National League pennant but lose to the New York Yankees in the **World Series**. The **Coors Amphitheatre** opens in **Chula Vista**, and voters not only approve of the convention-center expansion in downtown and the Padres' ballpark but also green-light $1.5 billion in city school bonds.

1999 **Legoland California** opens in **Carlsbad**. The **San Diego Presidio** ruins are once again covered up for posterity to preserve them for future archaeological digs.

2000 The population of San Diego hits 1,223,400. The San Diego County population is 2,813,833.

INDEX

INDEX

INDEX

RESTAURANTS

Only restaurants with star ratings are listed below. All restaurants are listed alphabetically in the main (preceding) index. Always call in advance to ensure a restaurant has not closed, changed its hours, or booked its tables for a private party. The restaurant price ratings are based on the average cost of an entrée for one person, excluding tax and tip.

★★★★ Extraordinary Experience
★★★ Excellent
★★ Very Good
★ Good

$$$$ Big Bucks ($21 and up)
$$$ Expensive ($16-$20)
$$ Reasonable ($10-$15)
$ The Price Is Right (less than $10)

HOTELS

The hotels listed below are grouped according to their price ratings; they are also listed in the main index. The hotel price ratings reflect the base price of a standard room for two people for one night during the peak season.

$$$$ Big Bucks ($250 and up)
$$$ Expensive ($175-$250)
$$ Reasonable ($100-$175)